The Structure of Personality

Modeling "Personality" Using NLP and Neuro-Semantics

L. Michael Hall, Ph.D.
Bob G. Bodenhamer, D.Min.
Dr. Richard Bolstad
& Margot Hamblett

Crown House Publishing
www.crownhouse.co.uk

First published in the UK by

Crown House Publishing Limited
Crown Buildings
Bancyfelin
Carmarthen
Wales
SA33 5ND
UK

www.crownhouse.co.uk

British Library of Cataloguing-in-Publication Data
A catalogue entry for this book is available
from the British Library.

ISBN 1899836675

LCCN 2002117317

Neuro-Semantics® is a registered trademark in the USA and other
countries by the Society of Neuro-Semantics.

Printed and bound in the UK by
Bell & Bain Ltd, Glasgow

Dedication

My life partner and co-author Margot Hamblett died of heart failure in February 2001 as this work was coming to print. Margot was an extraordinary change agent and initiated much of our written contribution to this book. Her own experience of personality transformation, based on the use of NLP techniques, gave her the confidence to guide hundreds of others to more satisfying lives. This current publication means that others who never met her will share her confidence, passion and love. I can think of no finer way to celebrate her life.

Richard

The Authors

L. Michael Hall, Ph.D.
A researcher and modeler, prolific author, and entrepreneur who lives on the western slope of the Rocky Mountains in Colorado. He originated and developed the Meta-States Model in 1994, and along with Dr Bobby Bodenhamer co-founded Neuro-Semantics®.

L. Michael Hall, Ph.D.
P.O. Box 9231
Grand Junction, CO. 81501
(970) 523-7877
Email: NLPMetaStates@OnLinecol.com
Web: www.neurosemantics.com
www.learninstitute.com

Bobby G. Bodenhamer, D.Min.
Director and trainer for the NLP Center in Gastonia NC for more than a decade, now director of the *First Institute of Neuro-Semantics*. An author of numerous books in NLP, Bob has used NLP and Neuro-Semantics in consultation work for many years, with hundreds of clients.

Dr Bob Bodenhamer
1516 Cecelia Drive
Gastonia NC. 28
Email: bbodenhammer@carolina.rr.com
Web: www.neurosemantics.com

Dr. Richard Bolstad and Margot Hamblett
Richard Bolstad is an NLP Trainer and developer of the *Transforming Communication Seminar*. Margot Hamblett was also an NLP Trainer, co-developer with Richard, and life partner until her recent death.

Dr. Richard Bolstad
26 Southampton Street,
Christchurch 8002
New Zealand
Phone/Fax +64-3-337-1852
E-mail: nlp@chch.planet.org.nz
Home Page www.cybermall.co.nz/nz/nlp

Table of Contents

Foreword

Challenging a Long-Established Paradigm
Are Personality Disorders Really "Fixed?"

I first became interested in clinical approaches to personality disorders while completing the U.S. Navy's Submarine School in Groton, CN. In 1970 I volunteered for a USN longitudinal study of "personality factors" which impact sailor success aboard nuclear Ballistic missile submarines (which remain submerged for 90 days at a time). The research suggested that those best qualified (i.e. who could best adapt) to serve as submariners strongly evidenced three distinct DSM "personality disorders:" Obsessive-Compulsive (OCPD), Schizoid (SPD), and Avoidant (APD). Those labels meant little to me at 18, but would significantly impact my professional perspectives for years to come.

This research was replicated by the USN in the 1990s[1] and the findings were the same. The implications are staggering: behaviors which were typically labeled as "disorders" actually proved to be *strengths*, especially within the context of submarine warfare. After all, don't we all want sailors who harness unimaginable nuclear power to be "preoccupied with orderliness, perfectionism, and control" (OCPD), are "socially independent" (SPD), and are able to "fully function even in total isolation" (APD)? Thus, personality is ordered and disordered within context and reflects client strengths.

The implications of this "strengths perspective" (first espoused by Hankins in 1939) have haunted me across my career. While completing four graduate degrees in the social sciences (counseling, sociology, social work, and psychology) along with post-graduate studies in education and post-doctorate work in both biophysical psychology and clinical psychology, I was able to scrutinize issues surrounding personality and its disordering. I funded my formal education by working with various in-patient psychiatric hospitals and out-patient clinics. These experiences reinforced many of my academic concerns about the predominant DSM paradigm and

iii

its perspective of Axis II personality disorders, their diagnosis, treatment and long-term outcomes. In the early 1980s I decided it was time to conduct my own research on personality disorders.

In 1986 I pulled together data I had collated earlier regarding cognitive and contextual variables impacting personality and decision-making. This research culminated in my dissertation, The Impact of Role-Expectation Cognitions Upon Test-Taking (October, 1989; Arlington: The University of Texas). One hundred and six non-clinical volunteers participated in this modified pretest-posttest comparison group design with repeated measures. The study explored the relationship between role-expectation cognitions and concomitant subject responses to a popular trait-based personality assessment tool. Subjects in the experimental group repeated measures while purposely thinking of their roles as a child, a spouse, and an employee. The control group repeated measures while thinking of their life "in general" (i.e. no assigned roles). The results indicated that reliability and validity of this personality assessment tool could be confounded under the conditions stipulated by this study.

The lesson? Personality traits (a psychoanalytic construct) are not fixed, but vary depending on contexts and perceptions (cognitive and semantic constructs). The implications for personality disorders are far too many to include in this Foreword, but here are a few:

I Personality and its disordering is fluid, not static or fixed (for instance, many paranoid patients function very well in highly structured work environments).

I Assessment of personality disorders has been paradigm-bound and thus self-limiting (e.g. a rigid disease model).

I Perceptions used to diagnose PDs reflect clinical projections regarding pathology, disease, malady, and limited growth and change potentials (i.e. PDs are traditionally viewed as negative, crippling, and impervious to change).

I Resulting clinical labels ignore cultural, cognitive, and semantic variables (e.g. the belief that one cannot talk rationally with a delusional client leads us to ignore the semantic patterns used by every client).

ı Disease concepts of PDs result in many secondary effects (e.g. Hawthorne, Looking-glass, Pygmalion and Galataea effects, etc).

Our Profession Changes Paradigms
From 1989–1994 I served as Program and Clinical Director for two affiliated in-patient psychiatric units (one for adolescents, one for adults). The psychiatric industry was battling new managed care paradigms and shrinking funds. Prior to 1989 many insurance companies paid for lengthy in-patient treatment of DSM personality disorders (e.g. it was not unusual for "borderline" patients to be in-patients for many months at a time). Insurance carriers up to that time were in league with the predominant medical and analytic paradigms¼but things were about to change!

About 1989 managed care providers discovered that the personality disorders took 75% of the available resources (both time and money) to treat 2% of the psychiatric population. They also began to argue that one's personality could not be "diseased." Independent (APA) research additionally revealed that the diagnosis of personality disorders had the least inter-rater reliability of all DSM maladies. The mushrooming managed care paradigm began asking a difficult (and long overdue) question: Do we have the knowledge, tools, experience, and resources to effectively treat personality disorders? The oft verbalized suspicion was that current paradigms were quite impotent in dealing with personality disorders and many of these clients were greatly harmed by the treatment they did receive. I witnessed and feared the same.

Another critical historic piece fell into place in December, 1989 when Public Law 101-239 mandated the development of clinical practice guidelines for use by all (mental) health professionals. The Agency for Health Care Policy and Research (AHCPR) was founded to formulate these guidelines and depression was selected as the first mental health need to evaluate. The Depression Guideline Panel (AHCPR Pub. No. 93-0551. Rockville, MD: U.S. Dept. of Health and Human Services) found that cognitive, behavioral, and brief therapies had the highest efficacy rates (46.6%, 55.3%, and 34.8% respectively). *The Clinical Psychologist* (Vol. 47, 1994 – Vol. 49, 1996) the *American Psychologist* (Vol. 49, 1996), and Bergin & Garfield (1994) reported much of the early meta-analyses surrounding these clinical guidelines.[2] The outcome? Brief therapies and cognitive-behavioral processes are in. Does this mean, however, that our paradigms have really changed?

"Changing paradigms" is likely an errant response if by it we mean, "going from *the wrong perspective to the right one*" (this is, after all, a dualistic paradigm itself!). Our disciplines are shifting away from long-term therapies which have questionable outcomes, but the focus remains fixed upon outcomes, not processes. Earlier neuro-linguistic and neuro-semantic research (anecdotal, in vivo, and in vitro) has clearly illustrated that our clinical paradigms must focus on contextual and semantic processes. For instance, Axis I clinical disorders are identified and cataloged by various "behaviors" while successful treatment (outcome) is gauged by changes in those behaviors. The therapeutic processes leading to these changes, however, have been studied from traditional, very limited, and often exclusive paradigms. For instance, psychotropic medications, representative of the medical model, have revolutionized the way some disorders are managed. But there is a key difference between managing manifest behaviors and "curing" the patient. Many of our disciplines no longer look to cure, only to manage. Can we re-order the dis-ordered personality?

How we perceive Axis II clinical needs reflects an assumed etiology. If genetics under gird personality disorders, then management by psychotropic interventions is the best we can hope for. If personality disorders are fixed and unyielding, then clinical treatments are offered in vain (a premise now clearly held by managed care providers). But what if personality disorders can be unlocked, ordered and reordered? What if neuro-semantic keys exist which help us to understand the personality ordering process?

These and other questions surrounding personality were the focus of a week long "think tank" in 1997. During that week, I shared the USN research, my dissertation outcomes, and my growing clinical concerns with my colleague, Michael Hall. At the end of that week,

Michael and I came to the same conclusion. A text was needed which could:

ı   help practitioners understand and treat personality disorders using a neuro-semantic model which explores the semantic maps that have historically shaped the ways clients view themselves and their world and

ı   work from an agenda that emphasizes strengths and abilities.

I am thrilled to introduce you to this book which does just that!

Why Read this Book?

You can expect many great things from this book. First, this text offers you a new conceptual model. The authors challenge and revolutionize the way we conceive and perceive the dis-ordering of personality. They explore this etiological paradigm by succinctly pulling together the foundational constructs and strengths of many and varied models (e.g. behavioral, brief, cognitive, force field, gestalt, human engineering, learning, linguistic, schema, semantic, sensory, etc). They then innovatively cast these against the backdrop of cutting-edge research regarding neuro-linguistic (mind-body) and neuro-semantic (mind-culture) processes. Part I of this book (chapters 1–12) reviews the applicable conceptual and clinical models necessary to re-perceive personality disordering. The genius of this book is that it provides a map by which to unpack and re-pack clinical perceptions of the personality disorders.

Second, this book offers you clear, pragmatic clinical guidelines. Part II (chapters 13–24) applies the neuro-linguistic (NL) and neuro-semantic (NS) models to 14 personality disorders (DSM, Axis II). Clinical vignettes, intervention guidelines, and various NL/NS patterns and routines are clearly detailed (thus making it very easy to assimilate into current practice needs).

This hands-on, pragmatic approach is both innovative and empowering. If you've ever had a sense of failure when helping those with personality disorders, this book will unlock ways to see these failures as meta-state stepping stones. We in the helping fields have spent so much time and energy learning to recognize and diagnose personality disorders (which any first year graduate student can do) that few really know how to meet these client needs. The glorious news is that personality disorders can be effectively treated! *Personality: Ordering and Disordering* tells you how!

Third, the authors offer you brief therapy techniques capitalizing upon current neurological and psycho-biological knowledge. These techniques are based upon holistic, systemic, and ecological frames and rely upon design, feedback, and strengths models. Thus, this book addresses a myriad of needs across the micro-, mezzo-, and macro-levels of practice (and it's the only one I've come across which does so!).

Finally, this is a well written, authoritative, informative how-to book of extraordinary interest to anyone dealing with clients whose personality dis-ordering is driving everyone around them nuts! It is impressive both in scope and depth, staggering in its implications for treating personality disorders, giving the clinical world an utterly new way of looking at the etiology and treatment of personality disorders.

This belongs on your "must read" list.

Carl Lloyd, Ph.D.
(Full) Professor, tenured
George Fox University
Newberg, OR
August, 2000

---

[1] During my first year at George Fox University (1994) I had an office next to Brad Johnson, Ph.D. Brad had just resigned his commission as a USN psychologist to accept his first teaching post. Our adjoining offices enhanced daily conversations about mutual research interests and shared experiences. One USN project Brad led was the replication of the 1970 study I participated in. The results were the same. Brad now teaches at the US Naval Academy in Annapolis, MD.

[2] It is important to realize that these clinical guidelines are derived from *outcome* research, not *process* research. Outcome research evaluates the presence and magnitude of clinical changes (i.e. results, outcomes) which result from specific clinical interventions. Process research evaluates what occurs *in* therapy.

Preface

ı   Can we *change* "personality?"

ı   What *is* this thing that we call "personality" anyway?

ı   What does the NLP model say regarding "personality?"

ı   What NLP models and techniques transform personality?

ı   What Meta-Stating and Neuro-Semantic models expand and extend the art of transforming "personality?"

As a Cognitive-Behavioral psychologist, when I first discovered NLP (Neuro-Linguistic Programming), I felt immediately excited. And during the past fourteen years, my exploration of the model has not waned or disappointed me. I quickly recognized that its powerful techniques and processes would revolutionize the way we work with people. And so it has.

Further, NLP arose from *modeling* the therapeutic "magic" of three therapeutic experts involved in three very different disciplines, *Virginia Satir* of Family Systems, *Fritz Perls* of Gestalt Therapy, and *Milton H. Erickson* of Ericksonian hypnosis. It was out of modeling those different fields that a Cognitive Behavioral Model arose. This speaks about the precision of the modeling skills of the two co-founders, Dr John Grinder as a linguist and Richard Bandler as a patterning genius.

At its essence, NLP describes *a communication model*—how we use language and how we "make sense" of language. From there, NLP refers to a model of human functioning—how we operate in the world making mental-emotional maps that give us a "program" for navigating life. From there, NLP references an entire meta-domain that examines the *structure* of experiences in general and provides modeling tools for unpacking the strategies, refining those programming strategies, and then replicating exemplars of excellence. And yet, as you will discover in this work, NLP is even more than all of that.

Here we focus on *NLP and Personality.* As such, this work extends the current research and practice of the Cognitive-Behavioral Model. That's because as a meta-domain, NLP cares very little about theory as it focuses primarily on *processes* for change and on those patterns that work to bring about transformation. Given that, NLP studies processes that work in many different fields without a compulsion to create some unified field theory. This makes NLP extremely practical and focused on *solutions* and *results.*

While it cares little about theory, that doesn't prevent many of us in the NLP field from exploring the epistemological foundations of the model. The terms "Neuro-Linguistics" and "Neuro-Semantics" actually originated with Alfred Korzybski (1933/1994) founder of General Semantics. The focus on Meta-Levels and frames originated from anthropologist Gregory Bateson (1972, 1979) who set the foundations also for cybernetics, meta-cognition, and systems theory.

Here we also present more than NLP, we present *Neuro-Semantics.* This represents an extension and expansion of the NLP model using the Meta-Levels model, the Levels of Thought. This refers to the self-reflexivity that drives the Meta-States model. In the past few years, we have discovered that the most powerful NLP patterns operate due to the frame-setting power of state upon state so that "mind" or "consciousness" becomes textured and layered with higher level awarenesses. This, in turn, leads to a richer and more resourceful kind of mindfulness in moving through the world.

NLP/NS and "Personality"

Early in the development of NLP, it became apparent to many that this model of human functioning which involved understanding and exploring the cognitive maps that people develop and use for navigating "reality," had tremendous implications for "personality."

Lewis (1982) describes how he titled his original from his studies under Richard Bandler and John Grinder as *"A Model for a Process*

Theory of Personality." He understood, as many who followed, that when we change someone's *reference structure* (i.e., one's "model of the world") "personality" itself changes. It has to.

In 1988, Wyatt Woodsmall and Tad James wrote the first book on one of the most exciting NLP domains, time-lines. In *Time Line Therapy: The Basis of Personality* they presented NLP patterns regarding how we code and process the concept of *"time"* and showed how this mapping or programming plays a central role in "personality." They also identified other key components of personality in addressing the NLP domain of the *Meta-Programs.*

When Dr Bodenhamer and I co-authored our work on Meta-Programs (1997), we sought to extend the perceptual filters by integrating facets of Cognitive Psychology, General Semantics, and Developmental Psychology. *Figuring Out People: Design Engineering Using Meta-Programs* (1997) most essentially addresses *personality*. The research and writing that went into that work renewed in both of us an interest in applying NLP to *personality disorders*. As it did, we began thinking and planning a second volume of *Figuring Out People* with the focus on personality.

In that discussion, we agreed about the value of following up *Figuring Out People* with a more scholarly work, and specifically one that would apply the numerous domains and models within NLP to the more serious problems of "personality disorders." As a result, while I began writing a text to that end, Bob used his counseling practice to think through and apply the concepts on a daily basis with people suffering from many different kinds of "personality disorders."

During the next year, as we continued to think about the approach we wanted to take in applying NLP to personality and "personality disorders," we happened upon many new applications of the Meta-States Model. This led to the introduction of several new sub-models and distinctions in NLP. We have included these in this work as *the Three Meta-Domains Model, Values as a Meta-Level Phenomenon, etc.*

Then the work got bogged down.

And so it stayed until I met two of the most respectable NLP Trainers and Thinkers, Dr Richard Bolstad and Margot Hamblett. Meeting them for the first time at the NLP Health Conference in Denmark in 1999, our common interests in applying NLP to personality quickly became obvious. Richard and Margot, in fact, were at the time writing a series of excellent articles on depression, schizophrenia, and other major personality disorders in the NLP Journal, *Anchor Point*. I asked them to collaborate with us on this project since their writings obviously put them at the cutting edge of NLP in forging new applications and patterns.

Consequently I have collected in this work the differing approaches from Bob and myself and Richard and Margot as we have utilized our knowledge and experience in applying NLP to transforming the structure of personality from limiting patterns to enhancing ones.

The four of us share a belief in the exciting and dynamic nature of NLP as a cognitive model of human functioning. We all appreciate the richness of NLP to provide many ways to map things. We recognize that there's no "one right way" to understand or do things. If a map enables us to navigate a particular territory and achieve certain objectives, then it works for that purpose. And another mapping may also empower us to do the same. We do not see this as a contradiction, but as a complement, especially when dealing with the systemic features of the human mind-body system. It does not mean that someone is right and someone else has to be wrong, but only that we have several choices. If you find differences in our approaches in the following chapters, we have left that intact to illustrate this richness.

Regarding this work, Richard has noted this:

> In this work, we likewise approach personality disordering from two different perspectives. In a sense, our (Margot and Richard's) chapters could be likened to Axis I, and Michael and Bob's chapters to Axis II. The interweaving of these two perspectives gives you choices in making sense of the clients you assist.

We have noted in the Table of Contents which chapters belong to whom and yet as you read the text, the difference in style will make that abundantly clear. Throughout the text we have summarized various domains of NLP and Neuro-Semantics as well as providing additional references. I have also added a final page after the last chapter for recommended books with other NLP and Neuro-Semantic Patterns.

Who Should Read this Book?

I have primarily directed this work toward the mental health worker (social workers, professional licensed counselors, family and marriage counselors, etc.). Yet it is equally directed toward anyone coaching and consulting with people, working with troubled people, and using the latest patterns for re-directing consciousness. In view of that, we highly urge anyone who wants to use these NLP and Neuro-Semantics patterns with skill and expertise to consult professionals who provide qualified training.

L. Michael Hall
Colorado, USA
Spring, 2000

Preface 2

When we first came upon NLP in the 1980s, the claims of its founders seemed preposterous. As psychotherapists we knew that such simple techniques could not possibly effect the fast and lasting change that they appeared to.

Now, we are in the position of having validated those claims in real life thousands of times. In 1998 and 1999, as the Balkan wars still raged, we taught NLP processes to psychiatrists and emergency aid workers in Sarajevo, confirming that the apparently profound personality disturbances of Post Traumatic Stress Disorder could be reliably solved by a 30 minute NLP-based intervention. In those same years, the first controlled study of NLP-based psychotherapy was published in Austria by Martina Genser-Medlitsch and Peter Schütz (1997). They showed that NLP interventions reduced anxiety, depression, paranoia, aggression, compulsive behaviors, social insecurity and a number of other personality problems. They also demonstrated that NLP left clients more in charge of their own life, and equipped them with more effective life skills.

Our work in NLP consulting centers on three models: The NLP Model of Strategies, the overall model of the Process of Change that we designate as the RESOLVE Model, and the Personal Strengths model, which we also developed.

In 1980, Robert Dilts, John Grinder, Richard Bandler and Judith DeLozier first presented NLP as a unified structure, organizing their model around the notion of behavioral "strategies" (i.e., sensory specific sequences of behavior). With that they promised that NLP would provide practitioners with

> a set of tools that will enable him or her to analyze and incorporate or modify any sequence of behavior that they may observe in another human being. (p. 3)

In this work, we have contributed specific chapters that examine some strategies which lead to disorder and distress in people's lives. We find this truly exciting. How? It means that there is a system or structure to how people create depression, anxiety, frustration, and confusion. And understanding *that system* enables us to more effectively find the opposite results of satisfaction and fulfilment for ourselves and for others that we work with. Perceptive human beings have often been able, perhaps after many years of experience, to detect and use this system to create positive results. The *NLP Strategy Model* enables the rapid delivery of such perceptive skill to those who need it most.

For those who want to use NLP-based processes to help others change, NLP provides a bewildering array of different methods. Many new NLP Practitioners report that they feel overwhelmed by the sheer expanse of choices available when a client walks in the door. While preserving this sense of abundance, we aim to simplify the selection of skills for such practitioners. NLP trainer Steve Andreas says (1999),

> I think that someone who uses the NLP methods exceptionally well has several ways of gathering all the different skills and techniques under a single overarching framework of understanding.

To date there are only a few published models which offer this form of clarification. Robert Dilts' Unified Field model (O'Connor and Seymour, 1993, p. 88–92) first categorized NLP interventions by three intersecting parameters:

1) "neurological level" (the "depth" of the intervention, from processes aimed at simple changes in the person's environment, through changes in behavior, capability, beliefs, identity and spirit;

2) time orientation (past, present and future); and

3) perceptual position (experiencing the world from the position of self, of observer and of the other person).

Since Dilts' work, a small number of other overall models have been presented. Veli-Matti Toivonen proposed a second detailed grid called the Subsystems Inventory of Psychological Phenomena, based on the interaction of language, sensory experience and physiology (1993). The development of *the Meta-States Model* (Hall, 1996, 1997, 1999) enables identification of the Meta-Level at which interventions operate and the consequent fields of application. This has led to the development of Neuro-Semantics. Steve Andreas (1999) proposes sorting NLP interventions by whether they promote joining or splitting of neurological phenomena, and by their application to the sequencing of a "problem".

The *Personal Strengths model* (Bolstad and Hamblett, 1995A) provides an NLP-compatible answer to both "diagnosis" and intervention choice. It equips one to quickly choose NLP processes that match the strengths a client already uses in generating "problems." This provides an advantage over models which categorize interventions only from the perspective of the practitioner. The Personal Strengths model enables us to know not only what choices we have, but whether each is likely to succeed with this particular client.

Finally, *the RESOLVE model* (1995B) can be used to replace traditional models of the "therapeutic process." We developed this model based on Bryan Royd's extension of the General Model For Behavioral Intervention (Tad James, 1995). One of Tad James' most important achievements was to identify the reliable sequencing that NLP developer Richard Bandler used in his work with clients. The RESOLVE model answers the question, *"In what order do I use all these skills?"*

In this book we explore the application of our models to some of the most challenging "personality structures." Our hope is that, interwoven with Michael Hall and Bob Bodenhamer's work, we can offer an adequate framework for therapists, NLP Practitioners, and consultants to use their skills in a way that is simple, elegant, and proven useful by research. This may require some departures from both orthodox psychotherapy and orthodox NLP use.

Richard Bolstad and Margot Hamblett
February 2000

Part I

*NLP and NS Models
for Understanding
the Structure
of "Personality"*

Chapter 1

"Personality" and the Meta-Model

De-Nominalizing "Personality" for Clarity

We *are* not things, traits, entities—yet we do respond and act as we perceive, think, feel, and act.

- What do we mean when we use the word "personality"?
- What does this concept of "personality" refer to?
- What determines a "good" personality that is healthy and effective?
- What causes a personality to go "bad" and become sick?
- Can we change "personality"?
- Can we reverse a "personality disorder"?

Many people in the psychological field of mental health and psychotherapy do not think so. We differ from them. Believing in actual *personality transformations*, we (among a host of others) have been busy making it happen. That's what this work is all about. And to do that, we will first present several of *the NLP Models of Personality* that enable us to think this way and to take actions that give us the ability to manage and affect "personality" itself.

The Language of "Personality"

We begin with language. We begin with the symbols and symbolic system that we have inherited in order to clarify what we mean and don't mean. The precision and specificity that this will give us will then govern most of the pages that follow. This accesses the first Model of NLP, the model, in fact, that initiated the Cognitive-Behavioral model of NLP. "The Meta-Model of Language in Therapy" (Bandler and Grinder, 1975, 1976) provides a way to think through complex concepts (like "personality") by examining *the language itself*. This gives us the ability to speak with more precision.

To fail to do this means accepting the language we have inherited from more primitive times and all of the ill-formedness incorporated into the linguistic terms and structure. Yet as we have learned in the Twentieth Century, and as so aptly put by General Semanticist Wendel Johnson:

> *The language of science is the better part of the method of science.* Just so, the language of sanity is the better part of sanity. (p. 50)

In the following statement Johnson further notes what this implies and means as anyone who has engaged in research design knows full well:

> The terminology of the question determines the terminology of the answer. If there is one part of the scientific experiment that is more important than any other part, it is the frame of the question that the experiment is to answer. (p. 52)

If this plays a central role in the "hard" sciences, it becomes an even more dominant concern in the "soft" sciences like psychology. Why? Because while words have no effect whatever on external phenomena, they play a creative and governing role inside the human nervous system. So while cursing a car all day long will not affect the car's mechanical functioning, you only have to curse a human being for a few moments before you begin to see effects! You will quickly see *neuro-semantic reactions.* And these reactions to the cursing may go on for years.

That's why the realm of human functioning and "personality" involves a very different kind of reality and a different kind of logic. It is *psycho-logical* reality and language itself enters into this realm. So languaging and re-languaging will play a central role in forming (ordering) and disordering "personality" as you will see in the chapters to come.

It also plays a major role in how we talk about "personality" itself. Listen to the language that we have inherited, to the sentence I just wrote. The symbol "personality" (a verbal noun or nominaliza-tion) allows, and even encourages, us to speak about human func-tioning as if it were a *thing.*

"Just look at her! She's got a great personality!"
"His personality stinks, that's all I can say."
"I can't stand her personality; she's so self-centered."
"You can't change a person's personality."
"Come to this workshop and you can change your personality!"

What impression does such talk give? It gives the impression that *"personality"* "is" an actual *thing,* does it not? Yet we know better than that. It is not a "thing" at all, but a concept about a set of processes.

Speaking about it in this way does not make it so. Speaking about a process or set of processes as if it "is" an inner, hidden, and static *thing* only turns *a verb* into *a noun.* We put a name on this living, moving, breathing, thinking, feeling, and relating organism. This reveals one of the many limitations of any linguistic system.

So we begin with an innocent enough term, another verbal noun, *"person."* But we didn't stop there. We used that noun to name all of the hundreds if not thousands of processes of an individual to describe an even higher level concept. And so another noun came into being, "personality." In the end, however, *this linguistic nominalization process* completely hides from our view the actual referent.

- What are we talking about?
- What are we referring to?
- Can you point to it?

No. It is not finger-able. This leads us to begin thinking of "per-sonality" as *a thing,* rather than a whole set of activities. Conceptually we reified the concept and began to suffer from what Whitehead called a "misplaced concreteness."

So what noun lies inside the word "personality" and comes prior to it?

"Person" is the first noun. This word stands for, and does duty for, the whole class of actions and behaviors that comprise the person's style of thinking, emoting, valuing, believing, relating, etc. So we use this term as *a metonymy* (Lakoff and Johnson, 1980).

> The language form of metonymy refers to using one well under-stood or easy-to-perceive aspect of something in a way so that it *stands for the thing as a whole* (or for some other aspect or part of it). When we say, "The White House issued a statement today about the war…" we use "White House" as a metonymy. So with such phrases as, "Hollywood isn't what it used to be." "Wall Street fell into a panic, but recovered later in the day."

The term *"person,"* as a metonymic model for *all of the processes* experienced inside a human being and expressed outside, *stands for* all of the *verbs* describing various actions and processes. Describing this enables us to bring back some specificity into our thinking, understanding, and speaking. It *de-nominalizes* the two nominalizations ("person" and "personality") and thereby gives us a much more specific behavioral focus in our questions about *the class of functions* that we experience and engage in that makes up our "personality." Doing this allows us to operationalize the term so that we can then specifically ask questions that enable us to identify the actual "components" and structure of what we put under the label "Personality."

- How does s/he think: value, perceive, reason, understand, believe?
- How does s/he feel: physically experience his/her body's sensations?
- How does s/he emote: meanings given to sensations and experiences?
- What reference experiences does s/he use to attribute meanings?
- How does s/he speak: language patterns, usage, syntax, content?
- How does s/he act: behaviors, actions, gestures, etc.?
- How does s/he relate to others: style, nature, intent, etc.?

Ultimately, to understand "personality" we have to move back to these *functional processes*—to the internal and external *actions*.

Then, and only then, can we develop an informed understanding and comprehension of the unique phenomenological world that we experience and live in as a "person" with a "personality." Then, and only then, can we get a good "reading" on the person's "personality" style and nature.

The power of the NLP and Neuro-Semantic models and patterns that you will find in the following pages will empower you to work with *ongoing processes*, with mental-and-emotional and bodily processes. That's what "personality" is all about. If you forget the referent and confuse it with a static thing, you might fall into the trap of "misplaced concreteness" and then begin to think in more deterministic ways, "Well, that's just the way she is."

"Personality" has a Structure and Strategy

We begin then by de-nominalizing *the kind of phenomena* that we will search for and identify as we explore the concept of "personality" for several reasons.

First, it enables us to avoid getting distracted by looking for "things" or "entities" inside people. "Personality" is not that kind of a thing. It's not like a kidney or a facet of brain neurology. As we turn away from that, we are then enabled to turn to think of "personality" in terms of *processes*: actions, movements, ongoing and dynamic behavior. In *Neuro-Linguistic Programming* (NLP), we define "behavior" as involving both the micro- and macro-levels.

Macro-level behaviors refer to those actions and responses that we see externally in how a person acts, relates, and responds.

Micro-level behaviors appear as subtle gestures, thoughts, emotions, etc. By calibrating to minute movements like eye-accessing cues and other responses of the autonomic nervous system we can detect these small unit behaviors.

Dilts, *et al.* (1980) wrote about this:

> In NLP behavior is defined as all sensory representations experienced and
> expressed internally and/or externally for which evidence is available

from a subject and/or from a human observer of that subject. ... Both macrobehavior and microbehavior are ... programmed through our neurological systems. Macrobehavior is overt and easily observable, as in driving a car, speaking, fighting, eating, getting sick, or riding a bicycle. Microbehavior involves subtler though equally important phenomena such as heart rate, voice tempo, skin color changes, pupil dilation and such events as seeing in the mind's eye or having internal dialogue. (p. 4)

There is more. Because both micro- and macro-behaviors involve neurology,

... all behavior—from learning, remembering, and motivation to making a choice, communication and change—is the result of sys-tematically ordered sequences of sensory representations. (p. 6)

Dilts, Bandler, Grinder, Cameron-Bandler, and DeLozier (1980) received this strategies model of human functioning from a classic work by Miller, Gallanter, and Pribram (1960). In their work, *Plans and Structure of Behavior*, they developed the TOTE Model (Test-Operate-Test-Exist) to articulate a flow-chart diagram of the ordered sequences of processes involved in *a "strategy"* that describes some facet of personality.

As *persons*, we develop, manifest, and order our "personality" by means of our mental actions as well as our larger-level external actions. As we *behave* in the way we think, perceive, feel, talk, and act—so we become.

Dilts, *et al.* enriched the TOTE model to create a neuro-linguistic *Strategies* Model. Thereafter they used it for analyzing, under-standing, and working with human personality, for *modeling* both excellence or genius as well as pathology. Today we refer to it as the *strategies model* in NLP. This model gives us the ability to iden-tify the component pieces and order that goes into the very struc-ture of a piece of behavior (kind of like the pieces and order that comprise a recipe).

(See Chapter 3 for an extended description of this model. In that chapter, Richard and Margott show how we use the Strategies Model for understanding structure and for effecting change.)

Acting Your Way to "Personality".

With this focus and emphasis on *processes*, on sets of actions and behaviors at various levels, we can now say that *we "do" personality*, and that we *act* our way to personality. This provides a very different way to think about this concept of "personality." What does this mean in terms of working with people?

It means that the very way we sequence our micro- and macro-behaviors creates, organizes, and structures what we experience as our "personality."

These behaviors generate an overall gestalt or configuration of something "more than the sum of the parts." This gestalt then expresses our "personality," that is, our nature and style for coping, navigating life, mastering challenges, processing information, relating, etc.

- How do you *"do"* your personality?
- What sequences of sensory representations and responses do you utilize to create your "personality"?
- What behaviors and actions give *expression* to the style and tone of your "personality"?

I've run through this quickly. Let me run through it again in summary since this offers a very new and different way to think about "personality."

We do not *"have"* a "personality" in any static way as if it consisted of an entity inside of us. "Personality" does not describe "the way we *are*" in that kind of way. Rather, we *"perform"* our "personality." In fact, we *learn* to *perform our "personality."*

Cultural "Personalities"

This model of personality explains why people born into different cultures and family environments *learn* to form, pattern, and "do" *personality* in very different ways. Given the cultural, family, and racial environment into which we were born as well as the given predispositions within our DNA and physiology, over the years we have *learned* how to think-feel, value-believe, speak and act *as a person*. It explains how someone from one race or culture can be born into a very foreign culture and develop a "personality" as structured by the new culture.

This interactional model integrates both *nature and nurture* to explain the gestalt of personality that results.

- How does a person learn to *"be"* an Italian, Russian, American, British, German, etc.?
- How does a person learn to *"be"* (think like, feel like, speak like, act like, etc.) a "city slicker," red-neck, cowboy, urban-ite, jet-setter, an aborigine, suburbanite, soccer mom, etc.?

It depends to a great extent upon the *inter-personal context* within which a person is born, and from which we learn to *become* the kind of person we become. Ultimately, *we learn to do "personality."* We learn to become, think, act, and relate as an Arabian, a gym-nast, a Hollywood star, a Wall Street financier, a Southern Belle, a rape victim, etc. We all *learn* how to think-emote, speak and act in ways that fit these kinds of classifications. No one *"is"* one of these *things* in any static or permanent way. Rather we learn *how to func-tion* in these ways (using these formats) in our thinking-emoting, speaking, behaving, and relating. The point about all of this?

"Personality" is very malleable. If we learned to do our "per-sonalities," we can take charge of our actions and behaviors to "do" our personality in a very different way. In other words, we can change our personalities.

Even the seemingly more "concrete" facets of personality, "race," and "gender" do not operate so concretely. People, with or with-out sex-change operations, can adopt (in any given culture) the ways of thinking-emoting, speaking, behaving, and relating of a male or female—and so develop more masculine or feminine "per-sonality" styles.

The same applies to those distinctions that we sometimes attribute to "race." As we meet people of a particular "race" who think-feel, speak, act, and relate in ways not characteristic of that "race" —we

10

become increasingly aware that "race" itself exists as *a category* of the mind. It exists as a concept that we have created focusing on certain characteristics that we then over-generalize and nominalize.

As we begin, we find that we have to struggle against the every-day language patterns that we typically use in thinking about *persons and personality*. We have to fight against the tendency of nominalization and reification. We have to also resist the temptation to use "is" language: "She *is* an Italian." "He *is* a red-neck right-winger." "She *is* an over-emotional woman." "They *are* hot headed Irish."

"Personality" Profiles, "Traits," Characteristics, etc.

Just as we began by de-nominalizing the over-generalized class term "personality," we also need to de-nominalize many of the associative terms that have arisen in the course of the centuries, many folk terms, that continue to influence the field of "Personality" research, development, and transformation. Without paying attention to our language maps in this area, we can easily fall into using vague words and referents without really knowing *of which* we speak.

> Personality may be conceptualized as a relatively stable organization composed of systems and modes. Systems of interlocking structures (schemas) are responsible for the sequence extending from the reception of a stimulus to the end point of a behavioral response. (Beck, 1990, p. 32)

Characteristics

The nominalization *"characteristics"* similarly sounds like *a thing* or entity. It is not. Actually it describes *how* a person *characteristically* thinks, feels, speaks, and acts. The language about *the character* of one's thinking or one's feeling reifies it into almost a thing. Yet when we think more specifically about the specific *character* of the person's thinking, feeling, speaking, and acting (i.e. characteristics), we simply refer to an attributed perceived *quality* that we impose upon the set of actions. This quality arises as an interaction between the actions and our evaluations of it. Thus, a "characteristic" ultimately arises from the *quality of impression* that we get and create about a set of actions.

Traits

Someone originally derived "character" from *the act of engraving* or inscribing. Interestingly enough the term *"trait"* referred originally to the touch, stroking, drawing, etc. of an engraver. As a result of such, it left a distinguishing *quality or trait*.

If the nominalization, "personality," leaves the impression of a static, frozen, and unchangeable entity, how much more the nominalization phrase—*"personality disorder"*? To make matters worse, the psychological community has solidified these specific nominalizations for each "personality disorder" in the DSM-IV (Diagnostic and Statistical Manual of Mental Disorders). Beck (1990) noted that:

> ... the very terms that we use to describe these disorders (narcissistic, compulsive, dependent, etc.) carry a pejorative taint. Once the therapist has made the diagnosis, it is much better to avoid labels and think in terms of beliefs, sensitivities, meanings, and so forth. (p. 65)

That statement will govern the reasoning, descriptions, and processes in this book. *"It is much better to avoid labels and think in terms of beliefs, sensitivities, meanings, and so forth."* Accordingly, we have sought to focus our attention on *processes* and sensory-based behaviors. Beck further suggests this as part of how we should deal with this nominalizing of "personality." He suggests that we translate the labels into *operational terms*.

> The schizoid style, for example can be described and discussed as the patient's being 'very individualistic' or not being 'dependent on other people.' The dependent personality disorder can be discussed in terms of 'having a strong belief in the value of attachment to others,' or of 'placing a large emphasis on the importance

of being a more social person.' In every case, a nonjudgmental description modified to fit the particular belief system can be offered to the patient. (p. 84)

When we do this, we thereby *dismantle the gestalt configuration* of "personality" and "personality disorder." This allows us to view *the process* of how a given person *disorders* his or her own way of thinking-emoting, valuing, believing, speaking, behaving, relating, etc. In both theory and practice, we find that this denominalizing of the *"thing" language* provides a level of empowerment. After all, it enables us to address all of the cognitive, behavioral, and affective schemas that drive and influence the person rather than feeling overwhelmed by the overly abstract idea of a "personality disorder."

About this, two NLP writers, Lewis and Pucelik (1982), have said:

This model and the labels associated with it are only generalizations about people. They delete a great deal of information: this is a part of how they are supposed to function. They can make it easier for us to perceive, understand, and predict behavior. However… 'Labels intended to be merely descriptive may also come to be regarded as explanations of the problem.' (p. 50)

In this work, we have attempted to speak often about *the ordering* and *the disordering* of personality in order to focus on it as *a set of actions and processes*. We will even go further and de-nominalize other conceptual "entities" that we so easily postulate and install in consciousness: beliefs, values, will, meaning, conscience, etc.

Strategies of Healthy and Toxic Personalities

Just as a person can sequence his or her micro- and macro- behavior to think-emote, speak, behave, and relate (the five most basic "personality" functions or *powers* of our "person") to take on various "personality" qualities, so in this process we do so in both healthy and unhealthy ways. This initiates the psychological and psychotherapy questions about whether *our "personality" strategy* enables us to operate in sane, unsane, or insane ways. Do we sequence our sensory representations and create an internal "model of the world" (mental-emotional map) that allows us to make *a good adjustment to reality* or *a poor one*?

Alfred Korzybski (1933–1994) founder of *General Semantics,* used the map/territory distinction. As an engineer, he explored the fields of neurology and language to understand how our nervous system *abstracts* from the world of energy manifestations (the territory "out there") to create a map-like replica (representations) of that territory. Since we move through life using our "understandings," representations, "ideas," or *strategies* about the world, this informs us about how to think-emote, speak, behave, and relate to that world. Our internal maps enable us to make either good adjustments to that world or poor ones. Korzybski used the terms "sane, unsane, and insane" to describe the continuum of adjustment.

A good adjustment to "reality"—physical reality, inter-personal reality, cultural, social, conceptual, etc. enables us to think-emote, speak, act, and relate in ways that fit. We experience this as "health"—wholeness, soundness. We feel alive, vigorous, open, curious, etc. It brings out our best.

"Unsane" or "unsanity" describes a not-so-good fit to "reality." One's thoughts, feelings, speech, actions, and relations enable us to get along in the world, but at the cost of a lot of friction, stress, distress, worry, confusion, fear, anger, etc. Depending on the degree of unsanity, we seem at odds with "the facts of life," frequently in conflict with our expectations and understandings about what "should" be. This corresponds to our psychiatric term "neurotic," which originally refers to "being full of nerves."

"Insane" (as used by Korzybski) refers to a complete break with reality, which psychiatric literature refers to as *psychotic.* Here a person's way of thinking, perceiving, understanding, valuing, believing, etc., and therefore his or her way of feeling, emoting, and meaning-making, which comes out in speech and behavior does not *fit* at all. We label such individuals as suffering from various kinds of "personality disorders."

So how does a "Personality" Strategy Work?

Richard Bandler and John Grinder began the meta-psychology field of NLP by *modeling* three psychotherapeutic wizards and their models. The three wizards of these arts were Fritz Perls, Virginia Satir, and Milton Erickson. And their fields were Gestalt, Family Systems, Hypnotherapy. They sought to find the strategy of healing that subsumed these three geniuses. In doing so, they adopted *a modeling attitude.*

A modeling attitude?

Yes, *a modeling attitude* refers to looking at human experiences and phenomena as accomplishments and skills. From there one begins to wonder:

- *"How* do you do that?"
- "What would I have to do at both the micro-level and macro-level of behavior in order to replicate that?"
- "What internal representations, filters, beliefs, values, understandings, responses, etc. play a role in generating this response?"

While this seems very appropriate and informative when applied to phenomena that we evaluate as forms of excellence or genius, many have found this strange when applied to those that we evaluate as "bad," psychotic, insane, etc. Yet Richard and John took *that same modeling idea* and applied it to such strange human phenomena as schizophrenia, multi-personality disorders, obsessive-compulsiveness, agoraphobia, etc.

In this way, they approached such phenomena, not as something "bad," "evil," "demonic," nor even as "crazy," but as *human accomplishments.*

- "What a skill! How do you do this?"
- "How do you know when to hear voices come from the wall sockets?"
- "What kind of pictures do you have of that invisible and imagined rabbit?"

- "What do you tell yourself to get yourself to split off a part of yourself and become someone else?"
- "What cues you to experience your body full of fright?"

These modeling questions invite us right into *the process of "personality."* They do not assume that a person engages in such processes *consciously*. These questions, and this attitude, rather start from another basic assumption, namely, that the person does such *in order to adapt the best he or she can* to their environment. If we would describe anything as "bad" or "crazy," we would designate the environment or context that invites, evokes, and encourages such adaptive responses.

Summary

- "Personality" is not a *thing*, but a way of talking about a set of behaviors, ways of responding, thinking, coping, relating, etc.

- The *language* that we use in referring to "personality" governs our thinking and conceptualizing. It's therefore important to de-nominalize our everyday language that presupposes things and entities. Using a non-identifying language about "personality" will help us to think more clearly.

- Here our most fundamental focus will be on the specific functioning as *a person* in thinking, emoting, speaking, behaving, and relating.

Chapter 2

The Meta-States Model and "Personality"

"Personality" as a Gestalt of Higher States

To order a "Personality" Structure we have to "Go Meta" to create Meta-Level Phenomena— Beliefs, Values, Identity, Self, Time, Cause, Destiny, Purpose, etc.—

"I have observed the psychotherapy scene
since the days when Freud was the main voice.
Later brief psychotherapy took a mere six months.
Now we have the thirty-minute and even five-minute cures of NLP.
Speed is not the real issue.
We must be closing in on the actual design of people."
(Wilson van Dusen, Ph.D.)

In the first chapter we established the basis of this work, namely, that *"personality"* emerges from *the specific functioning* of a *person* in the context of his or her environment. As a practical consequence of this, at birth we do *not* have a *"personality."* "Personality" develops. Over a period of time, we *learn* and grow ourselves a *"personality."* We *learn* how to be a person in relation to other persons in a social context.

We engage in this project using our five most basic human *powers* that we noted in Chapter 1 (i.e. thinking, emoting, speaking, behaving, and relating). And we do this in numerous *contexts:* cultural, familial, friends, school, etc.

What determines and governs and influences a particular *personality* style or orientation? Certainly our *style* of thinking, emoting, speaking, behaving, and relating. These *components* of our cognitive style, emotive style, relational style, etc. certainly provide us

17

with a starting place in understanding any given *personality*. And yet they do not bring the search to a conclusion by any means. Many other factors also play into the mix. In this chapter, we will begin the process of extending that exploration into *the structure of personality*.

"Personality" as a Learned Phenomenon

We *learn* to become *persons* and to *grow* our "personalities." At birth, we do not have a "personality" in the sense of having a style of thinking, valuing, believing, emoting, speaking, behaving, or relating. Instead, at birth we only have a few basic processes available to us and a few basic genetic predispositions. It takes years of development and response within the various contextual environments until we form and mold our basic *"style of being a person"* in thinking, emoting, acting, etc. And we inevitably learn certain things in familial, cultural, and societal contexts and continue to do so as those contexts change.

Within such *contexts* we slowly learn how to think, emote, speak, and behave. Those who nurture and protect us (or fail to do so) create *the relational contexts* within which we make our learnings. Our nurturers also set up pain and pleasure reinforcement processes for us as they bring various ideas, beliefs, values, and experiences to bear upon our experience. This provides us with our original *learning environments* in which we learn what brings pain, what brings pleasure. Such then sets many of the initial directions and orientations for our way of navigating through life. These become our first formative understandings about ourselves, the world, others, responsibilities, risk, friendliness, danger, etc.

Thus, "personality" *arises*, not from any deterministic or fated human "instincts" as such. At best they arise from the forming of our *"instinctoids"* (Maslow's 1950 term) for *instinct-like* tendencies. At the primary level of experience (i.e. our primary see, hear, feel states), we experience *drive-like energies*—maturational, sexual, cognitive-emotional, etc. These basic primary energies define and describe our everyday experiences—pleased, upset, contented, frustrated, angry, fearful, joyful, playful, curious, pained, etc.

Then, via the processes of habituation, belief formulation, and self-reflexive consciousness, we construct *the Meta-Level phenomena of "personality."* This involves numerous *meta-frames of references* (or schemas): frames of meanings about our Self, about Others, about Coping, about the World, and about other conceptual realities. As these beliefs and belief systems (beliefs embedded in higher belief frames) develop, grow, and become organized they function as the over-arching factors in consciousness. Then at even higher logical levels, the beliefs about these become meta-schemas that govern the first level meta-schemas.

In terms of psychotherapy, these Meta-Level phenomena will concern the great portion of our work as the chapters in Part II will show. We change personality when we alter the Meta-Level phenomena that structures our processes of mind, emotion, talk, and action.

As a self-organizing system, our Meta-Level *understandings* (i.e. our Meta-States) govern and stabilize the organization of our "personality." In other words, the feedback and feed forward systems empower our internal *structuring* of personality. They give *meaning* to the primary level experiences and set up a self-reinforcing process in order to eliminate whatever cognitive dissonance that may arise. This allows the "personality" schemas (belief systems, Meta-Level frames) to protect themselves against change.

Later in this chapter, as well as in the chapters to come, we will more fully distinguish between primary and Meta-States. For now, a primary state typically involves a primary emotion and relates to the outside world. In it we reference and respond to some event "out there." When we reflect back onto our state itself and entertain thoughts and feelings about our own experience, we have conceptually moved to a higher level ("meta") which has reference to something "inside," i.e., our own experience.

NLP's Three Meta-Domains and "Personality"

Three domains or broad areas of concern govern the NLP model with regard to *the structure of experience*. We have introduced one of these, the domain of language (i.e., the Meta-Model), now for the other two. Each of these domains operates at *a "meta" level* and so provides for us some useful models as we think about *personality organization*.

These three meta-domains describe three different models, namely, the Meta-Model, Meta-Programs, and Meta-States. Though different in focus and area of concern, all three domains describe *the same referent*, namely, our *subjective human experience*. As such, they provide us *three* avenues for exploring, playing, and transforming human experiences and therefore "personality." These three meta-domains provide the structural genius of the NLP model.

By way of explanation and description regarding these three models, we have:

1) The Meta-Model of Language

NLP itself began with this model as Bandler and Grinder detailed the specific linguistic patterns that set apart and distinguished the excellence in Satir, Perls, and Erickson. As a linguistic model, "the Meta-Model of language" provides a way to hear the cognitive structuring through the kind and form of words and sentences used. The model provides a way to move a person back to the experience out of which their linguistic structure arose. It does so by asking for specific referents.

Using the Meta-Model of language, we can identify the form and structure of *mental processing*, or a person's cognitive functioning. It provides an understanding of the linguistic magic that blesses or curses our lives. And, as an explanatory model about how words work in human consciousness and neurology, we can use the Meta-Model to identify the hypnotic trances that a person has received and lives in. The model also puts into our hands *challenges* to linguistic vagueness which in turn empowers us as we challenge mental mappings that are ill-formed and dis-empowering. By tapping into the structure of precision, it shows us how to de-hypnotize ourselves and others from non-productive trances.

The Meta-Model governs all forms of *languaging*. This includes the primary *representational domain* of sensory-based language (the VAK-visual, auditory, kinesthetic). It also includes the meta-linguistic domain of evaluative words. These generate and govern our primary states.

You will find us repeatedly using the Meta-Model and *meta-modeling* questions as a therapeutic intervention in the following chapters. Questions that ask for more specificity from a person essentially force the person to examine their linguistic mapping and to create a fuller linguistic representation. This typically enriches the client's experience.

This explains why the heart of psychotherapy is "a talking cure." The therapist who provides a caring, respectful, and empathetic environment that enables a person to *feel safe* then provides a service so seldom experienced in today's busy world—a place for thinking through the mental structures about meaning. Often that's enough for transformation. Frequently, people *talk* themselves into more resourceful ways of functioning as they get a chance to *step back*, examine their lives in terms of their larger goals, and are helped along by a skilled clinician.

Sometimes it takes a little more. In *meta-modeling*, a person has to "go back to the experience out of which he or she drew up the original maps." Frequently doing that *from a more adult perspective* updates the old maps. That's all that was wrong. "So back then, your fear of speaking up in that abusive situation made a lot of sense. Does it still make sense today?"

Further, because meta-modeling essentially asks, *"How* do you know?" it forces a person to break down the old mapping into component pieces and to trace the logic. More often than not, the "logic" no longer holds. It breaks down. "How do you know that she intends to insult you?" Frequently, we have jumped to conclusions and not applied a more adult form of "logic" to our neuro-linguistic emotional states. "Does his tone of voice *have to* 'make' you feel bad?" "Has there ever been a time when you didn't have that fearful feeling in response?"

The "common sense" questions in the Meta-Model summarize the kind of magical questioning that alters internal subjective reality. And you'll find these kinds of questions in most therapies. NLP has simply collected and codified them for easier access. (See Bandler and Grinder, 1975, 1976, Hall, 1997.) In Chapter 12 we have the basic format of the Meta-Model and the indexing questions that elicit precision and that therefore can de-construct ill-formed and toxic formulations of meaning.

2) The Meta-Programs

The second meta-domain model in NLP is what we call *Meta-Programs*. These "programs" refer to our perceptual filters, the glasses we use as we view the world, and the structure of how we pay attention to things.

As we come to habitually think and sort in a particular way, we develop Meta-Programs or our favorite ways to perceptually view things. We want the Big Picture (Global) or the Details (Specifics.) We Match what we see and hear with what we already know (Sameness) or we Mismatch and sort for Differences. We sort for Visual input (what things look like), Auditory input (what things sound like) or Kinesthetic input (sensations, feelings). These are but 3 of 50-plus Meta-Programs that have been identified.

The Meta-Programs show up in language. As we all talk, we express our Meta-Programs or Perceptual filters. We will talk about matching or mismatching. "That's kind of like X, isn't it?" "That seems really different from what you said earlier." Because of this, we can find the counterparts of our Meta-Programs in the Meta-Model. For example, we have favored *Modals* which describe our basic *modus operandi* (modal operators) for operating: necessity, impossibility, possibility, desire, etc. These show up in the Meta-Model as the Model Operators. And you can hear people linguistically mapping their reality in these ways. "I have to go to work." "I must get to work." "I get to go to work." The language describes not only perception, but also the mental-emotional world that a person lives in.

Where do Meta-Programs come from? From Meta-States. The kind of thinking and feeling that we use at the primary level (i.e., matching or mismatching, wanting options or procedures, the big picture or details) as we interact with people and the environment does not stay there. We eventually begin to bring that same kind of thinking and perceiving back onto ourselves and our states. Then, after we use that same kind of thinking habitually for a portion of time, and as it continues to reflect back onto itself, it becomes our "program" for thinking and perceiving. It becomes our Meta-Program. It is "meta" because that way of viewing things now governs our perceptual states. Metaphorically, think of them as your operating software programs for what and how you "perceive." (See James and Woodsmall, 1988, Hall and Bodenhamer, 1997).

Meta-Programs, as solidified and habituated Meta-States, emerge as a mind-set that controls perception. Eventually, a way of thinking, feeling, and perceiving becomes so habituated, so regular, and so patterned that it becomes "set" as a way of sorting for things. It becomes a Meta-Program. This highlights the fact that we can "set" a higher level of awareness and take it with us for years.

3) Meta-States

The third NLP Model that marks out a meta-domain is *Meta-States*. This model refers to the higher mental and emotional states that we adopt and develop by means of our self-reflexive consciousness. It describes the domain of all of our meta-cognitions: our thoughts about thoughts, feelings about feelings, etc. Our Meta-States arise and emerge because we do not just think about things, we think about our thinking, we feel about our thinking, and this goes on level after level, layer upon layer, so that we can "texture" our states (our mental-emotional states) with many layers.

In this way we apply thoughts-and-feelings (a neuro-linguistic state) to other states, experiences, thoughts, feelings, memories, imaginations, etc. As we bring one layer to bear upon another layer, we move up the levels (conceptually) and embed our states within states.

This Meta-Level structure of states describes the origin and source of our Meta-Programs. And it shows up in language since most of our higher level states (Meta-States) are languaged into existence. So a gestalt thinker who sorts for the big picture when reading a book or listening to a talk has framed his or her thinking with the value of believing in seeing the big picture. A necessity sorter brings a state of compulsion to bear on every other thought-and-feeling state. In this way, *driver* Meta-Programs (those that powerfully influence perception and thinking) reflect the Meta-States that structure our personality.

Which Meta-States order personality so that we feel confident in self, free to explore, excited about using our skills to the fullest, and compassionate with others? Which Meta-States disorder personality with frames of distrust of people, fear of being wrong and embarrassed, shame of feeling angry and so repressing awareness of values? In the following chapters we will utilize this state-upon-state structure to identify how the vicious spirals and loops can get set up that create a living hell in personality. (See Hall, 1995, 1996, 1999.)

Three Avenues to "Personality"

When we put these three meta-domains together, we have a three-fold way of describing our *experiential reality* in everyday life (i.e., our *mind-body states)*. Uniting them lets us describe our states as *systems of interactive forces* that generate our felt "force fields" within which we live, think, perceive, feel, and act. Each of the meta domains speaks about the structure of subjective experiences, looking at such through three different lenses. It provides the therapist or consultant with three models and avenues.

- **Language:**   The Visual, Auditory, Kinesthetic (VAK) neurological languages by which we represent things and the Linguistic meta-representational systems.

- **Perception:**   Perceptual filters that govern our thinking styles and patterns and that determine our perspective.

- **States**: State dependent neuro-linguistic experiences—the mind-body or thought-feeling states in which we live and from which we operate and which set the higher frames of concepts, beliefs, values, identifications, expectations, assumptions, decisions, etc.

The *linguistic distinctions* that we have in the Meta-Model will occur in the Meta-Programs as *perceptual distinctions* and also show up in the *thought-feeling distinctions* of one's Meta-States. A person's experiences have all of these facets and dimensions: linguistic, perceptual, and state distinctions working *self-reflexively.* So *over time* these dynamics create *a system of interactions.*

This theoretical model thereby offers a paradigm of systemic development of *human consciousness* and *"personality"* in terms of these three Meta-Levels. What follows describes how *mind-body consciousness* in all of its dimensions (concrete, abstract, somatic, intuitive, etc.) grows and develops over time adding more layers of complexity and *growing* our particular *personality style.*

Stage 1: *VAK Representations of the World from World of Stimuli.*

First we track over from our sense representations of the world into a mental world of sights, sounds, sensations, smells, etc. This represents our primary level or primary state of experience. At birth we do not have this ability. Piaget explored "constancy of representation" as it develops in the infant. This refers to the growing maturational ability of an infant to "hold images and representations" in mind even in the absence of the object.

Representational consciousness enables us to manipulate sights, sounds, sensations, words, etc. in our mind and to thereby create new arrangements and combinations.

Stage 2: *Meta-Representation of Representational Map.*

The next stage involves how we can say words *about* our representations of VAK stimuli. Prior to words, as very young children, we see, hear, feel (sense), smell, taste, etc. the world and represent such. Later we move into the linguistic stage of development and begin to use *a symbol system* wherein we let a symbol *stand for* something else.

This describes noises and marks not as *signals*, but as *symbols*. And as such, this distinguishes the basic difference between human consciousness and other kinds of consciousness. Animals almost entirely use and create *signals* but not *symbols*.

The Meta-model as described in *The Structure of Magic, Vol. I* describes the meta-representational map—the mental mapping we do linguistically.

Stage 3: *Meta-Programming—the Thinking Styles we Habitually Use.*

With VAK representation and perception and the use of language, we develop our first *styles* of sorting information. As this habituates, our thinking-feeling becomes a *perceptual style*. Perhaps we always sort visually, or auditorially, or kinesthetically. Perhaps we favor sorting for sameness or for difference, for what we have to do or what we get to do, etc. Eventually these ways of perceiving and languaging our world *coalesce* into the primary level. As they do, they become our perceptual filters, or Meta-Programs. They get into our eyes. This describes how we style our thinking.

Stage 4: *The Meta-Stating Process.*

As consciousness learns to make these meta-moves it not only creates Meta-Programs (perceptual filters), but also layered states: states-about-states. As we access thoughts-feelings about other thoughts-feelings, we organize our *personality* in states-about-states structures, Meta-States. As we do this, we thereby generate new *gestalts.* We generate new systemic configurations of layered consciousness, a "second-order abstraction" (Korzybski, 1933).

Suppose a two year old has a bad experience in potty training. Suppose constipation makes that primary experience painful. Even at two years of age, that child may then become *afraid* of that experience—dread and hate going to potty. And what if a

26

caretaker then *shames* them for *dreading* that? This creates embedded consciousness about consciousness.

Stage 5: *Meta-Level Coalescing.*

The experience continues. Via the habituation of the Meta-States, the Meta-Level frame of references of thoughts-feelings becomes so streamlined that it eventually "collapses" or coalesces into the primary state. When it does, the layeredness and embeddedness of the state merges with the primary level to become undistinguishable.

What happens then? The Meta-State of thought-and-emotion governs and *qualifies* the primary state. "Shame of fear of potting," or "joyful learning," or "compassionate anger," or "disgust of body parts," etc. Meta-levels operate as the frames-of-references that *set the frame* in our lives. And when this happens, the higher frames always govern, organize, and modulate the lower levels.

Stage 6: *The Process Continues.*

Since we can always think about any thought and feel about any feeling, this process of generating more and more Meta-Level frames continues. As it does, it generates more Meta-Programs and Meta-States. With every thought-about-a-thought, feeling-about-a-feeling, idea-about-an-idea, etc., we become more and more layered and embedded in a dynamic, system flow of consciousness. This creates more and more of our *domains of knowledge* or frames-of-reference that we use to navigate life. When we "go upward" (the Transdiveration Search in early NLP literature), we go "up" to these Meta-levels.

And it also continues to *coalesce* into the primary state. As it does, we fill up the personal "space" around us (the bubble of our state at the primary level) as our *neuro-linguistic reality* or model of the world with 3-D holographic structures. This refers to how we project out from our inner world in actual 3-D space our time-lines, values, beliefs, Meta-Levels, affirmations and negations, etc.

Figure 2.1

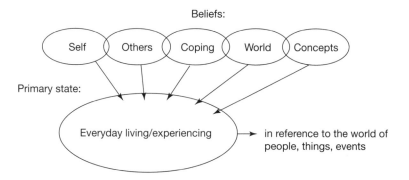

Meta-schema frame of reference

The Ordering and the Disordering of "Personality"

The three meta-domains of consciousness give us a picture of how we *order and disorder* "personality." These domains provide an explanation of how we generate an *ordered* (or dis-ordered) format (frame-of-reference) for our person. How do we *order* and *align* ourselves so that we create a healthy "personality?" How could we *disorder* and *mis-align* it?

We do so in terms of our innate *powers* of thinking, emoting, speaking, behaving, and relating. We may do so by using these *personality functions* to create an internal map of reality—and of how to navigate the various realities that we encounter (cultural, familial, personal, etc.). This results in our model of the world, a cognitive map or schema.

- To the extent that we have a nicely ordered map that accords fairly close to the territory and that productively enables us to cope with it, we have a good map, and hence a good productive, healthy *personality*.

- To the extent that we have a disordered, disorganized, chaotic, and toxic map that doesn't fit the territory very well and that doesn't allow us to move out into it in a productive way, we have an unproductive and unuseful model of the world and a *disordered personality*.

This suggests several things. The *quality* and *nature* of our personality depends upon our model of the world. Behind every tortured person who suffers from some *personality disorder* lies a disordered and probably toxic map of the world. Behind every highly successful genius and *healthy personality* lies a well-ordered, fairly accurate, and highly useful map.

This leads to several NLP presuppositions about human functioning or "nature." These distinguish the NLP model from most other models of psychology. These hold true except for those rare occasions when someone is truly suffering from neurological and/or brain damage.

> **"People are not deficient, damaged, and 'the problem'."**

Human problems do not normally emerge from innate genetic disorders but rather in the *mapping processes* that a given person has learned and used in coping with life.

> **"People are not broken; they work perfectly well."**

In terms of "personality" and "sanity," this puts the burden on map *accuracy, correspondence, usefulness,* and *practicality.* Korzybski (1933–1994) argued this throughout the 830 pages of that massive work. In doing so, he did *not* make map *accuracy* any kind of god or absolute. We *only* deal with the world indirectly, through our maps. And, a map never "is" the territory. It operates at a different logical level. The value of a map lies in both its similarity (never "sameness") and its usefulness. This explains why metaphorical maps (totally inaccurate) can play a very valuable role in sanity.

The Factors that Enter into "Personality"

As we have noted, numerous factors enter into the *growing* or learning of *personality.* We mentioned many of these in the previous section about the three meta-domains. Here I repeat some of that and extend the discussion.

1) Experience

It all begins with *experience*, namely, the events, situations, and inter-personal relations that we experience as we move through life. This describes *what* happens to us. *Experience*, however, does not only apply to first-hand see-hear-feel events, it can also include *vicarious* experiences (i.e. stories, learnings, movies, fantasies, imaginations, etc.). What drives experience so that it becomes fodder for *personality ordering or disordering* involves the activation of representation. Go through anything and *not* represent it—forget it, ignore it, etc. and it will not play a significant role in *personality*. Of course, if we *forbid* representation itself (a Meta-State), this paradoxically and ironically *amplifies* the effect. This speaks about the power of *negation* to increase human pain—a central factor in the neurotic process that we will explore later (Chapter 4).

2) Representation and Evaluation

Once we have an experience, we inevitably do two things with it: we represent it and we evaluate it. In *representation* of events, we internally present to ourselves the visual, auditory, and kinesthetic components that comprised the situation. Then in *evaluation* we think *about* it and attribute various meanings to it. This begins the *human ordering (structuring)* process.

> How do we think about the event, situation, conversation, etc.?
> What causation meanings do we give the event?
> What identity meanings do we attribute to the event?
> How do we respond to the event?
> What do we think about our response to the event?

How we evaluate a situation depends upon our beliefs about things. These beliefs function as over-arching *frames-of-reference* that guide our thinking. Beck, *et al.*, wrote:

> Those beliefs are embedded in more or less stable structures, labeled 'schemas,' that select and synthesize incoming data. The psychological sequence progresses then from evaluation to affective and motivational arousal, and finally to selection, and

implementation of a relevant strategy. We regard the basic structures (schemas) upon which these cognitive, affective, and motivational processes are dependent as the fundamental units of
personality. (p. 22)

3) Adaptation

As we think and emote about the situation, and think about our
thinking-and-emoting, *we respond to it*. We respond to it in order to
cope with it or to avoid it. We do so in adaptive and maladaptive
ways. Our response may effectively enable us to cope with the situation, or it may not. This *responding* to things occurs at all levels
of our *personality functions* (thinking, emoting, speaking, behaving,
and relating). Thus we may:

deny	avoid	repress	suppress	feel guilt
depress	whine	aggress	fear	blame
distract	pretend	excuse	rationalize	wish
explore	empathize	question	gather information	
etc.				

4) Genetic Predispositions

As we find ourselves moving through various events and experiences in life and responding with (and to) our innate powers of
thinking-emoting, speaking, acting, and relating, our response
patterns uniquely given to each of us via our DNA structures come
to light.

> There is strong evidence that certain types of relatively stable tem-
> peraments and behavioral patterns are present at birth (Kagan,
> 1989). These innate characteristics are best viewed as 'tendencies'
> that can become accentuated or diminished by experience. (Beck,
> 1990, p. 28)

> Similar developmental processes may be assumed to occur in
> humans (Gilbert, 1989). It is reasonable to consider the notion that
> long-standing cognitive-affective-motivational programs influ-
> ence our automatic processes: the way we construe events, what
> we feel, and how we are disposed to act. (Beck, 1990, p. 24)

We speculate that these dysfunctional beliefs have originated as a result of the interaction between the individual's genetic predisposition and exposure to undesirable influences from other people and specific traumatic events. (Beck, 1990, p. 23)

5) *Reflexive Thinking-Feeling*

Behind each and every one of these responses (adaptive and maladaptive) we generate other thoughts-and-emotions. Some of these support our responses, some of them contradict them. By such reflexive thinking we create various Meta-Level structures that organize our personality forces. These responses also come out of some schema or rule-guided map that explains for us *why* doing things this way will make life go better.

Yet because the map does not exist as the territory, a map may inadequately and even erroneously guide a response. Maps vary in different degrees of usefulness and accuracy. Adler described such "private logic" as the determinant of personal experience.

- What thought-feeling lies behind a given response?
- What do you hope to accomplish by that response?
- Why?
- How do you evaluate your response?
- What thoughts do you have about the thoughts that guide your first thoughts?

These questions enabled us to realize that thoughts-behind-thoughts, the unconscious level of thoughts, frame our thinking-and-emoting at the primary level. These all point to the beliefs embedded in the schemas that direct our life and form our "personality."

What we call *"personality traits"* (and "personality disorders") ultimately express themselves externally as *different coping and adaptive styles of behaving*. We respond to events characteristically with dependency, by withdrawing, by shying away from, by extraverting, aggressing, arrogating, etc. As a result we develop "personality" *styles* that involve thoughts, feelings, values, behaviors, habits, etc. of:

dependency	withdrawnness	extraversion
intraversion	narcissism	anti-social
passive-aggressive	paranoid	histrionic
schizoid	obsessive-compulsive	sociopath

When we de-nominalize these "labels" that indicate a nominalized process, we can then identify how these attributes function as *a basic strategy* whereby a given person actually functions.

In other words, these do *not* describe what the person *"is"* in any essential or final form, but simply *how the person has learned to operate*. By so de-nominalizing our language, we can remain clear about our subject and see the behavioral component elements that make up the "personality." This also empowers us to recognize specific "personality disorders" that arise when a person over-emphasizes or over-does some response that doesn't work in terms of helping him or her to adapt to reality.

If a person negates their self this may lead to a dependent personality, avoidance personality, a passive-aggressive personality, or a narcissistic personality. If a person fears and lets the fear grow and get out of hand, this can lead to a paranoid personality, a panic disorder personality, etc. So with other maladaptive processes: avoiding, competing, exhibiting, arrogating, denying, intellectualizing, etc.

6) Needs, Impulses, and Wants

Our *felt impulses, needs, and wants* lie at the center of how we order and disorder "personality." This comprises our primary state and many of the internal events or experiences to which we respond.

Freud thought of such as our *motivational forces* that shape and mold our everyday life. These express themselves at the kinesthetic level as our "feelings." Maslow (1950) distinguished such *feelings* as *deficiency "needs"* (the survival needs: air, water, food, shelter, etc.) and *growth needs* (security and safety, love and affection, self-esteem, self-actualization, etc.). These "needs" operate as *the drivers* of "personality." As we develop and grow, we become aware of some of the things that we evaluate as pleasurable and desirable.

What *energized felt passions* drive you? What do you seek to experience or feel? These "states" comprise both basic and primary states as well as some of the most existential and conceptual states known. These include a wide range of things:

Achievement	Accomplishment
Love & Affection	Romance
Acknowledgment	Recognition
Power/Control	Leadership
Peace & Quiet	Challenge
Excitement/Fun	Sex
Mental Challenge	Food
Variety	Travel
Etc.	

7) Cognizing, Thinking, Reasoning about our Needs

Our kinesthetic impulses (needs, wants, desires), as such, do not form or govern personality apart from our understanding of them. Alone they just provide a general energy. Cognitive formats or understandings form and mold these "needs." If we give too much power to them—we become especially prone to various *cognitive distortions*. Our reasoning and thinking skills become vulnerable to all kinds of errors.

Personalizing	Awfulizing
Emotionalizing	Discounting
Should-ing	Catastrophizing
Blaming	All-or-Nothing Thinking
Over-Generalizing	Labeling
Mind-reading	Can't- ing

Such cognitive distortions cause us to develop some very poor strategies for coping with the stresses of life, with psycho-social stressors, and with interpersonal stress. If such thinking continues, it becomes our very way of "seeing" (perceiving) things so that it becomes a Meta-Level frame-of-reference. This perpetuates our difficulties and makes the "personality" structure more resistant to change.

Such cognitive distortions contaminate our beliefs so that we begin to code our beliefs as *extreme* ("all", over-generalized), as *rigid* (all/nothing, black/white, inflexible), and as *imperative* ("must," "should"). These patterns for thinking-and-emoting then begin to shape our innate intelligences.

Over time our beliefs become even more fixed as they solidify into *stable self-states or our "personality."* Thus our inner predispositions plus our environmental factors plus our inter-personal interactions with reality lead to the re-inforcement and/or extinguishing of our beliefs. These beliefs contain "do's" and "don'ts" (commands and prohibitions) about living and adopting. They guide how we internally communicate with ourselves as we do self-monitoring, self-evaluation, self-warnings, self-instructions, which all add to the ordering and/or disordering of our "personality."

When exaggerated or deficient, this leads to "personality" disorders. This highlights the role that self-languaging plays in creating and driving "personality" structures. How we talk to ourselves about the events of life ultimately forms and molds our style of "being a person."

Figure 2.2

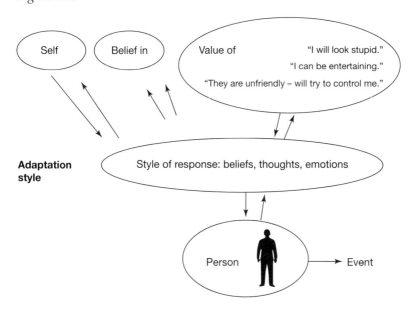

8) The Inter-Personal Context

The inter-personal context that we grow up in also plays a crucial role in how we order and disorder our "personality." The states of our parents and other significant adults create the first context within which we develop. What characterized these states?

Depression	Negativity
Accusatory (blaming, critical)	Hatefulness
Jealousy	Suspicion
Anger and hostility	Curiosity
Fear/worry	Religiosity
Curiosity & learning	Respect
Disrespect	Frustration
Fatigue and tiredness	Playfulness
Dignity	Care
Sadness (grieving)	

The quality, nature, and kind of states that we grow up in *set the context* for personality development. It offers a map of what one can expect, of possibilities, of taboos, etc. As we explore the inter-personal context within which we made our maps, learned how to cognize (think about) the world, we discover the "personality" styles that our environment predisposes us to.

These contexts also provide us with what we have responded, or reacted, to that has formed and molded our perception. Our perceptions thus come *embedded* in specific contexts. We then store our information as "meaningful configurations" (i.e. beliefs, values, understandings, etc.). From this we then build Meta-States about things—our interpretations and attributions of meanings. We do this to cope, to adapt, to defend ourselves.

Figure 2.3

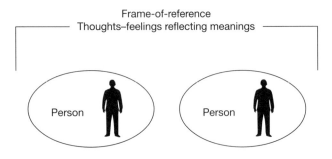

Frame-of-reference
Thoughts–feelings reflecting meanings

Person   Person

Figure 2.4

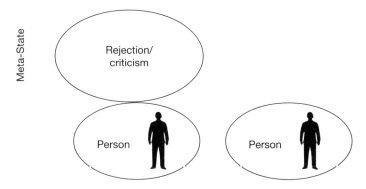

In addition to the emotional and meaning contexts in which we grow up, our parents and others bring other states to bear on our responses. Using the Meta-States model, we refer to this as *inter-personal meta-stating*.

We developed Meta-States, beliefs, responses as we processed information and thereby developed self-concepts, and self-schemas. If our states and Meta-States become characterized by rigid rules ("I must always do a perfect job") so that we feel a constant evaluation, this leads to inflexibility. Eventually over time, our beliefs broaden and become more absolute and extreme.

9) Habituation and acceptance of habituation

Figure 2.5

As we then become used to these states, we come to *accept them* (dysfunctional though they be) as our "reality," fate, and future. Then as we come to accept our dysfunctional beliefs, this sets up an ever larger level frame. The result? We lose our ability to reality-test them!

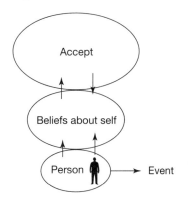

This *acceptance* of our "self" beliefs about our everyday life (a meta Meta-State) then solidifies as our "personality" structure. *Beliefs*, which exist as a Meta-State structure, create our basic orientation to reality. Thus once we have constructed, installed, and accepted various beliefs about our self at a Meta-Level, we use that Meta-Level awareness to perceive and interpret things. Nor will we give up or relinquish these self-constructions ("personality" structures) until we have deframed them and invented new and more adaptive beliefs as our strategies for "being."

These Meta-Level over-arching beliefs (as our "personality" schemas) become deeply ingrained and entrenched. They form the very framework of our "personality."

"Personality" as Meta-States

"Personality" then begins as a primary state of thoughts-and-emotions as we experience the sensory based world of events. At this point in our development, we experience very primitive states of pleasure or pain driven by hunger, thirst, wetness, dryness, etc.

From there we develop ideas and concepts. We develop concepts *about* our experiences, "time," purpose and destiny, people, "human nature," "self," etc. The overall configuration of all of these states and Meta-States begins to order our basic *personality*. Adler described the result as our *"life-style,"* i.e. our way of being in the world.

As Meta-Level phenomena, these higher level states give us a sense of stability. Our concepts (especially those concepts of "self") stabilize us. These frames, beliefs, values, etc. also begin to feel and seem so "real." Via our state-*about*-state structuring of consciousness, we *set frames of reference* or frames of meaning and then use them as our referencing system. This generates our neuro-semantic structures. It goes beyond the associative meaning of stimulus—response patterning. It goes beyond one event, feeling, or thought associated or linked to another. Now we move up and create another kind of meaning making, *Contextual Meaning or Frame Meaning.*

At the primary level our thoughts-and-emotions go *out* to the world to assess the territory. We use our thinking-and-emoting to become aware of the world and to make our preliminary maps about it. But then consciousness does what consciousness does best—it *reflects back onto itself.* We think about our thinking. We think about the products of our thinking (our former thoughts-and-feelings). As we do this, we move to a higher logical level and our consciousness now discerns, not things "out" there, but things (concepts, feelings, values, beliefs, etc.) "inside."

When we do this about our "self" (our concepts of human nature, personhood, identity, purpose, destiny, etc.) we create *"Self" Meta-States.* By doing so we generate Meta-Level maps (concepts) about ourselves as a Self. These Meta-Level Self states become our personality strategy for how to "be."

As these Meta-States develop, they take on more and more *the characteristics of stability, out-of-consciousness, chronicity, consistency, etc.* The stability of these states give our lives a sense of consistency. Chronicity speaks about how they become so consistent, and operate so continually that they seem always present, that they have an inertia within them. When over-done, we experience these Meta-Level states as rigid (giving us less flexibility), compulsive, and severe in how strong and pronounced they become.

This enables us to analyze *personality* in terms of dual levels. First we have the primary level structure of "personality." At this level we have the basic *functions or powers* of "personality," i.e. thinking-emoting, speaking, acting, and relating. Here we will find various "personality" symptoms: manifest problems, dysfunctional feelings and behaviors, etc.

Second, we have the Meta-Levels and the over-arching structures that make up those facets of "personality" that, for the most part, operate outside of consciousness. At this level we have automatic thoughts, beliefs, and emotions. We have our incorporated assumptions and frames of life.

The cognitive psychology model (Beck, 1990) posits that our "cognitive structures are categorically and hierarchically organized." Beck has labeled these meta-structures that organize "personality" as *schemas,* or rule-guided behavior. "Schemas provide the instructions to guide the focus, direction, and qualities of daily life and special contingencies." (p. 4)

He has also noted that these schemas involve cognitive distortions or errors, that they have attributional biases within them which create problems for us in terms of our experience of "personality." The rules within these schemas govern our information processing (p. 8). Yet these schemas, as meta-frames, operate at unconscious levels. So in terms of personality disorders, Beck notes that those who suffer from them—"usually have little idea of how they got that way, how they contributed to their own problems, how to change" (p. 6). Yet at the essence of "personality disorders," these schemas as meta-frames "cause," motivate, and explain why the person processes information selectively and dysfunctionally (p. 36), which then keeps the person perpetuating the very "personality strategies" that disordered them in the first place.

The Strategy of Doing "Personality"

Given that *personality* arises as a set of interactions between (or within) a person and his or her environment, it not only constitutes a *learned* and *grown into* phenomenon, but a phenomenon that has *a structure.* We describe this sequence of representational and meta steps as a *strategy* in NLP.

The strategies model also indicates that when a person has *a strategy* for any subjective experience, eventually the strategy will habitualize and streamline. When it does, then any initial cue of the strategy can immediately set off the whole strategy. As it does, it puts a person into *a particular state of consciousness.*

For example, at first we may have to build and practice the "driving a car" strategy, but after it streamlines via habituation, merely sitting in a car activates all of the programs of thoughts-feelings, behaviors, and responses involved in that strategy. We access a "driving the car" state and don't have to even think about it. It seems to have "a life of its own."

This same process applies to *personality strategies*. Once we practice a certain way of thinking-and-emoting, of valuing, believing, speaking, behaving, and relating—it habituates and streamlines. As it does, it also moves outside of consciousness awareness and becomes, at a Meta-Level, simply our basic *frame-of-reference*. In this case, it becomes our frame of reference for *being*.

Now we don't have to even think about how to "be"—how to think, emote, value, believe, act, or relate. The sub-programs within the larger frame-of-reference operate at a Meta-Level as our context. When our *personality strategy* has reached this level of development, we have incorporated our contexts, perceptual filters, and meta-frames and simply take them with us everywhere we go.

Texturing our States

Suppose you could *texture* your mental and emotional states. Suppose you could add various *tastes, feels, qualities* to your current frame of mind. Suppose you could make the way you move through the world *richer and fuller* and radiating with a delightful and fascinating *aroma*. Suppose that you're not stuck or limited with just the plain vanilla states…

If we begin with, and use, these *supposing* questions regarding the quality and nature of our everyday mind-body states, we can then begin to *design* and *engineer* the very quality of our lives. When we do this, we move to one of the most exciting and captivating features of *Meta-States*.

Plain Vanilla States

Consider the nature and quality of some of the following mental and emotional states. Examine the following list of terms that summarize these common everyday states and take a moment to explore them in terms of how you experience the *quality* of these states. You could ask about their—

- Intensity and Strength

- Accessibility and Development
- Features and Feel
- Ecology and Balance

Confidence	Anger	Joy
Clarity	Fear	Playfulness
Commitment	Anxiety	Respect
Courage	Sadness	Interest
Congruence	Discouragement	Enthusiasm
Curiosity	Tension	Relaxation

What kind of *texture* do you experience with these states? What are some of the qualities and properties that characterize them? Perhaps you experience:

- Hesitating confidence; courageous confidence; foolish confidence; playful confidence; bold confidence.
- Slow clarity; dull clarity; bright and brilliant clarity; developing clarity; curious clarity.
- Fear of commitment; total commitment; stressful commitment; playful commitment; miserable commitment.
- Aggressive curiosity; rigid curiosity; humorous and silly curiosity; serious curiosity.
- Hostile anger; dreadful fear of anger; shame about feeling guilty for being angry.
- Shameful fear; bold fear; curious fear; playful fear.

Flushing out our Neuro-Semantic Structures

The fact that we have and experience our mind-body states in terms of other qualities and properties informs us that we have, and carry with us, *Meta-States*. Typically, however, we don't experience them as "meta," as "above" or "beyond" our thinking. It all seems part and parcel of one state—one experience. This only means that the higher level thoughts and feelings that we have applied or "brought to bear" upon the plain vanilla state has completely *coalesced into the state and now comprises its texture.*

In this way, our Meta-States get "into our eyes." They coalesce and percolate into our muscles. Of course, when this happens, we cease to notice them as separate or apart of our regular everyday states. They become *a part of* the state and no longer *apart.* They enter into the state as the higher level qualifying and governing frames-of-reference. And in this way, our Meta-States seem hidden and invisible to us even though we never leave home without them.

Yet we can easily tease out the higher levels. We can use the qualities of our states as a way to *flush out Meta-States* (whether your own or those of someone else). Simply inquire about the quality of a state.

> Say, when you get angry, what's the quality of your anger?
> Would I like you angry?
> Are you respectful and thoughtful when you're angry?
> Or do you lose your head and go ballistic when you get mad?
> Can you maintain civility and patience when you're feeling upset and angry?
> Or do you become impatient and insulting?

The answers and responses that emerge from the *quality question* about a state *flush out* the higher frames. And typically, there are many of them. You can also ask about other Meta-Level phenomena.

> What do you believe about anger?
> What memories in your personal history inform you about this?
> What values or dis-values do you have about experiencing anger?
> What moral judgments do you make about this?
> How does this affect who you are?
> How does anger play into or fail to play into your destiny, mission, and vision?
> What do you expect about anger? About people when they get angry?

Understanding the Meta-Levels in our States

Far from exhausting the subject, these questions just get us started in this domain of the Meta-Levels in our Neuro-Semantics. Yet to fully understand what we mean by Meta-States and their importance, we need to step back and think about our everyday states. At first reckoning, they seem ordinary, plain, and of vanilla flavoring. But they are not.

They are textured. They have properties and features and characteristics that go far beyond "plain vanilla." Over the years, via everyday experiences, we come to *qualify them*. We set them inside of various frames-of-reference. And every time we do, we thereby create a Meta-Level state. And remember, we're using the term "state" here as a holistic and dynamic term that includes state of mind, state of body, and state of emotion.

So, using "anger" as a prototype, we come to experience *thoughts-and-feelings and neurological somatic sensations about* the state of anger. We like it or dislike it. We fear it or love it. We dread it or long for it. We believe it can serve us; we believe it only turns things ugly. All of these are Meta-States. *Dynamic, ever-moving and changing mental and emotional states about* other states.

Structurally, a Meta-State stands in special relationship to our states. It relates to the primary state as a higher state of awareness *about* it. This makes it *about* the lower state as a classification of it. The junior state functions as a member of that class. The higher or Meta-State functions as a category for understanding and feeling *about* the lower.

That's why "fear of our anger" (fearful anger) differs in texture so much from "respect of our anger" (respectful anger).

That's why "shame about getting angry because it only turns things nasty" differs so much in texture to "appreciation of my powers to get angry because it informs me that some perceived value or understanding feels violated and allows me to respectfully explore the situation *anger.*"

At a higher logical level, the mental and emotional *frames* that we bring to our primary experiences represent *the governing influence* in our lives. The higher frame as a message about the lower experiences modulates, organizes, and governs. It functions as a self-organizing attractor in the mind-body system. That's why Meta-States are so important. In your Meta-States, you will find all of your values, beliefs, expectations, understandings, identifications, etc.

The Systemic Nature of Meta-States

While I have teased apart the structure of our higher frames-of-references (or Meta-States) from the primary experiences, we can only do that for sake of analysis and understanding. In actual practice primary and Meta-Levels of experiences or states merge into *one unit*. Research scientist Arthur Koestler introduced the term "holons" many years ago to describe what in reality is composed of *"whole/parts."* These whole/parts *holons* refer to any "entity" that is itself *a whole* and yet simultaneously *a part* of some other whole.

Consider our "states" as holons. We experience our "states" as a whole. Confidence, courage, commitment, playfulness, joy, flow, etc. We experience each as a whole within itself. And yet, they also all exist (and actually *only* exist) as a part of some larger whole. We would have no state without a body, a functioning nervous system, a thinking brain, "life," oxygen, an atmosphere, etc.

A mind-body state operates as a holon also in terms of all of the higher mental and emotional frames (beliefs, values, expectations, etc.) that support it. The state of confidence is *a whole* and it is also *a part* of many other higher level frames.

Ken Wilber speaks about holons in terms of *agency and communion, and transcendence and dissolution. Each holon has its own identity or autonomy.* It has its own agency or identity as a whole. Yet as a *holon* within a larger whole, it also communicates and has communion with other wholes (i.e., confidence with respect, within esteem for self, within possibilities, etc.). This allows it to *transcend* itself and to go beyond what it has been to become more of what it can be. It can add novel components to itself. Or it can dissolve. A holon can be pulled up or pulled down.

Yet when a state as a holon moves up and experiences a transcendent of itself (self-transcendence) something new *emerges*. This occurs, for example, when we develop a compelling outcome so that we're empowered to boldly face a fear. In this case, *courage* emerges. And while the lower was transcended and included in the higher, this continuous process produces discontinuities. Yet the *leap* upward does not work in reverse.

In systems theory we say that the new *gestalt* is "more than the sum of the parts." Some new configuration has *emerged*. And merely *adding* all of the parts together does not, and cannot, explain it. *Emergence* has occurred. There was a leap upward to a higher form of organization and structure. Wilber (1996) writes:

> So there are both discontinuities in evolution—mind cannot be reduced to life, and life cannot be reduced to matter; and there are continuities. (p. 24)

He also says that "holons emerge holarchically." (p. 27) This term, holarchical, also comes from Koestler and replaces "hierarchical." Holarchically describes what we mean by a natural hierarchy, not the ones that we create which involve dominations. Natural hierarchies describe an order of increasing wholeness: particles to atoms to cells to organisms or letters to words to sentences to paragraphs. The whole of one level becomes a part of the whole of the next.

Each higher level *embraces* and *engulfs* the lower. That's why when we take a primary everyday state like anger or confidence and set various frames on it, we create new emergent properties to nurture the mind-and-body on.

Imagine embracing your anger with acceptance, appreciation, and then wonder. Imagine engulfing it in love, respect, and honor. Imagine applying mindfulness, values, and patience to it. Imagine bringing ecology concerns, moral uprightness, and honor to it. Mix well. Put into the oven of your mind, let it bake for awhile…

Imagine embracing your power to take action in the world with acceptance and appreciation. Imagine engulfing it with ownership, excitement, and joy. Imagine applying hope, desired outcomes, willingness to take intelligent risks, love, and concern for others, to it. Mix all of these well in a state of contemplative relaxation. Let it bake as you learn and explore and develop…

Texturing occurs. With *Meta-States,* you can now take charge of the process and design the kind of quality states that will turn you on to life in new and exciting ways.

States Plus: Transcend and Include

To transcend any everyday plain vanilla state, we begin at the primary level of consciousness as we notice our thoughts and feelings *about* something "out there" in the world. This defines a primary state. Our awareness focuses on something external to ourselves. We fear driving fast, closed in places, particular tones of voices. We get angry at violence, insults, and threats to our way of life. We delight in and enjoy the beauty of a scene or a piece of music.

We *transcend* this experience while *including it* as we move up to a higher level of thought, emotion, and awareness. This creates a new level of organization. We have something *higher* that still contains the essentials of the lower *plus something else.*

In respectful, considerate, and patient anger—we still have anger. We still have the sense of threat or danger to our person or way of life, yet the *anger* is now textured in larger levels of mind and emotion. That causes something new to emerge. We have the Anger State *Plus* something that transcends "mere" anger (that is, animal-like, brute anger). Now we have a higher kind of *human* anger, even spiritual anger.

We have hierarchy (levels) of states or holarchy because as Aristotle first pointed out:

**All of the lower is in the higher, but not all of
the higher is in the lower.**

Molecules contain atoms, but atoms do not contain molecules. As we move up levels, the higher level *includes* the lower and *transcends* it. As it transcends the lower, it *adds* new features, qualities, properties, and characteristics to it. In Meta-States this provides us with the ability to engineer new emergent properties for our states. It gives us the key to the structure of subjectivity as experiences become more complex and layered.

When our learning is *taken up into* playfulness and appreciation, when we *engulf* it with passion and the intention to improve the quality of life—something new emerges. We have a passionate learning state that's much accelerated and that's a real turn-on. It takes on more of the qualities of "genius." Each higher level has added new components that enrich the emergent gestalt. Now something bigger and more expansive arises. Now we have the Learning State *Plus*.

Meta-State Permeation

When I first wrote the text for *Meta-States* (1995), I made numerous mistakes in conceptualizing and theorizing about the structure of the model. These have been completely updated and the mistakes eliminated in the totally revised edition (2000). One of those mistakes involved thinking that the higher levels could not be anchored kinesthetically. At the time I didn't understand how the higher levels operate as holons, how they not only *transcend* but also *embrace and include* the lower levels. I now understand how they *permeate* the lower levels giving what had been a plain vanilla state all kinds of rich textures, tastes, aromas, etc.

Accordingly, we have recently been developing a whole series of patterns and processes for "mind-muscling" the mind-body integration that fully allows the higher levels to percolate down through the levels. This completes the process by which we layer thought upon thought and feeling upon feeling so that in the end we have holons—whole/part states within a hierarchical or holarchical system. These *State Plus* experiences then offer us topnotch high quality states that we have textured with the very best of resources. And when you get to this place, you have entered into the highest of design engineering with Meta-States. Now we have a powerful process for texturing our states so that they respond to our intentional designs.

Summary

Having recognized *the process nature of "personality"* we next turned to the micro and macro *behaviors* that make up such structures. This led us to look at numerous facets as we sought to model the patterning:

- Internal representations of information: sensory and language.

- Contexts and Environments within which such patterning arises and makes sense.

- Meta-levels of awareness and representation—higher level "meanings" that a person attributes to various concepts: time, self, causation, persons, relationships, purpose, destiny, responsibility, etc.

- Thinking patterns and styles (Meta-Programs) that govern the person's perceiving and filtering.

From this initial list of component features we have begun to recognize *how "personality"* works.

Chapter 3

The Strategies Model and "Personality"

"Personality" as a Strategy

In the previous chapters, we have mentioned the NLP Strategies Model and have even sketched out a brief outline of it. The time has now come, however, to provide a full description of this model. To that end, we now turn the pen over to Richard and Margot.

What do we mean by "Personality Strategy"?

We can describe "personality" in practical terms as a series of frequently used strategies. When we do this, then the process of assisting people in changing their personality "disorders" becomes the process of assisting them in altering less successful strategies or of adding more useful strategies. You can find the fullest description of the NLP Strategies Model in *Neuro-Linguistic Programming Volume 1* (Dilts *et al.,* 1980). The developers describe a "strategy" in this way:

> The basic elements from which the patterns of human behavior are formed are the perceptual systems through which the members of the species operate on their environment: vision (sight), audition (hearing), kinesthesis (body sensations) and olfaction/gustation (smell/taste). We postulate that all of our ongoing experience can usefully be coded as consisting of some combination of these sensory classes." Thus, human experience was described as an ongoing sequence of internal representations in the five sensory systems. (p. 17)

We write these senses using NLP notation as:

V (visual)
A (auditory)
K (kinesthetic)
O (olfactory) and
G (gustatory).

More precisely, the visual sense includes *visual recall,* where I remember an image as I have seen it before through my eyes (V^r); *visual construct,* where I make up an image I have never seen before (V^c); and *visual external,* where I look out at something in the real world (V^e).

So if I look up and see a blue sky, and then remember being at the beach, and then feel good, our notation would go: $V^e \rightarrow V^r \rightarrow K$. Even though at each step, I have *all* my senses functioning so that I can still feel my body while I look up, yet *my attention* shifts from sense to sense and does so in a sequence. That's what we mean by "strategy."

The developers of NLP used the TOTE model to explain the sequencing of these sensory representations. This model was developed by George Miller, Eugene Galanter and Karl Pribram (1960) to explain how complex behavior occurs. Ivan Pavlov's original studies had shown that simple behaviors can be produced by the stimulus-response cycle ($S \rightarrow R$). When Pavlov's dogs heard the tuning fork ring (a stimulus or "anchor" in NLP), they salivated (response). Yet there is more to dog behavior than stimulus-response.

What more is there to it? If a dog sees an intruder at the gate of its section (stimulus anchor), it may bark. However, it doesn't go on barking forever. It actually *checks* to see if the intruder has run away. If the intruder left, the dog stops performing the barking operation and goes back to its kennel. If the intruder is still there, the dog may continue with that strategy, or move on to another response, such as biting the intruder.

In Miller and Pribram's model, the first stimulus (the anchor of seeing the intruder) is the *Trigger* (the first T for *Test* in "TOTE") for

Original NLP Strategies Model

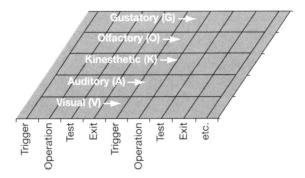

the dog's "scaring-intruders-away" strategy. The barking itself is the *Operation* (O). Checking to see if the intruder has left is the *Test* (second T). Going back to the kennel is the *Exit* from the strategy (E). We can write this as:

$$V^e \rightarrow K^e \rightarrow V^e/V^c \rightarrow K^e$$

Notice that the checking stage (test) is done by comparing the result of the operation (what the dog can see after barking) with the result that was desired (what the dog imagines seeing, a person running away).

Let's take another example. When I hear some music on the radio that I really like (trigger or anchor), I reach over and turn up the radio (operation). Once it sounds as loud as I enjoy it sounding (test), I sit back and listen. The strategy, including the end piece where I listen (another whole strategy really) is:

$$A^e \rightarrow K^e \rightarrow A^e/A^r \rightarrow K^e \, A^e$$

Meta-Representational Systems

We also process information in *words* and using words. The co-founders of NLP described this type of information as *"auditory digital,"* distinguishing it from the auditory input we get, for example, in listening to music or to the sound of the wind. As we think in words (or talk to ourselves), we pay attention specifically to the "meaning" coded into each specific word, rather than to the music of our voice. This moves us *up* to a higher level. Dilts *et al.* (1980) write:

> The digital portions of our communications belong to a class of experience that we refer to as 'secondary experience.' Secondary experience is composed of the representations that we use to *code* our primary experiences—*secondary* experiences (such as words and symbols) are only meaningful in terms of the *primary* sensory representations that they anchor for us. (p. 75)

NLP Strategies Model With Meta-Levels

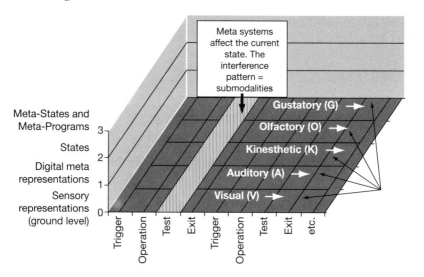

When we use words to talk about "anchors," for example, what we say only has meaning depending on your ability to be "anchored" by the word "anchor" so that you can see, hear, and/or feel actual sensory representations of an anchor. Recognizing how we use "anchor" in NLP to refer to a stimulus or linkage, that term now probably creates a set of different internal pictures for you.

Words (as the auditory-digital representation system) function as a meta-sensory system. They operate as symbols *meta* to ("above" and "about") the sensory systems. In other writings, we have pointed out that there exists at least one other meta-sensory system in common use—*the Visual Digital System*. Many scientists, composers like Mozart, and computer programmers heavily depend and use *the visual digital system* (Bolstad and Hamblett, 1999). In visual digital thinking, visual images or symbols take the place of words. This would include diagrams, cartoons, icons, etc.

Einstein says (quoted in Dilts, 1994–5, Volume II):

> The words or the language, as they are written or spoken, do not seem to play any role in my mechanism of thought. The psychical entities which seem to serve as elements in thought are certain signs and more or less clear images which can be "voluntarily" reproduced and combined. (pp. 48–49)

We have incorporated the digital senses into the NLP Strategy Notation in order that we can describe one of the common strategies people use to create a state of depression. It goes as follows:

$$K^i — A_d — K^i/K^c — A_d$$

K^i	Feel some uncomfortable body sensations;
A_d	Tell themselves they should feel better;
K^i/K^c	Check how they feel now, having told themselves off;
A_d	Tell themselves off for feeling that way, and repeat, ad nauseum.

Digital senses do not just meta–comment on "stable" primary representations, of course. They actually alter those representations. When we learn the words "foot" and "leg," we actually come to perceive those areas of our body as visually and kinesthetically distinct units. It enables us to punctuate reality in this way. Yet this distinction does not occur in the New Zealand Maori language, where the leg from the thigh down plus the foot is called the wae-wae, and they consider this entire structure as one unit.

In this way, *the meta-senses* create what physicists would call an interference pattern with your primary representations. In physics, an interference pattern occurs when two wave motions of the same frequency "collide" with each other.

So if we drop two stones into a pool of water, circular ripples move out from each stone. As these ripples cross each other, they create a complex weave of mutual interference. The complex water movements in the pool now result from an interaction of both the original sets of ripples. In the brain, the primary strategy can be thought of as like one pattern of ripples, and the meta-sensory responses can be thought of as like another pattern of ripples. Together they create what we consider to be the "meaning" of each event.

Using *Meta-States*, the higher representational pattern of language tends to govern the lower since it creates classes and classifications for the lower. In this way language can actually blind us from seeing what actually exists before our eyes. We come to see the world in terms of our labels, classifications, and terms.

Meta Responses

Even the basic sensory systems (VAKOG) can be used to create meta-responses. In describing strategies, the NLP developers noted:

> A meta response is defined as a response about the step before it, rather than a continuation or reversal of the representation. These responses are more abstracted and disassociated from the representations preceding them. Getting feelings about the image (feeling that something may have been left out of the picture, for instance) would constitute a meta response in our example. (Dilts *et al.*, 1980, p. 90)

Michael Hall has pointed out that such responses could be more usefully diagramed using a second dimension (Hall, 1995, p. 57) as shown below. This visual digital representation incorporates the meta-dimensions as the higher classification. And we do not have to necessarily experience it as more "abstracted or disassociated." If my K^i is a sensation of fear "about" some imagined picture, I may even experience that fear so intensely that I can't even look *in my mind* at that picture without going into a panic. In such a case, the higher meta-representation of the meta-feeling could overwhelm the strategy.

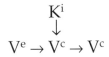

$$K^i$$
$$\downarrow$$
$$V^e \rightarrow V^c \rightarrow V^c$$

This emphasizes that the TOTE model is only a model, and a linear one at that. Real neurological processes are more network-like as noted by O'Connor and Van der Horst, (1994). Connections are being continuously made across levels, adding "meaning" to experiences. Hall (1995) has noted that this creates a layering or texturing of states so that our states become richer and more complex.

States and Strategies

What do we mean by "State" in NLP? O'Connor and Seymour (1990) define the term *"state"* as:

> How you feel, your mood. The sum total of all neurological and physical processes within an individual at any moment in time. The state we are in affects our capabilities and interpretation of experience. (p. 232)

Many new NLP Practitioners assume that state is a purely kinesthetic experience. A simple experiment demonstrates why this is not true. In research experiments, we can inject people with noradrenalin and their kinesthetic sensations will become aroused (their heart will beat faster etc.). However, *the emotional state* that the person enters will vary depending on a number of other factors in the environment. They may, for example, become "angry," "frightened," or "euphoric." It depends also on the person's primary representations as well as on meta-representations. That is, it depends upon what they tell themselves is happening (Schachter and Singer, 1962). The same kinesthetics do not always result in the same state. This highlights the power of the higher language level to "set the frame" for how we interpret the primary experiences.

Robert Dilts suggests that a person's state results from the interplay between the primary accessing, secondary representational systems, and other brain systems (1983, Section 1, pp. 60–69, Section 2, pp. 39–52, Section 3, p. 12 and pp. 49–51). Older theories assumed that this interplay must occur in a particular place in the brain; a sort of control center for "states." Yet by the time of Dilts' writing, it was clear that this was not true. A state (such as a certain quality of happiness, curiosity, or anxiety) is generated throughout the entire brain, and even removal of large areas of the brain will not stop the state being able to be regenerated. The brain is much more holographic than we first suspected.

Ian Marshall (1989) provides an update of this idea based on the quantum physics of what are called "Bose-Einstein condensates." The simplest way to understand this idea is to think of an ordinary electric light, which can light up your room, and a laser, which with the same amount of electricity can beam to the moon or burn through solid objects. The difference is that the individual light waves coming off a normal light are organized, in a laser, into a coherent beam. They all move at the same wavelength in the same direction. So it seems that states in the brain are a result of a similar process: protein molecules all across the brain vibrate at the same speed and in the same way.

This forms what is called *a Bose-Einstein condensate* (a whole area of tissue which behaves according to quantum principles; see Bolstad, 1966). This vibration results in a coherent state emerging out of the thousands of different impulses processed by the brain at any given time. Instead of being simultaneously aware that your knee needs scratching, the sun is a little bright, the word your friend just said is the same one your mother used to say, the air smells of cinnamon etc. (like the electric light scattering everywhere), you become aware of a "state." This "state" sort of summarizes everything ready for one basic decision, instead of thousands.

States, as Dilts originally hypothesized, are still best considered as meta to the representational systems and even to the digital representational systems. They are vast, brain-wide commentaries on the entire set of representations and physiological responses present. Just as the digital senses meta-comment on, and create interference patterns with, the primary senses, so do our states meta-comment on and alter the representations (primary as well as digital) "below them."

How does this play out in personality? An example occurs when a person becomes so angry that he or she may actually become physically *unable* to hear his or her partner or spouse expressing their love. The interference pattern from the state reduces the volume of the auditory external input. This often results in a completely different strategy being run.

Meta-States and Meta-Strategies

There are many other Meta-Levels of functioning in the human brain. Beliefs (as opinions about what is true), and values (opinions about what is important) are Meta-Level phenomena. Certain states can only occur as Meta-States, an example being "courage" which can only occur once there is a primary state of "fear" to be courageous in response to. The person who "knows no fear" is not feeling courageous; just naively relaxed.

Some strategies for sorting sensory experience are inevitably run almost continuously and unconsciously at a meta-level. The developers of NLP used the term *Meta-Programs* (the second meta-domain of NLP) to refer to the more basic sorting processes we use to decide what we pay attention to, and how we process it. An example would be whether we pay attention mainly to "the big picture" (global) or the details (specific). Meta-Level phenomena such as beliefs, values and strategies frequently interact. Hall and Bodenhamer (1997) observed:

> When we find a global person, that person not only processes information globally and deductively, but also *values* global thinking, *believes* in it and would argue against "watching the pennies in order to take care of the dollars." (p. 230)

Meta-Programs are sometimes described in NLP as "strategies which run our strategies." This suggests that they begin as ordinary, sensory level strategies. The *global thinking* Meta-Program may begin as a representational system level strategy, where the person checks what the overall "picture" is at the Test stage of the TOTE.

An example might be a child who:

1) sees a confusing set of interactions between their parents;

2) says to themselves "I wonder if they love me; what would it look like if they loved me?";

3) compares the external images of their parents seen at the start with the constructed image that those words of self talk "created"; and finally

4) agrees that the images fit the constructed image and says to themselves "Yes, they do love me!"

$$V^e \rightarrow A_d \rightarrow V^e/V^c \rightarrow A_d$$

And simply because a successful strategy will be run again and again, perhaps even millions of times, once the strategy runs often enough, it begins to run unconsciously. It happens just as our strategies for walking, once meticulously learned, eventually begin to run in a fully unconscious way. Accordingly, in precisely this way, *such strategies become the basis for "personality."* And like the other meta-phenomena, they create interference patterns with the sensory information accessed in our primary level strategies.

I may have a brilliant strategy for tidying up my living space. It may run perfectly in my work and home situations most of the time. However, if I tend to respond to challenges by associating into the situation (a response related to the Meta-Program called "Feeler" in the Myers-Briggs list), I may find that when I have a conflict happening at home, I continuously associate into the feelings of that conflict as I attempt to tidy up things. The result can easily derail my tidying strategy. On the other hand, if I responded to challenges in a more dissociated way, the tidying up strategy might continue to run perfectly well (though my relationship strategies might be at a higher risk).

Hall and Bodenhamer have focused their attention on these Meta-Levels in NLP, integrating the meta-phenomena such as values, Meta-States and Meta-Programs with the basic level strategies model of NLP. We believe that by emphasizing the importance of these aspects, they are nourishing holism in NLP.

Submodalities as Interference Patterns

In NLP, the interference patterns by which meta-phenomena alter primary sensory representations are known as "submodalities." Yet as Hall and Bodenhamer have rightfully said, submodalities are not *"sub"* to anything. We can better describe them as those *qualities* of the representations resulting from the interaction of "higher" brain processing and those primary representations.

If I *value* friendship, and prefer to recharge my batteries with other people (both meta-phenomenon) then it may be that when I see my friends in everyday life they actually look a little larger than other people and things, and my life seems to suddenly brighten up. These changes in my perception are submodality shifts, and "level of brightness" and "size" are submodality distinctions. Through such submodalities, meta-strategies and Meta-States "drive" our primary strategies from step to step. And, of course, this will become crucial as we look at specific personality disordering in later chapters.

Consider my strategy for washing the dishes at home. It is triggered by my seeing the bench untidy. How does just seeing certain things on the bench "trigger" this whole strategy? By those things being visually prioritized so that they literally stand out from the background (a submodality distinction).

This description of "submodalities" seems to reverse the description given by Richard Bandler and Will MacDonald, who say (1988):

> When Neuro-Linguistic Programming (NLP) first began to study subjective experience, the structure of meaning was found to occur in the specific sequence of representational systems a person used to process information. These representational system sequences

were called strategies. (pp. 1–2) (See *NLP Volume 1* for a detailed discussion of representational systems and strategies.)

Later it was discovered that the intensity of meaning held a direct relationship to the sub-modalities, or the component elements, of a given representational system. For instance, as you remember a pleasant experience, the degree of pleasure you have in that memory operates as a direct consequence of the color, size, brightness, and distance of the visual image you hold in your mind's eye. This description only appears to oppose our own description because it describes a cause-effect relationship. Actually a systemic, feedback-based relationship exists. If submodalities affect states, then states affect submodalities. The brain works in this systemic way with both feed back and feed forward loops.

For the same reason, we have no problem expecting that submodality shifts can alter personality programs or other meta-phenomena. Changing any element in the system must change all others. The type of change which results is, of course, debatable, and we can expect that meta-phenomena will demonstrate a resilience if a submodality shift in one meta-phenomenon violates some even more important meta-phenomenon. We typically refer to this understanding as "ecology" in NLP.

For example, I may shift the submodalities on images I have related to a belief that I have a poor memory. That belief may have been installed almost "by accident" when I overheard someone mentioning my "poor memory" at primary school ("programs" can be installed in us that easily and affect us for the rest of our lives!). In this situation, a submodality shift could occur very successfully. It would change how we code the information and "stick."

Imagine another case. Suppose someone had become accustomed to telling him or herself that "I have a poor memory," and used that for motivation to study harder at school. The *valuing* of this "away from" motivation (a meta-phenomenon) now has a lot of vested interest in it. While "negative" in one way, it has a long history of useful service. So in this case, a submodality shift would probably not "stick," but be reversed by the meta-strategy. That higher frame would not allow for the change.

This leads us to believe that before making any submodality shift, or any other NLP-based alteration to a person's strategy, for that matter, it is appropriate that we linguistically explore and redefine the meta-background to the change. Think of this as opening up the person's model of the world. In doing so, we also explore if there are any higher frames that would prevent the change.

To explain the neurological basis of submodalities, Graham Cairns-Smith uses the example of how we see the moon (1996, p. 195). When the moon is low down in the sky, it looks bigger than usual. This perceptual phenomenon is extremely resistant to conscious change, because the brain has determined that, generally, when something is near the horizon it is far away and needs a bit of magnification. We generally do not notice our helpful brain doing this enlarging of objects, yet it becomes obvious with the moon. This action by the brain is done based on a considerably complex understanding of perspective; one we are not born with. This means we can and do develop Meta-Level concepts that then affect our perceptions.

Many other similar submodality shifts occur with each image we see. In one study, office workers in a room repainted blue complained of the cold, even though the thermostat remained constant, and they stopped complaining when it was repainted yellow (see P. Berry). The color blue creates a cross-sensory system response in the kinesthetic representations.

The brain performs all this processing for us long before we become *conscious* of what we are seeing. Data from the eyes goes back into the brain through the optic nerves and is distributed to at least twenty separate areas for analysis (Cairns-Smith, 1996, pp. 160–171). One area analyzes color in the incoming images, one analyzes brightness / darkness, one area analyzes movements, and so on. Next, some more sophisticated meta-analysis of the images occurs. There is a huge area of the brain which has referred to it any images which might be human faces, for analysis and face recognition.

Another higher level processing area creates the sense of something seen being "familiar" or "strange." To analyze even something as simple as the color of something you looked at, data from a number of adjacent cones (cells in the retina of the eye that first "saw" the image) must be compared and computed. There is continuous cross-referencing of data with other areas of the brain *before* the messages are recombined and delivered to your conscious mind.

What does this mean? It means that submodalities are separately added to the image before it is available for you to examine. We know that constructed and recalled images activate many of the same pathways, and thus involve the same complexity of analysis and submodality control.

Meta-assessments such as the sense of familiarity do indeed seem to be generated by the images we take in, *once they have their submodalities adjusted by our brain.* Many of the assessments are clearly learned, and can be unlearned. As I type this on a computer, my brain stabilizes the image of the screen. If I look out of the corner of my eye at the screen, the submodality adjustment stops, and I see the screen for the constantly rolling sequence of flickering images a TV screen is (as you see when you try to video-film a TV screen).

Seeing the TV screen as a steady image is a learned submodality adjustment. Altering submodalities can create changes in our meta-assessments such as the sense of familiarity. It might then be said that the very submodality changes made at the first level of processing the image are the result of previous meta-judgments. That is also true.

What is our point in all of this? All of this neuro-linguistic processing in our brain operates as a system. If we alter any part of it, other parts will adjust. Electrically stimulating the area of the brain where "familiarity" is created produces a sudden "Ah-hah" experience, where the viewer will report that they have just made some important new connection about what they have been looking at (Cairns-Smith, 1996, p. 168). This new meta-response is as resilient as any of the "natural" ones. The person knows that it results from artificial stimulation of the brain, but still remains convinced that they have a new familiarity about what they are seeing!

Summary—Strategies: The Full Model

- A strategy is a sequence of internal representations, both primary (VAKOG) and Meta-Level (A_d, V_d). It can be conceived as having a trigger (the stimulus that initiates it), an operation, a test where the results of this operation are compared with the desired results, and an exit which is the result of this test.

- A strategy is also influenced by higher level phenomena such as states (coherent patterns of brain activity, experienced as "emotions"), Meta-States (states created in response to other states), Meta-Programs (strategies which function so regularly that they are triggered by almost every event in a wide context), values and beliefs.

- The interference pattern between the basic strategy and the Meta-Levels produces submodality alterations in the sensory experience. To change a strategy, one can change any of these elements; the strategy trigger and sequencing (changed by anchoring), the submodalities (changed by submodality shift), and the Meta-Levels (often changed by reframing processes and trance processes). Put another way, changing any of these elements successfully also involves changing all the other elements.

Chapter 4

Meta-States,
Design Human Engineering
and "Personality"

"Personality" Embodied
as an Energized Holographic Force Field

Using the NLP and Neuro-Semantics Models that we have to this point, we have learned a number of highly significant things about "personality." For instance, we have discovered that:

- Personality isn't "innate" but that we "learn" our *personality* style.

- Personality involves *a structured process* involving representations at multiple levels and evaluations, states and Meta-States.

- We *organize* personality by languaging and creating various Meta-Level frames.

- *Personality* involves layered consciousness and multiple embedded energies—Meta-States and Meta-Programs.

- We have a "strategy" by which we do personality.

In all of these considerations, NLP offers a study of the structure of subjective experience. This makes it clear that there is rhyme and reason to our experiences and therefore the possibility of altering it. We now want to add yet another distinction about "personality," namely, that because our personality involves the inseparable mind-body relationship, *personality involves embodiment.*

Embodiment? What does that mean? Embodiment refers to the fact that as *neuro-linguistic* and *neuro-semantic* beings, we experience our *personality* and its ordering and disordering *in our bodies.* This makes our neurological equipment (central nervous system, autonomic nervous system, digestive system, immune system, etc.) and our physiology crucially important. All of this gives rise to *the kinesthetic feel of personality.*

Pure Kinesthetics

We probably do not experience the *pure kinesthetic sensations* very often after our first few days or weeks as an infant. Pure kinesthetic sensations consist of hot/cold; tense/relaxed; rough/smooth; soft/rough; throbbing, burning, twisting, etc. We don't experience them *purely* because we soon develop responses to such—like, dislike, pleasure, pain, acceptable, unacceptable, desired, undesired, etc. We also get them linked together with other things and with ideas. When we do, this gives rise to an "emotion."

Dr Robert Plutchik (1980) defines an emotion as "a complex sequence of events having elements of cognitive appraisal, feeling, impulses to action, and overt behavior." In his book *Emotion: A Psychoevolutionary Synthesis* he posited eight primary emotions: fear, surprise, sadness, disgust, anger, anticipation, joy, and acceptance (receptivity). He theorized the emotional process in terms of "a chain reaction"—

Stimulus Event → Cognition → Feeling → Behavior → Function
Threat by Enemy → Danger → Fear → Run → Protection
Loss of Parent → Isolation → Sadness → Cry for Help → Reintegration

He then attempted to map primary and mixed emotions (*Psychology Today*, Feb. 1980, pp. 68–78):

anticipation and joy → optimism
anticipation and anger → aggressiveness
joy and acceptance → love
acceptance and fear → submission
fear and surprise → awe

> surprise and sadness → disappointment
> sadness and disgust → remorse
> disgust and anger → contempt

In NLP, we speak about *"emotions"* in terms of being meta-kinesthetics (K_{meta}). This speaks about a combination of kinesthetic sensations along with evaluations in the form of words *about* the kinesthetics. That makes an *emotion* a Meta-Level phenomena inasmuch as emotions consist of *evaluative judgments, meanings, values, and beliefs.*

This even applies to the *primary* emotions. Even anger, fear, joy, sadness, surprise, disgust, etc. already operate as Meta-Level phenomena. We could therefore tease out a *lost level* inside the primary state level. The primary emotions, since they already involve cognitive evaluations, result from that previous Meta-Level having collapsed or coalesced into a primary state. This demonstrates how Meta-Levels collapse and thereafter generate Meta-Level synesthesias.

Territoriality: our Sense of "Space"

One meta-kinesthetic sense that tends to develop in *personality* involves what we call our own *"personal space."* This refers to that "territory" which surrounds us that we feel belongs to us. It may encompass the territory that radiates out from our body from 12 inches away to 3 feet away. Most people sense this as their own "space," their personal territory. Intrude into it, stand too close, "get in someone's face," as we say, and they will take it as a personal affront. Into this field we also *project* many facets of our personality and personal constructs of reality.

This *sense of personal space* tends to differ in quality, nature, dimensions, etc. in different cultures and between different people. Some people experience it as wide-open and without any sense of protection or boundaries. Others experience their space as safely behind layers of ego-boundaries.

Into this *sense of space* we also project much of our internal *model of the world.* We do this in a systematic and patterned way most people don't notice in themselves or others. Bandler and Grinder revolutionized the fields of psychology and communication in 1975 by pointing out the presence of "eye accessing cues" as patterned external behaviors for representational system processing. Later, they and other co-developers of NLP specified the patterns for how people present (project) their representations of "time," their Meta-Programs, submodalities, etc.

In common parlance we say that different *personalities* give off different vibes—energy vibrations. Various alternative models in health and psychology have studied these auras and vibrations. Each operates from the presupposition that as personality becomes *ordered* (or disordered), it operates as a small force field— emanating various *energies* (somatic, neurological, psychological, spiritual, etc.).

We can undoubtedly explain much about these energies in terms of mental-emotional states. We don't have to claim esoteric powers to pick up on the *vibrations* generated by states of anger, fear, joy, love, gentleness, frustration, pleasantness, disgust, etc. Each state feels different to us—whether we speak about it as our neuro-linguistic state, or someone else's.

Personality, then, operates as *a gestalt of energies* that come together to form new and strange configurations. It thus not only operates as the result of various *models of the world* but also manifests those models. So conceptualizing *personality* suggests that we might discover useful information about ourselves and others if only we open our eyes and ears and notice our patterns of communication.

I have developed this idea of *personality as projective* of its own model and internal "reality" from various facets of the NLP model (as I'll reference in the following sections) as well as from similarities in Freudian, Adlerian, Gestalt, Family Systems, and other schools of psychology.

Projecting "Time" as a 3-D Holographic Image

In NLP, we talk about projecting into that space our "sense of 'time'" and talk about this using the metaphor of *a "line,"* as in *time-line.* Thus we bring the image, metaphor, and perceptual configuration of "time as a line" to bear on our concept of previous events, current events, and future events. This sets the frame for how we think, feel, and experience the concept of "time."

The metaphor and icon of *a time-line* then serves as a meta-language for "time." It allows us to code this *concept* using "sub-modalities," that is, the qualities and features of the visual, auditory, and kinesthetic representations of a "line," "circle," "boomerang," "curve," etc. As we metaphorically use various icons to symbolize "time," we can thereby encode "time" using space, distance, movement, directionality, intensity, etc. This allows us to talk about "time" in terms of its *direction and space:*

"Which way is your future?"
"Where is your past?"

We can speak about "time" in terms of *size.*

"How big is 'today?'"
"How much room do you have or experience until next month comes?"

That we *encode* and then *project* this Meta-Level concept of "time" out into actual space reflects our wondrous and powerful *semantic* class of life. It also means that if we watch carefully, we can actually detect a person's *internal* coding of "time" (past, present, future) in how a given person uses space, movement, gestures, etc. We can watch where a person gestures to when talking about something yet to happen (the "future"), something that has happened (the "past"), something now occurring (the "present").

If we then consider this as *a 3-D holographic image,* something that we create and use as we orient ourselves in the time-space continuum, we shall learn to see marvelous things. It gives us an ability to see a given person's "relationship" to these temporal concepts. Where and how does a person relate to his or her "future," "past" or "present?" Does the person have a sufficient and adequate way to sort out life's events? What kind of symbolic system does the person use to separate what has happened from what is happening and those from what will or could happen? If a person has these concepts all messed up, confused, and tangled together, he or she will probably have a very difficult time being "on time," using the past for learnings and wisdom, and making appropriate plans for the future. The person could end up "living in the past," feeling doomed and fated by it, and unable to see "a bright future." That would create a certain "personality" structure. Another person might have so large a space for the "present" that he cannot even anticipate the "future." Such a person would then undoubtedly live completely "in the now." This, in turn, would probably lead to the personality structure of being impulsive and reactive to immediate stimuli.

The person who has the "past" so much "behind" them that she cannot even see it, on the other hand, might not be able to use it as learnings. We have found that this structure typically leads to the personality structure of someone constantly making the same mistakes again and again.

This and many other facets of "personality" emerge from how we encode "time." As reflexive beings who can remember what has happened and anticipate what will, could, and might happen— how we conceptualize the temporal dimension greatly affects the form and shape of our "personality." NLP has an entire domain of study about this. In Time Line Therapy™ (James & Woodsmall, 1988), and Time-Lining Processes (Hall and Bodenhamer, 1997), there are multiple patterns for—

- Destroying Old Decisions that we have set and carried with us that limit and sabotage us: The Decision Destroyer.

- Recoding, reducing, and eliminating phobias and other negative traumatic events, from violence to one's person (rape, molestation, abuse, Post Traumatic Disordering, etc.) to violence and trauma against one's family, groups, race, nation, etc.: The Phobia Cure or V-K Dissociation Pattern.

- Re-Orienting one to "time" in ways that are more productive and enhancing: Changing One's Time-Line.

- Transforming our memories and encodings of the past: Re-Imprinting Pattern.

NLP has developed this spatial nature of "time" more extensively than any other concept. The Time-Line Model originated from Richard Bandler and was then developed by Tad James and Wyatt Woodsmall (1988).

This model gives us an explicit way to *elicit* a person's way of *representing "time,"* and the submodalities symbolically *stand for* the concept. In terms of the ordering and dis-ordering of personality, this provides us with a way to practically work with people.

Projecting Meta-Programs Holographically

As we metaphorically use various icons, symbols, and structures to encode a concept like "time," and then project out into our actual, physical space, we do the same with other concepts. This holds true for many of *the Meta-Programs.*

For instance, in global thinking, a person will move back or look up as if to see a bigger picture. In specific thinking, a person moves forward to look at the details. This suggests that in the 3-D actual space before us, we have coded these structures. What lies within our minds as our "model of the world," we have a tendency to project as a 3-D holographic image. Once we have done that, then we tend to act, feel, relate, gesture, etc. to it as if it were "real."

And, typically we don't know that we're doing this! Before you learned about Time-Lines did you know that you have a certain place in your personal space where you put the future, past, and present? Were you aware whether your symbolic structure of "time" went through your body (associated "time" representation; called "in" time) or stayed on the outside (meta "time" representation, called "through" time)?

This outside-of-awareness facet of our neuro-semantic nature means that we typically do not notice. Nor do we notice these symbolic structures in others. We don't notice how others systemically and methodologically *act out* their own symbolic structures. Typically, we all tend to get so caught up in the content of *what* we're thinking that we seldom, if ever, think about what we must be projecting, or how our symbolic structures affect our thinking, feeling, acting, skill, etc.

What Else do we Encode and Project into our 3-D Space?

What else lies coded as a 3-D holographic image that we project outward into our "personal space?"

Is it possible that we also encode and project into actual space other concepts? If we explore this, would we find a place in actual space where we typically store such "things" as values, beliefs, yes/no (affirmations/negations), background knowledge, decisions, self, etc.?

In one facet of NLP, co-founder Richard Bandler has explored this question. Calling it "Design Human Engineering™" or DHE, he has taken the field of *"submodalities"* (all of the specific features, properties, and qualities of the visual, auditory, kinesthetic, etc. sensory systems) and sought to discover where in actual 3-D space people put things. Bandler has suggested that if we pay attention to *the spatial location* of things, we will see and find there the person's decisions, beliefs, doubts, values, etc.

While there are many weaknesses and problems with this entire approach (Hall and Lester, 2000), there are also many strengths. In *Persuasion Engineering*, Bandler and LaValle (1996) use this hypothesis to elicit and work with a person's decision strategy, belief and convincer strategy. This occurs in the context of persuasion and especially selling. Believing that people put these mental constructions in actual space, that we hallucinate them there, then gesture to them in those spaces, and operate as if that's where we have put them, Bandler and LaValle set out to engineer "persuasion" that takes these holographic hallucinations seriously and uses them for persuasion.

How does this affect a salesperson's speech and performance?

It would mean that we would *not* want to put our product or service in a person's "doubt" location. Rather, we would want to put it in a person's space for "strong beliefs" and "feeling convinced." It means that we would want to stay out of another person's pictures and representations when we are talking with them so that the person can freely and easily visualize. It's easy to work with this one. Simply ask someone to visualize something in front of them and while they do, flail your arms in wild and chaotic ways. Typically this "tears up" the person's pictures and prevents him or her from holding the images steady.

Bandler talks about stepping to the side of a person and then gesturing to the places where that person represents an idea or belief. He can then gesture in a way as to bring the picture in closer, push it out further, move it up or down, etc. In these ways (and many more), we can then work with a person to create more or less intensity of emotion, encode something as more or less believable, more or less compelling, etc. By cupping and/or flatting our hand as we talk, we can relate to and treat a person's 3-D mental representations with more "reality," much the way a pantomime forms imagined walls, doors, windows, etc. in "space" and gets an audience to respond to such as "real."

Hallucinating Meta-Levels

As *embodied* persons, we hallucinate our mental concepts of "time," "self," belief, values, etc. by using various symbolic representations. Once we build or inherit from our culture various metaphorical styles for conceptual thinking, we *project* such into actual spatial locations.

The *deceptive* thing about *the spatial location* of a *concept* like "time" involves how we think and represent "time" using a see-hear-feel (sensory based) *metaphor*. In other words, we have an easy and readily accessible *cultural metaphor* that provides us with a concrete way to think about a concept.

Consider the implications of this.

Lakoff and Johnson (1980) describe the nature of metaphors from a cognitive and linguistic point of view. They not only suggest that all human *thinking* and *languaging* operates metaphorically, they also say that when it comes to abstract concepts, we humans have a predilection for using *concrete metaphors.* Doing so gives us a handle on things when it comes to thinking about the realm of conceptual ideas which inevitably are less definite and more vague. They argue that this arises from the nature of our *physical embodiment* in the world and the nature of how our bodies interact with the world as we find it.

So wherein lies the *deception?* It occurs because of how easily we can forget (or not recognize) *the operational metaphor* that governs our thinking and representing. And when we forget, we nominalize.

Look at the nominalization of the term "Time-Line" itself. We talk about it and relate to that "line" as if it were "real," actual, and literal:

> "Where is your Time-Line?"
> "Float above your Time-Line and go back..."
> "Now float down into your Time-Line and quickly zoom up to the present..."

Steve and Connirae Andreas (1987, 1989) have provided a much needed service regarding time-lines in their work as they have identified *other metaphorical images and icons* that people use. From boomerangs, to vertical spirals, to filing cabinets, to rolla-dexes, to floating lily-pads(!), the idea of a "line," although the most dominant metaphor, only represents one potential metaphor. For this reason, Hall and Bodenhamer (1997) have consciously attempted to de-nominalize the metaphor of a time "line," and so have used the term *time-lining.*

As a *metaphor*, we have simply taken a *concrete see-hear-feel* item and framed our concept of "time" with it. This has given us much more flexibility and more choices in understanding and relating to "time." Of course, as with every metaphor used as a frame-of-reference, it not only offers isomorphic relations, but also new associations, and it creates its own limitations and problems.

Figure 4.1

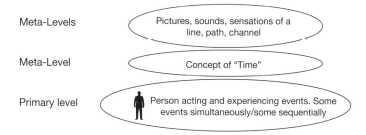

Meta-Levels — Pictures, sounds, sensations of a line, path, channel

Meta-Level — Concept of "Time"

Primary level — Person acting and experiencing events. Some events simultaneously/some sequentially

Concepts and Metaphors

The problem we have with so many, if not most, of our *concepts* springs from the fact that we do not have easily accessible and usable metaphors as we do with "line" for "time." This becomes exceedingly clear when we ask the representation question regarding *concepts*. What *concrete* object do you use for the following? What *actual tangible item* could you use?

How do you represent the idea of "Self?"
How do you represent the idea of *responsibility?*
What do you see, hear, feel, etc. about the idea of *human destiny?*
What about *mortality, purpose, love, dignity, values, trust, etc.?*

When we move up from the *primary level* (or state) where we use our VAK representations and sensory-based language and where we experience the empirical *see-hear-feel world*, we enter into a meta-domain of consciousness. Making that meta-move takes us into *conceptual states of consciousness*, Meta-States, where we use evaluative language. Here immediate *embodiment* vanishes. At this level we have to Shanghai images and icons from the sensory-based world and make them do duty for work at the Meta-Levels.

Gregory Bateson (1972, 1979) distinguished primary and Meta-Levels by designating the first level *Plethora* and the second *Creatura*. In describing the first, he said this is where the forces and energies of the world of physics occurs. He described the second, the Meta-Level, world of concepts as "the world of communication, mind, and organization." In the first we can properly use the word "dynamic," but not so in the second. In the second, it serves more as a metaphor and so we have to use the term more carefully.

He noted that in the first world, *energy* makes the difference. In the second world, however, *difference* and *information* describe "the difference that makes a difference."

Korzybski (1933–1994) explained these levels as "levels of abstraction." Following the pathway by which our nervous system *abstracts* (summarizes, deletes, generalizes, and distorts) from the energy manifestations "out there" in the world, and brings them in, he noted that they only bring in a *transform*, or representation, *of* it. Never the thing. Only the symbol. In the higher levels, we only have *ideas*, never things.

This *neurological mapping* gives us our first level "sense" of things—our VAK sensory modalities (the representation systems). From there we *abstract* again, saying words *about* the sights, sounds, sensations, smells, etc. Thereby we make our first level *linguistic maps*. And this process continues as we continue moving to higher and higher (meta) levels of abstraction, saying more words about previous words. This moves us into higher and higher levels of abstraction, thereby creating our *conceptual worlds.*

But how do we represent such? Primarily in *propositional* conceptual language.

But not exclusively. We also create and use other kinds of *conceptual language*. We use non-propositional language as poetry, proverbs, koans, paradoxes, stories (narratives), songs and music, art, sketches, diagrams, metaphors, etc. We do so in order to *see and hear and feel* the concept. Thus, the "time-line."

Making our Concepts "Real" in a Sensory-Based Way

When we take a meta position regarding a *concept* like time, self, dignity, purpose, responsibility, morality, mortality, etc. and frame it metaphorically—we *bring it down*. We embody it. In doing this, we make the *concept* more "real" to ourselves. We can then begin to relate to it as if it were *a thing*. As we thus "reify" the concept (endow it with "thing" like qualities), we create nominalizations. We take *processes* and name them. In this case, we take the mental process of conceptualizing an idea (a mental action) and concretize it with an embodied symbol. This then gives us a way to *project it out onto the world*.

We first of all describe this by the linguistic term *nominalization*. But we don't leave it there. We soon put the nominalization within yet another linguistic structure as we think about and conceptualize what that named-concept means, what causes it, etc. This leads us to using the linguistic distinctions of *cause-effect statements* and *complex equivalences.*

When we do this, of course, we have married the world of mind and the world of perception. We have brought more conceptualizations down to the ground and embodied them. Here *Creatura* meets and merges with *Plethora.* Here we combine some *Internal State or Significance* (which we denote and abbreviate as IS) with some *External Behavior* (EB). This gives us an equation or equivalence, a "complex equivalence," which describes a see-hear-feel behavioral equivalence about internal meaning.

As we create these *Complex Equivalences,* we have a way of *hallucinating* (or projecting) our internal worlds of ideas and concepts onto the external see-hear-feel world. From this comes our language. In other words, if we listen carefully for these linguistic structures, we can actually *hear* people describing their *embodied* concepts.

> "His harsh tonality equals feeling insulted, put down, threatened."

"When she softens her eyes and looks directly at me I know
I can trust her."
"I hate it when a person rolls the eyes when I talk; that tells
me that he or she is rejecting my ideas."

As we practice this way of *thinking*, our Complex Equivalence
becomes streamlined so that we don't even recognize *the EB = IS*
formula. We move on to *direct hallucination*. This means that we
can look out onto the world of people, events, actions and *see ideas,
concepts, and evaluative processes*:

"She's so *rude* when she does that!"
"He's just a *selfish person*, that's all there is to it!"
"She's *irresponsible*. Anybody can see that."
"I can't buy that. That would be *selfish*." (stupid, arrogant,
wasteful)
"Yes, he fired me *for no good reason*. That's why it's so *unfair!*"
"She's so *immature*."

Here we have *full blown hallucination*. We certainly do not describe
this to ourselves as a "hallucination." We typically save that term
for the mentally disordered. This use of the term "hallucination"
doesn't describe hallucinating six-foot rabbits, demons, little green
men, or Elvis Presley. It refers to hallucinating *ideas* and *projecting*
them into actual 3-D space.

Bandler and Grinder (1981) described *how* nominalizations lead to
this kind of hallucination.

When you give process instructions, you use a lot of words like
'understanding,' 'resource,' and 'curiosity.' We call these kinds of
words *nominalizations*. They are actually *process* words that are
used as nouns. If you turn a word like 'understanding' back into a
verb 'You will understand…' you realize that a lot of information
is deleted. If someone uses nominalizations when they're speaking
to you, it forces you to go inside and access meaning. If a client
says to you, 'Well, I'm looking for *satisfaction*,' you can turn satisfaction back into a verb and ask, 'You are trying to satisfy yourself
how?' … But if you don't do that, then you have to fill in the missing pieces yourself. That's what most therapists do with what their
clients say. They hallucinate what the person means. If all I say is

'I'm looking for *support*' you have to go inside and get your ideas of what it means for someone to support someone else. (p. 106)

In *Frogs Into Princes*, Bandler and Grinder (1979) further describe this use of the term:

You all hallucinate. You all hallucinate that somebody's in a good mood or a bad mood, for example. Sometimes it really is an accurate representation of what you are getting from the outside, but sometimes it's a response to your own internal state. And if it's not there, sometimes you can induce it. 'Is something wrong?' 'What's bothering you?' (p. 53)

When Sally used the word 'pensive' earlier, she was hallucinating with exactly the same formal process that a schizophrenic does. (p. 52)

One of the most powerful tools that I think is useful for you to have as professional communicators is to make the distinction between perception and hallucination. If you can clearly distinguish what portion of your ongoing experience you are creating internally and putting out there, as opposed to what you are actually receiving through your sensory apparatus, you will not hallucinate when it's not useful. (p. 54)

Hallucination can be a very powerful, positive thing. Anybody who has ever done a workshop with Virginia Satir knows that she uses hallucination in very powerful and creative ways, for instance in her family sculpting. (p. 60)

So with this usage of the term "hallucination," let's explore…

Seeing Hallucination Spaces

Where do we typically *see*, hear, and feel our hallucinated images? Using the time-line metaphor of "time" as a model, we do so in our immediate *personal space* about us. This personal space thus functions as a reflection of the internal model of the world. We can think of it as operating as our *Personality Space or Field* wherein we store our "reality."

If we therefore think of this *energy field* as a reflection of the internal model of the world, this gives us a way to understand our own internal mental structures as well as those of others. We do this with *time-lines;* now we can do it with values, beliefs, yes/no structures, etc. Once we do that, we can then begin to interact with the holographic Personality Field of others in order to pace and work with their reality structures. Since people project them out and then treat them as "real"—as we do, we enter their reality and work within their energy field.

Learning to Recognize Meta-Levels

Because the DHE model grew out of the *submodality model*, it assumes almost exclusively that *submodalities* operate as "the mechanism" for explaining contrastive differences between subjective experiences. This makes that model inadequate. It prevents the DHE development of NLP from recognizing the presence of Meta-Levels. As a result, that model has become "deaf and blind" to Meta-Levels in numerous subjective structures.

For example, a person has to *go meta* in order to *believe* and *understand* something. *"Beliefs"* and *"Understandings"* contain and involve Meta-Levels. To recognize this, simply think about *how* you can *represent* something that you don't believe. Do you believe that "Hitler was a good man"? No? Yet can you *represent* it? Of course you can. Now the submodality model and some NLP Processes would have you believe that if you simply map over the submodalities of a "strong belief" to that representation—you will believe it.

Well, go ahead. Try it. Make your pictures bigger, brighter, colorful, closer, whatever. Make your sounds more and more compelling.

Now test. Do you believe that Hitler was a good man? No? I didn't think so. Well, use the belief change pattern, get your disbelief about Hitler, turn it into the submodalities of "doubt" and then into belief. Does that make you believe it? I didn't think so.

Why not? Go inside and listen to yourself and to your *meta-voice about* all of that. At a level *meta* to your representation you have a higher level frame, you have a frame of reference that *outframes* the representation. You have a *"No! No way!"* that sets the frame for that thought, do you not? And that *negation frame* of "No!" sets the frame for what you think about that thought. Think it you can; believe it you cannot. To believe it you would have to say "Yes" to that thought. But you do not confirm it.

How do you know that you *believe in* something that you believe in?

Again, represent it and attempt to turn down all of the submodalities and to use the submodalities of disbelief or doubt. I have a guess about what will happen. Even if you turn down the quality, brightness, closeness, loudness, etc. of all your representations and make your representation small, distant, black-and-white, etc., you will still believe it. You may not have as much *juice*. But you still believe it. So listen, again, for your *Meta-Level Voice* that affirms the representation—that says "Yes!" to it.

To believe something we have to bring a higher level frame of reference of *validation and affirmation* to bear on the representation. To disbelief, we have to bring a Meta-Level voice of *dis-confirmation or negation*. To doubt, we have to frame it with a higher level frame of *maybe yes, maybe no.*

The same thing holds with the conceptual level of Background Knowledge or *"understanding."* Representation alone will not lead to "understanding." You can represent lots and lots and lots of details and, in fact, the more details you represent, the more confused you may feel. To *understand* you need an *organizing structure or format.*

Anytime we have a thought-or-feeling *about* a previous thought or feeling, a state of mind about a state of mind, we have a Meta-Level operating. And since higher logical levels always drive, modulate, govern, and organize the lower levels (Bateson, 1972, Dilts, 1980, Hall, 1995), this means that

Meta-Levels describe a central difference that makes a difference in human subjective experiences.

To recognize the presence of a Meta-Level, look for and notice *thoughts about thoughts, emotions about emotions, and thoughts in the back of the mind.* The richness of human consciousness—that we forever *abstract* about previous abstractions, that given any state or experience we will have thoughts-and-feelings about it means that we can expect and should look for the presence of Meta-Levels. [For more about this, see Hall and Bodenhamer's *The Structure of Excellence: Unmasking the Meta-Levels of Submodalities (1999)*.]

Seeing the Invisible (Unconscious) Levels

Expect also the Meta-Level to operate mostly in an *unconscious* manner. Bandler and Grinder (1979) mentioned this in *Frogs Into Princes.*

People have almost no consciousness of any Meta-Levels if you distract them with content. (p. 62)

This explains why we can (and do) so easily miss the Meta-Level frames—the Voices, Pictures, Metaphors, etc. that outframe our experiences. In those meta-frames we have all of our personal history, previous mapping that has dropped out of consciousness, our assumptions, presuppositions, higher level beliefs about Kant's *a priori categories* (i.e. time, space, purpose, destiny, causation, God, etc.).

- If we miss or ignore Meta-Levels, we miss most of the good stuff in human subjectivity!

- If we attempt to model without incorporating the meta-levels, we miss *most of the controlling, governing, and organizing principles and structures.*

When people "go inside" and engage in the trans-derivational search to their internal world of meaning, they go to their Meta-Levels, their frames-of-references. In other words, they go *in and up* (to use the operational metaphor in the Meta-States model).

They go to their "domains of knowledge," their "categories of understanding," their belief references, their assumptions about causation, meaning, identity, and spirituality. Count on it.

- If we attempt to understand a person without understanding their Meta-Level *meanings and structures*, we miss their presuppositions, "core" beliefs, and ultimate meanings.

Seeing and Using the "Field" of "Personality"

We have noted that the conceptual embodiment of our internal mappings affects and influences our understanding of things and has an effect on our "personality." By it we encode and solidify our sense of self. The following sections provide information along this line as we work with others in the way they have ordered and disordered their "personality."

Without utilizing Meta-Levels, but only submodalities, Bandler believes that we can learn to see *where* in actual 3-D space people put such structures as beliefs, values, decisions, convincers, etc. To learn to do this, begin with yourself and a few others. Elicit your *experience* of any of these complex and layered with Meta-Levels structures. As you do—notice several things:

- *How* do you represent such?
  VAK, words, evaluative words, etc.

- *What metaphors* do you rely upon to assist with the representation?

- *Where* in space do you put it?

The Space of your Meta-Level Affirmation/ Negation

Begin with your representations of "Yes" and "No." I believe that this will represent a major and significant "space" inside your Personality Field and carry lots of psychological charge. Notice how and where you represent Affirmation and Negation, Confirmation and Dis-Confirmation.

Remember, it will come *after* a representation, and will function as a response *to* the previous representation. Go through a list of items. Represent them and then notice *your response* to that.

I have my *Affirmation/Confirmation* space to my right, I gesture with my right hand to it mostly. It occurs just to the right of my body, mid-body height and it goes up so that the more I say Yes to something, the higher I have that Yes. My Yes voice begins with a matter-of-fact tonality, and moves up a scale of enthusiasm until it almost shouts an excited "YES!"

I have my *Negation/Dis-Confirmation* space to my left, I gesture with my left hand to it and, interesting enough, use a backhanded movement that I gesture to the left turning the hand over as I move. It begins with a slow movement and gets faster and more definite as the No becomes more definite. The No voice in a similar way begins with a matter-of-fact tonality, and becomes more and more definite, stronger, and angrier as the No increases.

Accessing your "Values" space

Think of something that you value, then of something that you feel is *very, very important.* Now of something that you don't deem as having much importance one way or the other. Now think of something that you very much dis-value. How do you know the difference?

Undoubtedly you first *represent* something: keeping the house clean, running, studying, reading, a ball game, watching a movie, working, achievement, recognition, being loved, sexual intimacy, etc. When you think about what you value, you *represent* it, and then you probably hear that *meta-voice* affirming at some degree of intensity.

Where do you experience all of this happening at? You may do so "all over the place." Get a memory, construct a representation, do a little of both, then put it up on your *representational screen*, then access your Meta-Level Affirmation or Negation, then store your Value somewhere else.

I do. After the previous steps, I then use the metaphor of a ladder, a hierarchical ladder so that the higher the value, the higher up in space I code it. I have found this structure with most of the people for whom I have elicited their values.

Accessing Beliefs and Strong Beliefs and Ultimate Beliefs

Think about something that you believe, something that you *really, really believe,* and something that you consider as one of the *ultimate, unquestionable beliefs* that you hold. Do a contrastive analysis by thinking about something that you *think,* that you have begun to make *an opinion* about, and something that you *just don't know.* If you think about a doubt, realize that a doubt functions as a "not-belief." You believe it "is not."

Again, notice your strategy: how you get it, put it together, how your Meta-Level Yes or No voice speaks *about* it. Then, notice where you put it after you have accessed it fully.

Do you have "down right" important beliefs? If so, you probably use the spatial metaphor of "down is more." In other words, a *foundational* metaphor. This represents the foundation of my life. Do you have "high" beliefs? Then you use an "up is more" metaphor, a *transcendence* metaphor. Do you have "core" beliefs? Then you probably have a "center" metaphor; "the more central a thing, the more it operates as the core."

Recognizing Decisions

The strategy for making a decision, for *deciding between two or more choices,* involves a set of comparisons. You have to represent something and perhaps something else. Then you have to access your values—your standards and criteria by which you make your decision. Once you *apply* the Meta-Level constructions of

"Valuable/ Not-Valuable," "Important/Not-Important" (and all degrees in between) to it, then you *make the decision.*

You do, *if* "you" as a "person" have permission to make such a decision. Here other Meta-Level processes play into the mix. Do you have a higher level frame of reference that gives you *the right* to make a decision? If not, if that *right* has been taken away from you or tabooed, you may feel "not right" about making the decision. This will then lead to indecisiveness. A part of you wants to; a part does not.

Have you constructed your self-definition as "I'm a decisive person," or do you operate under the frame of reference, "I'm an indecisive person; I can't make up my mind"? Here the meta-frame of Self and self-definition comes into play.

Think about some time when you made a decision and felt strong and definite about it. Think about a time when you couldn't make up your mind. Notice the process and how you know each experience. *Where* do you store your decisions? To what extent do you use a *scale metaphor* in the process? How do you experience yourself as "weighing" this decision or choice against this other one?

Self as a Meta-Level Structure

Having mentioned the subjective experience of "self," notice first how you represent yourself as a person, then in terms of all of the other facets of self that you can use in building up an overall self-image or definition:

Esteem, Dignity, Value
Confidence: skills, abilities, achievements
Social-Self: self as reflected in the eyes of others
Historical Self: who you have been up until now
Relational Self: self in intimate relation with others
Career Self: self as a worker, employee, wage earner
Recreational Self: self when playing, relaxing, enjoying
Musical Self
Artistic Self
Spiritual Self

Health Self
Exercise Self
Bodily Self
Sexual/Gender Self
Etc.

The complexity of "self" arises from all of the many facets that we can use to "identify" ourselves. Go through the elicitation process and then finally notice *where* do you store or posit or experience your *everyday self?*

Where do the boundaries of your self begin and end?

> *What kind* and quality of boundaries do you have?
> How much self-consciousness do you experience?
> How much self-forgetfulness do you experience?
> What degree or condition of self-esteem (as a mental evaluation of worth)?
> What degree or condition of self-confidence (as a feeling of ability to take pride in something that you do)?

What *metaphor* do you use for self? "Self is reflected in my face." "Self as my body." "Self is my sense of my emotions." "Self as my overall 'space.'" "Self as a core." "Self as a ghostly vapor deep inside—or an aura around me."

Summary

- Our *neurologically energized states* generate a **force field**—a real live, actual, and physical *field* comprised of mental energy, emotional energy, somatic energy, etc. This explains the power of *state dependent* learning, memory, perception, communication, and behavior. It explains why our states and Meta-States operate as *self-organizing phenomena.*

- Combining the three Meta-Domains of NLP (the Meta-Model, Meta-Programs, and Meta-States) and unifying the sub-models within the NLP model of human functioning creates a systemic model. It offers a way of thinking about how these facets of experience come together.

- This allows us to see and work with three major avenues into the adventure of experience: **language** (both VAK language systems and propositional language), **perception and thinking patterns** (the Meta-Programs for sorting and filtering, and the meta Meta-Programs of higher conceptual levels), and **states and logical levels** (the Meta-States and higher conceptual phenomena).

Chapter 5

The RESOLVE Model and "Personality"

Using NLP for Resolving Problems

From Personality Understanding to Transformation

If we construct "personality" through our thinking, feeling, deciding, valuing, believing, etc., and if there is indeed *a structure* to how we "do" personality, then can we *change* our "personality?" Can "personality" be transformed?

Yet bet it can.

How?

One way to assist someone to change successfully involves finding and altering the strategy which the person uses. And sure enough, there is even a *"strategy"* for this, "an organized sequence of internal representations and external actions" that we can perform to assist someone in changing. The RESOLVE Model was developed by Bolstad and Hamblett as a way to summarize many of the NLP presuppositions and processes. From here, we'll let them describe it in their own words.

The RESOLVE Model

The RESOLVE model describes *a helping sequence* in terms of a simple seven stage model using the acronym RESOLVE. It takes a truly skillful and knowledgeable Practitioner to actually deliver the personal transformations promised by NLP. Using NLP in a helpful way involves much more than just a set of techniques. We also have to have a map of the process of change, a map that's meta to the individual change processes that allows us to keep track of the process and where we are at any given time. To that end, we here introduce *the 7 stages of the RESOLVE model:*

1) **R**esourceful state for the Practitioner
2) **E**stablish rapport
3) **S**pecify outcome
4) **O**pen up model of world
5) **L**eading to desired state
6) **V**erify change
7) **E**cological exit

"R"—Resourceful State for the Practitioner

The first stage in this model aims simply to access a confident and competent state with regard to our abilities to embody the NLP presuppositions and to adopt a clear awareness about our role with a client. What does that involve?

In the 1960s and 1970s, counseling developers Robert Carkhuff and Bernard Berenson published a number of research studies showing that helping interactions tend to influence clients either for better *or* worse. They identified a number of measures of successful human functioning which showed that helpers who function well on these dimensions are able to assist others to function well on these dimensions too.

They discovered that helpers who function poorly on these dimensions actually influence clients to deteriorate in their functioning (Carkhuff and Berenson, 1977, pp. 5, 35). Carkhuff and Berenson likened most psychotherapists to professional lifeguards with extensive training in rowing a boat, throwing a ring buoy, and giving artificial respiration, but without the ability to swim.

"They cannot save another because, given the same circumstances, they could not save themselves."

Effectively using NLP in consulting with clients means that we congruently use the same processes for accessing resourceful states ourselves that we coach our clients to use. This enables us to congruently convey to clients that change is possible. So, we anchor ourselves into positive states of curiosity, fun, and creativity when we work with clients. We build rapport without getting caught in the same patterns that our clients are accessing.

We also develop the following NLP understandings and attitudes (or presuppositions) and make them our frame of mind:

1) *The Map is not the Territory.* All beliefs boil down to maps. As the client's map about how events happened is only a map, so is each and every therapeutic map we use to navigate this territory, including the NLP map.

2) *"Resistance" to suggestions indicates the need for more adequate rapport building.* Every time a client resists a suggestion it calls on us to design suggestions which more fully pace the client's world and emotions.

3) *Actions are always motivated by positive intentions.* The positive intention behind a given behavior may be to simply meet one's needs at that time. Recognizing the actions as based on the best choices available to a person at the time creates a positive place to begin as we then simply expand the person's choices that will enhance future actions. We don't have to make the person "wrong" before pursuing a solution.

4) *People already have all the resources they need.* This transforms the role of the consultant so that we simply help people access and apply the needed resources.

5) *Human beings exist as systems, as neuro-linguistic systems, so that change in one part affects the whole.* All change work needs to consider the ecological results on their body, psychological life, spiritual life, and social life.

6) *All results, both "positive" and "negative," are useful feedback that we can use as we adjust our next communications.* This attitude totally alters the way we think about the responses we get. There's no failure, just feedback information.

7) *Change is easy if you know how.* Actually, it is not "changing" that takes time, it's "not-changing" that takes time. When we know *how* to make significant transformation, the change process becomes easy.

8) *Our expectations profoundly affect what is possible for the client.* The states, Meta-States, perceptual filters, etc. all communicate and affect the client. We cannot *not* communicate.

In their search for a term not tainted by the expectations of "counselor" and "psychotherapist," Carkhuff and Berenson (1977) used the term "helper." In our chapters, we will use a variety of the terms like practitioner and helper, but we will mostly use *consultant*. In the business context, CEOs and managers hire a "consultant" to suggest strategies that enable the client to meet his or her goals. We find that there are several implications to this arrangement, which we consider appropriate in working with people for personality changes.

- The consultant should have expertise in the area of the desired change and expertise in connecting and co-operating with clients.

- The consultant needs to be "hired" (either formally or informally). We offer our expertise in response to a request. Consulting is not just a sadistic enjoyment of interfering in someone's life.

- The consultant elicits, clarifies, and works with a primary focus on the client's goals, not his or hers.

- The client is ultimately in charge of his or her own business. The client must assume responsibility for acting on the suggestions or not. Unless the client recognizes that the consultant doesn't solve the problem, but works mostly as a coach and consultant, "solutions" will carry little significance.

- Because the client pays for the consulting, the consultant should use his or her time with the client efficiently.

- While the consultant takes charge of the process, the client remains in charge of the content.

- Consultants operate with certain explicit professional guidelines like confidentiality, avoidance of double relationships, avoidance of sexual contact with clients, etc. Similarly, clients are also expected to operate with some guidelines that make the relationship professional: turning up to arranged meetings on time, etc.

There's yet another essential quality which we believe that all successful psychotherapists, Practitioners, and consultants must bring to the process of working with people. This one is rarely mentioned, yet it actually plays a very important role. This is the quality of *love*. Of course, our focus here concerns theories, models, and skills in the end love usually plays a more important role. About this, Virginia Satir once said:

> The ability to give and receive love is as important to the soul as inhaling and exhaling air is to the body. (Satir and Baldwin, 1983, p. 168)

Love cannot be faked therapeutically. Clients are far too perceptive for that to work. Nor is love merely rapport, although effective rapport is an expression of love. Love is not merely the ability to focus on positive aspects of a client's exploration, though that too is an expression of love. Love is more than just an attitude, more than just a strategy or a Meta-Program. It is not adequately expressed in any of the research on psychotherapy or change, because it cannot be so simply measured. And yet it is there, every time someone assists someone else to heal.

"E"—Establish Rapport

In the establishing rapport stage we establish the *personal* foundation upon which we can then truly work in a cooperative way with a client. Matching the client's model of the world, emotions, perceptions, etc. enables us to thereafter verbally and non-verbally lead the client to new experiences.

Bandler and Grinder (1979) noted that as we first elegantly join the other's reality, this increases our chances of being able to lead someone to change a strategy.

> When you join someone else's reality by pacing them, that gives you rapport and trust, and puts you in a position to utilize their reality in ways that change it. (p. 81)

An example. One of the set of strategies that often create anxiety involves making scary internal visual images. If I talk with the visually anxious person about what they can see as they sit beside me, chances increase that when I gradually shift my comments to talk more about kinesthetic relaxation, the person will follow this lead into the new strategy of relaxation (Yapko, 1981).

Examination of films and videotapes of therapy sessions and other conversations by communication researchers (Ivey *et al.*, 1996, p. 60; Condon, 1982, pp. 53–76; Hatfield *et al.*, 1994) now confirms the significance of what researchers call "interactional synchrony" or "movement complementarity." This same process is variously referred to in the NLP literature (e.g., Bolstad and Hamblett, 1998, pp. 68–72) as "non-verbal matching," "pacing," or "rapport skills."

What are these non-verbal rapport skills? NLP developers propose that when conversation flows smoothly, people breathe in time with each other, and co-ordinate their body movements as well as their voice tonality and speed. The more this matching of behavior happens, the more the other person gets a sense of shared understanding and at-one-ness or "rapport." Also, the more this matching happens, the more the other person will be open to useful suggestions, and adopt the emotional responses of the helper or therapist. All learning and change depends on this willingness of the client to be open to new responses.

William Condon has meticulously studied videotapes of conversations, confirming these patterns. He found that in a successful conversation, movements such as a smile or a head nod are matched by the other person within 1/15 of a second. Within minutes of beginning the conversation, the volume, pitch, and speech rate (number of sounds per minute) of the people's voices match each other. This is correlated with a synchronizing of the type and rate of breathing. Even general body posture is adjusted over the conversation so that the people appear to match or mirror each other.

Elaine Hatfield, John Cacioppo, and Richard Rapson, in *Emotional Contagion*, show that matching another person's behavior in these detailed ways results in the transfer of emotional states from one person to another. If I feel happy, and you match my breathing, voice, gestures and smiles, you will begin to feel the same emotional state. This is the source of empathy, and also of much therapeutic change.

What does this mean for us as consultants? Firstly, it means that we benefit from developing the skills of breathing in time with clients, adjusting our voice tonality to match theirs, and adjusting our posture and gestures to match theirs. Secondly, it emphasizes the importance, once the sense of rapport has been established, of having the flexibility to gradually shift back to a healthy and resourceful style of breathing, speaking and acting. The purpose of getting in rapport with our clients is to then assist them to move towards their goals; a process called "pacing and leading."

Building rapport in NLP terms also includes *pacing a person's core Meta-Programs and values* during the process when the person reveals them. Clients have been shown, for example, to prefer a counselor whose word use matches their own representational system (visual, auditory, kinesthetic or auditory digital) by a ratio of three to one (Brockman, 1980).

We can also enhance building rapport by the use of "artfully vague" language (i.e., use of the NLP Milton Model patterns). A study by Darrell Hischke showed positive effects from both representational system matching and nonspecific language. Chunking up verbally to generalized descriptions gives us the structure of agreement. Examples of language structures used while establishing rapport:

"So what happened for you was…"
"Sounds like you really want… "
"Can I check; the way you see it…"

"S"—Specify Outcome

Once we have established rapport, it's time to get at least one sensory specific and ecological outcome for the session. This means we shift to "chunking down" on the person's goals and outcomes to create more detailed plans. Why is this important? Because part of the system by which many clients maintain problems involves the use of vague language. In this stage of helping, we use the Meta-Model to create more precision of outcome.

Thomas Macroy (1998) found that when he analyzed family communication in terms of the NLP Meta-Model, those families who were most dissatisfied also used the most deletions, distortions, and generalizations in their language (especially deletions). Research on the *Solution Focused Therapy model* (a model closely allied with NLP) confirms that clients improve when they receive questions which focus on their specific outcomes. Also, there is another strong correlation. The amount of discussion of solutions and outcomes in the first session is strongly correlated to the chances that the client will continue with the change process (Miller *et al.*, 1996, p. 259).

William Miller has over-viewed the research of successful psychotherapy. In it he identified that enabling clients to set their own goals for therapy significantly increases their commitment to therapy and that, in turn, enhances the results (Miller, 1985).

With all of that in mind about the importance of specifying precise goals, there are two steps to this process: sorting outcomes and making them well-formed.

First, *Sorting Outcomes.* We sort outcomes in order to identify one or more goals from the array of problem-based information which the client presents. This sorting process includes asking solution-focused questions to shift their sorting from "problems" to "solutions." It also includes checking which outcomes will be easiest or most significant to deal with first in this session.

Second, *Making the Outcomes Well-formed.* We have detailed this check using the acronym SPECIFY. While we do not need to actively question all the aspects of this SPECIFY model in each case, we should keep this model in mind as we assess outcomes when working with a client. By identifying the first step the person would take to change, and by inviting the person to access relevant resourceful states, we actually begin the process of change. This means that setting an outcome is not something we do *before* helping someone change. It's better to view setting an outcome and changing as two aspects of the same process. Here are some examples of the language structures used when we engage in SPECIFY-ing an outcome with someone:

Sorting Outcomes
> "What has to be different as a result of you talking to me?"
> "How will you know that this problem is solved?"
> "What is this problem an example of?
> > What other examples are there of this larger issue?"
> "Which of these issues will, when you solve it, let you know that all the others can be solved?"
> "Which of these will be the easiest for you to change first?"
> "When is a time that you noticed this problem wasn't quite as bad?"
> "What was happening at that time? What were you doing differently?"

Sensory Specific.
> "What specifically will you see/hear/feel when you have this outcome?"

Positive Language.
> "If you don't have the old problem, what is it that you will have?"

Ecological.
> "What else will change when you have this outcome?"
> "What situations do you want this outcome in and what situations do you not want it to affect?"

Choice Increases with this Outcome.
> "Does this outcome increase your choices?"

Initiated by Self.
   "What do *you* personally need to do to achieve this?"

First Step Identified and Achievable.
   "What is your first step?"

Your Resources Identified.
   "What resources do you have to achieve this outcome?"

"O"—Open up Client's Model of the World

With rapport and outcome setting, we next move to the fourth stage in transformation as we assist a client in discovering how he or she has generated the old strategy. In doing this the person begins to experience him or herself *as capable of generating* a new, more useful strategy. Undoubtedly, more of *the "art"* of NLP happens at this stage in consulting than at any other.

The one core factor in the client's "personality" that reliably predicts how well they will respond to the change process involves whether they experience themselves as having *an internal locus of control.* Clients who believe that they are in charge of their own responses, that is, *"at cause,"* do far better in numerous research studies with a variety of different models of therapy (Miller *et al.*, 1996, pp. 319, 325).

Furthermore, it should be noted that research shows that this sense of being in control is not a stable "quality" that some clients have and others do not. Instead, it varies over the course of a client's interactions with the helper. Successful therapy has been shown to result first in a shift in the "locus of control," and then in the desired success (Miller *et al.*, 1996, p. 326). In their study of NLP Psychotherapy, Martina Genser-Medlitsch and Peter Schütz in Vienna (1997) found that NLP clients scored higher than controls in their perception of themselves as in control of their lives (with a difference at 10% significance level).

This means that when we deal first with this Meta-Level change, we dramatically increase our chances of enabling someone to change. We have specified three steps to putting someone "at cause" with their situation. These include:

1) Demonstrating the general possibility of change.

2) Demonstrating the specific possibility of changing the client's current problem.

3) Demonstrating the possibility of using a selected, specific change technique to change that problem.

First, give a concrete physical demonstration of change happening easily and quickly as a result of changing internal representations. For example, we have every client do a visualization exercise as we start.

> We invite them to turn around and point behind them with their arm, and then come back to the front. Next we have them imagine themselves going further, and notice what they would see, feel and say to themselves if their body was more flexible and they could turn around further. Then they turn around again and notice how much further they can go, instantly and without any extra effort (Bolstad and Hamblett, 1998, p. 81).

Second, access, elicit, and alter the person's problem strategy. There are three parts to this:

A) Pre-test. Tad James (1995, p. 28) emphasized that in the process of helping someone change (like all strategies) involves a test before the change intervention and then a related test after the intervention.

> "When you think about it now, do you get enough of a sense of that problem so you would know the difference if it changed?"

Until they can, it would be risky to go on. Why? Because *how* will they know whether they have succeeded? Of course, some clients will say they only experience the problem in certain situations. If that happens, we immediately say with conviction, "Okay, lets go there now!" Only after we have a pre-tested response which we can check against the post-test regarding a change can we develop "evidence of a difference."

B) Run a standard strategy elicitation. When a person produces the "problem" we typically say,

> "Wow! That's impressive. *How* do you do that? *How* do you know it's time to start?"

Consider the power of the presuppositions in these questions. They presuppose that the client "does" something. When the client answers them, he or she has established that if a change process didn't work, it's because they are still "doing" the old behavior well enough to get the problem.

Within this whole stage of opening up a client's model of the world we are engaged in the process of reframing. We are engaged in Meta-Level change that prepares for the simple shifting of the strategies which then occurs. Hall and Bodenhamer (1997) in *Mind-Lines* catalogued the vast array of choices available for reframing in NLP. A skilled NLP consultant will generate a number of these "strategy loosening" patterns at this stage.

C) Have the person dissociate from and experimentally alter the strategy. Working with Susan, a woman who experiences panic when her family are late home, Richard Bandler (1984) said:

"Let's say I had to fill in for you for a day. So one of the parts of my job would be if somebody was late I'd have to have the panic for you. What do I do inside my head in order to have the panic?" (p. 9)

Susan replies "You start telling yourself sentences like ..."

Richard interrupts, "I've got to talk to myself."

She continues, "...so and so is late, look they're not here. That means that they may never come."

Playfully, Bandler asks "Do I say this in a casual tone of voice?"

When Tad James modeled this pattern, he renamed it, "The Logical Levels of Therapy." James points out that in doing this, Bandler has achieved, by linguistic presupposition, a number of shifts:

- Susan agrees that she causes the panic. She is now "at cause."

- Susan acknowledges that it takes a specific strategy to do so.

- Susan agrees she is expert enough to teach Bandler how to do it.

- Susan describes the process in second person, as if someone else does it.

- Susan, in order to answer the last question above, has to consider what would happen if she ran her strategy differently to the way she usually does.

Third, pre-frame the specific change techniques identified that we use. This includes answering the questions:

"How does this technique relate to my problem and my outcome?"

"Does this technique work?"

One elegant way to do this is to tell stories about other clients who have benefited from the change technique. We can also rehearse the client through the process. Examples of *language structures used when opening up the client's model of the world:*

"When you think about it now, can you get the feeling, so you'd know if that changed?"

"How do you do that? How do you know it's time to start?…"

"If I was going to do that for you, how would I do that?"

"If I did it slightly differently [give an example of this], would it still work?" "So would it be okay to change that now?"

"Here's how we can alter that. Does that sound useful?"

"A client I had last week wanted to … I used a technique where we …."

"L"—Leading to Desired State

We are now ready to facilitate the client in actually changing his or her strategies, and enabling the client to reach the carefully crafted desired outcomes. By this stage, we have elicited the client's key physiology styles, Meta-Programs and values (while establishing rapport), outcomes, resources (while setting an outcome) and the old strategy that creates the problem/s.

Taking this all together, this provides an excellent base from which to select formal NLP change processes. Yet in doing this we need to recognize three of the variables relevant when choosing change techniques. These include:

1) *Ourselves as a consultant.* Obviously, we will tend to choose the change processes with which we are familiar, trained in, and can facilitate congruently. Generally this means that we will choose change processes which we enjoy ourselves.

2) *The client's framing of problem and desired outcome.* A client with a phobia who asks to get some "distance" on his or her anxiety obviously is pointing us to the *Phobia Cure Pattern.* This particular NLP pattern, also called the *V-K Dissociation Pattern,* teaches the brain to *distance* itself, or "dissociate" visually from disturbing memories.

We can also recognize that the client who uses the phraseology, "On the one hand… and on the other hand…" has already moved half way through a *Visual Squash,* or *Parts Integration* process. This refers to the NLP process in which we fuse into one two conflicting "parts" of the personality.

[In addition to many of the patterns that will be provided in this work, you can find an extensive list of NLP Patterns in *The Sourcebook of Magic* (1997, Hall and Belnap), and in *The User's Manual for the Brain* (1999, Bodenhamer and Hall).]

3) The client's style and personality. Over the twenty-five years that psychotherapists, psychologists, and others have been using NLP patterns for therapy, we have found that some clients find that anchoring works really well while others tend to prefer the use of submodality processes. Some clinicians will attempt to fix about anything using Time-Line patterns (James and Woodsmall, 1988, Hall and Bodenhamer, 1997), while others don't feel right until they do a parts integration. In other words, both clients and clinicians tend to have favorite patterns.

Having found that there is a structure behind these preferences, we have noted this in *the Personal Strengths model* (see Chapter 7). Some NLP techniques require the ability to "chunk up" while some require the ability to "chunk down." Some techniques require the ability to associate into experiences, some the ability to dissociate. Clients have varying strengths in relation to these skills; strengths that they also demonstrate in generating their "problems."

"V"—Verify Change

When we come to the sixth stage in the RESOLVE model, we move to assisting clients in consciously recognizing and identifying the occurrence of the change.

Studies in Solution Focused therapy have examined *the difference in the way* clinicians *ask* about the results of change processes when a client returns for the next session. In studies replicated several times, they have found that if they ask questions which imply the possibility of failure (e.g., "Did the change process work?"), they get a different result than if they ask questions which presuppose success (e.g., "How did that change things?"). When asked a question that presupposes change, 60% of clients will report success. If the question presupposes failure, 67% will report that their situation is the same as it was before (Miller *et al.*, 1996, pp. 255–256).

This recalls and confirms Johnson's (1946–1989) comment quoted earlier that "The terminology of the question determines the terminology of the answer."

One way we can presuppose change is to ask clients to notice what else has changed, or even what else they want to change next.

> "A lot of people go away and only check for results with the things we were intending to change. In fact, when one aspect of your life changes, several other aspects tend to change, and it's a good idea to find out just what has happened. So over the next week I'd like you to notice what else has changed in your life as a result of this process."

This approach also has the added advantage of directing the person's attention away from experimentally de-constructing their change.

Many times a client will say, "Nothing has changed" only then to go on and report the next minute that they have actually achieved every goal they set to achieve during our time together. What causes the shift? Our willingness *not* to assume that their memory of events *is* reality, but instead to ask persistently,

> "So what has changed in your life (or in your experience of the situation that was a problem)? No matter how small the changes seem at first, what is different?"

We then follow that question up by genuinely congratulating them:

> "Wow, that's great. How did you do that?"

Then thirdly, we keep asking:

> "And what else has changed?"

We have derived these three questions from the Ericksonian school of *Solution Focused Therapy* (Chevalier, 1995). In asking them, we are coaching the client to sort for solutions. This key strategy in Solution Focused Therapy describes a method which has 75% of clients achieve their goals in as little as four one-hour sessions.

Milton Erickson emphasized that change is an unconscious process, and that the conscious mind needs re-assuring that change has occurred. He says (Erickson and Rossi, 1979)

> Many patients readily recognize and admit changes they have experienced. Others with less introspective ability need the thera-pist's help in evaluating the changes that have taken place. A recognition and appreciation of the trance work is necessary, lest the patient's old negative attitudes disrupt and destroy the new therapeutic responses that are still in a fragile state of develop-ment. (p. 10)

Erickson here refers to pacing a client's strategy for being con-vinced. Similarly in NLP, a client may need to be convinced by checking for the change. He or she may do this one time, a num-ber of times, or over a period of time. They may even have a "con-sistent convincer" and never be fully convinced about anything. If they have a period of time convincer, we can ask them to go out into the future, past that time, and enjoy the changes. If they have a consistent convincer, we may choose to reframe this by saying, "Since you know you'll never be completely sure this has changed, you might as well accept it now."

Examples of language structures used to verify change:

"Remember that problem you used to have. Try and do it now and notice what has changed."

"Try again, and find out how much you've really changed now!"

"Notice what else is different as a result of this change you've made."

"What do you want to change next?"

"So what changes have happened since we started; big or small?"

"E"—Ecological Exit

At this seventh and last stage of the RESOLVE model we want to simply anchor the changes to the actual situations where the client needs access to them.

A number of studies have led helpers to recognize *the importance of future pacing* the changes that clients initiate. This means inviting the client to imagine him or herself in the actual life situation using the new skills. This process functions both to check out the appropriateness of the plans, the "ecology," and also to install the expectation of success in the person's future (Mann *et al.*, 1989; Marlatt and Gordon, 1985).

Allen Ivey and others have their clients write a "future diary" of their success a year into the future. Alan Marlatt has clients step into the future and fully consider what might make them change their mind about their changes, and then has them plan to prevent that. Both approaches have been shown to deliver far more robust change than parallel programs which skip this step of future pacing. Of course, if any undesirable consequences of the change are detected at this stage, the process shifts back to clarifying outcomes.

Examples of language structures used in future pacing:

> "Think of a time in the future, when in the past you would have had that old problem, and notice how it's changed now."

> "So as you think of the future, is it okay for that to be changed in this way now?"

> "Is there any way you could you stop yourself automatically using the solution to your problem?" (If they say, "I can't"; say "I guess you're stuck with the solution then.")

Adapting the RESOLVE Model

You can practice using this model by running through an imaginary session or by using it with a client as a practice session for a new consultant. You can take a challenging session with a particular client and review it using this RESOLVE model for the purpose of identifying important choice points and generating more options. This works well in a peer supervision situation. It provides a way to use this model to expand awareness of its usefulness and its logical sequence in a reality which may be neither logical nor sequential.

When so using this model, there are four ways the actual session could differ from the map that we have presented.

1) The actual use of skills is cumulative rather than sequential. Once rapport is established, you will want to maintain it throughout the other steps. Once you've begun using the Meta-Model, you will often challenge Meta-Model patterns at later stages as well.

2) The real process of therapy may end successfully at step 2 or 3 or 4. Just elicit the contributing strategy so that the problem disappears. Life is often like that—a lot easier than we expect!

3) You may cycle through the RESOLVE model several times, or run through it as a subroutine of one step in a larger RESOLVE process.

4) Occasionally you will successfully leap several steps at a single bound, or apparently reverse steps. No generalization is ever totally true for all times and circumstances. Once we know a town, we don't carry a map every time we leave home. Yet it sure helps people new to the town.

Summarizing the RESOLVE Model

The RESOLVE model sequences a number of key tasks which research has suggested are an important part of effective change-work. These tasks include the following:

Resourceful state for the Practitioner
- Adopt the presuppositions or principles of NLP.

- Negotiate a consulting relationship.
- Access and anchor oneself into a resourceful state.
- Cultivate the quality of love as a meta-frame.

Establish rapport
- Pace client non-verbally.
- Pace client's sensory system use and other Meta-Programs.
- Use generalized language.
- Verbally pace client's dilemma.

Specify outcome
- Reframe "problems" as "outcomes."
- Sort outcomes, and outcomes of outcomes.
- Ensure outcomes are sensory specific, and ecological.
- Identify resource states and exceptions to the problem.

Open up model of world
- Demonstrate the possibility of change.
- Pre-test the problem strategy.
- Elicit the strategy.
- Frame or reframe the client as "at cause."
- Invite the client to step aside from the strategy and experimentally alter it.
- Demonstrate the specific change techniques (Pre-frame change techniques).

Leading to desired state
- Select change process based on consultant skills, client skills, client's outcome.
- Run change processes.

Verify change
- Ask questions presupposing change.
- Use client's convincer strategy.

Ecological exit
- Future pace change.
- Check for ecology issues.
- Future pace past any "relapses."

Chapter 6

"Personality" as Meta-Level Phenomena

Central Meta-Level Phenomena Structuring "Personality" i.e., Beliefs, Values, etc.

- What plays a critically *important role* in your life?
- Does achievement, power, love, affection, spirituality, honor, sex, family, success, health, or fitness?
- What do you *value* as most significant and meaningful in life?
- How does our *valuing* something as important affect our personality?
- Does our *dis-valuing* similarly order our personality?

Raising questions like these directs our attention to the mental-emotional phenomenon that we call *"values"*—another nominalized term that though it sounds like an actual *thing* or entity, is not. Our so-called "values" do not refer to external objects. They arise instead from how we mentally and emotionally *value* something, attribute importance to it, and then respond to it as meaningful and significant.

We generally recognize this internal evaluative of "values" as playing a central role in "personality." What a person values obviously forms and structures his or her interests, emotions, motivations, behaviors, etc. What we value *drives* our lives and makes us the kind of people we are. So much of the way we live seeks to fulfill various *values.* When our external experience in the world of things, events, and people confirms and fulfills what we *value as important*—we feel good. Our positive emotions of joy, satisfaction, completeness, safety, dignity, love, appreciation, etc. provide us a *reflection* and *cue* about the fulfillment of our *values.*

Conversely, when our external experience in the world of things, events, and people disconfirms, fails to fulfill, and even violates what we *value as important*—our negative emotions *in-form* us about that as well. We then feel upset, angry, afraid, disgusted, frustrated, stressed, discounted, unfulfilled, threatened, etc. These emotions indicate the violation or failure to fulfill our values.

Positive and Negative Emotions and Values

What we experience as our *positive* and *negative emotions*, then, serve as signals *about our values*.

Good feelings come when we experience the fulfillment of our values and bad feelings emerge when we feel the violation of our values. Good feelings provide us with the somatic and personal energy to *keep doing whatever we have done that has brought about the fulfillment of our values*. This explains why the *positive* emotions seem more gentle, discreet, and easier to "live" in.

Bad feelings provide us with the *emergency kind of energy and response* that grabs our attention, knocks us about the head with a two-by-four, and alerts us to immediate and unacceptable danger. Such emotions alert us with bells and alarms and lights that something has gone wrong and that what we value and hold as meaningful is in danger. This explains why we experience more intense energy with negative emotions. Such negative energy provides a tremendous *power surge* within—good energy for the immediate moment and for the short-term. But such are not to maintain and "live" in. Living in fear, bitterness, stress, etc. wears on a person and eventually distorts personality.

Positive emotions operate like the acceleration pedal in a car. They give us the *Yes! signal* for continuing and sustaining our present direction. Negative emotions operate more like the *No! signal* of the brakes and of all the dashboard lights that alert us to the fact that *something has gone wrong*. We need *both* of these energies and signal systems to operate productively, maximally, and healthily. Yet they serve different purposes and so we have to sequence them.

To drive down the highway of life without any brakes or warning system invites disaster. We need our negative emotions to alert us to the endangerment of our values. To drive through life by riding the brakes and only looking at the warning systems invites burnout, misuse of such systems, and a missing of the journey.

Backtracking to the Source

Where do these *Go For It* and *Stop, Look, and Listen* signal systems of our positive and negative emotions come from? From our *thoughts*. We construct them over time by our thinking, reasoning, representing, and evaluating. Consequently, this explains how and why positive and negative emotions may become misaligned, distorted, and irrational.

Emotions only reflect the *e-valuational thinking* that sets up our *value programs*. They indicate a higher level processing, an evaluating of our feelings in a given life context.

To the extent that we have *valued* something in a distorted way, in a way that undermines our well-being, health, or productiveness, to that extent our emotions will not operate as a useful *rewarding and warning system*. Emotions do *not* have an inherent rightness or wrongness. Nor do they always give us accurate or useful information. Their value depends upon the *thinking* that generated the *meanings of value* in the first place.

As adults, we often have *values* driving and governing our lives which reflect childish or adolescent thinking rather than up-to-date adult values.

Recognizing and Appreciating "Values"

We learned our "values" and built them over time as we viewed various experiences, people, events, concepts, etc. as contributing to our experiences of pain and pleasure. Thus to ask, "What do you *value*?" also essentially asks, "What do you believe brings pleasure to you?"

Thus, *values* and *value systems* generally arise from what we *think* will contribute to our well-being, safety, excitement, and pleasure. We, conversely, *disvalue* what we believe will bring us pain, illness, hurt, danger, threat, etc.

This understanding gives us a model for how to regard the nature and role of *valuing* (hence, evaluating) in human personality. What we value or do not value inevitably results from the learnings that we have made as we have moved through life—and the pain and pleasure that we experienced with regard to various events, experiences, people, ideas, etc.

Show me someone who does not *value* reading, studying, and learning, and I'll show you someone who has probably had numerous experiences with that category of experiences that have caused them pain. A nun may have struck the back of her hand really hard with a ruler time and time again, or some other kids may have laughed at a particular student for not getting it, "Billy's a dummy! Billy's a dummy!" Either physical or psychic pain will lead a person to "rightly" conclude (and feel) that "learning brings pain." So no wonder the child does not value it. [I said "rightly" conclude because given *that* situation, this probably represents an accurate learning. The problem arises when we assume that our experiences comprise all of the possible experiences possible or that our experience represents the best of experiences.]

Our *values* explain and summarize our *learning history* about pain and pleasure. Do you value or disvalue "authority figures?" It all depends, doesn't it? What kind and quality of experiences have you had with someone who fell into that conceptual category? Did it result in pleasure (protection, dignity, excitement, admiration) or in pain (insult, punishment, distress)?

To therefore know the *values* of another person gives us a deep insight into the model of the world that orders things, what makes that person tick, what he or she moves toward and moves away from, etc. To *not* know what another person truly and deeply values means that we do not know that person very well at all. This prevents empathy, understanding, rapport, connection, and persuasion. Andreas and Faulkner (1994) wrote,

> Persuasion is the ability to offer compelling value to *others*. (p. 162)

But how can we offer something of *compelling value* to another if we don't know what they value?

Motivation also grows out of and demonstrates our *values*. We *move* toward what we value as producing pleasure, significance, and meaning, and we move away from what produces pain and violates our values. The degree, quality, and nature of a person's *motivation* therefore emerges from their values. Value little, have little or few *motives* (reasons or values) for *moving*, and you will experience little or at least very shallow *motivational energy*.

Where do we Fit "Values" into the NLP Model?

We begin by recognizing the term *"values"* as a nominalization, which arises from the verb (and process) of *valuing*. NLP generally studies "values" and our "hierarchy of values," as a separate domain. Yet where in the NLP model itself do we locate this domain?

- Should we think of "values" as simply internal representations?

- Or should we think of them as existing and operating at a higher logical level to our basic representations?

- How do "values" relate to another mental phenomenon, that of "beliefs?" If I *believe* in my *values*, does that put beliefs above *values?* If I *value* my *beliefs*, does that put *values* above *beliefs?*

- How do *values* relate to our Meta-Programs? Do we use our *values* as part of our perceptual filters for sorting information? If so, how do *values* differ from Meta-Programs?

- What relationship do *values* have to Meta-States? Does our thoughts-and-feelings of *valuing* operate as a state of consciousness above other states? If so, how do *values* differ from Meta-States?

Denominalizing "Values"? Valuing

Values identify and determine our standards (or "criteria") by which we make judgments, decisions, and *e-valuations*. Our *values* show up as nominalizations. Among the nominalizations that we use to code our "values" we have:

being right	happiness	fun
enjoyment	success	relaxation
sex	learning	usefulness
beauty	accomplishment	power
excellence	saving time	health
pleasing others	money	the past
security	discovery	exploration
love	family	praise
neatness	spirituality	humor
learning	autonomy	dignity
perseverance	truth	playfulness
self-reliance	wisdom	solving problems
creativity	freedom	courage
caring	contributing	mastery
order	simplicity	synergy
etc.		

Make a list of your *values*. What do you *value?*

- For a person who very highly values fun and enjoyment, he may give such criteria so much importance that he may find it very difficult to ever get around to accomplish much. The work, discipline, struggle, etc. may really put him off.

- For a person who highly values success, achievement, the struggle of accomplishment, he may find it difficult if not impossible to kick back, relax, and enjoy the benefits of his success.

The Meta-Level Nature of "Values" Makes them Neuro-Semantic

When we *denominalize "values,"* we discover *the process of valuing.* How does that process work? What does that refer to? How do we actually *value?* And, how does *the process of valuing* relate to Meta-Levels of consciousness?

Generally, whatever we *bring to bear upon our Thoughts-Feelings* (at a Meta-Level) has some *value* (importance, significance, meaning) to us.

This describes the essential process of meta-stating. Mere *representation* at the primary level of experience does not equate with or create a "value." We represent lots of things that we do not value.

You can go through a list of states and values that you do not value and represent them in such a way that you "know" what they stand for, can you not?

Can you represent the following: boredom, stupidity, dishonesty, over-seriousness, hurting, disharmony, legalism, slavery, imprisonment, sloppiness, just getting by, entitlement, ugliness, death, injustice, being stuck, disorder, danger, threat, etc. and still not *value* them?

When we do *value* something, we inevitably *represent that item repeatedly, again and again and again.* Doing this causes it to *habituate.* Our mind frequently goes out to that referent (event, person, concept). This *predisposes* us to it. Because in some way or another, we give that referent *meaning* of importance (whether positive or negative—important to esteem or important to avoid). Thus we have *important toward values* and *important away from values.*

At a Meta-Level, when we keep *bringing to bear* the same thought or representation to frame something, that frame of reference holds meaning to us. It may simply represent the value of "familiarity." But usually, it holds meanings that increase our well-being, pleasure, purpose, etc.

Thus, to *value* ultimately represents a Meta-State experience. We have meta-stated something at the primary level (or at any Meta-Level) with *thoughts-and-feelings of importance and meaning.*

This creates the *value.* And this process can continue indefinitely. We can value a value. I can value my loved one (= love and appreciate). Then I can value my loving and appreciating. Then I can value my identity as a loving and appreciating person.

To *value* means that we *believe* in the value or importance of something. I believe in the importance of loving, of living life with vigor and purpose, I believe in enjoying the process of taking on a challenge.

A *value* therefore simply represents one kind of belief—a belief in the value of something.

We can also *believe* in our values. Do you *believe* in the importance of having, knowing, and articulating your values? Valuing (at whatever level) involves the believing in the importance of something. Believing in that value moves you to the next highest level and solidifies the valuing.

There exist no values in the brain or mind as *entities*. Thinking of this mental-emotional process in that way locks us into a nominalized static world. Rather, we use our mind-body consciousness to *value*. "Value" operates as a multiordinal term, having no specific meaning until we specify the level at which we use it. For this reason we can easily confuse low level values with high level values and forget that we construct values within values. [If *multiordinal* is new to you, it refers to the self-reflexivity within language itself. As a nominalization, we can test for multiordinality by checking to see if we can use the term on itself. Can you *love* love? Can you *fear* fear? Become angry at anger? Yet each higher level usage of the same term introduces new connotations and meanings. See Hall, *The Secrets of Magic*, 1998.]

The Quality of our Values

How much *intensity* do you endow your internal representations with? Suppose we measured *the amount of energy* that you invest in *your valuing*. We could then range the energy level from low to high: from worthless, trivial, frivolous, to compulsive, serious, supreme.

This speaks about the relative *importance* of numerous items that we value. We do not value all of our values alike or with the same degree of importance. This results in our *felt sense of its degree of importance. How* important do we consider this or that item?

118

"Values" as Frames-of-References

Every frame-of-reference we create *structurally* operates as a value since we treat that frame as significant and meaningful. This explains *how* we can get "values" installed in ourselves that we do *not* consciously value any longer. As a child we might have really *valued* being the fastest, best, smartest, etc. We valued competing and beating others. If that value became really, really high, it may continue to operate at the highest Meta-Level to our detriment and chagrin. And if it does, it may undermine our ability to get along with others, play as a team member, and align ourselves with others.

In this, not only is it *Beliefs all the Way Up*, and *Frames all the Way Up*, but inasmuch as we value each belief and frame, it's *Values all the Way Up*. Neuro-Semantically, the meaning of treating something as valuable, significant, important, contributing, etc. turns all kinds of mental frames into the nominalization of "values."

Value-Frames Elicitation Pattern

Use the following pattern to help you identify your values: the things you highly value, the things you do not value, and the things you value moving away from.

Pattern for Eliciting "Values" and Value-Frames

A) *Think of something of great importance to you.*
    Think of something that you very much deem as important, of lasting importance, and of durable importance. Think of something that you really *go toward and really want.* How do you represent this? As you represent this, notice also if you have any *other* thoughts "in the back of your mind" *about* these thoughts?

B) *Think of something trivial.*
    Think of something that you consider *un*important, neutral, something to which you respond with a ho-hum kind of attitude (e.g. a plastic cup, a pencil, a discarded sheet of paper). How do you know that you think of this represented item as

*un*important? Any voices, pictures, thoughts, feelings *about* this represented item?

C) *Think of something important for you to avoid.*
This could be something like driving fast and recklessly, reacting with defensiveness, putting your hand in fire, driving without insurance, etc.

D) *Think of something that you feel driven toward, compulsive about.*
Use the phrases, "I have to have…" "I must have this…" to cue you about something in this category. What do you feel that you have no choice about? What "submodality" driver causes it to stand out, to leap out, (halo, brighter, glowing, close)?

E) *Think of something once deemed as un-important.*
Think about something that you once deemed as *not* valuable but that you now experience as valuable. It has moved from unimportant to something that now matters. What "thing" do you "have to have" and do you drool over?

F) *Run a Contrastive Analysis of these in terms of Submodalities.*
How do you distinguish between important and trivial? Identify the submodality continua that you use to gauge the intensity of an experience: close-far, left-right, up-down.

For me, desirable wants: color, close, 3-D, movie, immediately in front of me or to my right.

My trivial items: black-and-white, dim, still, to my left.

G) *Identify your Meta-Level Structure/s designing Important/ Unimportant.*
How do you cue yourself, say to yourself, "Important!" "Not important"? After you have represented the item (valued or not) what enables you to know which category to put it in?

For me, I have the words "Important" or "yes, that's true" "I value that." In a matter-of-fact tonality which grows to an enthusiastic affirmation in a moderate volume.

For me, for "unimportant" I have numerous verbal expressions coding this: "no," "unimportant," "not important," "Don't care about that." The tone is matter of fact—growing to a more emphatic and stern tone as it increases for some things, and more of a nonchalant tonality for others.

NLP Modeling: It All Lies in the Coding

Given that *structure* governs experience (the NLP model), then detecting and identifying *how we code "values"* plays a very important role in dealing with such. How do you represent *value or importance?* How do you signal your brain so that you know the difference between important and not-important? What did you discover in terms of your:

- internal VAK representations;
- the submodality qualities of those representations;
- your Meta-Level Affirmations/Negations?

Regarding the *Coding systems for values*, we begin with the representation systems and submodalities to identify the differences. To which do we respond more strongly?

High—low: spatial locations.
High—low: auditory volume, pitch.
Real—unreal: big/small in size; color or b/w; close or far; clear/fuzzy.
Give it more "reality": closer, forefront, "closely held."
Light/heavy; tight/loose; firm/loose.

Neurologically, we all have a nervous system that innately moves us toward what we value and away from what we do not value. Therefore our feelings of *attraction* and *aversion* reflect the things (ideas, experiences, people, etc.) that we have previously decided as a value.

Values and Neuro-Semantic Meta-Levels

While we begin with "submodality" distinctions to code the difference between *important* and *unimportant*, we also use some *Meta-Level structures*. We use some frames of reference. By these we categorize one *concept* versus the other. We do this because, after all, *"importance"* and *"value"* and *"meaning"* do not occur (or exist) at the primary sensory-based level of existence. These things exist at a Meta-Level.

Beyond Mere Submodality Representation

What happens when you use "submodalities" and represent an item closer, brighter, and more to the right? Does it automatically cause the brain-body system to respond to it as "important?" Not necessarily. *Mere representation alone,* no matter how "juiced" up, will not make the shift and hold it. Sometimes it may invite one to think and feel that way, but it won't stay unless some Meta-Level shifts also occur.

Therefore somehow you will use some meta-frame to distinguish *"Important"* from *"Unimportant."* How do you do this?

Perhaps you use one or more of the "submodality" continua. If you do, you may thus code "less important" as further away, dimmer, and more to the left.

The Meta-level Governs the Representations and "Submodalities"

What inter-relationship exists between Meta-Levels and submodalities? How do Meta-Levels and "submodalities" inter-relate?

Since the Meta-Level occurs at a higher level than the submodalities, *meta-frames always govern submodalities.* If you use the metaphor "Up is more, down is less" as a frame-of-reference for gauging the idea of "more/less" then this will modulate your submodalities. So with other metaphors that you could use:

> "Heavy is more, light is less"
> "Light is more, heavy is less"
> "Up is more, down is less"
> "Down is more, up is less"
>   (the more you go down, the more you enter into hypnosis)
> "Closer is more, further away is less"
> "Further away is more, closer is less"
>   (see seminar participant in Andreas, 1987, p. 83)

In other words, *the metaphor* we bring to bear upon our thinking about the intensity of an experience ("more or less") determines how our submodalities will work. Metaphors, as Meta-Level structures, refers to thinking about one thing *in terms of* another thing. Lakoff and Johnson (1980) have written extensively on the existence of the "orientational metaphors" that lie hidden in our everyday language (in/out, up/down, front/back, etc.). That we do not think of such as "metaphors" does not reduce their metaphorical nature. They noted that we generally use more *concrete* and highly defined facets of our experience (facets that grow out of our embodiment and the physics of our nervous system) to explain the less well defined.

Frames Govern "Submodalities"

The realization that our *frame governs our submodalities* also explains the variations in people's submodalities and why submodality shifts can have different effects on subjective experiences—people have different Meta-Levels framing their understandings.

Generally, most people in Western cultures will use similar meta-frames. As a result, for most people, when they make a picture or sound closer, louder, brighter, etc. it *increases* the experience, makes it more compelling, important, etc.

Generally, also, most right-handed people in Western culture will sort out their "time-line" from left to right or back to front. Thus the more they move an internal representation into the "present" and "future"—the more real and compelling it becomes to them, therefore the more valuable and important. The more they move an internal representation to the left and into their "past"—the less compelling, real, and so more unimportant it becomes.

This underscores the ultimate importance of checking on a person's frames (their Meta-Level structures). Understanding their frames gives a clue to their submodalities. Understanding their submodalities also gives clues to their meta-frames.

At the *conceptual level*, if someone deems "the past as all important and determining," how will this affect *where* they put their past, how *close* or far it stands from them, the *direction* of their time-line, etc.? To change this, we can address it at the Meta-Level (i.e. belief change pattern) or at the primary level (i.e. a submodality shift).

Thus, when we put an internal representation up in a certain spot, the representation will *activate* the Meta-Level meaning, *"No, not important."* Conversely, when we put it in another spot, it will *activate* another Meta-Level meaning, *"Yes, important!"* Thus we can activate Meta-Levels via "submodalities" and conversely, we can activate "submodalities" via Meta-Levels.

In fact, if a "submodality" shift works, it works *because it has activated some Meta-Level structures.* For primary states we need to map across "submodalities." For Meta-States we need to map across the Meta-Level structure or frame.

Values Analysis

Relationship Faithfulness
When Bob thought about how he values "being faithful to my wife" he first made his representation of Linda. This evoked in him positive associated feelings. Then immediately from "the back of his mind" came a "thought" of enjoyment *about* that. That seems to operate as his "yes" to the value.

When he tried a "Clintonesque" with regard to this and "thought" about "cheating on my wife" he immediately went into the place where he has his "No" stored—he experienced a very strong negative K (kinesthetic) and then "bounced out of there."

Staying Fit and Healthy
When I thought about my value of "staying fit and healthy" I put it in my *space* to the right … as if in my immediate "future." I code it as a picture of my future self moving and taking physical actions that will bring that value into existence. I have the picture in color, close, 3-D, panoramic, with appropriate sound track … and "in the back of my mind" I have a resounding "Yes" echoing.

When I shift to the opposite thought, when I think about "getting out of shape, fat, and unhealthy" I picture it over to my left as if away from me in my "past" (even though that has never characterized me). I see a black-and-white picture, small, dim, flat, and I hear a resounding "No" in my mind dis-avowing it.

If I shift all of the submodalities of my "getting out of shape" picture and code it with the "staying fit and healthy" submodalities (in color, close, bright, 3-D, etc.), my "No!" voice gets louder and I have a sense of wanting to take my left arm and shove it back out of the way and further to the left as if "to make it go away." My Meta-Level awareness refuses to let it stay so coded.

Summary

- *What* and *how* a person *values* obviously plays a central role in *personality*. Given the nature of *cognition* in human functioning, our *valuing* in fact functions as part of our self-programming. As we *value*, so we become. As we value, we establish the meta-frames of references that we then use to guide our lives. This creates our *drives*, our motivational energies, our perceptions, and our very sense of ourselves.

- Understanding this about the relationship between *valuing* and *personality* leads us to ask several questions: 1) If I didn't *value* this or that experience, person, idea, etc., *what kind of a person* would I "be" in terms of my thinking, feeling, speaking, behaving, and relating?; 2) If I shifted to *value* this other thing, person, set of experiences, ideas, etc., *what kind of a person* would that transform me into?

- While we can map "submodality" distinctions across to make transformations that involve primary states, we usually cannot do this with Meta-States. It works well with hateful/disliked to liked/friendly, boredom to fascination, and serious to ludicrous. Yet this same process does not work when we attempt to map across Meta-States such as confusion to understanding, doubt to belief. To do that necessitates shifting to a Meta-Level.

- We can increase our "values" to make them more intense by using the "submodalities" distinctions. How do we make a value more or less important? We can recode *the quality of the representation.* This improves its submodality qualities as it shifts its frame of reference.

- Values relate to personal congruence. When we live and act in a way that fits with our values, others experience us as congruent. We also experience some higher gestalts as self-integrity, wholeness, integration.

- We all have a sense of our own "personal space." In different cultures and sub-cultural groups, this "space" or sense of "territory" differs. This governs how close or how far people stand to each other, the degree that someone may "get in someone's face," or intrude into their personal space, how comfortable or uncomfortable we experience some people, etc.

- Beginning with this construct and thinking about it as *a 3-D spatial reality*, we can begin to notice *where* in actual *space* people seem to put their *model of the world.* NLP has long worked with this and described this in terms of "time-lines." *Where* in actual *space* does a person put his or her "past," "present," and "future?"

- Now we want to expand this beyond just these *concepts* of "time," and begin to look for other concepts: beliefs, values, strategies, affirmations/negations, etc. Because not only do we project our 3-D holographic model of the world into actual space, so do others.

- What metaphors does the person use in his or her orientations: up-down, close-far, in-out, bright-dim, loud-quiet, etc.?

- Where does the first Meta-Level begin? How high off the ground? How does the person signal or gesture with regard to this?

Chapter 7

The Personal Strengths Model and "Personality"

People have all the resources they need.
They just need to learn how to orchestrate them for resourcefulness.

Why do particular techniques work well with some clients and fail completely with others?
What explains the difference in response to the same pattern?

If you would like to be able to identify the specific techniques or patterns that will work as you listen to a client describing a dilemma, you have come to the right chapter. Here we want to offer some suggestions for recognizing *how* every client who enters your office reveals his or her *strengths* by the very way the person claims to have a "problem." The flipside of the "problem" is a strength or skill. It reveals a mastery.

When the developers of NLP modeled the extraordinary hypnotherapist Milton H. Erickson, they incorporated many of his principles, attitudes, and processes into NLP. In Erickson they discovered that he continuously urged the identification and utilization of clients' "problem" strategies in therapy.

> The author has repeatedly stressed the importance of utilizing patients' symptoms and general patterns of behavior in psychotherapy. Such utilization renders unnecessary any effort to alter or transform symptomatology as a preliminary measure to the re-education of patients in relation to the crucial problems confronting them in their illness.

In this chapter Richard and Margot present a model they developed as a simple and easy-to-use format for quickly identifying a client's "pattern of behavior" and pacing and utilizing them for choosing various NLP processes. Based on an earlier model developed by Carl Jung, the Strengths Model utilizes the NLP pre-supposition that every "problem" is a skill run by a strategy. Later, in the chapters on specific "Personality Disorders," we will use this model as a basis for therapeutic intervention.

Jung's Model of Personality

Before NLP, most models of personality were explanations of the various ways in which human beings were considered to be "broken." For example, Freud's model lists various personality types, each being a variation on what he called the "psychopathology of everyday life" (Masson, 1992, p. 85).

In developing its various models of personality (Meta-Programs, Strategies, Meta-States, etc.), NLP started on a very different foundation. You can especially see this with the Meta-Programs model which began as one of the few exceptions to the psychopathology approach. It used some of the concepts from Jungian analytic psychology.

As he referred to "personality types," Jung first coined the terms *Thinker, Feeler, Sensor and Intuitor.* His model uses these terms to refer not merely to types, but also to skills for living, which people developed in varying degrees. He explained (1964):

> These four functional types correspond to the obvious means by which consciousness obtains its orientation to experience. Sensation (i.e., sense perception) tells you that something exists; thinking tells you what it is; feeling tells you whether it is agreeable or not; and intuition tells you whence it comes and where it is going. (p. 49)

Tad James and Wyatt Woodsmall (1988, pp. 95–106) describe the Thinker-Feeler and Intuitor-Sensor continua as measures of what percentage of time/energy a person invests in each of the four functions. They ask the following questions:

"Does the person use thinking or feeling more?"
"Does the person use intuiting or sensing more?"

Jung's original model allowed for a second type of question. Just because someone develops their thinking skills does not mean they have reduced their feeling skills. The second type of question is:

"For each skill, how fully has this person developed the skill?"

Jung suggests that every human being benefits by being able to fully use all four faculties. People vary in the extent to which they are skilled in each area.

Four Basic Skills from these Jungian Categories

We find the Jungian categories, as described by James and Woodsmall, immensely useful. As we think of them as rather non-specific, we describe this in terms of "chunking up" in NLP and "intuitive" in Jungian terms. NLP is especially valuable in how it can get down to actual sensory data. Accordingly, this allows us to think of these as four important analogues in Jung's skills as the ability for:

1) *Dissociating:*
   To distance oneself from experiences, seeing them from outside; corresponding to Thinker.

2) *Associating:*
   To step into experiences, feeling them from inside; corresponding to Feeler.

3) *Chunking up:*
   To be aware of the global "big picture"; corresponding to Intuitor.

4) *Chunking down:*
   To be aware of the specific details; corresponding to Sensor.

These four skills play an essential role in living an enjoyable life since they are necessary prerequisites for all other internal processing. And this includes processing the NLP techniques or patterns. For example,

> To experience *Anchoring,* a person needs to be able to associate into experiences.

> To run *the Phobia Pattern,* one needs to be able to dissociate.

> To set *a Well-Formed Outcome,* one needs to be able to chunk down.

> And to do the *Parts Integration Process,* one needs to be able to chunk up.

When clients come seeking change, they bring their own personal skills with them, the very ones they have developed over a lifetime. Certain upbringings support the development of skills for dissociating as those experiences encourage the person to step out of experiences in the way they encode them. Other upbringings support the development of skills for associating into and fully "living" experiences. And yet other upbringings nurture both abilities. The same occurs for chunking as well as all skills.

Designing Interventions to Pace and Lead a Client's Strengths

When you study the original Jungian model in its fullness, you will discover that Jung claimed that each function (each strength) had *an active expression* and *a passive expression* (Whitmont, 1991, pp. 140–147).

The active expression refers to healthy use of the skill in a conscious, directed way.

The passive expression refers to an unconscious, compulsive use of the skill (the way most clients will have been using the skills in their problem area).

Rather than pacing the person's "passive" use of a function, Jung aimed to directly access and use the opposite "active" skills in his analysis. NLP uses the notion of *pacing and leading*, which seems to describe this more elegantly. Here also we will essentially be *playing to the strengths* of our clients, not their weaknesses.

Anchoring processes require *associating* into a specific situation. Clients who are excellent at associating will generally find it easy to become skilled at anchoring. Such clients have been using the process, for example in creating phobias. So the skill is intact in their repertoire of responses. But they may, or may not, have acquired the skill to dissociate which is presupposed in the *Phobia Pattern.* If we use *Collapsing Anchors* before the Phobia Pattern, or Stack a Resource Anchor first, we are utilizing their strength, and so pacing, before leading them to new skills.

Conversely, submodality change processes require being able to dissociate somewhat from the experience for which you are eliciting submodalities. Some submodality processes (such as the Phobia or Trauma Pattern) specifically require making dissociated, constructed images.

In *Time-Line Processes* a person imagines floating up above the time-line of their life. This requires *stepping back* or dissociating from the experiences on the time-line. A client who is excellent at dissociating will generally have well developed skills necessary for Time-Line Processes (see James and Woodsmall, 1988). They may find checking an experience in the time-line less convincing, but will experience the change from being up above and before the problem event. Someone who "feels" cut off from their experience may appreciate healing their limiting decision (to be cut off) from above the time-line before coming back and anchoring themselves to a powerful resource state.

The same applies to "chunking." Using the detailed NLP questioning style of Meta-Model questioning to clarify your thoughts and set specific goals requires "chunking down." This deductive type of reasoning and thinking *extends* an idea down and out into specifics of everyday life. The person skilled at "chunking down" to the thousand details of their day and becoming anxious may appreciate setting a sensory specific goal before you do trance-work and "chunk up" to some generalized "change."

On the other hand, using the "artfully vague" language patterns developed by Milton Erickson to induce trance presupposes the ability to "chunk up." The same holds for the techniques which ask for the purpose or "higher intention" of a behavior. A client who gets depressed because "everything" is hopeless may find it easier to use Parts Integration before setting specific goals.

This means that some of the NLP techniques will work with certain clients and not with others. And yet none of this is random. Clients have strengths. So this four-skill model provides one method for "diagnosing" those strengths and then playing to them. Of course, when a client can do everything you suggest easily, you have one who has well developed all four skills, which speeds along the consultation considerably.

Figure 7.1

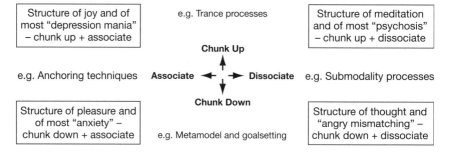

The Four Skills Combinations

In a sense, using NLP techniques with a client facilitates or coaches that person to develop *the skills* presupposed within that pattern. In this way, we not only transform the specific issue of the client, but the client also develops *a whole set of new skills* as required and presupposed by the technique. The great thing about this is that these skills are the very ones required to live an enjoyable life.

Jung noted in his model that people generally utilize *a pair* of the basic skills. In *the Personal Strengths Model,* a person may use skills to associate into a chunked up experience ("Everything feels like this") which could be used to create euphoria or "depression."

This person may benefit from developing their ability to chunk down and dissociate using submodality processes and dissociated goal setting.

Someone who uses skills to dissociate in a chunked up way ("Everything I'm conscious of is like this") could have used these skills to create a state of meditation or "psychosis." That person would benefit from taking on techniques of chunking down and associating such as strategy installation and associated goal setting.

If your client uses skills to associate into chunked down experiences ("These specific details feel like this"), which can be used to generate pleasure or "anxiety disorders," that person would probably benefit from learning how to chunk up and dissociate using a trance technique like the Time-Line Processes.

Lastly, the person who uses skills to dissociate in a chunked down way ("These specific details I'm conscious of in this way") which support planning successful action or extreme mismatching (what psychiatry might call a borderline personality disorder) could benefit from developing the skills of chunking up and associating into life with Parts Integration, Anchoring, and Trance Work.

The Polarity Swings

Using *the Personal Strengths Model,* two types of polarity swing can be understood and dealt with. Firstly, some swings, such as "manic-depressive disorders" can be understood as a person simply using the same skills with different content. Both the "manic" person and the "depressed" person will agree that "everything feels..." something (great or horrible!). What neither of them does well involves the abilities to chunk down and dissociate.

Secondly, some people develop strengths which focus on two categories "opposed" to each other, rather than two next to each other. We call this incongruity or "addiction." An addict may appear to oscillate between associating into one experience, part or set of values and behavior at one time, and dissociating from it totally at another. Neither skill is fully available to the person. This leaves the individual unable to successfully dissociate from undesired experiences and associate into chosen experiences.

In Isobel Briggs Myers' terms such individuals operate as *"perceivers"* rather than *"judgers"* (Briggs Myers, 1962). Their strengths are on the "perceiving" intuitor-sensor axis (chunk up/chunk down) rather than the "decision making" feeler-thinker axis (associate/dissociate).

How can the addict's skills be used in change work then? Chunking down to "one step at a time" and chunking up with Parts Integration are two examples.

Examples of Meta-Program Sorting

What does all this mean?

When clients step into your office and tell you that they have a "problem," consider *hearing* the information they then present as actually describing their *skills*. Listen to *how* they describe their difficulty. They will either say it affects everything or it affects specific things. They will say either that they feel intensely or that they have difficulty identifying their feelings. In each of these cases, they have thereby told you which strengths they are using and which they are not. And that, in turn, informs you which NLP Patterns they are already running. So within five minutes, you can begin to identify the NLP Patterns which will most likely help them change.

As we were developing this model, a client came to see Richard asking for NLP processes to help her create a sense of spiritual awakening. This, she said, was something she had never really had access to. Richard initially assumed that she wanted to experience processes such as *Core Transformation* (a process that "chunks up" to a profound "core state," Andreas, 1992). Yet in attempting to lead her through this, she continuously interrupted and disagreed with the instructions.

In describing her goal, she had actually described in intricate detail what needed to change for her to achieve "spiritual

134

awakening," but complained that while she could "think about it," the description had no feeling with it. As soon as Richard recognized her style (i.e., chunking down and dissociating), he changed his approach and went to another technique. She was delighted to be introduced to the far more detailed and dissociated submodality belief change, which she reported gave her the real experience of spiritual opening.

A client came to Margot complaining that he had a phobia of meeting people. This problem had been diagnosed by a psychiatrist, and he had heard that NLP had a Phobia Pattern which could resolve it in one session. However, as Margot listened to his description of the problem, it became clear that his "anxiety" was not the kinesthetic result of associating into traumatic memory (i.e., an NLP description of a phobia). In fact, he had never experienced the events he claimed to be phobic about (meeting women romantically) and was rather confused about what would happen if he did.

He rather felt disoriented by being with women, and tended to avoid these experiences. He complained that he did not know how he felt about the situation. His style of chunking up and dissociating prepared him for benefiting first from the use of *Time-Line Patterns*, and then from more fully associating into his body when he had been with women to rediscover his actual feelings.

These examples highlight that the diagnostic terms of "depression," "phobia," and "psychosis" only roughly correspond to the Meta-Programs which we are here sorting for. Here we have focused on which *strengths* people actually *demonstrate* in relation to this particular challenge at this particular time, rather than a label that someone has given them.

Expanding Personal Strengths

Not only can you pace and lead using *the Personal Strengths model* for selecting NLP Patterns, you can also design an exercise to facilitate your client's ability to achieve change and expand his or her repertoire of personal strengths. Such exercises can be given as between-session activities and include:

1) Practicing "chunking up:" stopping at specific pre-decided times in the day to ask,
   "What is this specific situation an example of?... and what is that an example of?"

2) Identifying general trends in life and asking, "What is a specific example of this trend?... and what specifically do I see/hear/feel as I recall that example?"

3) Taking a current or a remembered situation (an enjoyable one) and experiencing it from first position (associated), seeing it exactly through their eyes, hearing through their ears, having any internal voice in their throat, and feeling the feelings in their body fully (using overlapping of sensory systems to do so).

4) Using the same experience, see, hear and otherwise experience it from a "third position" (dissociated from first position), experiencing the "self" as simply another individual in the situation. Remember to have them associate back in after, and enjoy it again.

Other Implications

There's a lot more to understanding the four key skills of *Chunking Up/Down and Associating/Dissociating*. You may already have noticed that chunking up and associating form the basis of NLP processes which access the "unconscious mind," while chunking down and dissociating form the basis for "conscious mind" processes. Combining the two types gives us the key to multilevel communication in consulting.

You may also have noticed that chunking up and dissociating also give us two ways of meta-stating, while chunking down and associating access more original sensory representations.

Figure 7.2

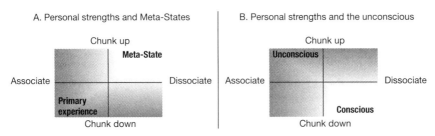

The Personal Strengths quadrants also correspond to time orientation differences. Ericksonian therapist Michael Yapko points out that human distress is a consequence of "temporal rigidity." When a person is unable to live flexibly from all three temporal perspectives (past, present and future), they suffer.

> The person with anxiety is stuck looking towards the future.
> The person with depression is stuck looking towards the past (even when they think they are considering life "now").
> The person with impulse disorders such as addictions is stuck in now.

Yapko explains (1992):

> A temporal component is a part of virtually every experience. For example, a structural component of anxiety disorders is a future temporal orientation: the anxious individual anticipates (orients to) the future in such a way as to create images (or internal dialogue or feelings) about events that have not yet occurred. In contrast to anxiety disorders, in impulse disorders, the overwhelming emphasis is on the immediacy of experience in a present temporal orientation. The person is not particularly attached to either past tradition or future consequences. Rather it is the emphasis on here-and-now experience that governs the impulsive need for immediate gratification. In the case of depression, the emphasis is overwhelmingly on a past temporal orientation. The depressive is continually hashing and rehashing old traumas, including rejections, humiliations, disappointments, and perceived injustices— and in essence all the hurtful things from the past. (pp. 118–120)

Figure 7.3

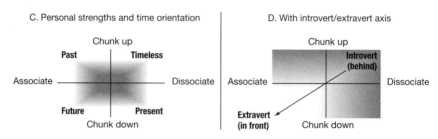

Finally, Jung's original model also contained another distinction which we could add to the *Personal Strengths model,* namely, Extraversion-Introversion (Whitmont, 1991, pp. 139–140).

Some clients describe their problems in *an introverted way* ("This is what happens inside me") and some describe their problems in *an extraverted way* ("This is what happens between others and me."). This makes up a third axis on the model, which then creates a three dimensional chart. This distinction has been less significant in NLP because we do most NLP processes internally. None the less, some variation along this continuum does occur. *Time-Line patterns* clearly describe a more introverted way of using time-lines than Dilt's *Re-Imprinting* on a time-line, where the person actually walks along the floor.

In general, the type of action methods and psychodrama developed by Jacob Moreno are more extraverted (as a Myers-Briggs assessment of the people at an action methods/psychodrama workshop will easily demonstrate). For a description of how to use these methods in the one to one consulting situation, see David Kipper's book *Psychotherapy Through Clinical Role Playing* (1986).

In NLP, another important place to find extraverted techniques is in the setting of tasks. Milton Erickson frequently set tasks which involved considerable interaction with other human beings and considerable movement. Describing how he routinely sent his clients in Phoenix to specific shops, and to the Botanical gardens, and to climb Squaw Peak, Erickson explains

> Because I believe that patients and students should do things.
> They learn better, remember better. (Zeig, 1980, p. 72)

Summary

- The *Personal Strengths model* gives us a model for planning interventions that suit each client. It is only a model and, as we say in NLP, "The map is not the territory." Using this model, we aim to use our ability to identify strengths in ourselves and our clients. This enables us to let go of puzzling over weaknesses, and build on strengths.

- This attitude of *respecting strengths* is crucial and the model gives us a tool to support it. When a client enters the room, we can ask ourselves, "As this person tells me his or her problem, do they describe chunking up or down; do they describe associating or dissociating?"

- Anxiety typically involves chunking down and associating, while depression involves chunking up and associating. Psychotic processes often involve chunking up and dissociating, while aggressive mismatching involves chunking down and dissociating.

- As soon as we know the answer to these questions, we know which NLP skills will be useful and successful for the client. Anchoring processes work best with someone who has the skill of associating, while submodality change processes such as the phobia process work best with clients who have the skill of dissociating. Meta-Model questions and goal-setting work best with someone who can chunk down, while parts integration and time-line processes are more easily used by someone who can chunk up.

- The *Personal Strengths model* allows us both to match the person's current strengths, and to help them build the opposite strengths.

- "Problems" can also be described in an introverted or extraverted way. Check with the client, "As this person tells me the 'problem,' does he or she talk about what happens inside or between self and others?" While most NLP patterns match the introverted skill, extraverted clients can be assisted to move around spacially as they do processes, and to "speak to" others involved in the situation.

Chapter 8

Modeling the Structure of Pathology

The Central Mechanisms of Disordering

The mental patterning within the "personality disorders"
always makes sense.
The person's mental map for navigating life and relationships
operates out of its own inner psycho-logics.

If we normally and typically *structure* our *personality* by our cognizing (representing, thinking, planning, hoping, interpreting, evaluating, believing, valuing, etc.), by emoting (valuing, giving meaning, feeling, somatizing, etc.) and by our actions (behaviors, relationships, movements, gestures, etc.), then what does it mean to *disorder* our personality? If *language* (our native language, symbol systems, stories and narratives, poetry, mathematics, music, etc.) and *routines* (habits, repetitive motor programs, life styles, etc.) *order* our experiences and, hence, *personality*, then what do we mean by "Personality Disorders?"

This chapter explores further into the very nature of "personality disorders," to look at the *disordering processes*, and to identify the structure or strategy of such.

What do we Mean by "Personality Disorders?"

Given the NLP models presented in the previous chapters, *disordering* does *not* mean without order, but having an order or structure that does not serve us well in terms of adjusting to the various realities with which we have to cope. If we experience *structure* by means of our mental-emotional *mapping*, which in turn governs the

141

powers and energies of our *personality*, then by *a "personality disorder"* we refer to those *structures* that prevent us from coping effectively or mastering the various environments in which we find ourselves. This includes all contexts: intra-personal, inter-personal, familial, business, cultural, etc.

Again, we do not have any *entity* on our hands when we speak about a "personality disorder," but *a way of functioning*. We have a *structured way of relating* ("being") in the world. We have a *set of sequences* of how we think, perceive, value, believe, emote, speak, respond, and act in response to the world. We have a programmed strategy of responses that *do not work* very well.

The Structure of a Personality Disorder

The very *structure and strategy* of such "personality disorders" involves how a person *disorders* his or her powers and functions via a sequence of representations. It also involves how the person then tends to *identify with* that sequence. In order words, they come to *believe* that *"that is the way I am."* Drawing this conclusion describes a meta Meta-Level of thinking-and-feeling. It speaks about making a meta-move that *sets an identity frame of reference* so that the person defines (and hence limits him or herself) according to his or her appraisals.

This *identification with* can involve a wide range of things: a style of coping or responding, a belief about self, some value, some idea, some need, etc. Korzybski (1933–1994) underscored this very process of *identifying* as the core of the *un*sanity. Arguing that the concept of "sameness" does not actually have reference to any-thing in a *process universe*—any and all kinds of *identification* man-ifests an inaccurate mapping and therefore prevents good adjustments.

This shows up predominately in *the "is" of identification*. This refers to all forms of the "to be" verb (is, am, are, was, were, be, been, being, etc.) by which we *over-identify* (actually, *identify*) our self (a Meta-Level concept) with any of our functions—our thoughts (beliefs, ideas, understandings), our emotions, experiences (actions, behaviors, relationships), etc. In other words, as

Korzybski said about the relationship of language to the world, "Whatever you say a thing *is*, it *is* not," so we can say with regard to the *self*.

"Whatever you say you *are*, you *are* **not.**"

Korzybski uttered this succinct truism to highlight the map—territory distinction. That our symbols *about* the world do not comprise the same referent as the world. Thus, the word *"cat"* cannot scratch you. The word *"hamburger"* cannot satisfy your hunger pangs. *Words*, as such, only operate as *symbols* **about** something else—and never exist *as* that referent. They cannot.

The same holds true for *the languaged symbols* that we use to make reference to our *selves as persons*. Whatever we *say* about ourselves, we *are* not. We exist as *so much more* than our thoughts, our emotions, our speech, our behaviors, our relations. Plus, we never stay "the same." We cannot. As living, growing, developing beings, we experience change moment by moment.

More accurately, our *sense of self* arises as emergent properties of all of these facts of our whole mind-body system. As we *reflect back* on ourselves thinking, emoting, believing, valuing, experiencing, talking, etc., we create a second-order level of thoughts-and-feelings (a Meta-State). And when we *reflect back* on that Meta-State, our consciousness moves to yet another Meta-Level. The "I" that performs these Meta-Level awareness moves exists as *more than* the thinking, emoting, speaking, behaving, etc. and yet it arises out of such.

This understanding enables us to **not** *identify* with any of these personality functions, but to recognize our *much more-ness*. Mapping our "self" as a person as an ever-growing, developing, self-reflective consciousness embodied in a specific time-and-place enables us to stay open, receptive, and flexible. We no longer have to feel *afraid* of our thoughts, feelings, actions, etc. We can recognize them as specific functions and energies, accept them as such, and not label ourselves according to them in a debilitating way.

When we do not avoid the danger of *identifying*, we create limiting Meta-States that lock us into a "sameness" that will prevent us from living effectively in a process universe. Then as we habituate this way of thinking-feeling so that it becomes "characterological," we then will tend to always behave according to that schema which we adopted. This gives us a sense of "security." But it also creates all kinds of limitations. These Meta-Level *identity* states supply us with our self-definition and identity. They allow us to stop evolving as we solidify our self-definition with, "This is who I am!" The *identity process* deludes us into thinking "we are done," "our personality is fixed by the time we are seven," "you can't change a person's personality," "this is who I am—take it or leave it."

Figure 8.1

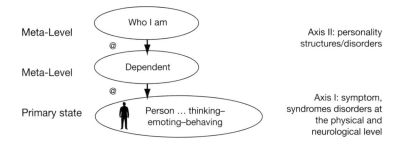

The Art of Changing Self-Definitions, Identity, and Personality
---

The Art of Changing Self-Definitions, Identity, and Personality

Solidification occurs when we set Meta-Level frames. This occurs because the higher frames govern and organize the lower frames. It occurs also because typically, the higher frames operate outside-of-conscious awareness. This gives them the *feel* of "reality." "This is just the way it is."

No wonder we experience difficulty with regard to *changing our personality structures,* to undoing "personality disorders," and to re-inventing ourselves. What causes this? It arises due to the stability of the Meta-Level structures of our constructed *self.* It arises because our strategies have become streamlined through habituation and have come to now operate as *unconscious* frames-of-reference. No wonder we find it difficult to challenge such, we have difficulty even in detecting such! Further, when this happens, then the natural *self-reinforcement mechanisms* within the structures keep them alive, protect them, and reinforce them.

Altering our personality structures necessitates numerous things. Beck (1990) says that we have to change and address our:

1) *Basic Life Schema*—our style of information processing and our basic paradigm of life (p. 9).

2) *Self-definition* that now feels familiar and has so often been re-enforced, and so over time accrues many short-term benefits. Here we have to address the numerous "secondary gains" that we have learned to enjoy via our "personality" structure.

3) *Tolerance for anxiety and distress.* Changing one's "personality" inevitably evokes anxiety. This will involve asking a person to *"face* your anxieties about your identity" (a Meta-State).

4) *Current self-definitions* that we have become used to, familiar with, as we develop new and more enhancing self-definitions.

5) *Cognitive processes.* Within all "personality disorders" we will find multiple cognitive distortions. *Cognitive distortions*, in fact, operate as the signposts to the schema" (Beck, 1990, p. 10).

More Defining of "Personality Disorders"

Theodore Millon has proposed the following summations as part of his "principles for conceptualizing personality and its disorders." I especially appreciate his emphasis against static entities and for systemic processes. As one of the foremost thinkers in this area, he has also stressed the importance of logical levels, complexity, and multiple or combinatorial modes of intervention.

Principle 1.   Personality disorders are not diseases.

Principle 2.   Personality disorders are internally differentiated functional and structural systems (or states), not internally homogenous entities.

Principle 3.   Personality disorders are dynamic systems (involving Meta-States), not static, lifeless entities.

Principle 4.   Personality consists of multiple units at multiple data levels.

Principle 5.   Personality exists on a continuum. No sharp division exists between normality and pathology.

Principle 6.   Personality pathogenesis is not linear, but sequentially interactive and multiply distributed through the entire system.

Principle 7.   Personality criteria by which to assess pathology should be logically coordinated with the systems model itself.

Principle 8.   Personality disorders may be assessed, but not definitively diagnosed.

Principle 9.   Personality disorders require strategically planned and combinatorial models of tactical intervention. (p. 7)

Millon (1969) proposed a "Biosocial-Learning Theory" model:

> Personality disorders are not fully understood by addressing cognitive preconceptions, or unconscious repetition compulsions, or neurochemical dysfunctions. Rather they are most fundamentally seen as expressions of evolutionary processes that have gone awry. Cognitions, unconscious structures, interpersonal styles, and neurohormonal dynamics are viewed, in this formulation, as overt

forms of expression or as underlying mechanisms that merely reflect and correlate with fundamental evolutionary processes. (p. 66)

For Millon (1969), the central continua of personality involve active/passive, subject/object, and pleasure/pain. From these he derived *personality coping patterns* that ultimately corresponded closely to the official personality disorders in the DSM-IV. By so differentiating people in these terms, he sought to understand them in terms of whether they primarily found reinforcement in themselves or others (dependent, independent), thus corresponding to the Meta-Program of Internal/External.

For him, the pain/pleasure continuum describes a person's normal, heightened, or diminished ability to experience either pain or pleasure. Being overly sensitive to stimulus (hyper-reactive to pain, the histronic patterns) or under-stimulated by such (the detached patterns) leads to either social isolation or obsession.

Active/passive describes another set of coping patterns. The active "tend to be characterized by their alertness, vigilance, persistence, decisiveness, and ambitiousness in goal-directed behaviors." Out of such states come planning, scanning for alternatives, manipulating people and events, circumventing obstacles, etc. The passive personalities by contrast "engage in few overtly manipulative strategies to gain their ends. They often display a seeming inertness, a lack of ambition and persistence, an acquiescence, and a resigned attitude." (p. 68)

The four components in his evolutionary model include: existence, adaptation, replication, and abstraction. Each has different survival functions. *Existence* functions for life enhancement or pleasure and life preservation (avoidance of pain). *Adaptation* functions for ecological modification (active) and ecological accommodation (passive). *Replication* functions for progeny nurturance (other), and individual propagation (self). *Abstraction* functions for intellective-reasoning (thinking) and affective resonance (feeling). The developmental tasks in each of these four categories: developing trust of others, acquiring adaptive confidence, assimilating sexual roles, and balancing reason and emotion (p. 110).

Early temperamental dispositions evoke counter-reactions from others that accentuate the original tendencies. In this way, a child's biological endowment not only shapes his or her own behavior, but also that of the parents and others.

The Over-arching Schemas of Personality — our Meta-Frames of Reference

As we develop and construct our understandings and beliefs about numerous concepts—self, others, coping and adaptive responses, pain and pleasure, purpose and destiny, etc. we develop our *personality structures*. These structures *order* how we think, feel, speak, act, and relate and thereby construct our personality structures.

Ultimately then, *personality* operates as a schema-driven *process, a strategy for existing, coping, mastering, and moving through the world.* If we accept or create the concept, "Others are devious, manipulative, and controlling," then we will respond via fear, dread, avoidance, mind-reading, etc. to others. Thus, we build our "personality" strategies in order to attain certain aspirations, ambitions, and emotional wants. "What specially do I want to get?" Being liked, perfection, honor, love, connection, relaxation, excitement, fun, curiosity, exploration, safety, freedom, space, etc.?

If indeed *our cognitive-emotional and behavior "schemas" drive "personality,"* then:

1) We should consider how our "personality" structure (ordered or disordered) and our *self* Meta-States interact as we encounter and respond to people, processes, things, learning, events, etc. How do they interact with the therapeutic process itself? (Beck, 1990, p. 64). What *perceptual filters* do they generate?

2) We should explore *the over-arching beliefs* that drive our experience of our "personality." Within these beliefs, we have meaning driven concepts that project onto the world the

Figure 8.2

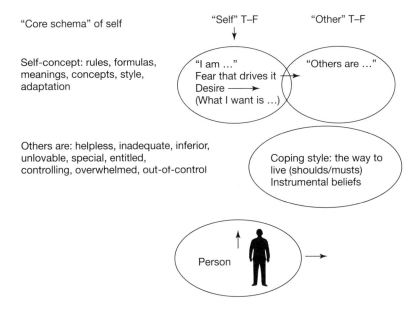

meanings that we have constructed. Given this, if we use our *emotions as signals* about our higher level meanings (Beck, p. 65) within ourselves, then we can begin the exploration of discovery of those meanings.

3) We can use *the phenomenon of "transference" relations* with a client as a window into his/her private world (p. 65). In doing this, however, we have to guard against our own projection (counter-transference), and carefully maintain a non-judgmental attitude. We should also avoid labels (pp. 65, 83–84).

4) We can use *a cognitive probe* (p. 81) as a means for searching a client's automatic thoughts and then on to the person's ultimate meaning. It inevitably comes from their over-riding schema. What cognitive fallacies and flaws do they manifest? What cognitive and language errors?

Personality Disorders Chart:

PD.	Patterning in Relationship Interpersonal strategies	Process/ Thought—Emotion
Paranoid	Away from	Self: mistrustful, over-vigilant, self-righteous, anger over, mistreated Others: devious, deceptive, assumed, treacherous Fear: being controlled and abused, manipulated, fear of mistreatment Belief: "People are dangerous."
Anti-social	Obstruct	Self: autonomous, strong, loner, anger World: dog-eat-dog Others: exploitative, deserved to be exploited; entitled to break rules Belief: "People are weak—take advantage of them."
Avoidant	Moves close then back Dampen E.	Sees self as inept, others as critical Dysphoria. Want to be close, fears being hurt Anxiety and sadness Introspective of anxiety and sadness but uses cognitive avoidance—won't look at their (MP) unpleasant thoughts. Lowers expectations and stays away Belief: "I may get hurt. So avoid people."
Dependent	Toward/Below Anxiety and depress.	Helpless, weak. Sees others as strong cultivate dependent relationships Belief: "I am helpless…" "I need someone to take care of me."
Obsessive-Compulsive	Be Above Anxiety—depression	Belief: orderliness is godliness! Control. Regrets, Disgust to control Shoulds. Self: inept, helpless Self-chastisement Others: irresponsible, self-indulgent, incompetent Fear: out-of-control, overwhelmed, disorganized MP: details Belief: "It's bad to make mistakes, be dirty."
Passive-Aggressive	Unexpressed anger	Oppositional Style: really wants support from authority figure, fears loss of autonomy Maintains relationship by passivity— if senses Rebellion Loss of authority— subversive. Self: vulnerable to encroachment by others Others: intrusive, demanding, interfering Belief: If I follow rules, I lose my freedom! Style: covert defiance, devious opposition, avoid competition, self-sabotaging behavior Belief: "I could get stepped on."

Personality Disorders Chart (continued):

PD.	Patterning in Relationship Interpersonal strategies	Process/ Thought—Emotion
Narcissistic	Be Above Anger Entitlement	Self: special, unique, superior, entitled prestigious Others: Less important, vassals Style: show superiority, seek glory, honor, wealth, competition, exception from rules Belief: "I am special, and must be treated as special!"
Histrionic	draw others to them	Self: glamorous, deserving attention! Gaiety, Mirth Others: Admirers of them! audience High spirits Romanticize situations Fear: themselves as unattractive, unlovable emotionalize Strategy: express self, go by feelings, dramatize, entertain, temper tantrums MP: global, impressionistic, (miss details) jump to conclusions, emotionalizing (52–53) Belief: "I need to impress people!"
Schizoid	Isolate Distance Sadness	Self: self-sufficient, loner Others: intrusive, don't want to be encumbered Belief: "World is dangerous. Don't chance significant relationships. Split self-instead."

Summary

- As we can *order* our "personality" in a way that allows us to effectively cope and master the situations of life, so we can also *disorder* our "personality." There's that much plasticity in our experience and nature. We can powerfully disorder our powers and turn life into a living hell full of tormenting internal demons.

- The *ordering* and *disordering* operates through various mechanisms:
  1) Cognitive mapping of the territory
  2) Somatic and kinesthetic mapping
  3) Self-reflexive building of levels upon levels of concepts

- In these ways, we can *disorder personality* so that we lack the resources for effectively coping with the various domains of reality that we face day by day. And yet, these same mechanisms provide us with the tools for pulling apart the old strategies and structures that don't work and re-mapping. Herein lies hope and the heart of psychotherapy.

Chapter 9

Modeling Pathology

The Central Mechanisms
for Disordering "Personality"

From what we have seen in the previous chapters, a whole range of ways lie before us by which we can *disorder* our personality powers. We can mess up and distort our thinking, emoting, speaking, behaving, and relating in a wide variety of ways.

This chapter proposes a few specific and central ways that we typically use in disordering "personality" so that it becomes *pathological*. Here we will explore the role of *repression*—the Meta-Level inhibition against one's experiences and emotions, the deficiency of learning, of ego development for reality testing, etc. These processes essentially operate as *the neurotic processes* which can disorder personality.

Accepting Thoughts-and-Emotions as Just Thoughts-and-Emotions

Near the beginning of modern psychology Sigmund Freud insightfully recognized the power that *repression* (repressing) plays in human personality. Accordingly, he developed several practical procedures for breaking up the power of repression on the structures of personality, namely, free associative thinking while in a relaxed and non-judgmental position, dream analysis of manifest content and latent content, Freudian slips, etc.

Since then other theorists have recognized the same. Carl Rogers talked about those feelings "denied to awareness." Harry Sullivan described such thoughts-and-emotions as facets of "not me." Cognitive theorists (Ellis, Beck, etc.) have described such as one's "automatic and unconscious thoughts."

If *consciousness* operates to process information and to then structure that information by creating schemas and mental maps—then when we create a mental map that banishes, rejects, and forbids *awareness*, we thereby have generated a self-contradictory structure. We have forbidden *awareness* to *awareness*. This tabooing of *knowing* (recognizing, acknowledging, feeling, taking something into account, facing what exists, etc.) results in our *repressing awareness*.

What motivates this? *Why* would we forbid awareness? Psychoanalysis describes it in terms of the lack of "ego strength." It proposes that we could not stand such overwhelming knowledge, that the ego would lose control and the self would disintegrate. Other theorists posit that it would overwhelm us emotionally and so we repress as a "security operation" (Sullivan), as a defense mechanism, to protect us, etc. Whatever the reason, repression suggests that we have *a vested interest against knowing*. We fear such self-knowledge and therefore push it away.

Where does this fear come from? Does this describe an inborn fear or a developed one? And how much accuracy does this view of repression hold? Do people "lose control" or disintegrate" by knowledge of the forbidden? Does it *always* happen? Does it happen to *all* people? If not, then what determines who caves in and who does not?

If the fear doesn't necessarily come built-in, then what factors, influences, and experiences play a role in its development?

Setting Up a Fear or Taboo Frame of Reference

Inasmuch as such *awareness of fear* does not occur universally, it must not arise as a genetic inherence of being human. After all, some people do not fear such knowledge. Other people, in fact, crave such. It must arise as part of *the learning environment* in a given person's family or culture. We then raise such questions:

- How, and in what way, do some families and/or cultures *forbid* certain awarenesses?

- What motivates them to so *taboo* certain thoughts-and-feelings?

- *What* thoughts-and-feelings, drives, needs, experiences, etc. do we find *tabooed* by certain people?

- What effect does such tabooing have in human personality?

Typical to most Western cultures in the past couple of hundred years, we find the *tabooing* of such human experiences as sexuality, anger, death, fear, anxiety, sadness, tenderness, and softness. Thoughts-and-emotions about these kinds of experiences have therefore received the most rejection and dislike. Societal and cultural *support* for such repression shows up in the sayings, mottos, values, and beliefs that predominate:

"Boys shouldn't cry."
"Don't talk about sex; it's a dirty subject."
"Only the low class talks about such things."
"People won't like you if you're angry."
"Don't be so emotional."
Etc.

With such *tabooing*, people easily and quickly *get at odds with their very nature.* A person experiences an upsetting event—something didn't go the way that he wanted it to go. Something violates one of his values (something he valued as important). So he feels either anxious, scared (fearful of loss), sad, angry, etc. But *if* he doesn't have inward permission to think and feel such, he then moves to a Meta-Level (consciously or unconsciously) and feels bad, ashamed, embarrassed, guilty, etc. for feeling one of the forbidden negative emotions.

So he *represses* his knowledge that he thinks-and-feels the particular negative feeling. With awareness or outside-of-awareness, he *forbids* himself to recognize and face the experience. But this does not make the experience of his thoughts-or-feelings go away. They only get detached from awareness and become inaccessible to conscious awareness. As such, they become *unconscious forces* (energies) inside and as such, they will take on different forms and expressions. They may become night terrors in dreams, they may become psychosomatic illnesses and diseases, they may become projected onto others, they may become dissociated into sub-personality "entities" (multiple personalities, demons, etc.). They may show up later in inexplicable feelings (depressions), thoughts (intrusion of thoughts), distractedness (inability to concentrate), stress, over-reactions, etc.

Turning One's Psychic Energies Against Oneself

Eugene T. Gendlin (1964) in *Personality Change* describes this dynamic along with some of the facets involved in its resolution.

> One client spent many sleepless hours each night with anxiety, shame, and resentment. He blamed himself for his reactions to a certain situation. He felt foolish and ashamed of the whole thing. As he tried to resolve it, he alternatively felt resentful (he would decide to confront them, fight it out, not back down, etc.), and alternatively he felt ashamed (he was a fool, and humiliatingly so, etc.). Only in the psychotherapy hour did it become possible for him to focus directly on 'this,' what it was, how it felt, and where it 'lived' in him. In 'this' he found a good many valid perceptions concerning the other people and the situation which he had not been able to specify before, and a good many personal aspects of himself. During a number of hours he directly referred to successive direct referents and felt meanings. Yet between hours he was unable to do this alone, but felt only shame or resentment. Only by moving temporarily "on by" these emotions could he refer directly to 'this,' 'what I feel' ... (p. 480)

Here we have a generic situation that triggered the person to feel anxious, shameful, and resentful. He had some kind of encounter with someone that turned out badly so that he felt angry—a part of him wanted to confront the person, have it out, fight it out, deal with it, etc. But then another part just felt bad—humiliated, foolish, embarrassed.

But worst of all, he "blames" himself *for his reactions* ... he judges his experience as foolish and feels ashamed of the whole thing. With this he moves to a Meta-Level and issues a judgment *against*

Figure 9.1

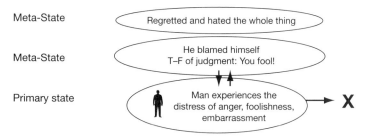

himself. In doing that, he brings his own psychological energies (thoughts, emotions, beliefs, values, etc.) *against* himself. When he does, he puts himself at odds with himself, so that he can't focus on the *content*.

Just as soon as he thinks about the episode, his mind jumps logical levels. He jumps up to various negative *meanings* that he levels against himself. When he can no longer stand that he jumps to another set of thoughts-and-feelings, wishing he had confronted the person and had had it out with them. And so around and around he goes. He loops around from one negative thought-and-emotion to another, never resolving anything.

Why not? Because he has forbidden it all and therefore "can't stand it." And as long as he does not *accept himself* and the negative emotions and experiences, he will not be able to use his ego-strength for facing his reality for whatever it is and deal with it.

The *therapy*, by its very nature, presupposed the very things which the man found curative. Unexpressed explicitly, and yet presupposed covertly, the *therapy process accepted* the negative emotions and the experience as such and simply, non-judgmentally, acknowledged them, and sought to explore them. So as the man focused directly on "this" (the event with all of his thoughts-and-feelings)—he got back to the experience and remapped it.

The *emotions* (as Meta-Level maps, cognitive interpretations) of some primary level kinesthetics were not the experience. His initial emotions resulted from his thinking, perceiving, and believing *about* the situation. But he got so caught-up in the emotions and felt so distressed *about* the emotions, that he didn't have permission to look at, face, or deal with the experience for itself.

Accordingly, his consciousness began looping around and around at the Meta-Levels regretting his shame, guilting about his embarrassment, blaming and condemning his self, etc. And as long as his awareness went there, he could only get glimpses of understanding about the experience itself. He had become *entranced* to his Meta-Level emotions, hating and rejecting them.

Not until he could *accept* and *welcome* those emotions and the thoughts which fed them, could he stop that Meta-Level looping and turning his psychic energies against himself. Nor could he do this alone. He needed the therapist, not so much to "straighten him out," as much as set a more enhancing frame of reference (i.e. acceptance, acknowledgment, calmness, reality testing, etc.). The therapist brought these states (or frames-of-reference) to bear upon the man and then directed consciousness back to the experience with his specific questions.

This illustrates the basic format and structure that begins the *pathological process*. Namely, rejection of one's own thoughts and feelings and rejection of reality existing as it exists.

The Failure of Repression

Given this Meta-Level analysis of pathology, Freud (1924) theorized one possible explanation for neurosis, namely, *the failure of repression*.

> There is nothing new in our characterization of neurosis as the result of a repression that has failed.

As evidence, he told the case history of a young woman who had fallen in love with her brother-in-law, who later stood at her sister's death-bed, and "was horrified at having the thought, 'Now he is free and can marry me.'"

This *horror of a thought* provided her with the motivation to forget the incident consciously. Forgetting it then led to hysterical pains (a psychotic reaction) and therefore a disavowal of the fact of her feelings, whereas if she had kept it in awareness or became aware again, she would suffer a nervous reaction.

> Both neurosis and psychosis are thus the expression of a rebellion on the part of the id against the external world, of its unwillingness —or, if one prefers, its incapacity—to adapt itself to the exigencies of reality, to 'Anagke' [Necessity]. ... Neurosis does not disavow the reality, it only ignores it; psychosis disavows it and tries to replace it. We call behavior 'normal' or 'healthy', if it combines certain features of both reactions—if it disavows the reality as little as does a neurosis, but if it then exerts itself, as does a psychosis, to effect an alteration of that reality. Of course, this expedient, normal, behavior leads to work being carried out on the external world; it does not stop, as in psychosis, at effecting internal changes.

Personality disordering then arises from a poor adjustment to the constraints of "reality." This "reality" includes both the external factors of the world at large —that many things necessitate effort and work, that dangerous situations, persons, and events exist out there, that just because we *want* something puts no *obligation* on the universe to give it to us, that we exist as fully fallible and mortal beings, etc. This reality also includes other kinds of "realities"—familial, cultural, interpersonal realities. This includes the fact that people often do things that countermand our wishes, that they do not live their lives to fulfill our every want, that they often do things that are hurtful and ugly.

It also includes all kinds of internal "realities." This means adjusting to the nature of thoughts and emotions, to drives, desires, hopes, expectations, cognitive processing styles (Meta-Programs), to negative emotions, etc.

The Gestalt of Rigidity

Lawrence S. Kubie (1957) presented an early analysis of *the neurotic process*. In doing so, he noted some of the overall configurations that result:

> The essence of normality is flexibility, in contrast to the freezing of behavior into patterns of unalterability which characterize every manifestation of the neurotic process, whether in impulses, acts, thoughts, or feelings. Whether or not a behavioral event is free to change depends not upon the quality of the act itself but upon the nature of the constellation of forces that has produced it. No moment of behavior can be looked upon as neurotic unless the processes that have set it in motion also predetermine its automatic repetition, irrespective of the situation, the utility, or the consequences of the act. (pp. 79–99)

The presence of *a sense of choice* or not, then plays a major role in determining the quality of a behavior as healthy or neurotic. For Kubie, the quality of *flexibility* in behavior demonstrates health whereas *rigidity* and *automatic reactions* ("semantic reactions") indicate a disordering from health.

> Wherever unconscious forces play the preponderant role in this constellation, dominating over the other two [conscious and preconscious forces], then for a variety of reasons the behavior which results from the interplay among these three groups of forces is subject to a tendency to automatic and obligatory repetition. This is, in part, because the unconscious conflicts and purposes are represented by symbolic patterns of activity through which their objectives can never be reached.

The mechanism that generates the neurotic process of inflexibility arises from *unconscious conflicts* which lie at odds with reality. Again, this speaks of turning one's psychic energies against oneself and then forbidding awareness to them. By contrast, healthy *ordering* of the structures of personality give one a sense of choice and flexibility.

> In contrast, wherever conscious and preconscious forces are in the saddle, the resulting patterns of activity are alterable by

experience. Since desired goals can be achieved through such patterns of activity, a state of comfortable satiety can be reached. …
Therefore, behavior which is determined by a constellation of
processes in which conscious and preconscious forces predominate is alterable by the impact of success and failure, rewards and
punishments, pleasure and pain, argument, logic, and exhortation.
It is a further consequence that such behavior is anchored in
reality and remains freely flexible. (p. 142)

The healthy adjustment here detailed operates primarily by the
feedback processes of how it interacts with the world. It openly
receives feedback and makes appropriate adjustments.

If we generalize from this to a concept of mental health in a
broader sense, it is fair to say that the greater health is achieved
whenever important areas of life can be brought under the domi-
nation of conscious and preconscious processes (never exclusively,
but to a major degree). Therefore, the goal of therapy is to shrink
those areas of life which are dominated by the inaccessible unconscious processes. (p. 142)

When a person has so ordered his or her personality forces so that
conscious and preconscious processes dominate, they thereby structure
these powers so that they can make ongoing adjustments in their
responses. In order words, they not only have choice, but they
have *choice of choice*. They can choose their choices. The NLP model
describes this as "running your own brain" or "driving your own
bus." The same appreciation for conscious awareness shows up in
Reality Therapy, Cognitive-Behavioral Therapy, and many other
schools.

Further, Dr Kubie also noted that his concept of *the neurotic process*
stood "far removed from the usually derogatory connotations of
the term." He said that he began from a different presupposition.
Namely:

there is a neurotic potential in human nature which is universal
because it is inherent in our psychological development, depending as it does upon the special role which symbolic functions play
in human development. It is the power of symbolic thinking and
feeling which endows Man with his unique creative potential, and

> it is also *the vulnerability of these symbolic functions to distortions* which gives rise to that aspect of the neurotic process which is peculiar to the human being. It is the symbolic process plus its vulnerability which gives rise to the neurotic potential. (p. 142, *emphasis added*)

Symbolic thinking here speaks of a Meta-Level where we construct our "reality" frames. Dr Kubie commented about "the vulnerability of these symbolic functions to distortions" and that such "gives rise to ... the neurotic process." This speaks about *disordering* that occurs at Meta-Levels by cognitive structures (ideas, beliefs, values, etc.) that distort our reality adjustment.

In other words, that we can construct screwball and toxic beliefs, ideas, illusions, deceptions, etc.—*therein lies the source of neurosis.* As fallible human beings, we inevitably build all kinds of infantile and childish thinking patterns and frames-of-references as we grow up. If at some point we close the door on our thinking, we can become mentally-and-emotionally *stuck* in such limitations and ignorance.

Typically, we "lock ourselves into" such frames by *believing* in our beliefs. This prevents an ongoing open-minded curiosity to *"what else lies out there?"* and "how I could have it wrong."

Kubie noted numerous cultural factors that may further solidify and reinforce the distorted symbolic thinking.

> Culture is one of the forces which determine if and when a patient will look upon himself as ill or at least as needing help and whether he will seek help. ... When we ask what role cultural influences play in the splitting off of unconscious processes from the mainstream of conscious and preconscious functions we face an issue which is not yet understood even vaguely. (p. 144)

Perhaps the primary *source* of cognitive distortions, erroneous ideas, misbeliefs, toxic ideas, etc. arises from our cultural environments. Do we have cultural *permission* to *own* our negative emotions? What taboos exist in our familial or cultural environment that forbid us from even acknowledging some of our thoughts and emotions? Or does our culture over-permit and even organize us to become overly concerned about acquisition, status, approval, material positions, idealized physical looks, etc.? Would it reward us for becoming compulsively obsessed about such? Do we *have to have* such things or experiences in order to feel happy and successful (conceptually)?

Learning Deficiency and Poor Ego Development

In addition to the Freudian concept of an overly inhibited super-ego, or an excessively severe superego, O.H. Mowrer (1952) theorized that neurosis primarily involves *a learning deficit* and therefore it arises due to an immature and underdeveloped ego. We thereby disorder our powers and create our personality structures based upon misguided, ill-informed, erroneous and poorly developed ego functions.

Relying upon the principles within Learning Theory, Mowrer applied to neurosis the principle that "all learning tends to undergo extinction unless it is at least periodically reinforced." Doing this then raised several questions as suggested by Freud (1936):

> Why do the unrealistic neurotic fears long outlive any real justification?

> Why do they stubbornly persist and even seriously incapacitate the person?

> Why are not all neuroses merely episodes in the individual's development which become a closed chapter when the next stage of development is reached?

> Whence comes the element of permanency in these reactions to danger? (p. 120)

If we normally tend to *un*learn ideas and concepts that no longer prove useful and replace them with *new learnings*, then what explains the stubborn persistence of unrealistic ideas, fears, beliefs, etc.? What provides these Meta-Level phenomena with such staying power, such stability, and such continuance long after "we know better?" Mowrer, suggesting that "mental health is a matter of attitudes," says that

> "it is with respect to *attitudinal learning* that the neurotic is most deficient. ... To put this matter somewhat paradoxically but succinctly, the neurotic is an individual *who has learned how not to learn...*" (p. 153)

This gives us yet another Meta-Level structure (and phenomenon) that *disorders personality.* Namely, *"learning how not to learn..."* For Mowrer, this describes the *learning deficit,* the *attitudinal* problem, and the factor that creates the permanence of the old learning so that it becomes locked in place thereby leaving the person rigid and inflexible.

The person has built a Meta-Level frame that organizes him or her to *not* learn, to inhibit learning, to prevent updating of old maps. This operates as an injunction at a Meta-Level,

> "Do not learn."

> "Do not look at this, think about that, talk about such. Bad things will happen if you do. You'll open a Pandora's box that will make things worse." "Too much learning will make you mad."

> "There are things that we just shouldn't know about or think about."

> "Leave it alone, you will only make it worse."

Mowrer says that this doesn't describe an overly severe superego, but simply *the lack of ego strength* to look and face reality forthrightly. And if our ego oriented ego cannot even look reality in the face, then it certainly cannot learn to deal with it. This Meta-Level frame of learning to not learn then prevents the "conceptual leadership" necessary for a person to give up "the dubious comfort of feeling no responsibility, no guilt."

Quoting Faust, Mowrer says that the neurotic has…

> bartered his sense of freedom to the devil for the dubious comfort of feeling no responsibility, no guilt. (p. 157)

This explains one of the *whys* regarding "learning to *not* learn." Learning leads to awareness which leads to *choice* which then begets *responsibility* to take action. The neurotic avoids all of these by *not knowing* in the first place. This gives him or her a false sense of security, comfort, okayness, "all is well with my soul," etc. To permit learning stirs things up, challenges one to keep growing, developing, adjusting, making changes, taking responsibility, recognizing wrong-doing and making corrections, etc.

Then more pointedly, Mowrer writes

> To the extent that our professional efforts are directed toward banishing guilt, not in the sense of helping the patient become guiltless but in the sense of diminishing his capacity for guilt, may we not be leading him further into the kind of helplessness, isolation, and enslavement of which the neurotic so often complains? (p. 157)

So what *attitude readjustment* does the person need here? He or she needs one that involves a change of mind *about* human existence, emotions, suffering, etc. It involves the welcoming, acceptance, and acknowledgment of such. It involves bringing unpleasant and disturbing thoughts and feelings into consciousness *so that* the person then develops the skills for effectively coping with such.

Erroneous Learnings

If we *order* our personality via learning, then we *disorder* personality by means of inadequacy, erroneous, and toxic learnings. To grow up in an early home environment where parents model and express a very faulty training in reality testing plays a detrimental role in ego development. If the early home environment contains multiple factors that make for confusion about self, identity, sexuality, purpose, etc., the child may learn various disordering ideas.

Summary

- To *disorder* your thinking, emoting, speaking, behaving, and relating (the behaviors that make up your personality), you only need to *reject these powers*. Reject, hate, dislike, and refuse to acknowledge certain facets of reality. Decide that you will tolerate no thoughts-feelings of anger, fear, anxiety, sadness, fallibility, conflict, frustration, insecurity, sexuality, closeness, tenderness, etc. Give such experiences higher level meanings that you feel highly averted to, threatened by, and upset with.

  It means I'm a sexual pervert.
  It means I could murder someone.
  It means I'm a bad person.
  It means I'm a lower class person.
  It means I'm doomed, condemned to hell...

- Conversely, to *reorder* personality and its powers, we only need to fully acknowledge and accept reality for how we find it. This doesn't mean we have to like it, condone it, or even tolerate it. It only means that we give our conscious awareness via our thoughts-emotions permission to function as information processors and energy producers.

- Making a general commitment to reality, to acknowledging the truth of whatever we find *so that* we can then decide how to respond, what to think and feel *about* such, enables us to use our powers effectively. This means that if we find ourselves feeling angry or afraid, we rejoice that we have these powers, and then we seek to discover their referents. "What do I feel afraid of or angry about?" This then allows us to reality check and ecology check our own thinking-and-emoting.

  "Should I take a stance of thinking-and-feeling angry or afraid of this?"
  "Do such thoughts and feelings appropriately access this situation?"
  "What other thoughts and emotions could I take with regard to this?"

"What other thoughts and emotions would bring out my best and more productively cope or master this situation?"

- Our emotions derive from our thoughts and our thoughts result from our learning history, and neither exists as an infallible absolute. Both operate as forms of neurological *mapping*. We mentally-emotionally *map* things. Thus, as human constructs, they exist as highly fallible maps and easily liable to distortion, deletion, and over-generalization.

Chapter 10

When Things Go Wrong

The Role of Trauma in Personality Disordering

As we have explored *the neurotic process* itself in the past two chapters, we have noted while not exploring to any depth the various kinds of trauma that motivate the process. Given the *norm* of a healthy body in a healthy environment, and healthy parenting by two loving and caring parents, the developing child makes good adjustments to him or herself, to the world of other people, the outside world of nature, the world of work and career, of school and learning, etc.

But things can and do go wrong.

Traumatic events can (and do) arise in our environment (natural disasters, wars, crimes, etc.), in our body (illness, disease, accidents, head injuries), in our families (divorce, abuse, rape, abandonment, neglect, spoiling, financial failure, refugee status, etc.) etc.

When things go wrong, in whatever way, in whatever domain, to whatever degree (intensity), for however long a period of time (acute crises, prolonged and chronic crises), however layered (one, a few, many), and at whatever developmental stage of the person (infancy, childhood, adolescence, etc.), the developing child has to *cope with it* with whatever resources (internal and external) available. Mentally we cope by trying to understand and figure out the significance and meaning of the crisis. Emotionally, we cope by dealing or not dealing with the emotions aroused by the event/s. We also cope verbally, behaviorally, and relationally.

Typically, the adaptive skills of a child will involve those *of a child* —magical thinking, personalizing, flight-fight, awfulizing, catastrophizing, tantruming, etc. As children we think and comprehend as a child, emote as a child, speak and respond as a child. We cope from an immature state, with under-developed ego awareness skills, unassertively, etc. Yet we do the best with can with what we have.

It's not surprising then that often the very ways in which children attempt to cope when things go wrong in their world create even more problems. The coping mechanisms used to adapt boomerang back upon the person, thereby layering problem upon problem. "I can't handle this ... therefore I must be stupid."

Coping/Adjusting by Map-Making

Out of the context of traumatic experiences, when "bad" things happen, the developing person does what humans do best—he or she responds by using the default program of Fight/Flight and then begins to mentally map out the meaning of the situation. The child thereafter draws conclusions about all kinds of things:

- The world (the kind of world he or she lives in, its level of safety or danger, its orderliness or chaos).

- People (the nature of people, whether one can trust them or not, what one can count on about "men" or "women," etc.).

- Oneself (one's value, worth, loveability, potentials, capacities, etc.).

As a person develops such cognitive awarenesses out of the painful and hurtful experiences, many of these mental ideas subsequently induce one into unresourceful states that we can only describe as *trauma states*. These trauma states can range from hyper-alertness and sensitivity, to hardness, numbness, dissociation, self-contempt, self-blame, etc.

These trauma states do not operate benignly, but actually perpetuate and intensify the trauma. They also operate, as do all states of consciousness, in a "state-dependent" way in terms of learning, memory, perception, communication, behavior, etc. (Rossi and

Cheek, 1988). This refers to re-accessing a trauma state and remembering, thinking, and perceiving trauma as if *in* it as a current situation. We will feel as if someone re-programmed for trauma. We will also communicate and behave in such a way as if still experiencing trauma. This describes the damage that trauma states can perpetuate.

Now one central difference between individuals who go through traumatic experiences and become traumatized and those who do not, but who stay resilient, hardy, and optimistic lies in *the conclusions they draw*. The traumatized tend to buy into the explanatory model of "learned helplessness" (Seligman, 1975). In doing this, such persons interpret the terrible things that happened to them using the following three templates:

- **Personal**: "I must be bad, unclean, worthless."

- **Permanent**: "This will last forever."

- **Pervasive**: "It will affect every part of my life."

Those who seem to survive the horrible things without a lot of psychological damage use an explanatory model of "learned optimism" (Seligman, 1991). They interpret the trauma using the very reverse patterns:

- **Non-personal**: "It speaks not about me, but about my environment, the people who perpetuated the pain."

- **Temporary**: "It concerns something that lasts for a period of time and then ends."

- **Limited**: "It had to do with only a specific area of life."

From the trauma state and this kind of explanatory style then arises the gestalt that Seligman has designated as *learned helplessness*. The "badness" that we experience and receive comes inside and concerns our inmost nature (personal). And this "badness" seems to cover everything (pervasive) forever (permanent).

The shift from that kind of trauma state to a more empowered state of mind-body will inevitably involve a shift in thinking and emoting. A person will have come to develop new and better understandings of the painful events through which they have come. They will learn to frame those experiences in such a way that they can live with them comfortably. Such indicates the resolution of trauma.

Meta-Stating the "Negative" or Unpleasant States

When things go wrong, when various kinds of unpleasant, undesirable, and even traumatic events occur, people typically then build Meta-States *about* the painful trauma state which then creates even more and worse difficulties. To the base or primary state, we then build Meta-Level structures (frames of mind and frames within frames) that increase and solidify the problem. We can all so easily do this. All we have to do is to "believe in our problem." If we "believe in the label" that pegs us, it gives more of a "sense of reality" to the difficulty, making it seem more solid and less changeable. It's a trick of language (nominalization) and a trick of the mind.

In this way, a person could not only feel violated, dirty, unclean, used, powerless, etc. (or any given primary state of consciousness), but also guilty *about* feeling violated, used, powerless, etc., or angry *about* feeling violated, used, powerless, etc. One's thoughts-and-feelings *about* the base experience (the bad thing/s

Figure 10.1

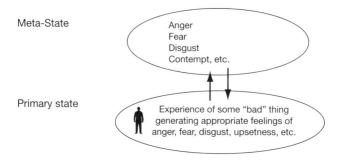

endured) now bring on some very destructive and unwarranted conclusions (frames) about the person's state. This describes where the real danger begins and does so for a number of reasons. Mostly, it prevents one from accessing one's full resources to deal with the base problem and at the same time creates a higher level frame of reference that maps or programs in a larger level problem.

Meta-Stating a Client's Sense of Trauma

Albert Einstein is often quoted for saying, "You can't solve a problem from the same space in which you created it." This speaks about the importance of moving out of *the trauma system* of thinking-feeling to a Meta-Level wherein we can gain better perspective. Typically, as long as a we stay *within* a traumatized state, we will probably not develop the skills for thinking, feeling, and responding in more resourceful ways. The state-bound learning, memory, behavior, perception, and communication will tend to keep us in the trauma.

We will therefore first need to *move to a meta-position*. From there we can begin to develop the resourcefulness by which to deal conceptually with the trauma and bring it to a good resolution.

"When you think about that younger you who went through those horrible experiences, what understandings, thoughts, and perspectives did you develop?" "As you think about those old ways of perceiving, how much accuracy would you attribute to them?" "As you think about those old beliefs, how well have they served you?"

"Allow yourself to sit back, to take a spectator's viewpoint, as in a movie theater, and put an old black-and-white snapshot of the you who suffered the trauma up on the screen. Meanwhile access a pleasant state of comfort, knowing that you can watch it from a distance. In fact, if you need more psychological distance, imagine floating back to the projection booth with the plexiglass between you and the theater. And there you can feel safe as you watch the old memories play out in the form of a black-and-white movie."

After a person takes a meta-position to the old traumatic experiences, one can access various resourceful states and bring such to bear (as a meta-message) on the primary trauma state. "As you watch that old movie, you can remind yourself that... (supply the new more resourceful awareness)...

"...you did the best you could and that you did survive."

"...you developed lots of erroneous ideas as you took things personally when it had nothing to do with you."

"...it represents only an experience that you went through, not the basis of your life or identity."

Additionally, this approach enables one to access various resourceful states and then begin to subjectively experience how such resources would have changed things.

"As you watch the old movie, suppose you imagined yourself as really assertive... how would that transform things? (Resilient, with strong personal boundaries, able to esteem yourself in high and positive ways, confident about your skills, etc.)

Bringing a positive and powerful resourceful state to bear on another not so resourceful state (like a trauma) changes things. It sets new frames-of-reference so that we can begin to see things *in terms of* those resourceful frames.

"And now suppose that you fully *accepted* that trauma... not that you would like it or desire it, but matter-of-factedly look at it from this distance and accept the fact that, 'Yes, I went through that.'" "And how would it change things if you *fully appreciated* the you who went through those painful experiences?"

Such "meta-stating" or frame setting enables us to build positive and enhancing meta-frames-of-reference for living rather than the negative Meta-States of self-contempt, self-blame, anger at self, rejection of some previous trauma state, etc. Inasmuch as we all will think *about* our thoughts and feel *about* our feelings

174

(Meta-State experiences), we might as well manage these Meta-State experiences so that we can stop building mental-emotional dragons inside.

Meta-Level Mathematics and Magic

How do meta-messages and Meta-States treat trauma?

In a provocative piece entitled, "The Group Dynamics of Schizophrenia," Gregory Bateson described "the world of communication" and how it radically differs from the world of physics and forces. He identified the "world of physics" as innately involving the cause-effect processes of Newtonian dynamics. In this world we find that actions or things become energized by the transference of energy from other actions and things. In this world, billiard balls move entirely and exclusively according to the physics of impact and gravity. You hit the ball with your cue stick and the ball moves in accordance with the energy transfer of that force.

But a whole different set of "dynamics" occurs in "the communication world." When we kick a dog, *the resulting movement* of that dog in response to our kick only partially partakes of a "Newtonian trajectory." What happens? Where does the dog land? To predict the trajectory of the dog, the intensity of his response as he lands, the "state" of the dog upon landing, etc. not only involves the amount of force applied, but also the dog's own metabolism, his internal energy system, his learning history, relational nature with the kicker, etc. Predicting it *only* upon the basis of Newtonian physics will miss perhaps the most important factors that will contribute to the situation.

Bateson (1972), in fact, commented that while we may use the word *"dynamic"* when referring to processes within psychological nature, we must remember that we use it in a different sense from the way physicists use the word in their domain of physics (p. 229). After distinguishing between these two realms, Bateson wrote,

> This, I think, is what people mean by magic. The realm of phenomena in which we are interested (psychological, mental, communicational, etc.) is always characterized by the fact that 'ideas' may influence events. (p. 229)

In so introducing the word "*magic*" into the realm of communication, Bateson may have provided the very inspiration for language and metaphor in the first NLP book, *"The Structure of Magic"* (1975). (Along that line, Bateson also used other such phrases, "the realm of magic," "the magical realm of communication" (231).)

Suppose we now ask, "What precisely did Bateson mean by the term *'magic'?*" Did he refer to some quick-fix gimmick? Some therapeutic "technique" to make everything better in one swell swoop? Obviously not. By keeping this term within the Batesonian context, we get an entirely different understanding.

> It might well be sufficiently confusing to be told, that according to the conventions of communication in use at the moment, *anything can stand for anything else*. But this realm of magic is not that simple. (p. 230, my emphasis)

Accordingly, Bateson first used the word "magic" in the realm of communication to refer to the cognitive-neurological understanding about *how ideas influence events*. And in this realm of symbolization, as Bateson recognized the flexibility of "ideas," and the plasticity of symbols, he warned that it does not go to the extreme position that "anything can stand for anything else."

Yet meaning making using symbols does involve a fluid, complex, and plastic arena inside the human nervous system that transcends the laws of physics. As such, it does allow us to set frames and then nested frames-within-frames so as to create higher and higher conceptual levels or states that govern and control the information within those semantic contexts. Bateson (1972) noted this "dynamic" of communication when he wrote:

> All communication has this characteristic—*it can be magically modified by accompanying communication.* (p. 230, my emphasis)

How can we "magically" modify one communicational message (set of representations)? By setting other communicational messages above the previous message.

As evidence, Bateson illustrated with examples such as speaking with your fingers crossed behind your back. The meaning of that symbolic representation *qualifies and modifies* the lower-level message of whatever verbalizations you make. In the structure of humor, the "punch line" often exists at a different logical level than the syntax of the joke set-up and predisposition sets the person up to expect. The sudden shift in logical levels jars consciousness thus producing humor.

In these examples, we see how *the role of meta-communicational signals* can play out in such ways that the meta-message modifies or qualifies the lower-level message "magically." To use mathematical symbols to convey this understanding, the meta-messages can operate as plus (+), minus (–), multiplication (×), or division (÷) *signals* of the original state.

Bateson (1972) asserted that this means that "the world of communication is a Berkeleyan world" (p. 250). This describes the world of communication as a world of mental representations, where no true "things" exist, only *messages* (i.e. ideas, concepts, understandings, beliefs, etc.). "Things" and events cannot enter into this world.

"I" as a material object (p. 251) cannot enter it, yet "I" as a message, as part of the syntax of my experience, can enter into it. External objects only enter into "the communicational world" as we represent or map them (correctly or distortedly) into the communication system. These representations, in turn, then drive or govern that world. In this way, our mapping can function in ways that seem absolutely "magical" to us. This provides the basis for the "word magic" and the languaging "wizardry" that we can do with ourselves and others.

The Magic of Meta-Linguistic Levels

What I found fascinating in these ideas involves how messages and messages-*about*-messages can structurally enter into a mathematical set of relationships with each other. Bateson commented that communication signals can operate as either pluses (+), minuses (–), multiplication (×) or even division (÷) processes. He described how messages can *interact with each other* in a mathematical way in the following:

> All messages and parts of messages are like phrases or segments of equations which a mathematician puts in brackets. Outside the brackets there may always be a qualifier or multiplier which will alter the whole tenor of the phrase. (p. 232)

I offer the following diagram to illustrate Bateson's concept.

Figure 10.2

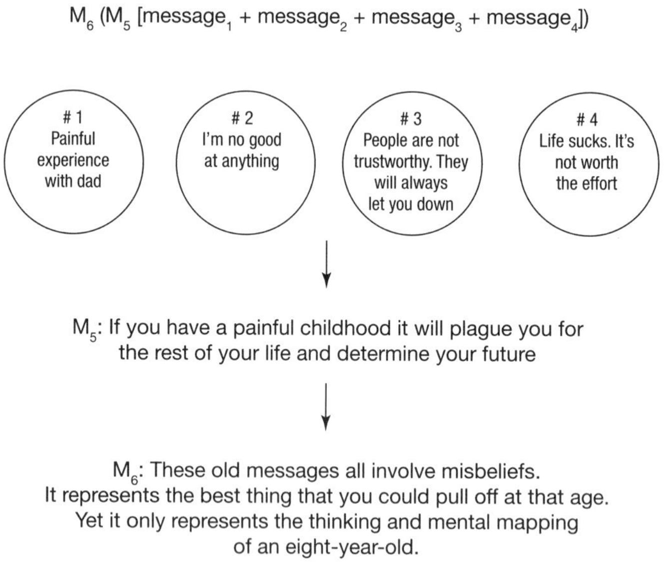

$$M_6 (M_5 [message_1 + message_2 + message_3 + message_4])$$

#1 Painful experience with dad	#2 I'm no good at anything	#3 People are not trustworthy. They will always let you down	#4 Life sucks. It's not worth the effort

M_5: If you have a painful childhood it will plague you for the rest of your life and determine your future

M_6: These old messages all involve misbeliefs. It represents the best thing that you could pull off at that age. Yet it only represents the thinking and mental mapping of an eight-year-old.

At the primary level, if we horizontally (linearly) experience messages #1 through #4, we experience them as comprising one *"addition"* of pain to another. Message after message (each comprising a primary state of pain, distress, and negative emotions) offers additional content messages which arose from the original experience and which addictively increase the person's mental-emotional pain. Each of these messages induces the sufferer into the appropriate mind-body state of distress. And each *adds* to the pain. Here we have simply *addition.* One state *added* to another state, etc.

Then along comes message #5. But it does not operate as yet *another message,* it operates rather as a meta-message, a message *about* all of the previous messages. Because of this, it does not function in the same way as just another additional message of trauma. As a message-*about*-the-other-messages, it provides communication and representation of another painful message at a Meta-Level. It sets a higher frame of reference. So rather than merely *adding* to the individual's misery, it *multiplies* that misery. As a meta-communicational message it multiplies the primary messages/states (#1–#4).

Message #5, as did the first four messages, represents a painful message *about* a trauma. Yet structurally its syntax provides a different kind of pain, one that actually *amplifies* the trauma. How does it accomplish this? It does so by amplifying and intensifying the lower-level messages framing those lower level messages with an understanding, perception, and belief that locks in the trauma at a higher level.

Consequently if the person later experiences a positive experience with someone, it will tend to "not count." If the person later learns that he or she can do something, that also will more typically be discounted. The higher perceptual frame-of-reference ("If you have a painful childhood it will plague you for the rest of your life and determine your future") now filters and controls all current experiences working as a vicious self-fulfilling prophecy. This illustrates the power of Meta-Level messages that we build and install in our minds.

Finally, we see another meta-message (actually, a *meta*-meta-message). Message #6 also operates in a way that multiplies the other messages. Yet instead of increasing pain, it has the effect of *negating* the personal distress. Structurally, its message about all of the messages at lower levels *reverses the sign* from – (minus) to + (plus).

This negation message multiplies a – (minus) to the lower level messages and thereby effects a transformational reversal. Bateson (1972) commented about these sets of relations:

> What exists today are only messages about the past which we call memories, and these messages can always be framed and modulated from moment to moment. (p. 233)

This means that inasmuch as the "past" does not exist as a "thing," but only as a set of internal memories and representations by which we structure our understandings, we can change these meanings by changing the frame within which they operate. And, *a meta-message always modifies lower-level messages.* It can do this in a way that effects positive or negative results.

We can think about these meta-messages as operating in a way very similar to the way *the procedural parts* of a fax message operate. Such procedural messages essentially *index* for the recipient the meta-information about the source, sender, intended recipient, date, time, etc. All of these "messages" in the text communicate *about* the text and thereby modify the text. In other words, they *frame the text* and create the *con*text of meaning for the text. An unlabeled fax, on the other hand, would offer a message, but one that the recipient might find confusing and ambiguous, thereby inducing a state of doubt.

Application

Running the "Magic" in our Minds

Since "states" of mind-body consciousness inherently involve internal representations which induce corresponding physiology, the thoughts-feelings of the primary messages (e.g. messages #1—#4 in our example) function as the primary states. *Above and over* these primary states the higher-level, or meta-message, then creates and reflects another state, a state meta (Greek for "above, beyond, about") to the primary state. Similarly, the message that qualifies it stands at a Meta-Level to it and a meta-Meta-Level to the beginning thoughts-feelings. We might diagram such as follows.

Figure 10.3

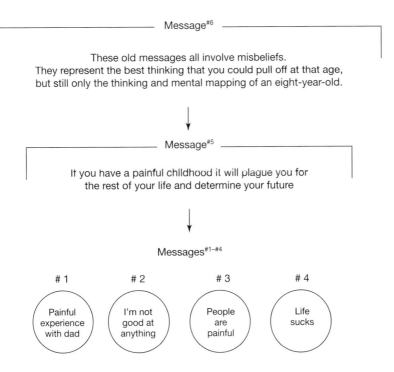

Bateson (1972) noted that psychotherapy involves a context of multi-level communications (p. 224). It involves multi-levels of meanings that involve such multiple levels as the immediate and direct languaging which the therapist does with his or her clients, the less direct languaging that arises from the therapist's particular theory which expresses a particular psychological paradigm, the languaging that the context of a particular problem, role, expectation, etc. provides (the languaging involved in the "script" of restaurant behavior, visiting the school principal, going dancing, applying for a job, engaging in conflict resolution with a mate, etc.), and the languaging that one's larger culture provides.

Levels of Thought or Mind

This description has fleshed out the *Levels of Thought* model that lies at the heart of the *Meta-States* model. Because we can think *about* our thoughts and feel things *about* our feelings, we have the power of self-reflexivity to set higher logical levels. These higher frames then take the *texts* of our lives and create internal mental-emotional *contexts* that govern the meanings that we experience.

With each higher frame we set yet another frame-of-reference that generates another layer of contextual meaning. When that happens, we experience more texturing of our neuro-semantic states.

Summary

- Thought at each level sets higher contextual frames and so controls the meanings and emotions that we experience in everyday life.

- As we learn to take messages into account at different logical levels, we can begin to note **how** one level of message can "magically" affect other levels of messages (lower-messages) providing us with a way to more systematically deal with such complexity of messages in human experience and subjectivity.

- This model now gives us the ability to use our powers of communicational "magic" described in the Meta-States model to alter the very structure of our "personality." Use this explanation to seed your awareness of how to create large-level generative change at Meta-Levels.

- This will give you the near-magical ability to **negate** old "messages" that used to generate intensive personal pain, **divide** old childhood pains in half and then half again, **multiply into our representational equations** new resources, **subtract** hurtful and irrational beliefs (e.g. some of the REBT irrational beliefs that make people neurotic) that serve no useful function.

Chapter 11

Re-discovering the Healthy "Personality"

An Alternative Model to "Personality" via the DSM-IV

Defining Normality

Before we look at some specific forms of "personality" "disordering," it's appropriate to step back and ask ourselves what we mean by *"disordered"* and what we mean by *"healthy."*

The Greek philosopher Theophrastus (370–285 BC) described 30 types of annoying personality (Rusten, 1994). In 1923, the German psychiatrist Kurt Schneider limited himself to ten categories when he wrote, *Psychopathic Personalities,* introducing the concept of "personality disorders" to the modern world. Schneider's labels, such as "wicked personality" and "fanatical personality" kept him fairly closely in the tradition of Theophrastus. In the East, categorizations of personality and personality disorders are generally body-mind based.

An example is the Five Elements System of Traditional Chinese Medicine, which we have previously described (Bolstad, 1995 C). This system suggests that for each personality one of the main acupuncture meridians and organ systems of the body tends to be more vulnerable to stress. The result creates both physical conditions and psychological problems. The five core psychological problems identified by this system are anger, frenetic activity, rigid thinking, sadness, and fear.

The most widely used diagnostic tool in Western Psychiatric care is the DSM-IV manual (1994) of the *American Psychiatric Association.* The APA lists ten personality disorders in the DSM-IV manual, while the World Health Organization currently lists eight in its ICD-10 system (WHO, 1992).

In its previous manual, the APA listed three categories which it has now dropped, and did not list four categories which are new to its fourth collection. This reminds us of just how changeable and arbitrary such classification systems are. All maps differ from the territory, and these classification systems are an excellent example of that principle. It is tempting to laugh at Theophrastus' list of 30 annoying characters. Yet in the end, DSM-IV "research" on which personality disorders exist comes down to asking a group of psychiatrists what annoying personalities they have met lately, and finding out which ones they agree on a label for (Caplan, 1995).

Dr Mark Zimmerman, who worked on the DSM-IV cautions, noted

> I saw firsthand the oftimes unscientific nature by which changes were made in the official diagnostic criteria. (Caplan, 1995, p. 232)

The view of many researchers, such as Hans Eysenck, is that there exist only a small number of personality traits (i.e., Meta-Programs) which can be demonstrated by research. *The Eysenck Personality Questionnaire* (Eysenck and Eysenck, 1991) sorts for just three Meta-Programs:

"extraversion" (extravert ↔ introvert),

"psychoticism" (egocentric/creative/eccentric ↔ controlled/rigid thinking),

"neuroticism" (emotional ↔ calm).

These three continua have the largest amount of neurological and cross-cultural demographic research to support them. In their extreme forms, Eysenck claims, these traits produce clinical disorders and in less extreme, but unbalanced, forms they produce personality disorders. (Eysenck *et al.*, 1993). They also account for much of the normal variation in personality. There is obviously a close correlation between Eysenck's research results and Carl Jung's three personality continua (Introvert ↔ Extravert; Feeler ↔ Thinker; Intuitor ↔ Sensor).

Research has also been done correlating the Eysenck questionnaire with self reported symptoms of the DSM personality disorders. The correlation was strong in two separate studies. This doesn't mean that the DSM categories actually exist, but as one researcher wrote:

> Eysenck's dimensional components of personality can account for the various personality disorders. (O'Boyle, 1995, p. 564)

Eysenck suggests that, if we can account for the range of human difference with three continua, then it makes a lot more sense than using the three hundred categories in the DSM-IV™.

The DSM-IV defines "personality" as an enduring pattern of relating to the self and environment, and a "personality disorder" as any such pattern that results in personal distress or social impairment. The theory of the DSM-IV states that whether someone has a *"personality disorder"* is a separate issue from whether they have a *"clinical disorder"* such as a phobia, depression, or psychosis. The two types of condition are coded on different "Axes" of the DSM systems.

Researchers independent of the APA have tended to find that most of the conditions listed in Axis II (personality disorders) overlap with conditions found in Axis I (clinical disorders). For example, the definition of Schizotypal personality disorder, in real life, is much the same as the definition of the clinical disorder Schizophrenia (Mathews and Deary, 1998, p. 211–213). Eysenck's research suggests that Axis I and Axis II are two different perspectives of the same subject matter.

In this work, we likewise approach personality disordering from two different perspectives. In a sense, our (Margot and Richard's) chapters could be likened to Axis I, and Michael and Bob's chapters to Axis II. The interweaving of these two perspectives gives you choices in making sense of the clients you assist and how to utilize the NLP models and patterns for strengthening and re-ordering the structures and strategies of "personality."

Boundary Conditions in the Mind

If experts can't agree on what makes for a disordered "personality," they agree even less on what makes a healthy one.

The English word *"health"* derives from the old English "hal" or "hael" and means "whole" or "complete and unitary" (Madjar, 1985, p. 113). When we take this meaning of the word, a healthy personality system then would involve one where information flows freely through the system without any barriers or divisions. Quantum physics suggests that the universe functions in a state of undivided wholeness (Bolstad, 1996). We therefore begin from the presupposition that this state of wholeness is natural, and we have to account for any deviation from it.

In the 1960s some curious medical research gave us a wonderful metaphor for understanding how the personality can become unhealthy (meaning fragmented, split, unintegrated, and conflicted). At this time, several patients with epilepsy had the two hemispheres of their brain surgically severed in the hope that this would reduce their epilepsy (Gazzaniga, 1976). Each hemisphere of the brain runs one side of the body (the left hemisphere runs the right side, and vice versa). The two hemispheres also have slightly different functioning styles, with the dominant (usually left) hemisphere running the digital senses (speech and complex symbolic communication).

Generally, the patients functioned quite well after this brain splitting operation, and there were no apparent personality changes. Their usual strategies were intact. However, closer monitoring revealed something odd. If a patient was given an object to hold in their left hand, and could not see that object, they often claimed that they were not aware of anything there; or else they knew that the object was there, and could point to similar objects, but could not name the object verbally.

If a picture of a naked woman was shown to the left hemisphere of the brain, the person usually blushed and laughed. If the picture was shown to the right hemisphere, the person would blush and laugh, but *not know why*. When asked they would explain something like, "Well, you know, it's a funny experiment." At home, the partners of these patients reported somewhat more disturbing problems. At times the patient might initiate sexual contact, but then push the partner away with their left hand. So while the person's usual strategies were intact, not all of their brain had access to these usual strategies. Further, at times their brain ran strategies which they did not approve of.

Physicist Dr Paul Goodwin, working for the NLP based firm Advanced Neuro Dynamics, has proposed a model for how functional (non-surgical) splits in the brain occur, paralleling the split brain experiments (1988, pp. 91–101). To understand his model, we must first explain the biological basis of memory.

When any experience occurs in our life, new neural networks are laid down to record that event and its meaning. To create these networks, the neurons grow an array of new dendrites (connections to other neurons). Each neuron has up to 20,000 dendrites. Steven Rose (1992) gives an example from his research with newly-hatched chicks. After eating silver beads with a bitter coating, the chicks learn to avoid such beads. One peck is enough to cause the learning. Rose demonstrated that the chicks' brain cells change instantly, growing 60% more dendrites in the next 15 minutes. These new connections occur in very specific areas— the "bitter bead neural networks."

California researcher Dr Marion Diamond (1988) and her Illinois colleague, Dr William Greenough (1992), have demonstrated that rats in "enriched" environments grow 25% more dendrite connections than usual. Autopsy studies on humans confirm the process. Graduate students have 40% more dendrite connections than high school dropouts, and those students who challenged themselves more had even higher scores (Jacobs *et al.*, 1993).

Paul Goodwin suggests that under certain conditions of stress, small neural networks become divided from the rest of the brain, by a boundary which interferes with the flow of electrical information between neurons, much as a pane of dark glass interferes with the flow of light (as diagramed overleaf).

This leaves the neural network functionally separated out from the rest of the brain. We will discuss later on the actual structure of

Figure 11.1

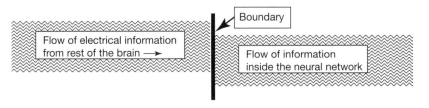

these boundaries. For now, it's useful to have an image of what happens, something like this:

Figure 11.2

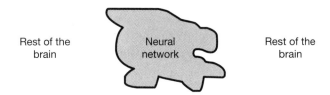

New brain scanning techniques begin to give us more realistic images of how this actually looks. Psychiatrist Don Condie and neurobiologist Guochuan Tsai used an MRI scanner to study the brain patterns of a woman with "multiple personality disorder." In this disorder, the woman switched regularly between her normal personality and an alter ego called "Guardian." The two personalities had separate memory systems. The MRI brain scan showed that each of these two personalities used different neural networks (different areas of the brain lit up when each personality emerged). If the woman only pretended to be a separate person, her brain continued to use her usual neural networks, but as soon as the "Guardian" actually took over her consciousness, it activated precise, different areas of the hippocampus and surrounding temporal cortex (brain areas associated with memory and emotion). (Adler, 1999, pp. 29–30)

The Most Basic Boundary of All: the Self

Philosopher Ken Wilber discusses this notion of boundaries at some length. He proposes that boundaries are routinely set up in the brain as a result of our childhood training in the separateness of self and other, body and mind, and conscious and unconscious. He further suggests that different therapies focus on healing different boundary conditions, so that psychodynamic therapy (e.g., Freudian analysis) was aimed at healing the conscious-unconscious split, humanistic psychology (e.g., Gestalt therapy) at healing the body-mind split, and transpersonal psychology (e.g., Psychosynthesis) at healing the self-other split.

Wilber says that our human attempt to control our experience leads us to create boundaries between what we want to hold on to and what we want to reject. We fail to notice that what we want and what we don't want are two aspects of one unitary information-flow.

For example, when we experience a craving to eat chocolate, and we have a goal to keep slim, we may separate off the "chocolate craving" in order to hold on to our other goal. We don't notice that both the craving and the goal are part of the same organism searching for enjoyment and fulfilment. The separation forms a boundary between our "self" (the rest of the brain) and the neural networks where our chocolate-craving-strategy is stored (Wilber, 1985, pp. 15–21).

One of the original developers of psychology, the father of American psychology, William James, says the "Self" is the name of the process which we could call "owning" or "appropriating" or "identifying." He explains:

> The I… is a Thought, at each moment different from that of the last moment, but appropriative of the latter with all that the latter called its own. (1950, Vol. 1, pp. 291–401)

Information flows into our neurology via the five senses from outside, from other areas in the neurology, and also as part of the various non-sensory connections between all life. From moment to moment, our thinking then divides this information into two sets. I see the door and I think "not-me." I see my hand and I think "me" (I "appropriate" the hand to myself, or "own" it; I "identify" with it). Or, internally, I see the craving for chocolate and I think "not-me." I see the ability to read this article and understand it and I think "me" (again, I appropriate or own it; I identify with it).

Actually, all these pieces of information are in one mind and operate as expressions of one mind. We have created the notion of self and non-self as an arbitrary division. Using the Meta-Program (or internal sort) similar to matching or mismatching, we have mapped things in terms of self and not-self. In a sense, *the self* is the ultimate Meta-Program or Meta-State, a Meta-Program that we then use to run all of our other Meta-Programs and Meta-States. This division of self/non-self may be useful metaphorically, but it is a division which has "taken over" and now thinks it runs the neurology.

Beyond Self

Like any Meta-Program or other internal sort, the owning of experiences as "me" and the disowning of other experiences as "not me" occurs largely unconsciously, although it is continuously active. The whole notion of strategies as we think of it in NLP depends on appropriating or owning one sensory experience after another in a sequence. A vast array of sensory experience is available at every moment in our experiences, and the Meta-Program (Meta-State) of *owning* selects out one section at a time as "mine."

It seems, for example, as if "I" am first holding a book, and then "I" am looking at the words, and then "I" am saying the words to myself, and then "I" am making pictures of the meaning. Actually, all of the senses are functioning all of the time, yet conscious attention continually shifts from one sense to another as the sense of "I" appropriates or identifies with each sense in turn.

The sense of self is the original model of a boundary condition in the brain. It separates us off from whole aspects of our experience, as surely as the split brain surgery separated those epileptic patients from large areas of their experience.

Similar boundaries separate the "conscious" from the "unconscious," and our experience of body sensations (as "body") from our experience of mental processes (as "mind"). Spiritual teachers have pointed out that when this process of internal division ceases, the action of the whole mind-body-environment gives a profound experience of joy, of meditation, of love. In terms of the sensory systems, as described in NLP, this "meditation" simply means the simultaneous awakening of all the senses.

The eastern teacher Jiddu Krishnamurti explains

> If you are so attending, all your senses are completely awake. It is not one sense attending, but the totality of all the senses. Otherwise you cannot attend. Complete sensory activity is a state of attention. Partial sensory activity leads to concentration. ... Can one see completely with all the senses? See not with the eyes alone, but with the ears; to listen, to taste to touch? ... Watch yourself one day. Look at the sunlight and see whether you can see with all your senses, completely awake and completely free. Which leads to an interesting fact. Where there is disharmony, there is the self. Attention is complete harmony. There must be a great volume of energy gathered through harmony. It is like the river Ganga. Attention is a movement to eternity. (Jayakar, 1986, p. 405).

Human beings have sought to recreate this sense of wholeness in every culture. Happold (1971) notes that such a state is described in all religions. In the Christian Bible, St Paul writes, "I live, yet not I, but Christ lives in me" The earliest Islamic poet of Iran, Baba Kuhi writes, "I passed away into nothingness, I vanished; And lo, I am the All-living—only God I saw." The Hindu saint Paramahansa Yogananda explained, "When one is illumined, he sees himself as the one Spirit throbbing beneath all minds and bodies."

The Taoist teacher Huai Nan Tzu says, "Those who follow the Natural order flow in the current of the Tao." In the Buddhist text Samyutta— nikaya it is explained that the feeling of "I am" has no corresponding reality, and that when this truth is understood then the state of nirvana is attained (Rahula, 1959). [For more about NLP processes which move towards this state, see *Anchor Point*, Bolstad (1998) Bolstad and Hamblett (1997).]

State Dependent Neural Networks

So far, we have considered two types of boundary conditions in the brain: the surgical split left-right brain experience, and the experience of self-other. Many smaller boundary conditions occur in the brain, and to understand them we need a more precise model to explain how boundaries actually happen in the brain itself.

Ernest Rossi and David Cheek first described the psychotherapeutic implications of the process by which a neural network becomes separated from the rest of the nervous system (1988, pp. 47–68). To understand their model, let's explain first that the transmission of impulses between neurons and dendrites occurs via hundreds of precise chemicals called "information substances," substances such as dopamine, noradrenaline (norepinephrine), and acetylcholine. These chemicals give us the basis for what we call *an emotional state,* and they infuse not just the nervous system, but the entire body, altering every body system. A considerable amount of research suggests that certain states are useful to learning.

J. O'Keefe and L. Nadel found (Jensen, 1995, p. 38) that positive emotions enhance the brain's ability to make cognitive maps of (i.e. understand and organize) new information. Dr James McGaugh, psycho-biologist at UC at Irvine, notes that even injecting rats with a blend of emotion related hormones such as enkephalin and adrenaline means that the rats remember for longer and better (Jensen, 1995). He writes:

> We think these chemicals are memory fixatives. They signal the brain, 'This is important, keep this!' emotions can and do enhance retention. (pp. 33–34)

However there is another important effect of the emotional state on the memory process. The particular mixture of chemicals present when a neural network is laid down must be recreated for the neural network to be fully re-activated.

For example, if someone is angry when a particular new event happens, they have higher noradrenaline levels. Future events which result in higher noradrenaline levels will re-activate this neural network. As a result, the new event will be connected by dendrites to the previous one, and there will even be a tendency to confuse the new event with the previous one. If my childhood care giver yelled at me and told me that I was stupid, I may have entered a state of fear, and stored that memory in a very important neural network. When someone else yells at me as an adult, if I access the same state of fear, I may feel as if I am re-experiencing the original event, and may even hear a voice telling me I'm stupid.

This is called *"state dependent memory and learning."* Our memories and learnings are *dependent* on the state they are created in. Rossi and Cheek (1988) write:

> Neuronal networks may be defined in terms of the activation of specifically localized areas of neurons by information substances that reach them via diffusion through the extracellular fluid. In the simplest case, a 15mm² neuronal network could be turned on or off by the presence or absence of a specific information substance. That is, the activity of this neuronal network would be "state-dependent" on the presence or absence of that information substance. (p. 57)

Actually, all learning is state dependent, and examples of this phenomenon have been understood for a long time. When someone is drunk, their body is flooded with alcohol and its by-products. All experiences encoded at that time are therefore encoded in a very different state to normal. If the difference is severe enough, they may not be able to access those memories until they get drunk again!

State dependent memory is the biological basis of many other phenomena which we work with in NLP. Anchoring works by triggering the release of the same chemicals as were present in the state where the anchor was set, and reactivating the same neural networks.

Post hypnotic suggestion is a similar application of this phenomenon. It is easily understood as a matter of anchoring (e.g. "When you hear me click my fingers you will feel a deep sense of calm and relaxation."). Submodality shifts are a method of reactivating a neural network by using the same submodality coding, or conversely de-activating the network by recoding a memory so that the memory no longer triggers the old networks. Hypnotic amnesia is also explained by the state dependent memory structure, as the neural networks established in the state of trance are deactivated by the very different chemicals present when the person comes out of trance.

Freud based his whole approach to therapy on the idea of "repression" and an internal struggle for control of memory and thinking. This attempt to explain the existence of "unconscious" memories and motivations ("complexes") can now be superseded by the state dependent memory hypothesis. No internal struggle is needed to account for any of the previously described phenomena. The "complex" (in Freudian terms) is simply a series of strategies being run from a neural network which is not activated by the person's usual chemical states. Rossi and Cheek (1988) note this:

> This leads to the provocative insight that the entire history of depth psychology and psychoanalysis now can be understood as a prolonged clinical investigation of how dissociated or state-dependent memories remain active at unconscious levels, giving rise to the "complexes" that are the source of psychological and psychosomatic problems. (p. 57)

Healing State Dependent Memories

A good example of this state-dependent process is *Post Traumatic Stress Disorder*. Persons with PTSD can have their memories of a traumatic event such as a motor vehicle accident reactivated by any future events that involve motor vehicles or any events that generate high levels of adrenaline in the body. The person has, of course, had many other mildly disturbing experiences that they have coped with effectively in their life before (by reframing the meaning of the event, and by dissociating themselves as they review the event, for example).

Yet in the case of their memory of the motor vehicle accident, they find themselves unable to use these healthy resources. This is because as soon as they begin to re-experience the traumatic event, they are operating from a neural network which has inadequate connection to their "healthy" state. When reliving the accident, they are unable to remember their usual skills. They can only run the strategies, Meta-Programs, values and beliefs (as Meta-States) that are associated with the neural networks laid down at the time of the crash.

Using techniques based in NLP, we have several choices for getting the resources from where they reside in the person's other neural networks, and shifting them into the neural network where the accident has been coded. For example:

1) We can directly teach the person the new and needed strategy and submodality encoding skills in order to dissociate from the event. We can use *Strategy Installation,* the NLP *Trauma Pattern,* or a *Time-Line Pattern.*

2) We can anchor the resourceful state they access at other times (create the chemicals of that state) and connect this anchor with the memory of the traumatic event (creating a chemical link between the two experiences, so that useful information can flow into the neural network holding the accident). We call this pattern *Collapsing Anchor.*

3) We can use *Parts Integration.* In this technique, we connect the "part" (or neural network) which runs the anxiety and the "part" (or neural network) which is resourceful. We base this on the higher intention which they share, such as enabling the person to feel comfortable.

4) We can use any technique which allows (or causes) the free flow of information across neural networks (e.g., *Eye Movement Desensitization and Reprocessing,* where the person quickly accesses visually from one side of the visual field to the other and back; see Shapiro, 1995).

5) We can establish signals which allow us to communicate with the traumatic neural network non-verbally (such as finger signals) and treat this network as a "separate personality" (a "part" or an "unconscious mind") which has its

own strategies etc. We can then enable it to learn more useful strategies.

6) We can verbally reframe the meaning of the events. If this seems a rather simplistic way to attempt to influence such a challenging situation, consider the research by Dr Lewis Baxter (1994) who showed that clients with obsessive compulsive disorder had raised activity in neural networks inside the caudate nucleus of the brain (demonstrated on PET scans of the brain). Drugs such as Prozac raise serotonin levels and the caudate nucleus activity is thus reduced. Baxter found that when clients repeated a simple reframe to themselves, the PET scan showed the same raising of serotonin levels and the same lowering of activity in the caudate nucleus. Precisely chosen words affect state-dependent neural networks.

The situation may be made somewhat more complex, however, because the rest of the person's brain will often have developed mechanisms to attempt to cope with the unpleasant experience of associating back into the accident. One example would be to use alcohol to numb the emotional responsiveness of the person, and protect them from adrenaline surges. This, in turn creates new problems and new state-dependent memories. Even more serious problems arise if the person experienced the accident when they were a baby, and had to try and solve the problem with the limited skills of a young child.

In our example, we considered a traumatic event. It is important to notice that the problem need not originate in an obviously "traumatic" event. Any event which is chemically separated from useful resources can create psychological problems. Consider the failure of many children to learn how to spell visually. NLP research shows that teaching them simply to look up to the left while they remember the word will solve the problem (Dilts and Epstein, 1995, p. 409).

Good spellers have learned to do this naturally. The neural networks which enable the strategy to work (visual memory) are there in *all* children (otherwise, teaching them to look up to the left would make no difference!). Something has directed the "poor spellers" away from accessing this resourceful neural network in the context of spelling words. The anxiety associated with school experiences is one possible cause for this state dependent memory. Another is simply that the person was told not to look up when spelling, and this instruction is re-activated (unconsciously) by the state they enter every time they go to spell a word.

Another important point about the healing of state dependent memories is that such healing, while it involves the free flow of information, need not require "conscious" awareness. All of us run a large number of our most resourceful strategies without any conscious awareness, including spelling words, reading books, and even breathing. These things can be done consciously, but are much more fluently done unconsciously. For that reason, Milton Erickson (1953) emphasized, in contradiction to Freud, that

> The unconscious as such, not as transformed into the conscious, constitutes an essential part of psychological functioning. (p. 2)

Summary

- The healing of "personality disorders" involves the healing of boundaries between state-dependent neural networks. The existence of such state dependent neural networks provides us with an alternative model for understanding the phenomena previously described as repression.

- In our experience, people who heal inner boundaries in this way will often still choose to be more introverted or extraverted, more emotional or more factual, more chunked up and creative or more ordered and chunked down. They will still access the unique strategies that they have learned in their unique life, based on the unique values and beliefs they choose to continue with. They will still have a "personality." But they will not live fragmented lives, puzzled by why they are propelled from one state-dependent disaster to another. Their preferences will be less extreme, and more flexible.

- Ultimately, their healing is a metaphor for all of us, reminding us to refuse to accept anything less than access to all of our resources. We can assist clients to access these resources by techniques such as Installing New Strategies, Collapsing Anchors, Integrating Parts, Communicating with the Unconscious Mind, and Reframing.

- What does it mean to be "normal" or "healthy?" Here we have described the healthy person in terms of qualities such as integration, choice, resourcefulness and awareness. These skills result from an ability to allow the free flow of information through the brain, integrating different emotional and cognitive responses appropriately for the ever-changing territory of the world each individual lives in.

Neuro-Semantics and the Concept of "Self"

As a short supplement to this chapter on defining, describing, and operationalizing our understanding about what makes up *a healthy personality*, I want to add something that differs from Richard and Margot's point of view. I derive the following primarily from Korzybski's use of multiordinality as well as from Bateson's understanding of "mind" and "personality" as an emergent property of an inter-connected system or network.

The "Self" Beyond "Self"

Another way of modeling this comes from tapping into the linguistic distinction from General Semantics of *Multiordinality*. Multiordinality refers to phenomena at multiple levels of mind as a distinction Korzybski introduced and that I've incorporated into the *Expanded Meta-Model* (*The Secrets of Magic*, Hall, 1998).

Because we have so many terms available to describe *mental phenomena*, *multiordinality* gives us a way to sort through the levels to understand more specifically their structure. *Multiordinal terms* mean nothing when taken out from their *level of abstraction*. We have to specify the level to determine their meaning.

We can and do build *thoughts at many different levels*. When we do not notice the levels, when we confuse levels, when we wish the levels would just go away, we create the confusion of category errors. All thoughts are not equal. They do not occur at the same level. "Thought" occurs at many different levels and we label such thought by different terms. This generates differences in emotions—there's primary level emotion (driven, determined, encoded, and structured by primary level thinking). Then there are meta-feelings (determined and controlled by Meta-Level thinking). We can also discover and sort out meta meta-feelings.

This means that in running our own brain and in assisting (coaching) someone else in running his or her brain, we need to take into consideration both mind and meta-mind levels. They differ. And they operate by different sets of principles. Our multiordinal "selves" thus refers to the layers of "self" in a self-reflexive system.

> *"Who* does the observing of that self who performs on the stage at the primary state level?" If we self-reflexively ask this question it typically generates *multiordinality confusion!* "My own self?" What self? Which exists as my *real* self, the actor or the observer? And who now observes my observer self?

As a multiordinal word, expect the term *self* to mean something different at each level.

1) At the primary state level, **Self₁** operates as the actor, doer, experiencer.

2) **Self₂** functions as the observer of the lower level self.

3) **Self₃** operates as the director of Self₂ and Self₁.

4) **Self₄** functions as the theorizer about the other lower-level selves.

We can now re-phrase all of this to say:

1) At the PS level, *I have thoughts-feelings about* various objects, events, people, and ideas in the world. From that primary experience I speak and behave (hence, *self as actor*, Self₁).

2) And as **I** do, **I** develop T–F about *myself* in that experience which indicates or represents Meta-Level consciousness. It generates another facet of self—*self as an observer of Self*. I (as $Self_2$) now have consciousness of $Self_1$.

3) Who then thinks-and-feels and observes *the observer Self*? This infinite regress arises because we can always entertain T–F about previous T–F states about states.

Self creating Self, etc.
This allows us to create and experience a new Self ("self" at various levels) every time we step back to talk about our previous conception. $Self_3$ *directs* $self_2$, and so on as $Self_n$ theorizes about the director Self about the observer Self about the experiencer Self.

$Self_1$, $Self_2$, $Self_3$, etc. simply operates as a shorthand version for *"I operating at level one," "I* operating at level two," etc. These Selves, functioning as our "personality" in all of its holistic and layered complexity, simply explains how we experience multi-levels and dimensions of abstractions simultaneously.

Figure 11.3

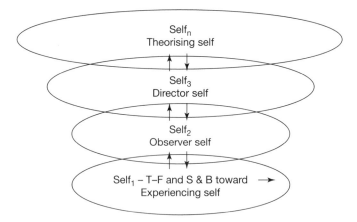

Chapter 12

NLP and NS Patterns for Transforming "Personality"

Throughout the previous chapters we have repeatedly referenced various NLP Patterns and suggested using them in working with clients. We will continue to do that in the following chapters. So, before ending this section of the book and beginning the next section that will address specific *personality disorderings*, we want to present some of the most basic NLP patterns. I say "some" because there are far too many to put into one chapter. Hall and Belnap (1997) collected 77 of the most commonly known and used patterns in their book, *The Sourcebook of Magic*. You can find the NLP patterns in many other sources as well.

Many years ago, psychoanalytic therapist, Dr Stephen M. Johnson took many of the NLP patterns that you will find here and integrated them into his work. *Characterological Transformation: The Hard Work Miracle* (1985) used 6-Step Reframing (pp. 111–115), Resource Accessing (pp. 116ff), Reframing (pp. 110–115), V-K Dissociation (pp. 119ff), etc. *Characterological Transformation* used these very patterns in addressing these stabilized difficulties within the context of the psychoanalytic model.

Patterns for Personality

In detailing specifically *how* "subjective experience" has structure in the previous chapters, we have simultaneously suggested that the particular *states* that we mean and address in psychotherapy operate according to a pattern or strategy. Our mind-body or neuro-linguistic experiences are *ordered, sequenced, and managed* according to a plan of some sort. When we *stop* running a particular plan, we can no longer *do* that experience. It's not that we don't have *the skill* to do so, but that we *do not run it*.

Conversely, *healthy personality orderings* also have a structure and form. Richard Bandler and John Grinder initiated NLP upon the basis that "brains go places" and that we can learn to "run our own brains," and teach them to go in the directions that will enhance our lives. That's the purpose of all of the following patterns.

You will find the following NLP patterns sequenced and described in terms of *step-by-step instructions*. These operate as the bare bones of the processes and, for the most part, they will get the job done. Of course, knowing the model and developing mastering with these forms enables one to do so with artistry, style, and elegance. And when a person moves to that level, the processes do not seem like "formulas" at all, but rich and meaningful communications between consultant (therapist) and client.

Collapsing Anchors Pattern

A state of consciousness always involves both mind-and-body. When we experience two states that radically differ (relaxing and tensing, feeling afraid and joyful) operating at the same time, they tend to interfere with each other. This pattern accesses both and then fires them off simultaneously to force them into *one neurology*. This typically causes each state to collapse and so disperses neurological energies. This frequently results in confusion, disorientation, interruption, and even some slight amnesia.

This pattern works especially well for changing feelings and behaviors resulting from prior experiences that are now unuseful. It utilizes "unconscious" processes and so does not depend upon a person understanding the process. Use this pattern when you have two states that conflict and sabotage each other, or when you have an unresourceful state (an old anchored experience) that creates serious interference.

The Pattern
  1) *Access an unresourceful state.* Invite, elicit, or just catch a person in a negative state and set an anchor for it. To do this with their conscious awareness, invite them to talk about it

while including the qualities of their sights, sounds, sensations.

2) *Break state.* Stop, interrupt and have them set that state aside.

3) *Access a resourceful state.* Ask the person to think about the state that they would prefer to operate from. "What would you like to experience when in that situation?" Describe it fully: "What would you see, hear, feel, smell, taste? What words would you say to yourself?"

4) *Amplify and anchor.* As the person accesses the resourceful state, have him or her double the size of their pictures, make the voice stronger and more intense, or make whatever submodality shift they need to do to amplify the state. When they eventually reach a peak in this resourceful state, anchor it.

5) *Again break state.*

6) *Fire off the unresourceful anchor and then immediately fire off the resourceful anchor.* Hold each anchor and let the neurological processing continue—asking the person to "just experience this state fully." Hold the positive anchor longer than the negative anchor.

7) *Test your work.* After you have broken state again, fire the anchor for the unresourceful state or ask the person to try and recall their previous negative state to see if it returns. If it does not, you have succeeded in collapsing that anchor.

8) *Refresh the resourceful anchor.* As a good ecology process, go back and re-access the resourceful state, making it stronger, brighter, bigger, or whatever submodality amplification that intensifies it and re-anchor it.

Parts Negotiation Pattern

When one "part" or facet of a person enters into a conflicting relationship with another part in such a way that it initiates self-sabotaging processes, they create an internal "fight" between these two parts. Frequently, people can live for years (or even a lifetime) with such internal conflict raging within. This wastes tremendous amounts of psychic energy, sabotages effectiveness, and creates incongruence.

This pattern gives you the technology to change that. Use it to stop the conflict between the parts and to negotiate a peace. View each "part" as having a valid purpose and function, one that simply gets in the way, and interferes with, the other part. Accepting that, simply construct a way that both parts can sequence their activities to create a win/win solution for both. First, find and access each part, discover the purpose, role, and positive intention of each, find out how the interruptions occur, and invite each to a new sequencing.

The Pattern

1) *Identify the parts.* "What part of you does this behavior?" "What part creates this emotion or thought?"

2) *Determine the desired outcome.* What does each part want? And what meta-outcomes does each obtain by the first level outcomes? Specify in VAK terms.

3) *Engage the parts.* Check to see that each part understands and values the role and function of the other part. Assist each part in realizing that the problem lies in how each interrupts the other (hence, a sequencing issue).

4) *Determine the positive intention.* If step two did not elicit and identify the positive value of each part, then continue asking each part, "What positive function do you serve?" Do so until each part can see and value the importance of the other part.

5) *Negotiate an agreement.* "Do you value your own function enough that if the other part will agree to *not* interrupt you, you will do the same in return?" Have the person check to see if he or she has an internal sense of "yes" or "no." Continue until the parts reach an agreement.

6) *Make a deal.* Ask each part if it will actually cooperate for a specified amount of time. If either part becomes dissatisfied for any reason, let it signal you that the time has come to renegotiate.

7) *Run an ecology check.* "Do any other parts play a role in this process?" "Do any other parts interrupt this part?" If so, renegotiate.

Agreement Frame Pattern

When two people conflict and lack agreement, they will continually butt heads. Disagreements arise when we look at things from different points of view and do so categorically. Achieve an agreement frame by moving to a higher logical level that encompasses all of the concerns, perceptions, and frames-of-reference. This pattern enables us to facilitate the process whereby people or groups in conflict reach quality agreements with each other.

The Pattern
1) *Identify the current frames.* Ask each person for a specific description of his or her outcome. "What do you want specifically?" "What values, beliefs, and criteria drive this goal?" "How do you evaluate this as important?" (These questions not only gather important information, but also pace each person so that each feels heard and understood. They also begin to construct meta-outcomes for an agreement frame.)

2) *Identify common elements.* Find a common element (at a higher level) that unites the outcome and see if you have agreement at this level. "Jack wants a blue chair and, Jill, you want a red one. It seems that, at least, you both agree on purchasing a chair, right?" By pacing the higher level want it moves the parties there.

3) *Identify a higher level category.* If you get a no, then move the parties up to the next category. In the example, you might use "furniture." "Do you both agree that you want to

purchase some piece of furniture?" Continue until you find some level (category) of agreement. "So you could both agree on an expenditure for the house, right?"

4) *Utilize the parties' meta-outcomes to formulate the larger level agreement frame.* "By purchasing X, what will that do for you Jack?" "And if you purchase Y, what will that do for you Jill?" "When you get that outcome, what does that do for you?" Continue this until the parties agree to the other person's higher level intent. "So you both want a comfortable and attractive home?"

5) *Frame the negotiation using the higher level agreements.* Move back down from the general frame of agreement to specific exchanges. "Would purchasing this blue chair meet the criteria of comfortable and attractive?" "Would letting Jack decide this one and Jill the next purchase meet your joint criteria of having equal input into decisions?"

6) *Confirm agreements.* During the process, continually identify and solidify all levels of agreement reached and their importance to each party.

Re-imprinting Pattern

Traumatic episodes and reactions arise from traumatic experiences and from negative stories, movies, and imaginations. And, once we map a "trauma," those representations will govern our functioning, believing, valuing, perceiving, etc. They "imprint" upon us so that it becomes a very solid program. "Imprints" can involve positive experiences as well as negative. By definition, "imprints" function in a very ingrained way and one not easily altered.

Imprints, as beliefs, work in a self-fulfilling way. When we try to argue with a belief, the person may have too much data, gathered over time, supporting the belief. By going back to the original imprint, we come to a time before the person's maps became cluttered by later confirmations. In imprint situations, often a person switches positions with a hurtful person and experiences the other's reality.

Obviously, children do not have a clear sense of their self-identity. They often pretend to think and act as someone else. Sometimes they take on the role model—lock, stock, and barrel—with very little discrimination as to what they accept it entails. Our adult selves, in many ways, involve an incorporation of the models we grew up with. *Introjection* of a significant other frequently, although not always, occurs in the imprinting process.

Re-imprinting works by updating internal maps, highlighting resources, and changing the old codes. In re-imprinting, we can even give the people who perpetrated the hurt the resources they needed to have not created the hurt in the first place. This doesn't excuse or condone the hurtful behavior, but maps out appropriate resources and behaviors. Often, victims of crimes build limiting beliefs that anger and fear then maintain.

The Pattern

1) *Identify the problem.* What belief, behavior, emotion, etc. do you want to change? What associated feelings go along with it? Inquire about what the person has done to change that belief or behavior. Ask, "What stands in the way?" "What stops you?"

2) *Locate the experience.* With the anchored feeling, initiate a search using your time-line, etc. to locate the imprint experience. "Allow the feeling to take you back, all the way back, to the initial experience."

3) *Using a time-line travel back with the emotion.* Establish a time-line and go back to the imprint experience. Have the person stay with the feeling (while you hold the anchor) and begin to remember the earliest experience of this feeling. When the person has gotten to an earlier experience, while associated in this regressed state, have him or her verbalize the beliefs (generalizations) formed from that experience.

"Take a moment and think about how frustrating (or whatever the negative emotion) everything has been. Take that feeling back in time… what do you experience? Does it involve anyone else? … Do you see the person looking at you? … Go ahead and put yourself inside 'the you back then' for just a moment. What beliefs do you make about this experience? … What beliefs about others, about the world, about God?…"

Sometimes when the person verbalizes the belief, this will consist of the first time he or she has become aware of it. The articulation of the belief itself will cause the misbelief to simply evaporate.

4) *Break state and review the experience.* Ask the person to step off the time-line and review the imprint experience, identifying the situation and the other participants.

"I want you to come back here to this room now, and to leave that past memory."

Then have the person experience the episode as if watching a movie of himself.

"Look back at that experience you had, put it way out there so that it completely leaves, so that you no longer find yourself in it at all… and watch that younger you…" "How has that experience affected you since that time?"

Ask the person to verbalize any other beliefs formed as a result of this imprint (those beliefs that arose "after the fact"). Sometimes people don't form beliefs at the time of the imprint, but later. We can build imprint beliefs both during and after the episode.

5) *Find the positive intentions in the feeling or belief.* Determine the positive intentions of the people involved in the situation. The person may have to ask the characters, "What positive intention did you have in doing this?" Did they seek to install this belief that you exist as a worthless person? Trying to screw you up? What intention did this party have in doing this? Would he like it if he knew what is now going on with you?

6) *Identify and anchor the needed resources.* Ask the person to identify and anchor the resources and choices that he/she needed back then and didn't have. Do the same for all the characters in the situation.

"What would you need to give those persons in order for them to respond differently?" "More acceptance." "So they need a realization that different people have different models of the world."

Get those resources. "I want you to vividly recall a time when you fully had that accepting feeling." Find a specific example. Anchor it.

7) *Apply the resource.* Ask the person to review the imprint experience, off the time-line, from the perspective of each of the characters involved. Holding the anchor, give each character in the situation all the resources they would have needed to achieve a desired outcome, back then.

"Take these resources and give them to this other person. This other person is in your brain right now—that image or memory comes from your brain. So take this and give it to him. What does he or she do differently? … What beliefs do you now build out of this experience? … Just go inside, and allow your unconscious mind to review each experience with this experience knowing that they now have the resources they needed. We know that this person didn't have that resource at that time, although as your resource, you can update that model now…"

"There is a younger self back in that experience that needs resources that he or she didn't have then. What resources do you have now that would have allowed you to build a different set of beliefs then?… What insights, skills, abilities…? What is the closest you have come to having that resource? Now take that light and shine it back through your history. Shine it on that younger you… so that as that younger you begins to feel this resource, you can allow yourself to imagine how that would have changed things. And you can now allow yourself to be relaxed and secure, calm and comfortable with yourself in that memory… see that younger self in front of you building resourceful beliefs and abilities."

8) *Associate and relive the imprint experience.* Becoming each character, have the person step onto the time-line (holding the anchor) with all the resources previously given to that character. Then have the person update and/or modify the beliefs associated with the experience.

9) *Receive resources.* Ask the person to step onto the time-line as their younger self and receive the qualities or attributes they needed from each significant character.

10) *Review and future pace.* Ask the person to step off the time-line and review the changed experience. When he/she feels satisfied with the outcome, have the person step back onto the time-line, and then move up quickly into his or her future. Then stop and use the resources to see how they will think-feel and live in a new and different way.

Change Personal History Pattern

The "past" only exists "in our mind." Externally in the world "out there" it no longer exists. It has passed. We keep it inside in our mind and body and call it our "memory." Yet even our memories continually change with every new understanding, development, and experience. Since it only exists as a construction, "It is never too late to have a happy childhood."

What we remember, *why* we remember, and *how* we use our memories involves our personal choices. You can "accurately" represent hurtful and traumatic memories but of course, that just empowers them to keep our body and emotions all stirred up. This is not a wise way to run our own brain. Use this pattern to *change personal history.* We have adapted the following version of this pattern in terms of Meta-States.

The Pattern

1) *Identify the problem event.* This will serve as the primary state. "Think about a time and place in your history that still troubles you." "How does it trouble you?" "What problem does it create for you?" "When you step into that memory, what emotion arises? What meanings?" Now step out of that problem state.

2) *Take an observer's viewpoint of that experience.* This represents a Meta-State about the primary state. Float above your time-line (dissociate) and go back to the problem event and observe it as a witness to it. From this meta-position, see that *younger* you going through that event. (If you have difficulty staying dissociated, put your representations up on an imaginary screen.)

3) *Gather learnings about the event from the observer position.* This allows you to move into another Meta-State about the primary—learning about the event. "What resources did that younger you need?" "What resources did the others in the situation need?" Identify the resources needed that would have changed it.

4) *Return to the present and fully access the resources.* From the position of the here-and-now, access and anchor each and every needed resource. Amplify these and then test your anchors for the resources.

5) *From the observer meta-position, transfer the resources.* When you have returned to the past event, give that younger you each resource as a gift from your present self. Visualize giving such resources to that younger you. Then let the event play out with the resources. Imagine the younger you now acting, thinking, feeling, etc. in a transformed way. From this position, you can also give the others in the movie the resources that they needed.

6) *Come forward through your history with the added resources.* Step into the movie and become that younger you for the moment, and then imagine yourself moving up through your time-line experiencing the resources so that as you

move through each subsequent year of life, the resources transform your history and enrich your life. Let the resources transform yourself and the others.

7) *Return to the present and run an ecology check.* Does this new edition of your memory provide you a sense of closure? Does it encode better learnings and responses? Does it enhance your life? Would you like to live with this new edition? Does it provide you a more useable map for navigating life?

8) *Future pace.* Look out into your future from the perspective of having made these changes in your sense of your personal history and imagine them continuing into your future…

Swish Pattern

Since "brains go places" and take us to thoughts-and-feelings that can create problematic and limiting states, this pattern enables us to identify the cues that *swish* the brain to go wherever it goes. Detecting such then enables us to re-directionalize our brain so that it goes to somewhere more useful and productive. This pattern can change the way we feel and behave.

The Swish Pattern represents an especially generative pattern. If you think about "the behavior that would change the old response," you program in a specific action or response. Yet if you think about *"the me* for whom this would no longer operate as a problem" you send your consciousness to a more powerful, positive, and confident You. Neurologically, we move away from pain and toward pleasure. So whenever we attach a *"pleasure"* meaning to a stimulus, we program ourselves to move toward that "pleasure." This directionalizes our mind.

The Pattern
1) *Develop a full representation of the cue picture* (or sound, sensation, word). The cue representation "triggers" the person into feeling stuck, unresourceful, or into problematic behavior. "What do you see, hear, feel just before you engage in

unwanted behaviors?" Make the cue picture *an associated image.*

2) *Develop a fully represented desired self image.* Develop a representation of a desired self that no longer has these problems. Put into this image all of the qualities and attributes (not behaviors) that you believe necessary to the desired outcome. Make this picture *dissociated.*

3) *Check for objections* and see that all parts want the desired self. Quiet yourself and go inside and ask, "Does any part of me object to this new image of myself?"

4) *Link the two representations.* We now want to create a linkage between the representations so that the cue always leads to the resourceful picture. In building this mechanism, we will use the person's *driving modalities.* Start with a cue picture big and bright, in front of the person and construct a small dark future self in the corner or in the middle of this picture. Always start with the cue image and then add the future self image.

5) *Swish.* As the cue image gets smaller and darker, have the future self image grow bigger and brighter until it fills the whole screen. Do this very, very quickly, in just a couple of seconds. Do it as fast as it takes to say, "Swwiissshhhhh." After this, ask the person to clear "the screen."

6) *Repeat* this swish 5 or 6 times, allowing your brain to go quicker and quicker with each swish.

7) *Test.* Ask the person to think about the cue image (or behaviorally test by creating the external cue for the person!).

8) *Future pace.*

[Note: If you don't find this works sufficiently well, then use "distance." Make the associated cue image big and close. Place the dissociated desired self-image in the distance. Then send as you let the cue picture vanish or fade away, bring the desired imagine forward very quickly so that it fills the screen.]

Decision Destroyer Pattern

Sometimes in moving through life, we just make some poor decisions. Afterwards, those decisions become part of our mental map and begin to operate as a major psychological force in our life (as a Meta-State). This pattern *destroys* such limiting, destructive, and unenhancing decisions.

"Decisions" function as part of our mental maps that provide specific instructions about what to do. And while a decision in one context and at one time may function very well for our benefit, as contexts and times change, these decisions can become out-dated and unuseful. This pattern allows us to alter the decisions that we have constructed.

The Pattern
1) *Identify a limiting decision that you still live with.* What did you decide? Fully express the decision and its meanings. When did you adopt this decision? How long have you lived with it? How has it become limiting to you? Fully elicit this information.

2) *Identify an enhancing decision you'd like to live life by.* By using the criteria of the Well-formedness Conditions (specific, stated in positive, small steps and stages, something you can take to, etc.), access fully a more enhancing decision that would serve you better now and in the future. As you access this decision state, anchor it fully.

3) *Float above your time-line back to when you made the limiting decision.* Observe it dissociatedly from above your time-line. Float down into the experience—and observe it associatedly. Anchor this experience.

4) *Repeat.* Float back to other instances of this Limiting Decision until you get to the earliest experience of using this limiting belief.

5) *Now float back up above your time-line and fully re-access your enhancing decision.*

6) *Go back 15 minutes prior to the decision.* Once you have your enhancing decision fully accessed from above the time-line, float back to 15 minutes prior to the earliest decision, then float down into that younger you, bringing with you that Enhancing Decision fully and completely.

7) *Experience the old situation with new resources.* As you do, bring these enhancing resources with you, letting them (in your mind and internal experience) completely change your awareness and feelings as you experience the effects of this new decision.

8) *Then quickly zoom up through your time-line to the present.*

9) *Stop at the present.* Fully integrate the experience and future pace.

Visual-Kinesthetic Dissociation Pattern—Phobia Resolution Pattern

We can process information *analytically and experientially*. When we "think" or read something experientially, we feel as if we have *entered into* the story so to speak. To do that we representationally *encode* it in such a way that we cue ourselves to *neuro-linguistically experience* it. Conversely, when we "think" or read something analytically, we hold the material at "arm's length" so to speak. We analyze it, think *about* it, and take a spectator's point of view regarding it. In the first instance, we **associate** *with and in* the content; in the second, we **dissociate**.

A caveat about this language. We use the term *"dissociation"* with caution because we do *not* (and cannot) literally step out of our body so that we do *not* experience an emotion. Even "dissociation" involves our body, and occurs *in* the body, hence somatic sensations and feelings. More accurately, we *conceptually* step aside from our emotions and *think* about them from a *meta* position.

Each of these perceptual styles has its strengths and weaknesses. *Association* empowers us to take the first perceptual position of self, to enter into a story, and to "know" it from within.

215

Dissociation allows us to take the second and third perceptual positions (the points of view of others, second, of the system, third, etc.) to apply scientific or personal analysis, to learn from it, to not let it activate our emotional responses, to know it from without. Too much association and we become emotional cripples, hysterical, unable to "think," emotional reactions, etc. Too much dissociation and we become intellectual eggheads, emotional incompetents, unable to relate emotionally and personally, etc.

With regard to hurts, traumas, and unpleasant realities, many people can't *even think about* such information. To do so re-traumatizes. Typically, such individuals eventually lose their willingness to even entertain painful thoughts; those in helping professions frequently burn-out. Others develop PSTD (Post Traumatic Stress Disorder). Because they cannot "think" without going into negative painful emotional states, they experience "thinking" as distressful and unpleasant. This robs them of an important resource: the skill of *thinking comfortably* **about** *unpleasant events.* So "reality" pains them. So they repress, suppress, deny, avoid, etc.

The *V-K Dissociation pattern* offers a marvelous technology for recovering from trauma states and from PTSD. It empowers us in learning how to "think" about unpleasant things *without* re-associating and re-experiencing the situation. We can stop signaling our body to respond to "thoughts" as if actually in the trauma again. By stopping the ongoing re-traumatization, we resolve the pain and move on in life.

The technology within this pattern works by moving, mentally/conceptually, to a different frame-of-reference (other position, third position, dissociated viewpoint) and viewing the information from a position of distance. This stops one from associating into the experience and accessing negative emotional states allowing one to bring new resources to bear on the situation.

We can now develop the *flexibility of consciousness* to choose when to step into an experience and when to step out—conceptually and emotionally. We can decide **how** to code and experience information: analytically, "objectively," and un-emotionally or experientially, "subjectively," and "emotionally." We can remember old events as a spectator to the experience—as a movie-goer, rather than as an actor in the movie. Use this technology for effectively managing "emotions" so that you learn from the past rather than use it to feel bad about. Use it to "switch off" any scene that you don't need to play any more in your inner theater.

The Pattern
1) *Create a dissociated representation.* Create a dissociated image by imagining yourself sitting in a movie theater. On the screen in this mental theater, put a black-and white picture of the younger you in the situation *just before* the traumatic events occurred. Freeze-frame, as a snap-shot, a scene prior to the movie. Now sit back to watch it, aware that you have taken a spectator's position to that younger you. Notice that you have stepped out of the picture, and have a position from outside. This will change how you feel *about* it.

2) *Identify your driving submodalities.* As a spectator to your movie, notice your VAK codings and their submodalities (another Meta-Level state). Play around with altering them. As you take this position to your younger self, look at the ways you internally represent that memory…

As you begin with the visual system, just notice how you have the picture—in color or black-and-white? A movie or snapshot? Bright or dim? Close or far? And as you make these distinctions, you can begin to choose which coding would enable you to *think comfortably about* that memory so that you can stay resourceful and thoughtful in a relaxed and comfortable way.

Begin to check out the auditory system regarding the sound track of your memory. Do you even have a sound track? What sounds do you hear coming from that movie? What quality of tones do you hear? At what volume, pitch, and melody? Now check out your language system. What words do you hear from that younger you? From where do you hear these words coming? Notice their tone, volume, and location. As you notice how that younger you feels, what sensations does that person have in his or her body up there on the screen? Where and at what intensity, weight, pressure?

What shifts in these submodality codings enable you to *think comfortably about* that old memory? As you make these alterations in your coding you can relax in the growing sense of distance and control this gives you. Notice the effect it has for you when you dim the picture of your unpleasant memory. Now turn down the brightness, further, further, until it doesn't bother you anymore. Send the picture off into the distance... Soften the tonality of the sound track.

3) *Move to a second-level dissociation.* Imagine yourself floating out of your body in the tenth row in the theater and float back to the projection booth. From this point-of-view you can see today's self (in the tenth row) watching your younger you on the screen. As you note the adult you sitting in the theater (seeing the back of his or her head) let yourself also see beyond that to the still picture on the screen.

At this second-level, if at any time you feel uncomfortable and need to remind yourself that you are not in the picture, but merely watching it, put your hands up on the plexiglass to remind yourself to feel safe and secure in the control booth.

4) *Let the old memory play out as you watch it from the projection booth.* Let the initial snapshot play out as a black-and-white movie as you watch the memory from the projection booth. Watch it from the beginning to the end, then let it play beyond the end to a time when the bad scene disappears and see that younger you in a time and place of safety and pleasure. As you keep watching after the passing of the trauma, move to a scene of comfort... whether it occurred at the same time or whether you have to fast forward your memories to some future event of comfort. When you get to that place, stop the action, and freeze frame the picture. [If the experience becomes especially intense, dissociate to a third level.]

5) *Step in and rewind.* The next step will occur really fast. So don't do it until you get all of the instructions about what and how to do it. In a moment, *rewind this memory movie* in fast rewind mode. You have seen movies or videos run backwards. Now rewind this movie backwards at a high speed rewind. This time, rewind it while **inside** it. From that vantage point, you might see a confusion of sights and a jumbling of sounds as everything zooms back to the beginning.

Now associate yourself into the comfort scene at the end of the movie and feel those feelings of comfort and okayness fully and completely, recode everything in color, close up, etc.

Do you feel that comfort scene? Good. Now push the rewind button an experience it rewinding ... zoooooommmmm. All the way back to the beginning.

It only takes a second or two to do that fast rewind, and how did that feel...

rewinding from inside the movie?

When you experience the fast rewinding, all the people and their actions go backwards. They walk and talk backwards. You walk and talk in reverse. Everything happens in reverse, like rewinding a movie.

6) *Repeat this process five times.* Having arrived back to the snapshot at the beginning, clear the screen in your mind. Take a break. Shift your awareness. Open your eyes and look around.

Now, go to the scene of comfort at the end again, and *as soon as* you step into it, feel, see, and hear it fully... rewind the movie even faster. As you do this over and over your brain will become more and more proficient and the rewind will go faster and faster until the rewind takes only a second each time. Zoommmm!

7) Test your results.

Break state from this exercise. Then after a minute or two, call up the original memory and see if you can get the feelings back. Try as hard as you can to step into the scene and feel the full weight of the emotions.

Threshold Pattern or Compulsion Blowout

Sometimes a way of thinking-and-feeling which doesn't serve us well continues to work simply because we still believe it will if we just work at it long and hard enough. So we stay in dysfunctional relationships, patterns, organizations, etc. Yet patterns of thinking, emoting, talking, and behaving can threshold. They can accumulate over time to the point that one has an internal sense of "Enough!" "No more!" We can experience "the last straw" about things. Then we "go over the top." "Something snaps" irrevocably.

Sometimes a person will hit threshold with a habit pattern such as smoking, drinking, cussing, putting up with a mate, enduring a job, etc. Then something snaps. Therefore, the old pattern cannot cohere in that person's life. They can't stand even the smell of a cigarette. The taste of alcohol no longer holds any appeal. The thought of a particular person repulses them! They've hit threshold. Source: Andreas and Andreas (1987).

The Pattern
1) *Identify your compulsion state.* What do you feel compulsive about? What do you obsess about mentally, emotionally, and behaviorally? Identify the problem.

2) *Identify a non-compulsion state.* Think about something similar to the compulsion, but unlike it in the sense that you don't become obsessive-compulsive about it. For instance you may feel compulsed about pistachios but not about regular peanuts, about ice cream, but not about yogurt.

3) *Run a contrastive analysis.* Compare the differences between these two items in terms of their *driving* submodalities. How

do you *code* the thing you feel compulsive about? How do you code the similar thing about which you do not feel compulsive?

4) *Blow it out.* Take the quality of the representation (the sub-modality) that drives the compulsion (size, closeness, color, etc.) and make it more and more so (bigger and bigger, closer and closer, brighter and brighter, etc.) until you blow it out! Exaggerate it until the experience cannot exist in that form.

   When you do this, expect that the feelings of compulsion will increase at first, and will get stronger and stronger… then, as it thresholds, it will pop, snap, blow out, etc.

5) *Test.* Think about the item. How do you feel? Is the item blown out?

6) *Ratchet the experience.* An alternative method for getting an experience to threshold involves ratcheting it like you would a car jack, making it go higher and higher. Take the experience and the driving submodality qualities that pump it up and ratchet it again and again. Do so repeatedly until you get it beyond threshold. Then pause for a few minutes and test.

7) *Swish to a new resourceful you.* After you have changed the compulsion, invite the person to think of the "you" for whom these contexts offer no problem. Then use the Swish pattern to move from the old cues that triggered compulsion to the new states of resourcefulness.

Breaking Up Limiting Synesthesias Pattern

We can get several modalities combined, fused, and stuck together in representing information. We call this merging, linkage, or synthesizing a *synesthesia*. This refers to an *overlap between the senses* of seeing, hearing, feeling, smelling, etc. Sometimes this creates problems as when a person sees blood and automatically feels horror, he or she has a V-K synesthesia (see-feel). As such, it can amplify traumatic memories.

This pattern breaks up such synesthesias and so adds behavioral choices in such contexts allowing us to create new responses.

The Pattern

1) *Identify a problem context.* Find a specific person, time, and/or place where you experience the problem behavior.

2) *Access, anchor and calibrate the problem.* As you access the problem behavior and state, anchor it to a specific location on the floor. When you do this, notice the physiology, breathing, eye accessing, voice tone, etc. in that problem state.

3) *Identify and step into a resource space.* As you specify a resource that would make the problem unnecessary, or prevent the problem, step into it and anchor that resourceful experience to a specific place on the floor. Calibrate by noticing the changes involved in becoming more resourceful.

4) *Step back into the problem space.* While you remember the problem situation again, take on the physiology of the resourceful state fully ... including voice, breathing, body positions, etc. Continue to hold the image of the problem while making the physiological changes.

5) *Adding more options.* Next, add an auditory digital and visual construct to this resourceful state by taping the left foot and moving the right finger to the chin. As you do, look up and to the right while saying "Mmmmm..." as if thinking of something profound. As you do this, *step back into the resource space.*

6) *Check out all representations.* Now think about the problem by moving your eyes through all of the accessing positions in a figure 8 configuration always moving up from the center. Then reverse the direction again moving up from center.

7) *Test and run an ecology check.* Break state, and test to see if you have a different reaction to the problem. Run an ecology check to determine if any part would object to using this more resourceful choice.

Meta-Modeling as a Pattern

We use the *Meta-Model* to listen to the statements made, respectfully enter into the person's constructed linguistic world, explore it, and curiously ask questions about it. When we then *pace and confirm* the person's mental maps, he or she feels understood. This elicits "trust" and rapport. When *meta-modeling* we coach people in enriching their maps and making them more well-formed.

The following distinctions present *the first Meta-Model of language.* The patterns fall into three map-making processes: deletion, generalization and distortion. This highlights the fact that we make our models of the world by leaving characteristics out (deletion), by summarizing or generalizing features (generalization), and by altering/distorting other features (distortion).

The Meta-Model of Language in Therapy

Patterns/Distinctions	Responses/Challenges

Deletions:

1. Unspecified Nouns or Referential Index (Simple Deletions).

"They don't listen to me."	Who specifically doesn't listen to you?
"He said that she was mean."	Who specifically said that?
	Whom did he say that you call mean?
	What did he mean by 'mean'?

2. Unspecified Relations (Comparative Deletions).

"She's a better person."	Better than whom?
	Better at what?
	Compared to whom, what?
	Given what criteria?

3. Unspecified Referential Index

"He rejected me."	Who specifically rejected you?
"People push me around."	Who specifically pushes you?

4. Unspecified Verbs

"She rejected me."	How specifically did she reject you?
"I felt really manipulated."	Manipulated in what way and how?

5. Nominalizations (Hidden or Smothered Verbs, Ambiguous Words).

"Let's improve our communication."	Whose communicating do you mean?
	How would you like to communicate?
"What state did you wake up in this morning?"	Use Co-ordinates to index:
	Specifically what, when, who, where, which, how, etc.?
	De-nominalize the nominalization to recover the hidden verb.

The Meta-Model of Language in Therapy (continued)

Patterns/Distinctions	Responses/Challenges

Generalisations:

6. Universal Qualifiers (Allness, Generalizations that Exclude Exceptions).

"She never listens to me."	Never?
	What would happen if she did?

7. Modal Operators (Operational Modes of Being).

(Necessity, Possibility, Impossibility, Desire).

"I have to take care of her."	What would happen if you did?
"I can't tell him the truth."	What wouldn't happen if you didn't?
	…Or what? What would happen if you did?

8. Lost Performative (An Evaluative Statement with the Speaker Deleted or Unowned).

"It's bad to be inconsistent."	Who evaluates it as bad?
	According to what standard?
	How do you determine this label of "badness?"

Distortions:

9. Mind Reading (Meaning Attributions and Cause-Effect Assumptions about Others).

"You don't like me…"	How do you know I don't like you?
	What evidence leads you to the conclusion?

10. Cause—Effect (Causational Statements of Relations between Events, Stimulus-response Beliefs).

"You make me sad."	How does my behavior cause you to feel sad?
	What evidence leads you to that conclusion?

11. Complex Equivalence (The "Is" of Identity, Identifications).

"She's always yelling at me; she doesn't like me."	How does her yelling mean she doesn't like you?
"He's a loser when it comes to business; he just lacks business sense."	Can you recall a time when you yelled at someone you liked?
	How do you create this equation in an absolute way between these things?

12. Presuppositions (Silent Assumptions).

"If my husband knew how much I suffered, he wouldn't do that."	This statement presupposes that she suffers, that her husband's behavior causes her suffering, that he lacks knowledge about her suffering, that his intentions would shift if he knew.
	How do you choose to suffer?
	How is he reacting?
	How do you know he doesn't know?

The Pattern

1) *Listen for ill-formedness or vagueness in representation.* As you listen for statements, cue yourself to stay in sensory awareness. Do this by noticing if the words themselves permit you to see, hear, feel, taste and smell the referents. Continually *track over* directly from the words to creating your own internal representations.

> When I track over, do I have a complete understanding of the person's referents and meanings?
>
> Have they left something out? (Deletion) What? Unspecified nouns, verbs, relations, etc.? If so inquire.

Continue also to check for other problems (generalizations and distortions).

> Have they generalized something so that it lacks specifics?
>
> Have they distorted some process so that I don't know how it works (cause-effect), what it means or how it came to mean that (complex equivalence), have they information about another person (mind-reading), etc.?

To Meta-Model, a person has to stay in *sensory awareness* and *not* project their own meanings, references, definitions, etc., onto the other person's words. To do this, adopt a "Know Nothing" frame of reference.

2) *Challenge the ill-formedness.* Any time you don't know how the person's internal mental map of reality works, inquire about it.

"How do you represent this 'rejection?'"
"Where did you get that information?"
"Does it always work that way?"
"What have you presupposed?"

3) *Continue checking for areas of unclarity and asking for more precision until you have a sufficiently adequate representation of the other's meanings.*

Changing Meta-Programs Pattern

Meta-Programs are not "written in stone." We *can* change them. In fact, in the normal process of growing and developing over our life span, we do change some of them. These stabilizing ways of thinking develop over time in various life contexts and become habitualized. So as we learn them, we can also unlearn them and develop more effective thinking styles.

Robbins (1986) says that one way to change a Meta-Program involves "consciously deciding to do so." Most people just never give a thought to the art of changing their thinking and perceiving patterns and so they don't.

Meta-Programs inform our brains about *what to delete.* If we move toward values, then we delete awareness about what we move away from. If we sort for the details, we delete the big picture. Directing our awareness to what we normally delete describes how we can shift focus and change our operating systems. The followings comes from Hall and Bodenhamer (1997).

The Pattern:
1) *Identify the Meta-Programs* that currently govern your sorting, processing, and attending. Specifically identify when, where, and how you use this Meta-Program that does not serve you well. How does it undermine your effectiveness in some way?

2) *Describe fully the Meta-Programs you would prefer to use as your default style of sorting in a given context.* What Meta-Level processing would you prefer to "run your perceiving and valuing?" Specify when, where, and how you would like this Meta-Program to govern your consciousness.

3) *Try it out.* Imaginatively adopt the new Meta-Program and pretend to use it in sorting, perceiving, attending, etc. Notice how it seems, feels, works, etc. in described contexts where you think it would serve you better. It may seem a little "weird" at first. Reckon its strangeness due simply to your unfamiliarity with looking at the world with that particular perceptual filter. Notice what feelings you experience while using this.

If you know someone who uses this Meta-Program, explore with them their experience until you can take second position to it. Then step into that position fully so that you can see the world out of that person's Meta-Program eyes, hearing what he or she hears, self-talking as he or she engages in self-dialogue, and feeling what that person feels.

4) *Run an ecology check on the Meta-Program change.* Go meta to an even higher level and consider what this Meta-Program will do to you and for you in terms of perception, valuing, believing, behaving, etc. What kind of a person would it make you? What effect would it have on various aspects of your life?

5) *Give yourself permission to install it for a period of time.* Frequently, a person can "install" a Meta-Program filter by granting themself permission to use it. After you give yourself such permission, go inside and see if any part objects. If no, then future pace. If yes, then reframe using the objection.

For example, suppose you have typically used the Other-Referencing Meta-Program (#14) and have given yourself permission to shift to Self-Referencing. Yet when you do, you hear an internal voice that sounds like your mother's voice in tone and tempo, "It's selfish to think about yourself. Don't be so selfish, you will lose all of your friends."

This voice objects on two accounts: selfishness and disapproval that leads to loneliness. So rephrase your permission to take these objections into account. "I give myself permission to see the world referencing centrally from myself—my values, beliefs, wants, etc., knowing that my values include loving, caring, and respecting others and that this will keep me balanced by considering the effect of my choices on others."

6) *Future pace the Meta-Program.* Practice, in your imagination, using this Meta-Program and do so until it begins to feel comfortable and familiar.

Troubleshooting. If you have difficulty, then do this procedure on your time-line. Float *above* yourself and your line to your meta time-line, then *float back* along the line into your past until you come to one or several of the key experiences wherein you began using the old Meta-Program.

Then ask yourself, "If you knew when you originally made the choice to *operate from the Other Referent (name the Meta-Program you want to change)*, would that have been before, after, or during birth?

Use one of the time-line processes to neutralize the old emotions, thoughts, beliefs, decisions, etc.: the visual-kinesthetic dissociation technique, decision destroyer pattern, etc. Once you have cleared out the old pattern, you can install the new Meta-Program.

Parts Integration Pattern

This pattern offers another option for dealing with "parts" conflict. In this case the conflicting parts are integrated into one unit. This unit has the function of meeting the higher shared intention of the two previous parts. The process is done in a relaxed or "trance" state.

The Pattern

1) *Access a relaxed state.* Begin by accessing into a relaxed, confident state. Use a relaxation process to get into the right state for communicating with your inner mind. Sit somewhere comfortable, and hold your hands out with the palms up, as if holding an object in each.

2) *Identify the two parts you will work with.* If the issue concerns some behavior you wish you could stop, then you have one part that wants to stop and another part that causes you to engage in the behavior. If you can identify one part, but not a second, just call the second part "the part of me that's most opposed to that first part."

3) *Begin communication with one part.* Take either part and ask which hand it would stand on if you knew, and where it would stand on that hand. Trust your unconscious response. Feel that hand: is it cool or warm, light or heavy? What would the part look like if you could see it? What kind of voice would it have? And what would it say, if you ask it now, "What do you want for me?" Whatever the part responds to the question, thank it for communicating. This is very important inasmuch as your aim is to discover what an even more important thing it will get by striving for what it wants. For now, when you ask the part what it wants, it may tell you something positive or negative. Either means you've begun sorting this out.

4) *Begin communicating with the other part.* Take the other part and ask where on the other hand it would stand, if it knew. Feel, see and hear it there, and ask it (as you did before), "What do you want for me?" Thank it for communicating.

5) *Find the higher positive intentions.* Start with either part and ask, "If you have that outcome, what do you want by having that, that's even more important?" Appreciate each answer. Go up the "ladder" of Meta-Levels of outcomes at least three steps with each of the parts, asking, "If you have that outcome, what do you want by having that, that's even more important?" In doing this, our aim is not about getting the details but about the larger, wider, and more useful result.

6) *Find a shared higher intention.* Sometimes it will quickly be obvious to you that the two parts have the same highest outcome. Sometimes when you've asked the meta-question about "the outcomes that are even more important" several times, you'll realize that you're so far up the ladder of outcomes on one side, that you need to go back to the other side

and climb up higher there. For example; working with a person who wanted to stop smoking we might find the following outcomes from the part that smokes:

Have better friendships
Be comfortable with friends
Not feel anxious
Satisfy cravings

We might then go to the part that wanted to stop smoking and get such outcomes as the following:

Get the most out of life
Be healthy
Part that wants to stop smoking

Even though 'get the most out of life' was only two steps up, we realize that it is higher up, more general than "have better friendships." So we go back to the part that wanted to smoke, and ask the meta-outcome question again. Suppose we then get the following:

Get the most out of life
Enjoy myself
Have better friendships
Be comfortable with friends
Not feel anxious
Satisfy cravings
Part that wants to smoke

7) *Invite the parts to integrate.* Once you've found the shared highest intention, then ask:

"Do these parts notice that they have the same highest intention?"
"Do these parts realize that they were once part of a greater whole?"
"Does each part realize that the other part has resources that would help it to achieve its higher outcomes?"

As the parts identify this truth, invite them to allow themselves to integrate now. Do not consciously move your hands together. Hold them up and watch closely for any subtle, tiny movements they make towards the center and say, "That's right" to acknowledge these movements as soon as you see them. Keep encouraging honest, unconscious movement of the hands together.

8) *Experience the new unity.* Once the hands are together, notice that the two parts are now one wholeness, with one weight and temperature; a wholeness with all the resources that the two parts used to have. Feel where in your body it would be right for that oneness to be placed, and put your hands there, just allowing that wholeness to spread from there through your whole neurology, your body. You may feel warmth spreading through you. Congratulate yourself, and think of a future time which, in the past, would have been a time of incongruity, but which you can now imagine yourself in, acting as a whole aligned person

Strategy Installation Pattern

A strategy is a sequence of internal representations which lead to a result. We can consider every personality problem as a result of a series of strategies which lead to undesired results.

For example, to create "anticipatory anxiety," a person needs to run a particular strategy. One might begin by noticing that a family member is thirty minutes late in arriving home (a visual trigger for the strategy). The person may then say to him or herself in a fast high pitched internal voice, "They're not here; they may never come. They may be dead!" (the Auditory digital operation phase). Perhaps the person then makes a big associated picture of life without that person, and compares that with a hoped for life together (the visual test phase). The person could then get a sense of panic about the drastic difference (the kinesthetic exit or "result" phase). There's a transcript of Richard Bandler working with a person using this strategy (Bandler, 1984, pp. 1–31).

In a sense, all the NLP change processes described here install new strategies. We can also directly design and install a strategy by rehearsal. This is the basis of most skills-based education, and is the NLP counterpart of many techniques used in cognitive psychology (e.g., Beck and Emery, 1985, pp. 210–231). A new strategy will begin with the same trigger point, but will lead in a new direction. It will be rehearsed by the person until it has been "installed" (that is, until it runs automatically in the challenging situation).

The Pattern

1) *Identify the trigger for the old strategy.* Clarify the specific behavior or feeling state the person wants to change. Ask, "What do you see, hear, smell, taste or touch that lets you know it is time to begin this behavior or get this feeling?" "Since you don't do this twenty-four hours a day, what specific event triggers it at the times when it does happen?" In anticipatory anxiety, a person might say, "I look at the clock and see that the person is thirty minutes late."

2) *Identify the desired result of the new strategy.* Ask, "What would you like to do, or what would you like to feel, at those times that were a problem?" This gives us the "Exit" of the new strategy. Check that this exit is "ecological" (i.e., it fits with the person's values, other outcomes, and preferred Meta-Programs). With anticipatory anxiety, the person might want to feel calm and relaxed, take any needed action to re-plan his or her time, etc.

3) *Find a series of steps which lead from the trigger situation to the desired exit.* There are several places to find such new strategies. These include:

- Where else in your life do you meet a similar challenge and yet get to the result you want here? What internal steps do you take to get the results you want? With anticipatory anxiety this may include times when the person was at a restaurant and noticed that their meal was late, or at a bus stop and noticed that the bus was late.

232

- Who else do you know who would manage to meet this challenge and yet get the results you want? What internal steps do you imagine they take to get the results you want? With anticipatory anxiety this might include a friend who stays calm and relaxed in such situations.

- What is the simplest way you could alter the internal steps you have been taking previously, so that they lead to the result you want? Beck and Emery (1985, pp. 210–231) suggest a number of ways to subtly change the anticipatory anxiety strategy. Bandler (1984, pp. 1–31) demonstrates some of these, which include:

  a) Altering the submodalities of the old strategy to more comfortable ones. For example, changing the internal voice to a slower and low pitched mode, or changing the images of life alone to smaller dissociated images.

  b) Exaggerating the strategy to create a sense of humor and amusement. The person might be instructed to imagine everyone in the world as having just died and left them alone on the planet. They could then let go of those images and think more realistically about what they'd like to do right now.

  c) Interrupting the old strategy with a sudden action (e.g., clapping the hands) or with a shouted command, "Hey! Lets get a more useful image here!"

  d) Inserting a meta-comment in the strategy. In the anticipatory anxiety situation this might include asking Meta-Model questions, "Has there ever been a time when someone was late and they didn't die or leave you alone?" It could include asking questions about the outcome of the feeling state produced, "Whatever has happened to make them late, what emotion is most useful for me to have right now?"

4) *Find a more useful comparison at the test phase of the strategy.* The final state in which someone leaves a strategy is a result of the comparison they make in the test phase. A useful

comparison is one that can give the person either positive feedback (I'm getting what I want) or negative feedback (I need to change what I'm doing).

Imagine I am buying a car. If I compare the image of the car I'm considering with an image of the most expensive car in the world, there's no way I'm ever going to get positive feedback. I'm guaranteed to feel disappointed in the car I'm considering. If I compare the image of the car I'm considering to an image of all the things I want to be able to enjoy doing in my car, I have a chance of getting positive feedback. This makes it a more sensible comparison. Much of the unhappiness people experience results from making inappropriate comparisons (e.g., "Am I as attractive as my favorite movie star?", "Did my life today provide me with the excitement of my best childhood birthday party?").

The panic in anticipatory anxiety results from the person comparing an image of living life alone and abandoned (the expected result of their imaginings) to the image of living life the way they want to. This kind of comparison is "setting themselves up to fail." There's no way to get positive feedback as a result of comparing these two things.

A very different feeling would result if the person compared an image of some possible immediate action (i.e., phoning up to check what happened with the relative) to the desired immediate result (i.e., of seeing themselves as doing something useful). In this comparison, the result may be negative feedback (phoning up may not look likely to produce any useful new information) or positive feedback (phoning up may seem like a useful action to take). This would be a useful comparison to make.

Here's another example of useful and less useful comparison. If I compare my financial success so far with that of Tony Robbins, and ask myself, "Am I doing as well as Tony?" I have "set myself up" (perhaps for feelings of hopelessness and depression). If I compare my actions today with the actions I imagine a financially successful person taking in my situation, the result may be negative feedback (I could have improved) or positive feedback (I did the best I can imagine doing). This is a more useful comparison.

Another example: If I compare an image of how organized my office is now, with an image of a perfectly organized office on an advertisement for new office spaces, I may be setting myself up for obsessional behavior. If I compare how organized my office is with how organized it needs to be for me to find most things within five minutes, I may have a useful comparison.

5) *Write out the new strategy and rehearse it until it runs naturally.* A good strategy is simple, uses more than one sensory system, has a test which checks whether the outcome has been reached, and fits with the person's other values, beliefs and desired Meta-Programs.

For the person who experienced anticipatory anxiety, the new strategy might run:

> Trigger (Visual): See from the clock that the other person is unexpectedly thirty minutes late.
>
> Operation (Auditory Digital): Interrupt thoughts by saying "Relax!" in slow calming submodalities. Curiously ask self, "What is a useful action I could take now to help me feel more in charge of the situation?" (Visual) Picture one possible action.
>
> Test (Kinesthetic): Step into that picture and compare the feeling I get from doing this action with the feeling I want to get (in charge of the situation and doing something useful).
>
> Exit (Kinesthetic): Take the action (or go back to the operation and picture another possible action).

To rehearse the person through this, simply ask them to imagine being in that situation with the clock, then have them say to themselves calmly, "Relax!" Have them ask themselves aloud, "What is a useful action I could take now to help me feel more in charge of the situation?" Have them make a movie of one possible action, step into the movie and check how it feels. If it feels good, have them imagine going ahead and doing that action. Repeat this rehearsal until just seeing the clock in their imagination starts off the process automatically.

6) *Future pace.* Have the person check what it will be like to use this strategy in future in the situations that they want to.

Neuro-Semantic Patterns

Neuro-Semantics® extends and expands NLP as it uses the "Levels of Thought" (or mind) model which lies at the heart of *Meta-States*. We have included the following Meta-State patterns in this work since we reference them frequently. See Bibliography for a much more extensive list of Meta-Stating (or Meta-NLP™ Patterns).

The Meta-Stating Pattern

In *meta-stating* we take one thought or feeling (as a state) and bring it to bear upon another. In so *applying* one to another, we move up and create a logical level structure. This use of our reflexive consciousness thereby enables us to set a frame at a higher level for the lower. It enables us to texture, qualify, and add new richness to our states.

1) *Access.* Access a resource state that you want to bear on the primary state (i.e. joy, pleasure, relaxation, love, confidence, etc.). State accessing involves two primary processes: memory and imagination. To use *memory*, simply ask about a referent experience and invite one to recapture it. "Think about a time when you felt full and completely confident... and step back into that memory, seeing what you saw, hearing what you heard, and feeling what you felt. ... be there again completely." In NLP we prefer to pick a referent experience that's small and simple in order to make the state more discreet and pure. To use *imagination,* simply ask and invite, "Imagine what it would be like if you were fully and

completely relaxed with just the right level of alertness. Step into that experience fully."

2) *Amplify and anchor.* Intensify the kinesthetics of the resource state and establish an anchor for it. Do it until it radiates with neurology. To make sure that we have a strong and intense enough state so that we can use it and leverage with it, we want to make sure that there's a strong emotional charge to it. To this end, we typically invite the experiencer to gauge *how much* he or she experiences the given state from 0 to 10.

3) *Apply.* Bring the resource to bear on the primary state. This creates anchoring at a Meta-Level. Think of the primary state, thought, stimuli, etc. *in terms of*, through the thinking-feeling of, the resource. Or we can embed a primary state experience into the higher resourceful state, "as you feel this inner strength, keep it fully in mind and let it grow only to the degree and extent that you begin to think about that challenging situation."

4) *Appropriate.* "Imagine using and having and experiencing this state in the days and weeks to come as you move into your future. In fact, as you stick these feelings and ways of thinking into your future, just imagine this frame as a way of being in the world."

5) *Analyze.* Check the ecology of this construction. "Do you believe it will serve you well? How will it enhance your life? What problems could it cause? Does any part of you object to having this state of mind and emotion?"

Meta-NO-ing & Meta-YES-ing

Belief Change Pattern

This pattern enables people to *disconfirm* an old limiting thought that has become a "belief" and to also take a new thought and promote it to the level of a belief. A belief by definition differs from a thought in that we have confirmed or validated it. As a validated thought it then becomes a "command to our nervous system" or an activated neuro-linguistic program. Prepare for this by identifying any limiting beliefs that get in your way. Then specify some thought that you would like to transform into an enhancing and empowering belief, one that you would really like to have running in your mind-and-emotions.

The Pattern

1) *Get a good strong representation of saying "No!" to something.* Make sure that the person's *"No!"* looks, sounds, and feels congruent and that it truly fits with the person's beliefs and values. *Anchor* this resource experience of congruently, firmly, and definitively saying *"No!"* to something. Invite the person to stand up and utter the **"No!"**

2) *Ask the person to identify* **the limiting belief** *that they no longer want to run their programs.* Meta-model the limiting belief to assist in deframing it, loosening it up, and preparing for the belief change. Find out how it has not served them well, how it has messed things up, etc. As you notice how they represent the belief, pace its positive intentions.

3) *Meta* **"No!"** *the limiting belief.* As the person accesses the limiting belief fully and has it, invite him or her to *go meta* to that belief. Then, *about* that belief, have them utter their strong and powerful **"No!"** Have the person do it congruently, intensely, and repeatedly.

   "And you can keep on saying 'No!' to that limiting belief until you begin to feel that it no longer has any power to run your programs."

   "And how many more times and with what voice, tone, gesturing, do you need to totally disconfirm that old belief so that you know—deep inside yourself—that it will no longer run your programs?"

4) *Get a good strong representation of saying "Yes!" to something.* Repeat as in step one, only this time with all of the internal representations and neurology of **"Yes!"** Once you do,

reinforce it by asking about it, and amplifying it so that the person has an intense experience of his or her **"Yes!"** Anchor with a touch, the way you say *"Yes!,"* where you gesture to, etc.

5) *Fully elicit from the person* **an enhancing belief** *that he or she wants in the head.* What specifically will the person think and say in the new belief. Write out the language of it. Get several versions and make sure that the person finds the expression of it compelling.

6) *Meta* **"Yes!"** *the enhancing belief.* After deframing the old belief, now let the person's mind swish to the content of what to believe. Have the person fully re-access the enhancing belief and then to *go meta* to it and *validate* it with a great big *"Yes!"* Have them repeat it with intensity and congruency.

7) *Complete with future pacing the new empowering belief.*

Meta-Stating Negative Emotions Pattern

Generally, to bring *negative emotional energy* (the psychic energy of negative emotions and thinking) *against* ourselves, or any conceptual facet of ourselves, puts us at odds with ourselves. It turns our psychological energies *against* ourselves in an un-useful way. While exceptions do occur to this, they operate as the exception rather than the rule. Use this pattern as a general process for handling "negative emotions and thoughts."

The Pattern:

1) *Identify an emotional state which you have difficulties handling, controlling, or managing.* For example: anger, fear, disgust, sexual, religious, etc. What negative emotional state of thought-or-emotion do you not like, can't stand, hate, wish you didn't experience? What negative states do you feel as "taboo?" Describe this state. How is this a problem? What do you think and/or feel about this?

2) *Check your permission level.* Go inside, quiet yourself and say, "I give myself permission to feel X." Upon doing this, notice your internal responses in terms of your VAK and language responses inside. Identify any objections that arise. What would happen if you did accept or experience this negative emotion?

3) *Design engineer a new Meta-Stating structure.* Go inside and give yourself permission congruently with a strong and resourceful voice that reframes the objections. For example. "I give myself permission to feel anger because it allows me to recognize things that violate my values and to take appropriate action early." "I give myself permission to feel the tender emotions because it makes me more fully human."

4) *Meta-State the negative emotion with a powerful out-framing resource.* For example, you can access each resourceful state (i.e., acceptance, appreciation, calmness, thoughtfulness, etc.) and then *apply* that state to the primary emotional state. In doing this, use the basic meta-stating format: Access, Anchor, Amplify, Anchor. "As you feel this calmness fully and completely... feeling this in just the way you find it most powerful and resourceful you... and keeping this in mind as yours, now apply this to your experience of *anger*... and just notice the transformation that occurs as you feel calm anger..."

5) *Check ecology and add needed reframes.* Imagine fully and completely moving into your tomorrows with this outframe on the negative emotion ... does any part of you object to letting this operate as your orientational style? If so, recycle back to step 3.

6) *Future pace and install.* Use what you know of the persuasion language patterns in NLP (the Meta-model and the Milton Model) to construct a nice induction for a more resourceful future.

Drop Down Through Pattern

This technique involves beginning with an emotional state and "dropping down" through it to a lower or deeper emotion or state. Doing this process can assist a person in releasing negative emotions in which they feel stuck. See *Adventures in Time-Lines* (1997); we have derived it, in part, from Tad James and John Overdurf.

The Pattern

1) *Identify an event or emotion that the person wants more control over.* "What memory or emotion are you struggling with? Do you know the root cause of this feeling, that is, the first event which, when disconnected, will cause the problem to disappear? Tell me about the first time you felt this emotion..." Name the state or emotion (i.e., anger, fearfulness, timidity, etc.).

2) *Drop down through.* "As quickly as you can, allow yourself to just drop down through the emotion as you *do a kind of kinesthetic 'free-fall' through it* and do this as quickly as you can... and say aloud the name of the emotion that you find underneath this first experience..."

3) *Continue dropping down through.* Continue to repeat this process until you have floated all the way down through and have reached the void. This will generally generate a chain of states. Go until you reach the "void," "nothing," an unspeakable stage, etc. and come out the other side to a positive kinesthetic state.

   "And as quickly as you can, just drop through that emotion, the emotion you found underneath the original one. And what do you find underneath that one? After you reach that unspeakable experience, just notice as you come out the other side to a positive experience. Then free-fall another time to a second positive kinesthetic."

   [Only go to two positive emotions. If looping occurs more than once, use an inductive language pattern to exit the loop to a deeper level of meaning. End the process when you reach the second positive emotion. You should see and experience an obvious physiological shift. This suggests the chain of emotions below or behind emotions have collapsed together.]

4) *Return to the original experience.* Then Meta-State the original state with the resource experience. "And now as you return to the resource state which you accessed in step 3, just be there calmly in that experience as you begin to notice how it has transformed..."

5) *Reorient yourself back to this present moment and test.* "Now, come back to now, and as you recall some event, any event, in the past where you used to feel that old emotion, go back there and try to see if you can feel it, or you may find that you cannot."

6) *Future pace.* "I want you to go out into the future to an unspecified time in the future which if it had happened in the past, you would have felt X (the name the emotion), and notice if you can find that old emotion, or you may find that you cannot."

Meta-Stating "Ownership" of your Power Zone

The design of this pattern is to recognize and own the very core "powers" or functions of neuro-linguistic functioning. By doing this, we thereby establish the basis for *personal empowerment, responsibility, proactivity,* as well as many other higher level Meta-States.

The Pattern
1) *Access a full experience of your four central powers.* Access an awareness of your two private inner powers. Namely, your powers of *thinking (i.e.* representing, believing, valuing, understanding, reasoning, etc.) and your powers of *emoting* (i.e., feeling, somatizing, valuing, etc.). Think about some recent situation wherein you operated with your *thinking-and-emoting powers* and just welcome these into your awareness.

Using the same experience, acknowledge a basic awareness of your two public and outer powers. These involve your powers of *speech* (i.e., speaking: languaging, using and manipulating symbols, asserting, etc.) and *behaving* (i.e., acting, responding, relating, etc.).

Step in and fully access, feel these, mime out these *powers* in your own personal "space" to create your *Circle of Power* and influence and responsibility.

2) *Access and amplify the resource state of ownership.* Think about a time or place when you strongly felt that something was yours. When every fiber in your being said, *"Mine!"* Keep it small and simple: "My hand." "My eye." "My cat." "My toothbrush."

3) *Access the states of acceptance and appreciation of "Mine!"* This move sets two higher Meta-States *about* the ownership of your power zone state. As you experience a sense of acceptance (i.e., welcoming, acknowledging), apply that to your power zone. As you experience a sense of appreciation (i.e., seeing value and delight in it), apply that also.

4) *Amplify these states until your neurology radiates.* Ownership: "I own these powers. They belong to me. They come out of my neurology, my body and so they are mine. I recognize them and own them."

Acceptance: "I fully accept and acknowledge these powers. I recognize that others equally have a thinking-feeling, speaking and behaving power zone."

Appreciation: "I appreciate and celebrate these powers as mine, mine to use as I navigate through the world. Nobody can take these powers away from me."

5) *Apply these states to your power zone.* Let your words emerge as you language it effectively.

"This is my *zone* of power. I am totally responsible for my *responses* of mind, emotion, speech and behavior…"

6) *Future pace.* Imagine moving into your future with these powers and being able to effectively distinguish between the things you are responsible *for* and those that you are responsible *to.*

Meta-Stating Dis-Identification

When we distinguish our sense of "self" from our powers and experiences, this allows us to get more in touch with our pure consciousness self (i.e., our core self) which can then direct, guide, and control our other expressions. Developed from Roberto Assagioli (1963) as an "exercise in dis-identification" which began by becoming *"aware* of the fact: 'I *have* a body, but I *am not* my body.'"

Korzybski (1933–1994) noted that *over-identifying* with temporal facets of our self or of our situation reduces us, creates unsanity, causes us to become "possessed" by the identification. We then become our roles, our masks, our emotions, our ideas, our beliefs, etc. And this, in turn, "tends to make us static and crystallized … prisoners." (p. 121)

Use this pattern when you or another has become *too identified* with some facet of personality, in order to construct a map of a higher transcendental self.

1) *Start with the supporting belief.* "You transcend your powers and expressions of personality as well as your circumstances." Shift from confusing and identify self and these facets of mind-body to make this more empowering distinction.

2) *Dis-Identify linguistically.* Use the linguistic environment, "I have… but I am not…" to frame any and all of your powers and functions and circumstances as not you. "I have a will, I am not a will," conscience, etc.

3) *Dis-Identify in trance.* Access a relaxed and comfortable state and induce yourself into this transcendental state *about* your psychological and physiological powers to further the distinction of these levels of experience. "If I lost any of these

powers, my core Self would remain." The following hypnotic language patterns provide an induction for accessing this state-about-a-state (the conceptual state *about* the state of our identity, hence a Meta-State). I have adapted the following from Assagioli (1965):

> [E]very time we identify ourselves with a physical sensation we enslave ourselves to the body … I *have* an emotional life, but *I am not* my emotions or my feelings. I *have* an intellect, but *I am not* that intellect. I *am* I, *a center of pure consciousness.* (p. 117)

> I put my body into a comfortable and relaxed position with closed eyes. This done, I affirm, 'I *have* a body but *I am not* my body. My body may find itself in different conditions of health or sickness; it may be rested or tired, but that has nothing to do with my self, my real 'I.' My body is my precious instrument of experience and of action in the outer world, but it is *only* an instrument. I treat it well; I seek to keep it in good health, but it is *not* myself. I *have* a body, but *I am not* my body.

> I *have* emotions, but *I am not* my emotions. These emotions are countless, contradictory, changing, and yet I know that I always remain I, *my-self*, in times of hope or of despair, in joy or in pain, in a state of irritation or of calm. Since I can observe, understand and judge my emotions, and then increasingly dominate, direct and utilize them, it is evidence that *they are not myself.* I *have* emotions, but *I am not* my emotions.

> I *have* desires, but *I am not* my desires, aroused by drives, physical and emotional, and by outer influences. Desires too are changeable and contradictory, with alternations of attraction and repulsion. I *have* desires, but they *are not* myself.

> I *have* an intellect, but *I am not* my intellect. It is more or less developed and active; it is undisciplined but teachable; it is an organ of knowledge in regard to the outer world as well as the inner; but *it is not myself,* I *have* an intellect, but *I am not* my intellect.

After this dis-identification of the 'I' from its contents of consciousness (sensations, emotions, desires, and thoughts), *I recognize and affirm that I am a Centre of pure self-consciousness. I am a Center of Will,* capable of mastering, directing and using all my psychological processes and my physical body.' (pp. 118–119)

'What am I then? What remains after discarding from my self-identity the physical, emotional and mental contents of my personality, of my ego? It is the essence of myself—a center of pure self-consciousness and self-realization. It is the permanent factor in the ever varying flow of my personal life. It is that which gives me the sense of being, of permanence, of inner security. I recognize and I affirm myself as a center of pure self-consciousness. I realize that this center not only has a static self-awareness but also a dynamic power; it is capable of observing, mastering, directing and using all the psychological processes and the physical body. I am a center of awareness and of power.' (p. 119)

4) *Distinguish Self and Function while in trance.* As you recognize more fully how each power, function, facet, circumstance, etc. differs from your core self, reframe its meaning as that of a function or tool that you can use in navigating the world and expressing yourself without over-identifying with it.

5) *Swish your brain to a Transcendental Identity.* Specify the You who exists above and beyond these powers—the user of the powers, the state of "pure consciousness." Represent this with a symbol or word to anchor it fully.

6) *Image this Higher Self as a Stable Center* out of which you can live and express yourself.

Summary

- This brief overview of some of the NLP Patterns gives you many of the key patterns that we refer to in this book and an idea of the range and extent of patterns.

- Human experiences have structure and if they have structure, then there are patterns that govern the sequencing and ordering of that structure. Knowing how to recognize, unpack, alter, and install such highlights the very heart of the NLP and Neuro-Semantic models.

Part II

*Specific
"Personality"
Disordering*

Chapter 13

Double-Binding and Schizophrenia

Schizoid Personality Disorder
Schizotypal Personality Disorder

What do we mean by the "Schizoid Personality Disorder?" The DSM IV provides the following diagnostic criteria.

"A pervasive pattern of detachment from social relationships and a restricted range of expression of emotions in interpersonal settings, beginning by early adulthood and present in a variety of contexts, as indicated by four (or more) of the following:

1) neither desires nor enjoys close relationships, including being part of a family.
2) almost always chooses solitary activities.
3) has little, if any, interest in having sexual experiences with another person.
4) takes pleasure in few, if any, activities.
5) lacks close friends or confidants other than first-degree relatives.
6) appears indifferent to the praise or criticism of others.
7) shows emotional coldness, detachment, or flattened affectivity."

A similar category is that of Schizotypal Personality Disorder. The criteria for that diagnosis includes the following.

"A pervasive pattern of social and interpersonal deficits marked by acute discomfort with, and reduced capacity for, close relationships as well as by cognitive or perceptual distortions and eccentricities of behavior, beginning in early adulthood and present in a variety of contexts, as indicated by five (or more) of the following:

1) ideas of reference (excluding delusions of reference).
2) odd beliefs or magical thinking that influence behavior and are inconsistent with sub-cultural norms (e.g., superstitious-ness, belief in clairvoyance, telepathy, or 'sixth sense,' in children or adolescents, bizarre fantasies or preoccupations).
3) unusual perceptual experiences, including bodily illusions.
4) odd thinking and speech (e.g., vague, circumstantial, metaphorical, overelaborate, or stereotyped).
5) suspiciousness or paranoid ideation.
6) inappropriate or constricted affect.
7) behavior or appearance that is odd, eccentric, or peculiar.
8) lack of close friends or confidants other than first-degree relatives.
9) excessive social anxiety that does not diminish with familiarity and tends to be associated with paranoid fears rather than negative judgments about self."

Bateson and the Palo Alto Group

A great deal of what we now recognize as *the NLP attitude* arose from the work of anthropologist Gregory Bateson (1972) and his team who explored schizophrenia in the 1960s. Gregory Bateson, John Weakland, Paul Watzlawick, Richard Fisch, Jay Haley, and Don Jackson took a new approach to schizophrenia. They started from the presupposition that the language and behavior of the schizophrenic "made sense." Assuming that, they began inquiring about in what formative world or social environment would the schizophrenic response *make sense*. This led them to ask the context question:

"In what environment or context would these kinds of responses make sense?"

As communication theorists, they postulated that the speech and behavior of the "schizophrenic" comprises "messages" and so backtracked to the context within which such "messages" would reasonably follow. So they also inquired,

"What kind of messages would elicit these messages?"

From all of this they formulated the "double-bind theory of schizophrenia." They also offered key suggestions for working with someone with a "schizophrenic personality disorder" for the purpose of re-ordering (re-structuring) the thinking-emoting, speaking, behaving, and relating of that person.

As Bateson (1972) worked on the nature, source, and quality of schizophrenia, he explored *the learning contexts* within which such strangeness of thought-and-emotion could arise. He concluded that in schizophrenia one fails to recognize and distinguish messages of different logical typing. It involves "… the absence of meta-communicative framing" that we generally notice in dreaming, but which typically characterizes the waking communications of the schizophrenic. (p. 190)

When the schizophrenic hears a message, and does not know of *what sort or order of a message* it consists, he or she thereafter gets into *a meta-communicative tangle* by developing an imperfect ability to discriminate the typing of the messages. In a now classic and seminal paper entitled, "Toward a Theory of Schizophrenia," Bateson wrote the following.

> Our approach is based on that part of communications theory which Russell has called the Theory of Logical Types. The central thesis of this theory is that there is a discontinuity between a class and its members. The class cannot be a member of itself nor can one of the members *be* the class, since the term used for the class is of a *different level of abstraction*—a different Logical Type—from terms used for members. Although in formal logic there is an attempt to maintain this discontinuity between a class and its members, we argue that in the psychology of real communications this discontinuity is continually and inevitably breached, and that a priori we must expect a pathology to occur in the human organism when certain formal patterns of the breaching occur in the communication between mother and child. We shall argue that this pathology at its extreme will have symptoms whose formal characteristics would lead the pathology to be classed as a schizophrenia. (pp. 202–203)

Because the person suffering from schizophrenia cannot discern logical levels, he or she also cannot tell "where he stands" with other people. This confusion becomes especially important in relation to an emotionally significant and/or powerful person. So when that person sends out contradictory messages, the person doesn't know what to do with it. The context of the schizophrenic involves a relational/conceptual world that forbids him or her from "going meta" to the frame-of-reference within which the messages occur. This locks the person in at a primary level with no context markers for knowing "how to understand" the events that transpire. So the person feels "crazy." He or she receives "yes" messages and "no" messages, but cannot sort them out.

Analogously, it means living in a world where one gets lots of faxes and emails, but no meta-information at the top of the sheets regarding *the sender, his or her purpose, time frame, subject, address, etc.* And if that lack of reference would confuse a person, then one begins to get faxes and emails contradicting the first emails, and then more contradicting those, etc.

Now since this *breaching* of the formal logical levels shows up in such communicational modes as humor, play, non-play, fantasy, sacrament, metaphor, etc., understanding *how messages and meta-messages interact* enables us to understand and work with such breaching. In other words, we not only send messages to each other, we send out messages-about-our-messages (meta-messages) to signal each other about *how to take us* and the sort of messages we send. Such meta-messages consist of a higher logical type than the messages they classify. And this *framing of messages and actions* "reaches considerable complexity" in us humans, *yet* "our vocabulary for such discrimination is still very poorly developed." (p. 203)

For Bateson, Don Jackson, Jay Haley, and John Weakland, who made this original analysis and offered their theory of schizophrenia, *the double bind* comprises the heart of the pathology. This not only involves messages and meta-messages, an intense relationship, a message of fear and/or danger plus a conflicting message of love and/or safety but most importantly, a tertiary message *about* those messages to *not* ask for clarification(!)

A tertiary negative injunction prohibiting the victim from escaping from the field. (p. 207)

The result of this?

We hypothesize that there will be a breakdown in an individual's ability to discriminate between Logical Types whenever a double bind situation occurs. (p. 208)

As an overview, we here have a picture of human subjectivity, both those forms that involve some of the most intense pathology and dysfunction—schizophrenia. In this we have a portrait of *the structure of that subjectivity* involving logical types or levels.

In fact, we cannot understand, identify, model, or replicate such human experiences without understanding the role of logical levels, frames, and meta-frames, messages and meta-messages, etc., and using such levels in replicating such. In other words, without building in the *meta-position* or *meta-move* in our strategies, we cannot accurately model those forms of human subjectivity that involve layers of learning about learning, thinking about thinking, states about states, etc.

For Bateson, the symptoms that we call "schizophrenia" involve a special case of epistemological error. The person has "learned" that response, and within its own contexts, it makes sense. But at a larger level, it doesn't make sense because it has failed to "go meta" and recognize the existence of logical levels.

Part of the context then that creates a schizophrenic response involves *the inability to meta-communicate*. As a result, the person lacks the ability to tell or discern the sort or order of message. The person then sequences his or her thinking-perceiving in a way that prevents the schizophrenic from being able to pick up the more abstract labels which most of us use conventionally (although we may not be able to tell how we make our discriminations).

Among the formal characteristics of the communication environment wherein a person would not learn to discriminate logical levels the following:

1) The person does not have permission or skill in meta-communicating.

2) The person constantly finds him or herself put "in the wrong" about identifying messages.

3) The person lives in a context where another constantly attacks them when he or she recognizes the message-identifying signals—those signals without which we dare not discriminate fact from fantasy or the literal from the metaphoric. (p. 199) No matter what the person does, it is a "no win" situation.

It is to this double-bind that persons develop the responses that we designate as schizophrenic symptoms.

In the past, psychological models have described the schizophrenic as having "weak ego function." They lack "the process of discriminating communicational modes either within the self or between the self and others" (p. 205). So the schizophrenic "exhibits weakness" in functioning in the communicational realm of identifying the correct mode of messages. By way of contrast, normal persons use *context* as a guide for mode discrimination and they learn this from the characteristic patterns. But not so for the schizophrenic. The person must live in a universe where the sequences of events where his or her unconventional communicational habits operate in some sense as appropriate (i.e. appropriate to the double-bind situation).

Replicating the Personality Disorder

If *a model* works, then if we follow the strategy for sequencing our sensory representations and imagine a context wherein we have lots of motivation to so perform, then we could replicate the structure of that subjective human experience. Let's see if this works.

Suppose a mother has a mental map from her history that makes her feel anxious when her child initiates closeness, bonding, connectedness, intimacy, etc. She operates from a frame that prevents her from experiencing such closeness. That then operates as the beginning context. Then, let's imagine that she typically with-draws when the child responds to her as a loving mother. Further, let's suppose that the mother not only feels *anxiety and hostility* toward her child, but that at a Meta-Level she believes/feels that having such feelings is unacceptable.

"Good mothers should be close to their children."
"It's not okay to feel anger, hostility, rejection, etc. to the child."

If we further imagine that this second program operates as so strong a taboo in her that she does not recognize it consciously in herself. In other words, that she has a motivation to repress her feelings of anxiety and hostility and so will deny them and not acknowledge them.

If the mother feels loving and behaves with affection to which the child moves close, then she will then begin to feel anxious and hos-tile. She will then communicate that non-verbally to the child. She could do this in a variety of ways: by a tone, gesture, posture, etc. Yet she doesn't allow herself to entertain awareness of this. She must deny it, first to herself. Yet she must also *simulate* affection and closeness because at a deeper level, the other feelings do not allow them to arise. Now this later experience of assimilated affec-tion exists on a different logical order than the former message (her feelings of anxiety and hostility). It operates as a message *about* the former experience.

Figure 13.1

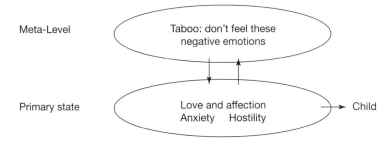

While the mother uses the child's responses to affirm herself as a loving person, and simultaneously simulate these feelings, this places the child in a position where he or she must not accurately interpret the communication from the mother. For the child to maintain the relationship, something highly motivated and crucial, he or she *must not discriminate accurately* between orders of messages. The child, in fact, must systemically distort his or her perception of the meta-communicative signals (pp. 213–4). In this way, the child learns to *split* consciousness, to not "go meta," and to develop two parts or facets of "personality" that have no means of communication between them.

Now suppose the mother feels hostile and wants to withdraw. She might say to the child, "Go to bed, you're very tired and I want you to get your sleep." Overtly this may even sound loving. "Good mothers" say such things. Yet here she says it to deny another feeling, "Get out of my sight because I'm sick of you. I feel hostile toward you." What a painful reality this makes for the child. So the child has a motivated reason to *not* recognize the double-layered messages.

If the child correctly discriminated the mothers's meta-communicative signals, the child would feel threatened beyond his or her abilities to handle that level of threat. Yet a child's ego doesn't have the strength to do that. To face the fact that one's mother both does *not* want us around *and* that she doesn't speak the truth, but deceives us with her loving behavior exists as far too much for a child to handle. Such awareness demands a much more highly developed ego that can hold two contradictory thoughts at bay simultaneously, that doesn't personalize, that can abstract, etc. Such would simply overwhelm in pain a little undeveloped ego. To discriminate orders of messages accurately and then get that would essentially attach massive "pain" for discriminating and learning!

The child therefore *accepts* the idea that he feels tired rather than recognize the mother's deception. Yet in doing this, the child must *deceive* him or herself. The child must *learn* to *not know* his or her own internal state. Doing that supports the mother in her deception. To survive with her, the child must falsely discriminate his or her own internal messages as well as falsely discriminate the messages of others. This process does the damage inasmuch as the child begins to disavow his or her own reality orientation. He makes a false map, but he disconfirms his map making ability.

It *seems* on the surface benevolent that the mother defines for the child how he feels. It *seems* like overt maternal concern. But it later works havoc in the personality. As the mother does this, she essentially controls the child's definitions of his own feelings, thoughts, understandings, etc. This undermines the child's response-abilities for thinking, emoting, speaking, and behaving. If the child fights for his or her own assertive right to know his or her mind, "I am not tired." The mother may respond, "You don't *really* mean to say that." And given her position of power, the child may very well buy into her "reality," namely, that she does have "loving feelings for me, and that I am just tired." Yet this acceptance offers no real solution. Ultimately, it creates more problems. For accepting the false discrimination, the child pays the price of sabotaging his or her own ability to sort messages at Meta-Levels.

How could the child escape from this situation? If he or she commented on the contradictory position his mother has put him in, the child could begin to sort and separate para-messages. Bateson noted that the child must meta-communicate in order to become saved from his distortion.

> "Mom, I'm getting two very different messages from you and don't exactly know where I stand. I get the sense that you feel anxious and angry about being tied down with a little child and yet that you value thinking about yourself as a loving mother. Which message should I go with? How should I integrate these messages?"

Yet, of course, the child cannot say that. Many adults don't know how to say that. Fear of a counter-accusation would hold the person back even if he or she was that clear in his or her own mind. Bateson concludes,

> So by preventing the child from talking about the situation, the mother forbids him from using the meta-communicative level— the level we use to correct our perception of communication behavior. The ability to communicate about communication, to comment upon the meaningful actions of oneself and others, is essential for successful social intercourse. (p. 215)

Characteristics of this Disordering

The most striking feature of the "schizoid" personality disorder involves the person's unemotional and unmotivated style. Such people typically manifest a lack of desire for relationships, lack of empathy, constriction of affects, and so they tend to withdraw, isolate themselves, and become reclusive. We noticed this in the DSM IV's diagnostic criteria that we quoted at the beginning of this chapter.

The *term "schizoid"* arises from Greek signifying "splitting" (schizo) and "like or representing" (-oid). Traditionally, such individuals carry themselves in a quiet, shy, reserved, and withdrawing way. This personality disordering differs from the *schizotypal* (an abbreviation of "schizophrenic genotype") and from *schizophrenia* itself.

> Schizoid personality disorder is not presently identified with eventual movement into schizophrenia; rather the schizoid individual is seen as chronically reclusive and isolated. (Regina Ottaviani in Beck, 1990, p. 121)

Meta-Programs Characteristics

Those with schizoid personality disordering consider themselves observers rather than participants in the world. This leads them to over-use the *dissociative* mode. And as "self-sufficient loners" whom others experience as dull, uninteresting, unresponsive, and humorless, they use the *non-demostrative sort* in inter-personal relationships.

Cognitively, they sort *globally* and so have a vagueness to their thinking that deletes significant details and cues in their environment and in their relationships. This results in a "poverty of thoughts" as well as in "defective perceptual scanning" (Milton, 1981). As a result they simply miss many of the subtle details.

Their unresponsiveness to things indicates *the inactive sort* and leads to their lethargy and unexpressiveness in their movements and monotonous speech (Millon, 1981). Missing so many important details, which leads to a disinterest in things, and their inactive response style, they end up with poor social skills.

The overall gestalt that results from this? They find very little interest in life and so continually complain about things, events, and people as *uninteresting.* This results in anhedonia. At the cognitive-behavioral level, they use a *dampening* style whereby they can discount and de-energize things that others would find interesting.

Typically, only dramatic events tend to evoke much of an emotional response in them. The only exception to this is in demands for participation in social events. Hence Ottaviani describes their social-phobias.

> Schizoid personalities are prone to anxiety disorders when situations demand social interaction. Although typically impervious to feedback from others, they may become overwhelmed by social contact that they consider excessive. (Beck, 1990, p. 129)

Supporting Cognitive-Maps for This Way of Functioning

The following describes the automatic thoughts typical for the Schizoid personality.

> I'd rather do it myself.
> I prefer to be alone.
> I have no motivation.
> I'm just going through the motions.
> Why bother? Who cares? So what?

Such "thoughts" discount, de-energize attention, dampen motivation, and move one to avoid and isolate. No wonder the person feels so little, experiences such a paucity of emotional richness, and doesn't want to become engaged in a healing process!

Once a person gets into this state of mind-body, he or she will then inevitably *reflect on* those thoughts with more of the same kind as they bring that kind of thinking and emoting to bear on their situation (how they naturally Meta-State themselves):

I'm a misfit and defective—what's wrong with me?
It's so much trouble to deal with people—it's not worth the bother.
Because I'm empty inside—I'll never find anything exciting.
Relating to people makes life too complicated and messy, why bother?

In this way, the person applies the discounting, dampening, and de-energizing thinking to their higher level concepts of life, relationships, self, destiny, etc. These constructions describe the Meta-Level formats that organize the person's experiences, perceptions, emotions, and behaviors.

"Although usually comfortable with a detached lifestyle, these individuals may become depressed over [a Meta-Level function] their awareness that they are deviants who do not fit into society. ... Further, their belief that life is meaningless and barren [a belief in a Meta-Level abstraction] can lead to or exacerbate depression." (Beck, 1990, p. 129)

Neurologically, Millon (1981) has noted that autonomic hyperactivity, deficits in reticular formation, congenital aplasia in the limbic system, and neurotransmitter deficits have been suggested as possible causes or contributing factors to this state.

Treatment: Reordering the Disordering

Given the nature of the schizoid's lack of motivation, constriction of emotion, dampening and discounting style of cognitive distortion, etc. the first and central issue in therapy involves *engaging* him or her in the transformation process. This disordering of one's powers suggests trauma in relationships that he or she has proven to be much more distasteful, painful, unrewarding than experiences of pleasure. The cognitive and behavioral strategies of the person (discounting and isolating) suggest a neurological sensitivity to "hurt" and so a protecting of self via these strategies.

This suggests a very gentle approach by the therapist initially by aligning with the person's need for safety and protection. Then, in that context of demonstrating empathy, the therapist can begin to activate the person's ability to think less globally and more specifically.

> Since the schizoid is unattentive to the emotional details that others perceive and interpret, the therapist can ask questions to help the patient attend to these emotional details. (Beck, 1990, p. 131)

This suggests using the NLP specificity-to-abstraction scale and inviting the client to attend to things, to literally put him or herself "in" things, the literal meaning of "interest" (inter and esse, "to be"). By redirecting consciousness and attention to the specific details, this shifts the schizoid's typical consciousness of viewing things in global, non-specific ways that glazes over "the differences that make a difference."

Recording such details—details in what others say and do, details in how others seem to experience themselves, etc., enriches the client's model of the world making it less impoverishing. One may begin this by pacing their disinterest and dislike of people. "I want you to make a list of the specific things that you don't like this week."

States and Meta-States

From the state of consciousness model, the experience of the schizoid makes lots of sense. The thinking and internal representations of vagueness, discounting, de-energizing, and dampening will result in bland, boring, and uninteresting movies. Who would have much energy or engagement if the internal world consisted of very fuzzy, black-and-white B-rated movies?

From the Meta-State Model, the schizoid makes his or her experience worse by bringing states of dis-interest, meaninglessness, futility, "why bother," etc. to bear on the primary states. This needs deframing and/or outframing. So we start with the structuring: "dis-interest and unsatisfying thoughts-and-feelings about life in general" (the Meta-State of the schizoid). We could then deframe it with "doubt and skeptical questions about what the person has missed." We could outframe with a state of "interest and curiosity."

> "What a skill—this ability to become totally impervious to the thoughts and opinions of others. How do you do this? Could you teach me this skill?"

Or a therapist could Meta-State it with an ecology check.

> "When you step back even further from this overall picture of your life—the way you think-and-feel; do you experience this as a very exciting or enhancing way to live? Do you like the mental maps that enable you to think-and-feel this way? How many problems has it generated for you? Would you like to alter this and experience life more like others do?"

If the client buys this and wants to begin the transformation process, the therapist can then future-pace and Meta-State antici-pated difficulties:

> "We know from experience that certain kinds of interfering thoughts will arise in your mind and give you some problems in following this pursuit for you, right? What automatic thoughts can you count on inevitably popping up and interfering?"

This question invites the client to go meta to the meta-structures—identify the cognitive-emotional distortions and prepare to deal with them.

Schizotypal Personality Disorder

Characteristics: This pervasive pattern of deficits in interpersonal relations involves peculiarities in ideation, appearance, and behavior. The DSM requires five of the following to make a diag-nosis of a person having a schizotypal personality disorder.

1) Ideas of reference.
2) Excessive social anxiety.
3) Odd beliefs or magical thinking.

4) Unusual perceptual experiences.
5) Odd or eccentric behavior or appearance.
6) No close friends or confidants (or only one) other than first-degree relatives.
7) Odd speech.
8) Inappropriate or constricted affect.
9) Suspiciousness or paranoid ideation.

The most striking feature in this disordering involves the oddities of cognition. These include "ideas of reference" which means believing that unrelated events are related to them in significant ways. Also lots of suspiciousness and paranoia, magical thinking—that others can read their minds, and illusions. They may think they can read others' minds, see people in shadows, etc. From this disordering of reality testing and distorting cognitions comes odd speech (i.e., tangential, circumstantial, vague, or over-elaborate).

Meta-Programs and Meta-Model Distinctions

Since at the heart of this disorder lie "oddities of cognition", recognizing these explains the subsequent responses in speech and emotion.

"Many schizotypals will engage in the cognitive distortions of emotional reasoning and personalization. In emotional reasoning, a person believes that because he or she feels a negative emotion, there must be a corresponding negative external situation. With personalization, the individual believes that he or she is responsible for external situations when this is not the case. These patients are often very concrete, and are unable to assess accurately the probability of an imagined outcome." (Ottaviani in Beck, 1990, p. 138)

Thus, *intuiting* the world via their emotions, these individuals jump to the conclusion that their feelings/emotions always and only (universal quantifier) tell them the truth. So they trust their intuitions and believe them over sense-experience (sensors). This undermines their ability to do "reality testing" or to develop what we call "ego strength." Using the over-responsibility sort, they interpret things "personally" and immediately associate into that position, blaming themselves.

Their strategy for coping involves isolating and withdrawing. Yet as they do, they increase their risk of losing what reality testing others could have provided for them. As they become more and more odd in their thinking, talking, and behavior, their social inappropriateness increases. This makes for more isolation and gives room for more fantasy.

Therapeutic Strategy: Reordering the Disordering

Establishing rapport and trust plays a crucial role as does offering a structured process so that they can learn to reign in their tangential thinking. Along with some social skills training, a therapist must begin with building up more and more ability and skill in reality testing. This means recognizing "thoughts" and "emotions" as just thoughts and emotions—and not reality, not the territory. It means to shift from personalizing and emotionalizing to thinking more objectively about one's thoughts (a Meta-State).

A patient who sometimes thinks of himself as "not real," will need to learn how to recognize that thought and then evaluate it. What evidence do I have for this? What do others say? Then to discount it as having no objective evidence. Beck suggests the use of pre-designed *coping statements* that the client can rehearse such as, "There I go again. Even though I'm thinking this thought, that doesn't make it real or true." Here a person Meta-States him or herself with a higher level realization of "thoughts" as just that— internal representations.

Such individuals can develop more awareness of their thoughts by noticing them, recording them, and then keeping track of their predictions. If one suddenly has a thought of some vividly imagined terrible thing going to happen (paranoid ideation), the person can write this down and make a prediction. Later, they can record what actually happened.

Together a therapist can help the person identify his or her cognitive style and then develop adequate responses to help manage and control such. Those who go too global and end up with only vague impressions can learn to specify. Those who lose their point in over-elaborate going over and over extraneous details can learn to summarize and condense.

Since mind-reading typically goes along with the schizotypal disordering, the therapist should assist the person to learn to challenge such, to recognize their intuiting, personalizing, and emotionalizing, and build up cues so that they can shift to looking for evidence and getting collaborative witness from others.

Such persons can learn to recognize the danger of isolating, giving in to too much fantasy, and the importance of social skills and appropriateness.

With all of that in mind, let me now turn the pen over to Richard and Margot.

Schizophrenic Personalities

In 1973 psychologist D.L. Rosenhan published a study in which his psychology students went to prestigious Psychiatric hospitals in their community and claimed to have one symptom out of the ordinary (e.g. hearing a voice in their head). They were all admitted, and most were diagnosed schizophrenic, although in every way apart from their one symptom they behaved normally. After one week, they reported the symptom gone and asked to be discharged. Their experiment was over.

Unfortunately, the hospitals would not release them. They would not that is until Rosenhan rang up and explained the situation. Rosenhan told the hospitals there were others who had not been named, who were in the experiment. Within a few days the hospitals found and released other patients whom they now realized were sane, although in fact there were no more psychology students (Rosenhan, 1973). These other patients, apparently as sane as Rosenhan's students, would otherwise have remained under treatment, diagnosed as having lifelong "incurable" illnesses. There may or may not be a real thing called schizophrenia. But at the very least, all that glitters is not gold.

The West's Most Expensive "Disease"

Schizophrenia is the most frequently discussed of the psychoses (disorders where the person is assessed by psychiatrists as out of touch with reality). Many psychiatrists consider that there may in fact be a number of different and overlapping syndromes which are being described under the one label of "schizophrenia" (Perris, 1989, p. 4). Perhaps one of the clearest areas of agreement though, is that schizophrenia represents a separate disorder entirely from split or multiple personality, with which it has previously been confused in the public mind. We can perhaps best describe schizophrenia as a disorder of thought and perception.

The DSM-IV lists its symptoms as delusions, hallucinations, disorganized speech, disorganized behavior or immobility, and loss of emotion or will. To be diagnosed, two of these symptoms need to be present in such a way as to damage achievement in social, career or self care areas, over at least 6 months duration. This requirement has been included partially as a result of concern over studies such as Rosenhan's (above).

The cost of current schizophrenia treatments is enormous. In the United States 0.5% of the gross national product goes into the treatment of schizophrenia (World Health Organization, 1996, p. 3).

In Canada (and probably elsewhere in the west) 8% of all hospital beds are taken up by people with this diagnosis, using up more hospital beds than any other single disorder (Long, 1997). 6.2% of prisoners in US jails have been diagnosed schizophrenic, and an estimated one in three homeless persons suffers from the condition (Kopelowicz and Liberman, 1998, p. 192).

Schizophrenia is not often enjoyable. Depression and self medication with drugs or alcohol are common amongst those diagnosed, and are associated with poorer chances of improvement. 25% of schizophrenics attempt suicide, and 10% succeed (Kopelowicz and Liberman, 1998, p. 192).

What Gets Someone Diagnosed Schizophrenic?

Cognitive research shows that in persons diagnosed schizophrenic, there are major problems with cognitive strategies (Perris, 1989, pp. 22–23).

1) Living in castles in the air

In NLP terms, we associate schizophrenia with a person having difficulty in "chunking down" (Perris, 1989, p. 43, pp. 148–151, p. 157, and Arieti, 1948). The person with this problem does not identify the distinctions between situations fully. Rather than chunk down to the sensory specific details of a problem event, they talk about it vaguely or metaphorically.

One client, discussing this very problem with the authors, said "Some days it hurts when I walk on the earth. I need to keep up in the air."

This illustrates the metaphorical communication. I might say that same sentence metaphorically, but this young man experienced it as a sensory fact. He was unable to explain what days, specifically, or how specifically it hurt, but he believed it to be true in the same way that one might say, "Some days my legs are a little stiff in the morning, and I need to stretch them out and exercise."

He believed that at times he physically floated in the air because the ground was too painful. We might say that this man was unfamiliar with meta-modeling his experience, with indexing it specifically. Having a conversation with someone diagnosed schizophrenic can be like immersing oneself in a festival of Milton Model patterns (i.e., mind reading, layered presuppositions, lost performatives, deletions, nominalizations, etc.). We have often had the experience where one sentence said by a client takes 15 minutes to carefully unpack before we can actually move on usefully.

One person came up to Richard at the start of a training day and said "Thank you so much for what you did last night. It was beautiful." Yet Richard had not had any contact with her the previous evening.

On another occasion, a client told us "I know what you are doing here. I know you've called down Pavlov's dogs."

In Ericksonian terms, the person diagnosed schizophrenic is experiencing a profound trance state (Donan, 1985, pp. 27–28). It's a standard joke in Psychiatry that neurotics build castles in the air, whereas psychotics actually live in them (and Psychiatrists collect the rent!).

2) Not thinking about thinking

The person diagnosed schizophrenic is often also unable to adequately classify situations from a meta-position. For example, they are not able to distinguish a real memory from a hallucinated one, or an internal thought from an external voice. Many cognitive psychologists consider this to be the core of the disorder (see Jacobs, 1980). Much of such meta-commenting on experience in "non-psychotic" persons is done using the auditory digital sense. This sense is the one most commonly experienced as "out of control" by the person diagnosed schizophrenic.

Contrary to popular belief, the most common form of hallucination in schizophrenia is auditory, and "uncontrollable" internal thoughts are also a frequent complaint of persons diagnosed schizophrenic. We would describe this in NLP as the person diagnosed schizophrenic lacking in adequate submodality distinctions between real and unreal, self and other etc. In a sense, the schizophrenic person is well dissociated from their internal experience (so that their own thoughts may not feel like "theirs"). But this dissociation is not a clear meta-position.

To use Hall's terminology (Hall, 1997), we might say that schizophrenia is a disorder resulting from the failure to develop adequate Meta-States. In discussing this with Michael, he pointed out that this view of schizophrenia has references back to the Bicameral theory of Julian Jaynes (1976).

Jaynes proposed that until quite recently in human history, most people experienced much of their auditory digital self talk as coming from real, externally existing voices (e.g., the voices of the "gods") and acted accordingly. He proposed that these external voices might be generated in the non-dominant hemisphere (though we now know that the person experiencing auditory hallucination has the "normal" speech areas of the brain active).

For our discussion, the important claim Jaynes made was that during most of human history, "hallucinated" voices were not meta-commented on by the hearer, but were accepted as the result of separately existing minds. This capacity is often rediscovered by the person diagnosed schizophrenic, says Ryan DeMares (1998) who describes his own experiences with auditory hallucination using Jaynes model.

3) Missing social subtleties

Interpersonally, people diagnosed schizophrenic behave much like you would if you were unexpectedly placed in a totally foreign culture. Their attempts to communicate subtly mismatch the cultural norms. Often they mistakenly assume that others share their own unique sensory experiences, values, beliefs, and Meta-Programs. They may use "socially unexpected" gestures, body postures, proximity, facial expressions, voice tonality and phrasings, without apparently noticing that these meta-communications appear or sound odd to others.

Such mismatching is so profoundly culturally determined that we as authors doubt the ability of a person from one culture to diagnose schizophrenia accurately in a person from another culture. People who move from one culture to another are in fact far more likely to be diagnosed schizophrenic (Pomare and de Boer, 1988, p. 120).

On the other hand, many people working with schizophrenia note that their own way of diagnosing the condition is not primarily by the classical symptoms but by the very strange feeling that they get when they are with the person diagnosed this way. This feeling is described as a "lack of affective resonance" (Perris, 1989, p. 5), and equates, in our experience, with the person diagnosed schizophrenic having great difficulty using socially normal rapport skills. Often, this difficulty emerges quite early in life, and some cognitive psychologists consider its effects on the parent-child relationship to be central in the development of schizophrenia (Perris, 1989, pp. 33–34).

It leaves the person especially vulnerable to confusion in any situation that involves meta-communication. An example is the "double bind" identified by Gregory Bateson (Perris, 1989, pp. 51–54), where a person might for example say to the client, "Come and give me a hug" while grimacing at the client with anxiety. Research has since shown that most families generate double binds, but the person diagnosed schizophrenic cannot process the two communications from a meta-position.

4) Other Symptoms

In persons diagnosed schizophrenic, there is also often a reduced attention span, reduced memory, impaired goal achievement skill, flattened emotional response, and reduced ability to learn from verbal sources (while visual and kinesthetic skills seem relatively good). This cluster of disabling symptoms could be considered the result of the primary difficulty meta-commenting and meta-modeling.

Schizophrenia often is first diagnosed when the person has an "acute" or "florid" state where delusions, confused activity and hallucinations are marked. This acute state often occurs in response to some social stress (such as starting a new job), and more fully approximates common expectations of "insanity." A prolonged cognitive confusion and social "ineptness" is the more fundamental pattern out of which this florid state emerges. Medication often reduces the florid state without affecting the core problems at all.

Personal Strengths

In the *Personal Strengths model*, when you hear clients tell you that they can't touch the ground, or that they know you're sending energy beams to attack them, recognize that such clients are demonstrating skill with chunking up and dissociating from experience.

Figure 13.2

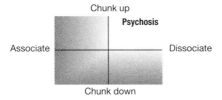

Causes?

Schizophrenia Societies, often set up as support groups for families of schizophrenics, are not always a reliable source of information about schizophrenia. In their drive to remove blame from families, they have frequently publicized erroneous and reductionist claims about the biological origins of the disorder.

For example, most say that schizophrenia is a disorder seen in the same prevalence throughout the world. World Health Organization statistics show that schizophrenia does not occur equally around the world. When diagnosed with the same careful standards, its prevalence ranges from one in a thousand, in many non-western countries, to one in a hundred in the west. Many non-industrialized societies have no incidence whatsoever (Kleinman, 1991).

Within western society, it is dramatically more prevalent in cities. A recent Danish study followed up 1,750,000 people born to Danish women between 1935 and 1978 (Mortensen *et al.,* 1999). In this group there were 2669 cases of diagnosed schizophrenia. The "population attributable risk" was 5.5% for a family history of schizophrenia, and 34.6% for having an urban place of birth. That is, living in the city has over six times more effect on the development of the disorder than genetics and family upbringing combined.

Even season of birth was twice as significant as family and genetic factors (the highest risk births are in late winter; February–March). The social and physical environment in which a person is raised is extremely significant in the development of the problem. It now seems clear that some kind of vulnerability from family/genetic and perinatal (around birth) factors leads to schizophrenia in the presence of social stresses which occur far more in some cultures than others.

Recovery rates from schizophrenia also vary depending on where people live. World Health Organization studies show that in Nigeria, 58% of diagnosed schizophrenics fully recover within two years, and in India 50% recover within two years. In Denmark, only 8% recover within two years, despite having vastly more drug treatment. (Jablensky *et al.,* 1992). Nonetheless, if we follow up even western people with "well diagnosed and severe forms of schizophrenia" we find that within 20–30 years a full 50% will be functioning normally (Kopelowicz and Liberman, 1998, p. 191).

Schizophrenia is certainly not usually a lifelong disorder. Most people with schizophrenia will recover fully. Western levels of drug treatment do not enhance their recovery (and may inhibit it). Family and social support, as well as simplicity of lifestyle, are clearly associated with more successful outcomes. With support, a calm lifestyle, and helpful feedback, the person diagnosed as schizophrenic will learn new skills which fully resolve their "problem".

There are differences in the child development of people who will later be diagnosed schizophrenic (Jones, *et al.,* 1994). The British national child development study followed up almost all children born in Britain in one week in March 1959. From these, 17,000 individuals diagnosed schizophrenic have now been identified, and their childhood results studied.

At age 7, these children had unusual difficulties pronouncing words and reading. At 11, they had less hemispheric dominance than the rest of the population (they could just as easily tick squares with their left as with their right hand). This suggests that something unusual is happening in the "schizophrenic" brain long before it is identified as unusual, impairing the auditory digital sense in particular.

New brain scan studies are beginning to shed further light on the differences. When a person diagnosed schizophrenic is having an auditory hallucination, the area of their brain called Broca's area is active (as shown on PET scan; Barnaby, 1995). This is true also for a "normal" person as they talk to themselves. But interestingly, if the "normal" person imagines an "alien" voice talking to them, a region of the temporal lobe is activated to monitor and distinguish between internal-external speech. This area is not activated by the brain of the person experiencing an auditory hallucination. Note that none of this tells us "how" these problems emerge. We know that they emerge more in the countryside than in the city, more in Europe than in Africa.

People also have different opinions about the precipitating factors that lead to the acute symptoms of schizophrenia. Those diagnosed schizophrenic tend to describe their primary concerns as involving identity and fundamental beliefs about life; issues which may well be raised more intensely in industrialized city environments.

Psychiatrist Peter Breggin says

> so called schizophrenics, especially during their initial crisis, almost always are preoccupied with the meaning of life, God, love and their own personal identity, often with cataclysmic implications about the end of the world or the disintegration of their own personalities.

He says that their metaphorical communication and behavior "can be understood as conflicts or confusion about … identities, values and aspirations rather than as biological aberrations." In a sense, the issues which the person is struggling with are meta-commenting issues.

Medication, Anyone?

Since 1954 a large number of medications have been used to treat the symptoms of schizophrenia. In general, American studies show that, given a placebo, about 20% of people diagnosed schizophrenic will have their perceptual symptoms such as hallucinations disappear (Sheitman, *et al.*, 1998, p. 168). Treatment with "anti-psychotic" drugs pushes this percentage up to around 60%, but does not generally affect the other symptoms of thought disorder and lack of interest in life.

Furthermore, it is important to understand that the extra 40% who benefit in this way from the drugs have only been given temporary relief. If they stop taking the drugs, their symptoms are likely to return. For this reason, we wish to emphasize that those on anti-psychotic medication should not come off that medication without medical supervision. On the other hand, several studies show that those treated with placebo show greater clinical improvement and less overall functional disturbance than those treated with anti-psychotic drugs (Breggin, 1992, pp. 77–83). In one study re-admission rates for those given placebo were 8%, compared to readmission rates of 47% for those given the actual medication.

The other concern with drug treatment is that typical anti-psychotic drugs are associated with long term brain damage. The 1986 Manual of Clinical Psychopharmacology says that the brain damage of tardive dyskinesia occurs in 50–60% of chronic users of these drugs. The June 1990 Clinical Psychiatry news updates this, saying that exposure for 15 years or more leads to "almost certain" tardive dyskinesia. (Breggin, 1992, p. 95). This causes the odd rocking motions, tremors, bizarre postures and twisting tongue movements we often imagine as features of long term psychiatric clients. It's the clinical end result of interfering with the flow of dopamine and other neuro-chemicals between the lower brain and the frontal lobes of the brain, a process which could be termed chemical lobotomy.

Long-term stays in the hospital environment are also clearly unhelpful in the treatment of schizophrenia. When someone is admitted for acute schizophrenia, assigning them to an 11 day hospital treatment with follow-up, this leaves them with better results than a 60 day hospital treatment with the same follow-up. Social functioning even two years later is better for those who return to normal support networks in the community (Kopelowicz and Liberman, 1998, p. 202).

Traditional psychodynamically oriented therapy (exploring the "causes" of the person's problems and their unconscious "dynamics") has also been shown to have little or even adverse effects on the course of schizophrenia, although occasional, rare cases of sudden success do occur, with any treatment tried, perhaps because they would have occurred anyway (Kopelowicz and Liberman, 1998, p. 202 and Perris, 1989, pp. 64–69).

Modeling Sanity in Insane Places

Surely, you might be thinking, someone will have studied how the vast majority of people diagnosed schizophrenic are recovering. Surely, someone will be organizing rural retreats with a promise of 50% recovery in two years. Not quite. However, there is increasing evidence that approaches based on cognitive and social education are successful in increasing the percentage of complete "cure."

What has been shown to work? Studies beginning in the 1960s show that behavior therapy (giving rewards for "appropriate behaviors") produce change in the in-patient situation, but the gains prove very difficult to transfer to community life where the rewards are no longer controlled (Kopelowicz and Liberman, 1998, p. 197). Training in Community Living programs (where training in life skills and direct assistance is given to people living in the community) have resulted in increased social functioning and less readmission.

Training in social skills combined with family assistance often reduces readmission to zero (Kopelowicz and Liberman, 1998, pp. 200–203). Training in the cognitive functions which are damaged in schizophrenia (attention span, verbal learning, memory, etc.) and training in identification of perceptual distortions (such as hallucinations) has been successful, but there is as yet little evidence that it affects social interaction and other outcomes. Shifting to teaching new skills by using the (unimpaired) visual and kinesthetic senses has also been tried with some success (Kopelowicz and Liberman, 1998, pp. 198–199, 205).

Traditionally, therapists have avoided the use of hypnosis with persons diagnosed psychotic, on the grounds that it may increase their dependency and confusion. As with depression, psychosis need not be considered a contraindication for hypnosis; rather it is an indication to use hypnosis educationally, to build inner resources, and to pace and lead the person carefully to reality based experiences.

Joan Murray-Jobsis (previously publishing under the name Joan Scagnelli-Jobsis; see Scagnelli-Jobsis, 1982) has reviewed the literature on the use of hypnosis with psychosis, and proposed a (non-Ericksonian) model of assisting the person to learn new ways of responding to life. She notes that while some studies find that persons diagnosed psychotic do not respond to hypnosis, others find that they respond normally, and still others find that they respond with a wider than normal variation. Ericksonian therapists have pointed out that arises because the person diagnosed psychotic is already in a deep trance state (Dolan, 1985, p. 128).

In the history of Ericksonian and Neuro-Linguistic psychotherapy, there has been a range of interventions used with people diagnosed schizophrenic. The anecdotal and research evidence from these suggests several useful strategies to assist the person in creating the type of successful change that naturally occurs in over 50% of "schizophrenics" world-wide.

Rapport: the Medium is the Message

From the core issues that we have identified, our goals with the person diagnosed schizophrenic will typically include helping them:

1) Chunk down,

2) Make meta-distinctions about their thinking (to "reality check", as it's called in Psychiatry),

3) Learn rapport skills.

Unfortunately, when we meet these people, *their* goals will often be chunked up, unrealistic and totally out of rapport with everyone around them. Yet if we respond to these chunked up, confused and mismatched goals by imposing our "vision" of sanity, we respond insanely (in an unrealistic and mismatched way) to the people who need sanity most. A therapist is unlikely to "win an argument" with a schizophrenic client about what is real. While you may choose to make it clear that you do not yourself perceive and believe what the client perceives and believes, it remains important to respect their "map of the world." The most successful initial move must convey powerfully your intention to get rapport with the client.

Many of the accounts of successful therapy with persons diagnosed schizophrenic begin with dramatic rapport building. Dr Karl Whitaker gives an interesting example of such an approach:

> "For instance, in one first interview with a family with a schizophrenic girl, I turned to the girl after I'd been talking fairly emptily with the parents and asked, "What are you here for?"
>
> She said, "Contact is good for colds."
>
> I said, "How long have your parents been cold?"
>
> And she said, "Twenty years."
>
> We went on talking schizophrenese like this without any hesitation." (Haley and Hoffman, 1967, p. 272).

Here Whitaker used the girl's own chunked up and dissociated (metaphorical) style of communication.

Yvonne Dolan identifies a similar pattern in the work of Milton Erickson (Dolan, 1985, pp. 58–61). One case involved a man who had only spoken six sensible words in the five years he was in hospital. Otherwise he spoke in "word salad"—a long jumble of sounds, words and syllables in no apparent order. Psychiatrists, nurses and others made numerous unsuccessful attempts to talk to him, or even find out his full name (his six words included "My name is George").

To begin, Erickson had his secretary record, in shorthand, a sample of the man's "speech". Erickson then studied this sample until he could improvise a word salad similar in form. Now he was ready. He sat down next to George and introduced himself. George spat out an angry stream of word salad. Erickson replied with an equally long stream of the same type of noise. George appeared puzzled and added more word salad, and Erickson responded in kind.

A few days later Erickson returned and again George spoke in word salad, this time for four hours. Erickson, aware that George was watching a clock on the wall facing them, replied in kind for another four hours, missing his lunch. George listened carefully, and they then traded another two hours. The next day George gave only two sentences of word salad. After Erickson returned his own two sentences, George did an extraordinary thing. In plain English, he said, "Talk sense Doctor!"

"Certainly, I'll be glad to. What is your last name?" Erickson asked.

"O'Donavan, and it's about time somebody who knows how to talk asked. Over five years in this lousy joint ..." and he lapsed back into word salad. But this was the breakthrough. A few months later, George O'Donavan left the hospital and found himself a job. Erickson followed his progress for some years and he was not readmitted.

Erickson's Pace and Lead to Sanity

Jeffrey Zeig identifies a sequencing in Milton Erickson's work (Erickson, M.H. and Zeig, J. "Symptom Prescription for Expanding the Psychotic's World View" in Rossi 1980), Erickson explains:

> No two people necessarily have the same ideas, but all people will defend their ideas whether they are psychotically based or culturally based, or nationally based or personally based: When you understand how man really defends his intellectual ideas and how emotional he gets about it, you should realize that the first thing in psychotherapy is not to try to compel him to change his ideation; rather, you go along with it and change it in a gradual fashion and create situations wherein he himself willingly changes his thinking. I think my first real experiment in psychotherapy occurred in

1930. A patient in Worcester State Hospital, in Massachusetts, demanded he be locked in his room, and he spent his time anxiously and fearfully winding string around the bars of the window of the room. He knew his enemies were going to come in and kill him, and the window was the only opening. The thick iron bars seemed to him to be too weak, so he reinforced them with string.

I went into the room and helped him reinforce the iron bars with string. In doing so, I discovered that there were cracks in the floor and suggested that those cracks ought to be stuffed with newspaper so that there was no possibility (of his enemies getting him), and then I discovered cracks around the door that should be stuffed with newspaper, and gradually I got him to realize that the room was only one of a number of rooms on the ward, and to accept the attendants as a part of his defense against his enemies; and then the hospital itself as a part of his defense against his enemies; and then the Board of Mental Health of Massachusetts as part, and then the police system—the governor. And then I spread it to adjoining states and finally I made the United States a part of his defense system; this enabled him to dispense with the locked door because he had so many other lines of defense. I didn't try to correct his psychotic idea that his enemies would kill him. I merely pointed out that he had an endless number of defenders. The result was: the patient was able to accept ground privileges and wander around the grounds safely. He ceased his frantic endeavors. He worked in the hospital shops and was much less of a problem. (pp. 335–337)

The same pattern is clear in the work of Doctor Patch Adams (Adams, 1998) as seen in the film *Patch Adams* staring Robin Williams. Himself a client in a Psychiatric hospital, Adams helps his roommate Rudy to deal with his terror of hostile chipmunks (which no-one else can see, but which prevent Rudy getting to the toilet or leaving his room). After acknowledging that he himself cannot see the chipmunks, Adams achieves success by joining Rudy in an imaginary shootout with them.

Zeig cautions:

If such an initial intervention were made in a sarcastic manner, or from a frame of reference of trying to trick the patient out of his symptom, the positive outcome would be limited. An attitude of empathy and respect on the part of the therapist is crucial to ensure successful change. (In Rossi, 1980, p. 336)

He explains,

This pattern can be divided into three major elements, which occur in the following sequence: (1) meeting the patient where the patient is; (2) establishing small modifications that are consistent with, and follow from, the patient's behavior and understandings; and (3) eliciting behaviors and understandings from the patient in a manner that allows the patient to initiate change.

What if you're not Erickson?

Erickson and Adams were both willing to go to considerable lengths to pace the metaphorical world of their clients. The same basic principle can still be applied where ethical or personality restraints inhibit you from talking word salad or shooting chipmunks with your client.

Steve Lankton gives a great example in his work with a client named Greg (Lankton and Lankton, 1986, pp. 128–135). Greg believed that the doctors at his hospital were killing people for experimentation purposes. He had never dated (he had decided that he wouldn't date until he had a Master's degree), and he couldn't read or write. But that isn't why he came to see Steve Lankton. He came because he wanted to be an ambassador. Lankton took on this goal. In twice weekly, three-hour trance sessions, he had Greg practice reading and writing.

One of the first things he had Greg do outside the therapy sessions was to go to a restaurant and order two desserts. After this he was to write a report on the two desserts. After all, one of the things an ambassador has to do is take out other diplomats and be able to tastefully recommend a dessert. In this way, Lankton had followed Erickson's model of

1) meeting the patient where the patient is;

2) establishing small modifications that are consistent with, and follow from, the patient's behavior and understandings; and

3) eliciting new behaviors and understandings. At the time Lankton was writing this, Greg had a Master's degree in Administration and Policy, and an MBA.

Another example of entering the client's model of the world with respect is given by Richard Bandler in his work with Andy (videotapes of his three sessions with Andy have been published by NLP Comprehensive). Bandler recounts the story thus (Bandler, 1993, pp. 107–108):

"One schizophrenic I worked with hallucinated people coming out of the television set and following him around. Think about that. When I heard this, I said, 'Wow! That's great!'

He looked at me and said, 'What do you mean it's great?'

I said, 'Well, what do you watch?'

He said, 'Little House on the Prairie.'

On that show there's a snippy little bitch named Mary. She kept coming out of the screen and following this guy around going, 'Aarrhh, aarrhh, aarrhh' just like she does on the program. She would bitch and moan until he would freak out and start screaming. Of course he was a paranoid schizophrenic! I said to him, 'This is a multi-million-dollar disorder!'

The guy looked at me and said, 'What are you talking about?'

I said, 'Does the term "Playboy Channel" mean anything to you?' I said, 'Think about it. We could run courses and train traveling salesmen in this. They could be monogamous and have the best time they ever had. This is a multi-million-dollar disorder that would give people the ability to never be lonely again.'

> I told him, 'I want to know how to do this.' And this guy, who had spent five years trying to get rid of a problem, began by saying, 'Well, maybe I'll tell you and maybe I won't.'
>
> Now that shows a changed attitude."

In this case, Bandler did not claim that the people coming out of the television are "real"—merely that seeing them could be useful. In this he offered a reframe. In the same way, Yvonne Dolan describes reframing episodes of catatonic immobility as a great way for a client to give himself some space. This results in the client almost immediately reducing his catatonic sessions from 4–5 hours down to 15 minutes at a time, and then even discovering that he could talk while still "giving himself some space." (Dolan, 1985, pp. 90–106)

This pacing and reframing of the "problem" can be done very lightly. When a therapist demonstrates that they can understand the inner world of the client, they do not have to talk as if they are stepping on eggshells. Carlo Perris encourages therapists who are challenging schizophrenic cognition to lighten up.

If the client claims their disorder is "always there" for example, he asks, "Do you mean you are crazy even when asleep?" When a client says during a phone call that she had previously believed that she was telepathic, but is now over the delusion, Perris says, "Then you could have saved the cost of the telephone call and got in touch with me telepathically." While arguing with the person's "delusions" is clearly counterproductive, aligning with the person to consider the delusions light-heartedly can be very effective. It communicates that the therapist is willing to "act normally" around the client. (Perris, 1989, pp. 141, 138)

Building Rapport with Metaphorical Communication

As mentioned earlier, schizophrenic communication itself can be thought of as metaphorical. Yvonne Dolan discusses the therapeutic use of metaphor with psychotic clients (1985, pp. 128–140). Her goals include relaxing the person, providing a context to intersperse positive suggestions, and allowing the client to respond to suggestions at their own pace.

She emphasizes two practical points about telling metaphors to persons diagnosed schizophrenic. The first is that being relaxed and confident yourself is a crucial starting place. The ability of psychotic clients to "pick up" anxiety or incongruity in therapists and others (their sensory acuity) is well known. The second point is that the topic of a metaphor told to a schizophrenic client is most usefully an actual life event, rather than a "fairy tale" or fantastical/theoretical story.

Dolan gives an example of her work with a client named Nathan, whose first psychotic episode had happened when he was 17 years old. Nathan hallucinated an experience where he received a message saying, "Your future is your past."

He believed that this showed that he was going backwards in life, and became extremely anxious and obsessed about this. Dolan told him a story about another therapist, Kate, who had lived out in the country when she was 17. At this time, her parents went away for the weekend, leaving her with instructions not to use the family car to go to a party. Kate and her friends eventually found a way to get to the party without it registering on the car's odometer. They drove carefully backwards on the quiet country roads. Dolan (1985) emphasized:

> You know country roads, so you know that you can carefully and very comfortably go pretty far backwards while going in the actual direction in which you really want and need to go forward. (p. 136)

Immediately after being told this story, Nathan got his first good night's sleep since his hallucinated experience. His obsession stopped from that point.

The basic principle of therapy with clients diagnosed schizophrenic is the same as with all clients: to pace and lead. So far, we have considered four main ways of doing this:

- *Accept the client's metaphorical communication,* and enter into it with them, e.g. Erickson's use of word salad with George, and Whitaker's comment about how long the girl's parents have been cold.

- *Assist the client in reaching their goals* (however "delusional" they may seem) in such a way as to offer a subtle shift in focus to more useful skills, e.g., Adams joining the struggle with the chipmunks, Erickson helping the man to reinforce his windows with string, and Lankton getting Greg to write a report on the two desserts.

- *Accept the strategies with which the client is generating "schizophrenic symptoms."* Then reframe them as useful skills, e.g., Bandler's offer to market Andy's hallucination skill, and Dolan's advice to the catatonic man to give himself some space.

- *Use real-life stories as metaphorical communication,* e.g., Dolan's story of going backwards into the future.

Overview of Therapy with Clients Diagnosed Schizophrenic

From our earlier comments about the nature of schizophrenia, it is clear that three central goals of consulting with someone diagnosed schizophrenic are likely to be:

To learn to chunk down.
To make meta-distinctions.
To use rapport skills.

The successful therapy process with clients diagnosed schizophrenic (as described by Lankton and Lankton, 1986; by Dolan, 1989; or by Bandler, 1993) is an educational one, rather than a therapeutic one in the traditional medicalized sense.

In the following sections we will consider each of these three central goals in turn and give examples of the more detailed "educational tasks" which can assist a person to reach them. Education is a respectful process. It does not require the therapist to assume that their client is "sick" or damaged". Merely that there are things they could learn.

1) Chunk Down

Cognitive therapists such as Carlo Perris recommend teaching the client the structure of their thinking, so that they can challenge their own Meta-Model patterns. Perris (1989, pp. 148–151) recommends starting with less emotionally laden areas, rather than the central delusions.

For example, earlier we mentioned one person (diagnosed schizophrenic) who attended our training and came up to Richard one morning to thank him for "what he did last night" (a time when Richard had no contact with her). As Richard looked puzzled, she quickly responded using the knowledge she had learned over the training, saying "Oh, I know! I'm using Mind Reading; thinking that you know what I was thinking about last night, aren't I." Having practiced Meta-Model questions in neutral situations, she was able to quickly unpack and Meta-Model what would previously have been a bewildering "delusion".

Garis Hagstrom (1981) studied the use of such confrontation by a therapist working with a single schizophrenic client over a two year period. The communication was analyzed for NLP Meta-Model patterns. Sessions later in the therapy showed that the client's communication changed to include more complete sentence structures (less use of deletion, distortion and generalization) as well as more congruent linking of nonverbal and verbal signals. Several studies of cognitive therapy show that the extent of delusional thinking can be markedly reduced in less than ten sessions (Perris, 1989, pp. 162–163). This provides evidence that persons diagnosed schizophrenic can benefit considerably from meta-modeling their own communication.

Perris identifies several types of "thought disorder" which benefit especially from Meta-Model style challenges. These include:

Generalization. Perris points out that, when asked how they came to stay in bed all day, the person diagnosed schizophrenic will simply reply "Because I'm lazy." or "Because I'm a schizo-phrenic." Such comments are very amenable to requests for specificity using the Meta-Model.

Identity assumed on the basis of identical predicates. This type of thinking is actually the basis of metaphor. One might say, using this type of thinking, that a) people grow and expand, and b) flowers grow and expand, so c) people are flow-ers. In schizophrenic thinking, this is treated, not as a metaphor, but as a fact. In the sentence "People grow and expand," "grow and expand" is the "predicate." The person using this type of thinking assumes that if the predicates are the same, the sub-jects of the sentences are identical.

One of our clients gave a simple example of this when he claimed that he was Jim Morrison of the rock group The Doors. He explained that he reached this conclusion because Jim Morrison was born on December 8th and he also had a signifi-cant experience on December 8. We describe this type of think-ing as a complex equivalent.

Premature assignment of meaning. As a person begins to say a sentence, the person using this type of thinking quickly assumes they know the end of the sentence and responds to their guess as if it was reality. This is a form of mind reading. The same premature assignment of meaning could be done in response to any sensory information (e.g., on seeing a car with writing on it, the person may assume that the car is a police car). In such cases, the result would be challenged as a complex equivalent.

Egocentric over-inclusion. This refers to the schizophrenic ten-dency to assume that all events have meaning in relation to them (as, for example, in our client's comment about Jim Morrison's birthdate). This pattern will also be stated as a com-plex equivalent.

Failure to distinguish personal meanings from causes. These are cause-effect patterns. In schizophrenic thought, the person assumes that some quality they attribute to a situation actually causes the events in that situation. They may assume that the reason they "didn't win the raffle" (an event) is because there's "a world-wide opposition to the spiritual truths they promote" (a quality they attribute to the situation).

Loss of symbolic thinking. Metaphorical statements may be taken literally. For example, on overhearing someone say "I can see through you" the client assumes that this refers to a concrete fact.

Thoughts transformed to perceptions. Just as in a trance state, thoughts produce sensations and motor activity (like finger signals); so in schizophrenic thinking, thoughts produce sensory images, sounds and sensations which seem real and externally produced. In this sense, schizophrenic thinking is trance-like. Perris lists this with the other cognitive patterns to be meta-modeled.

We should also emphasize that all these thought patterns also occur in people not diagnosed schizophrenic. They are normal results of generalization, deletion, and distortion. Nothing the person diagnosed schizophrenic does is "bizarre" in itself. Any normal person could learn to produce all the results of schizophrenia; generally, they have found better things to do with their life.

What's the aim of challenging these patterns? To give the client the ability to challenge his or her own beliefs and perceptions, to recognize them as maps. It is not to argue with specific delusions with which we as therapists disapprove. Arguing with delusions, which are by definition "fixed ideas," is rarely useful.

One of our clients was obsessed with a belief that he had been a Nazi in his previous life. He believed this because he had a nightmare where he was at a Nazi rally. In an attempt to prove how unlikely his conclusion was, Richard asked him how he felt at the rally. He said he was terrified.

Richard then said, "Nazis do not feel terrified at their own rallies. The dream may be an expression of a fear you have, but is unlikely to result from your having been a Nazi in some other life."

The man agreed. The next week he returned, pre-occupied with his new delusion that he had been a German Jew in his last life.

2) Make Meta-Distinctions

All of us, on occasion, engage in daydreams and flights of fantasy. When we are communicating with others, or when we are performing a set task, we usually manage to detect and stop such thought streams. This requires *a form of meta-awareness* which NLP training by its very nature enhances. (Meta-awareness refers to an awareness of one's own internal strategies, states, and the qualities of our modalities).

Several research studies from Cognitive Psychology also show that within ten or so sessions, clients diagnosed schizophrenic can be taught to identify cognitive distortions (such as delusions and hallucinations) as they are happening, and to interrupt them. They typically call this training in meta-awareness "cognitive rehearsal" (Perris, 1989, pp. 178–182).

Its use also reveals the presence of a strategy for hallucination (Perris, 1989, pp. 166–167). For example, auditory hallucinations are preceded by an expectant "listening attitude." The client actually turns up the submodalities of their internal voice until it can be heard. Once they become aware of this, they can just as easily be taught to turn the voice down or even off. This can be practiced in the therapy session, until the person is skilled at interrupting their old strategy.

In his work with a young man diagnosed schizophrenic named Andy (Bandler, 1988), Richard Bandler has him experiment with his submodalities of "Mary," a hostile person who he would see and hear in stressful situations. Bandler invited Andy to shift the visual position of Mary, put her on a screen and smash the screen, and otherwise alter the submodalities.

In the book *"Time for a Change,"* Bandler describes Milton Erickson's process of teaching a schizophrenic client to make meta-distinctions between real and unreal (Bandler, 1993, pp. 7–9). The woman and her psychiatrist made a two hour trip by airplane down to Phoenix to visit Erickson. However, when Erickson said to her, "And you left your house and drove here in a green station wagon and saw the countryside on the way, and how long did it take you to get here?"

She replied, "Twenty-six hours."

In this way, Milton determined that the woman was unable to distinguish between the images she made when he told her his story, and the images she saw when she remembered actual events. By contrast, Erickson had her psychiatrist review in his mind three things that he knew were true, then go inside and make up three other events. Erickson then asked the man how he knew which ones were which.

The therapist said of the real ones, "They seem square, whereas the other ones are vague and transparent and don't have a shape."

Erickson shifted back to the woman. He turned around and began to instruct her to review the events then occurring. He told her to put them into square pictures. Then he made up fantasies and told her to make them vague and transparent and without any shape. He began to instruct her unconscious mind to start to sort out all events this way. "Nowadays, TVs being mostly square, I recommend you make sure you have other ways to sort real from not real."

Fairly standard NLP techniques can be used to change submodality distinctions in this way.

One man we worked with, who had been diagnosed both schizophrenic and depressed, found it very disturbing to hear (i.e., to "hallucinate") his father's voice yelling in his left ear, telling him he was no good. After having run an auditory Swish a few times (having his father's voice fade into the distance while his own, more supportive voice came in from the same side), he reported that his feeling of depression disappeared. This brings up an important point. Nothing in the rules says that a person who uses schizophrenic thinking styles can't also use strategies of depression and anxiety. We have other chapters for dealing with these problems separately. Yet we have often found that when anxiety is solved, the diagnostic symptoms of schizophrenia are also dramatically reduced.

3) Use Rapport Skills

Much of the suffering of the person diagnosed as schizophrenic comes from their difficulty in building and maintaining rapport. This occurs in the specific situation of talking to someone, and in the more general situation of living in a social community. People diagnosed as schizophrenic are frequently puzzled by their inability to "get on" with people. When their actual mismatching is pointed out, they may become very defensive of it. Examples of social mismatching include not washing or dressing to the standards of the social group they belong to, avoiding contact with people by staying in bed all day or staying at home, and using socially unusual mannerisms and ways of talking.

It's easy for a "socially liberal" therapist to assume that such behaviors are the person's unique way of being, and should not be questioned. While everyone has the right to be odd, the question is what results they actually want. The person diagnosed schizophrenic does not always realize how precise their playing of the "social rules" needs to be for them to get the social results they want. Unfortunately, very few people in the client's social world will challenge these mismatched behaviors openly. The more unusual the behavior, the less useful feedback they will get! Further, clients who have recovered from schizophrenia often tell us that keeping out of rapport was a way that they protected themselves from a feared engulfment by others (a Meta-State).

Careful goal-setting is crucial for the therapist to have permission to challenge this social mismatching on behalf of the client, rather than attempting to change it as some sort of "social policing." Where the person would not themselves set "rapport skills" as a goal, training in this area must make sense for the client's other goals (as in the story of Steve Lankton working with the man who wanted to be an ambassador). Once goals are agreed on, the person can be taught the strategies they need to succeed.

For example, Perris describes the elicitation of a person's strategy for staying in bed all day, and its replacement by rehearsing through a new motivation strategy (Perris, 1989, p. 144). He also describes the cognitive rehearsal and roleplaying of specific social skills. In our experience, the person diagnosed as schizophrenic often needs considerable practice to maintain basic rapport skills such as matching body position. These skills can be practiced both in the therapy session, and then (once they are fluent enough) in home tasks.

It is important to respect the challenge that such new skills present to a person who has never used them. In particular, being able to adopt second position in social situations can be a rather scary experience.

Cognitive therapists note that the person diagnosed as schizophrenic will often assume that they know how others feel and think, because others feel and think just as they do (Perris, 1989, p. 174). Much of paranoia is a result of assuming that the attention of others is focused on the client with the same intensity as their own. It's the fear (which we have all had at times especially in social situations) that a stain on one's clothes is as obvious and central to others' perception as it is to our own perception. Most of us can pull out of this cognitive distortion with a brief reminder that other people live in their own world and have their own concerns; that people do not usually spend all evening scrutinizing every detail on everyone else in the room. People diagnosed as schizophrenic have had less practice with this ability to take second position and develop self-reassurance.

Another important aid to enabling social success involves anchoring resource states for social use. Yet this may pose particular difficulties for schizophrenic patients. The cognitive distortions of "schizophrenic thinking" make the accessing of resources more challenging. Yvonne Dolan gives a number of useful suggestions (Dolan, 1985, pp. 74–89). These include the therapist modeling the state desired, describing in detail the state desired to the client, asking hypothetically, "What would it be like if you could remember those good feelings?," describing someone else relaxing and feeling good (what Erickson called the "My friend John" technique), and asking what the client does for "fun." Dolan points out that when the client effectively dissociates from positive experiences, the best way to access one may be to actually go with them for a walk, to a restaurant, to a sports event, etc.

Like the person who is depressed or anxious, the person diagnosed as schizophrenic often has a Meta-Program of sorting for problems. A key to therapy then becomes helping them identify small successes and magnifying these. I mentioned earlier that many times I have seen a client tell me that "nothing has changed" one minute. Then, a moment later I hear them talk about having actually achieved every goal they set for our time together. I facilitate this shift by using my willingness *not* to assume that their memory of events *is* reality, but instead to ask persistently about what has changed in your life and then validate it.

An Example of Transformation

In preparing this chapter, we were fortunate to have the assistance of a skilled NLP Master Practitioner who had previously been diagnosed as schizophrenic. We will call him *John*. Throughout his childhood, John had the problems identified in the child development study: he was unable to spell despite numerous specialist attempts to teach him; and telling left from right was an occasional challenge up until his teenage years. As a young adult, he was under considerable stress, living in the city, with no money and little food, but access to large amounts of marijuana and hallucinogenic mushrooms. He said he felt like a fuse inside him could pop, and everything hardwired would need to find its own way. As a result he recognized that his best option to deal with the pressure at the time was "insanity." It created a safer, more enjoyable inner world for John to live in.

Living increasingly in "his own world," John became preoccupied first with the hopelessness of the world political situation, and then with a belief that he was one of the holy trinity of Father, Son and Holy Ghost. So he went on a search to create the unity of this trinity and to heal the world. Music and TV seemed to contain visual and auditory messages directed at him specifically. He heard different lyrics to songs and saw different words written. He also had frightening kinesthetic hallucinations where he believed he was electrocuting himself (the metaphor about a fuse popping becoming a physical reality at these times).

After an episode where John attacked someone violently, he was admitted for psychiatric treatment, and eventually diagnosed as schizophrenic. He resented the approach of his psychiatrist, whom he felt was transparently trying to build rapport with him (by playing pool, etc.) in order to change him. The first drug he was prescribed (chlorpromazine) had a paradoxical effect on him, keeping him awake, and unable to sleep at night. The second, stelazine, produced a marked reduction in his hallucinations. He also appreciated those individuals he met inside the psychiatric system who seemed motivated by a real love of human beings; people who were there for him when he needed support.

After almost a year, John began gradually to "loose the ability" to hallucinate. We asked what happens now when he imagines a strange voice talking inside his head. He explained that he never does that now; in fact that he *could not* do it! Any voice he imagines, even any song or music he hums, is translated into his own internal voice. In this way, he is incapable of confusing imagination with external reality. His only regret is that he also has reduced his auditory-visual imagination.

Currently, finding sane ways to improve this is one of his interests. John's story is a dramatic and clear cut example of re-coding the submodalities of imagined experiences differently, and using auditory digital as a meta-system. When asked how he changed, John explained that he knew while he was "schizophrenic," that it was he himself who was running it. It gave him a sense of the power of his own mind, which eventually drove him to explore new ways of running his brain, and new ways of relating to others. Eventually this led him to study the cognitive and rapport-building skills of NLP.

Now, John's psychiatrist has told him that he could not have been schizophrenic, and re-diagnosed his problem as a drug induced psychosis. In fact, John clearly fitted the DSM-IV definition of schizophrenia. Re-diagnosis is a way of avoiding facing the fact that someone can be diagnosed schizophrenic and then become fully "normal" again a couple of years later. It is comparable to the situation with cancer which, when "spontaneously" healed after NLP work, will often be re-diagnosed as a benign tumor. To someone who understands NLP, John's recovery is not so mysterious. It is a tribute to the skill of human beings to learn ever better ways to resolve inner challenges and find happiness.

Summary

- The model of Meta-Levels governing the levels of communication presents a facet of the layering and structuring of "personality." The levels of messages that we structure in our thinking and feeling obviously crucially affects how we experience our *personality.*

- These Meta-Levels of thought (Meta-States) also provide us with a way to disentangle the meta-muddles that our mind and emotions can get into. This highlights the role that *communication* itself plays in personality structuring and re-structuring.

- Schizophrenia is a psychiatric nominalization for a cluster of thinking processes including difficulty chunking down, a lack of meta-thinking enabling distinctions between real and unreal, loss of rapport skills, and resulting life impairments. It occurs less, and disappears faster, in rural societies, and may be exacerbated by long term psychotherapy.

- Working with the person diagnosed as schizophrenic requires an ability to pace unusual behaviors, goals, and metaphorical communications. It involves the ability to lead the client to new possibilities.

- New possibilities include the ability to Meta-Model one's own thought, the ability to recode the submodalities of experience so as to usefully distinguish real from unreal, and the ability to match others' behavior and respond based on a realistic appraisal of others' experience.

Using the RESOLVE model for therapy, the sequence of steps includes the following:

1) *Resourceful State:*
   Remain calm as you expect change since clients will pick up your states, confidence, emotions, etc. Remember that schizophrenia will spontaneously disappear for most people so diagnosed.

2) *Establish Rapport:*
   Aim to match the unusual behavior like word salad and metaphorical communication. Enter into the person's world of ideas, beliefs, feelings, and frames.

3) *Specify Outcomes:*
   At first this may involve accepting unusual goals (e.g. to be an ambassador). It requires reaching agreement on some type of outcome which enables learning to "chunk down," develop meta-distinctions and learn rapport skills.

4) *Open Up Model of the World:*
   As you view the "schizophrenic process" as the use of cognitive strategies this implies that these strategies can be changed and/or put into useful contexts.

5) *Leading:*
   Leading refers to an educational process including tasks to precisely index (or Meta-Model) the communications that the client engages in with him or herself as well as with others, especially generalizations, an identity based on predicates, premature assignment of meaning, egocentric over-inclusion, confusion of personal meanings with real causes, loss of symbolic thinking.

   It also involves marking out the unreality of hallucinations and delusions using the distinctions of the modalities (submodalities). By these you will be able to change the problem strategies, such as critical internal voice, using the Swish Pattern and other NLP patterns. Teach the use of a realistic second position in social situations, elicit and improve motivation strategies, access resource states and memories of success, use NLP rapport skills consistently.

6) *Verify Change:*

Coach the person to celebrate successes, however small, and to focus on solutions.

7) *Exit:*

By using a model of therapy as educational, prepare for client autonomy.

Chapter 14

Disordering "Personality" Through Paranoia

We now turn to *the disordering* of personality that involves mapping the territory of the world in terms of fear and danger. This shows up in what we have labeled as the **Paranoid Personality Disordering.** We have abbreviated this chapter due to the fact that we have recently completed a work, *Mastering Your Fears* (Bodenhamer and Hall) that's now being used as a training and will soon be put into book form.

Characteristics of the Paranoid State

The DSM-IV describes this disordering as:

> A pervasive distrust and suspiciousness of others such that their motives are interpreted as malevolent, beginning by early adulthood and present in a variety of contexts as indicated by four (or more) of the following:

> 1) suspects, without sufficient basis, that others are exploiting, harming, or deceiving him or her.

> 2) is preoccupied with unjustified doubts about the loyalty or trustworthiness of friends or associates.

> 3) is reluctant to confide in others because of unwarranted fear that the information will be used maliciously against him or her.

> 4) reads hidden demeaning or threatening meanings into benign remarks or events.

5) persistently bears grudges, i.e., is unforgiving of insults, injuries, or slights.

6) perceives attacks on his or her character or reputation that are not apparent to others and is quick to react with anger or to counterattack.

7) has recurrent suspicious, without justification, regarding the fidelity of spouse or sexual partner.

Most characteristic of the thinking and emoting of those who suffer from this disordering involves their habitual adoption of a persistent and unrealistic tendency to *interpret* the intentions and actions of others as demeaning or threatening. This makes sense.

It also makes sense regarding how a person might so map the world. Clients have typically experienced environments where they truly found other people to be hurtful, threatening, intimidating, and sadistic. They then use those referents to build a map of people, events, situations, etc. as comprising a danger and threat. The central problem with this lies in failing to specifically index *who, when, where, under what conditions, etc.* that the harm occurred. By *not* mapping with such precision, the person tends to over-generalize the "sense of threat" and make it his or her perceptual filter for all people and situations.

In doing this, such individuals use *the danger schema* as their central model for navigating inter-personal relations. As a consequence of this frame, they tend to *mind-read* the motives, thoughts, feelings, and agendas of others as malicious in intent. They project such onto others. And, as this persists to the point of habituation, they become increasingly unwilling to even consider alternative explanations.

Viewing the world and others as threatening and dangerous, they therefore adopt *the basic coping mechanism of vigilance* (and hyper-vigilance). This Meta-State of fear, suspicion, and negative anticipation then becomes their Meta-Program for sorting in their general perceptions.

"Is this person, event, or situation dangerous?"

"What could go wrong in this situation?"

"How could this person be trying to trick me, manipulate me, or control me?"

The paranoia map further encourages people to look, not to themselves for the source of problems or difficulties, but to others and to external events. This expresses and installs the Meta-Program of External (rather than Internal) in terms of their locus of control and authority.

James Pretzer (Beck, 1990) writes,

> paranoid individuals have a strong tendency to *blame* others for interpersonal problems, usually can cite many experiences that seem to justify their convictions that others are to blame, are quick to deny or minimize their own problems, and often have little recognition of the ways in which their behavior contributes to their problems. (p. 99)

Given this explanatory style about problems and conflicts between persons, they tend to come across in conflict situations as stubborn, argumentative, defensive, and unwilling to give. Why? Because they operate (almost perpetually) from a state of threat and danger. Their "defensiveness" makes sense to their model of the world even if it seems most preposterous to others.

Cameron (1959) wrote,

> The adult who is especially vulnerable to paranoid behavior is one in whom this process of socialization has been seriously defective. His deficient social learning and poorly developed social skills leave him unable to understand adequately the motivations, attitudes, and intention of others. When he becomes disturbed or confused under stress, he must operate under several grave handicaps imposed by a lifelong inability to communicate freely and effectively, to suspend judgment long enough to share his tentative interpretations with someone else, to imagine realistically the attitudes that others may have toward his situation and himself, and to imagine their roles and thus share their perspective. (p. 53)

Because those who use the paranoid map feel so much threat and danger in the world, they operate primarily in *moving away from* threat and danger (shame, humiliation, exposure, vulnerability, control, manipulation). Typically, they do not seem well organized to *move toward* their values or goals. As a result, this gives them "an eye" for dis-values and this shows up in the "negative" attitude, hence the Meta-Program of *pessimism* (rather than optimism). They see the world in terms of the negative, and so filter out the positive.

Other solidified Meta-States that have become Meta-Programs which further contribute to formulate this disordering pattern include:

- *Associated* (rather than dissociated). They truly and deeply *feel* danger (even where no danger truly exists) because they represent and so code it. This then makes it part of their neuro-semantic reality.

- *Defensive* in passive-aggressive ways due to their sense of threat.

Verbally and linguistically, this pattern of disordering shows up in several of the Meta-Model distinctions. Mentally, such people engage in *mind-reading* and jump-to-conclusions in a *global* way. They have developed the skill for taking any small sign of threat, control, manipulation, etc. as a sign of danger. Inter-personally, they operate from the *distrusting* sort and from the *non-demonstrative* sort so that they have difficulty expressing warm, tender feelings when in the paranoid state.

The *psychoanalytic view* sees the paranoid personality disordering as inaccurately perceiving in others "that which is actually true of him or her, and, as a result, experiences less distress than would result from a more realistic view of self and others." Hence we find that *projection* drives this disorder. The *cognitive-behavioral model* sees it as a set of strategies "directed toward minimizing or forestalling shame and humiliation." (Beck, 1990, p. 101).

Sources of Origin

We have already noted some possible origins for this kind of mapping. What else might give rise to this disordering? What factors and components contribute to the creation of paranoid disordering? Sources of origin for this disordering may arise from parents who teach children fearful ideas about the dangerous world of others.

> "You must be careful about making mistakes."
> "You are different from others."
> "It's a cruel and cold world out there—be very, very careful."
> "Don't trust people—they will manipulate you if they can."
> "People are cruel, malevolent and deceptive. Trust no one."

Experiences of hurt, betrayal, ostracization, humiliation, shame, etc. obviously operate as fertile soil within which any of us could draw such conclusions and then generalize them to all people.

Bandura (1977) develops a construct known as *self-efficacy*. This refers to subjectively estimating that we have the ability to cope effectively with the world, with people, and with problems.

Beck (1990) relies on this construct in understanding the central need of the paranoid personality disordered person. He or she needs a greater sense of personal confidence about seeing through deceptions of others, thwarting their manipulations, speaking up, handling problems, etc. Without a sense of self-efficacy, one assumes that he or she "must be constantly vigilant for signs of danger." This leads then to constant scanning for subtle cues— every one of which then reinforces the eye of living in a "dog-eat-dog" world.

State-dependency learning, memory, perception, behavior, and communication plug in when the person goes into the paranoid state.

> When one is vigilant for signs of threat or attack and presumes malicious intentions, it follows that any slights or mistreatments are intentional and malicious and deserve retaliation. When others protest that their actions were unintentional, accidental, or justified,

303

their protestations are seen as evidence of deception and as proof of their malicious intentions. (Pretzer in Beck, 1990, p. 105)

With an attitude like this, no wonder inter-personal conflicts eventually esculate as the paranoid person holds back, withdraws, looks suspiciously at others, treats them as suspect, ascribes negative motives to them, mind-reads them, etc. When they then get treated unfairly or badly—they take it as confirmation of the person's badness and fail to see the interactive system that they have participated in.

Treatment: Reordering the Disordering

How do we go about reordering and straightening out the distortions in thinking-feeling, speaking, behaving, and relating involved in this "personality disorder?" In treating this particular disordering, as a therapist, we must begin by fully accepting and welcoming the paranoid system. By seeking to understand it, how it makes sense, how the person designed it, the higher positive intentions of safety, protection, and stability that the person seeks to achieve, we make it safe to explore and examine. This means also including accepting the client's distrust of us, exploring that, curiously and respectfully asking lots of questions about it. In doing this, we slowly begin a defragmentation of the paranoid system itself.

First and foremost, by increasing the person's sense of self-efficacy regarding problem situations
This will result in the person feeling reasonably confident in handling problems, thereby reducing the intensity of the person's symptomatology. Beck (1990) writes:

> The primary strategy in the cognitive treatment of PPD is to work to increase the client's sense of self-efficacy before attempting to modify other aspects of the client's automatic thoughts, interpersonal behavior, and basic assumptions. (p. 108)

In NLP, we recognize this strategy as providing us with the central *leverage point in the system*. Thereafter, we can aim to do other things that will assist in developing a greater sense of self-efficacy.

1) *Person/Behavior Distinction*

   Facilitate in the client a strong sense of being so much more than his or her feelings and thoughts. That is, separate the person from behavior. This kind of *Dis-Identification* is central to NLP and to Neuro-Semantics and enables a person to step back from processes and to recognize the mapping for *mapping*. "You are much more than your thoughts, aren't you? Or, could it be that you truly think you are *just* your thoughts?" "Is that *all* you are?" "Whatever you *think*, you are?" Use the Meta-State Patterns of Dis-Identification and Ownership of one's Power Zone.

2) *Meta-Awareness about Beliefs*

   Once we have created the distinction between *person* and mapping at all levels (in thoughts, in feelings, etc.), then we can facilitate in the client a larger level awareness of his or her beliefs. "You're more than some of the ideas that you've confirmed, are you not? Or, is that *all* you 'are'?"

   This can then empower us to assist the client in identifying and challenging the beliefs (schemas, models) that govern his or her thinking-and-emoting. Now we can start sorting out *limiting* beliefs from *empowering* beliefs and coach the person to the point of choice. "Which belief would you prefer to entertain and use as your navigational guide as you move through life?' "You'd really like that one?": "How would that belief support you?" "So you'd like to say 'Yes!' to that belief?"

   Since a belief differs from a mere "thought" by being a higher logical level of *confirmation thoughts* about the primary thought, we transform "thoughts" into beliefs by confirming them. Use the Meta-*Yes*-ing and Meta-*No*-ing Meta-State pattern.

3) Outframe the person's old beliefs with doubts

We can fragment a person's way of validating and "proving" limiting perceptions and beliefs by seeding lots of doubts and questions about it. We can question its validity, usefulness, appropriateness, specificity, generality, etc. By questioning and planting doubts, we begin to erode the higher frame of absolute validation for the idea. We can restrict the scope of events acceptable for evidence. Or, we can bring counter-examples to the generalizations and inquire about how the counter-example fits into the larger schema.

4) Quality Control the paranoid belief

The NLP process of running "an ecology check," which we refer to as establishing a Quality Control frame of reference in Meta-States, invites a client to step back, "go meta" to the entire paranoid paradigm and to check out its ecology. From this higher level of awareness we can also engage in some reality testing and evaluation about its usefulness.

A Sample Therapeutic Conversation

I have adapted the following from Beck (1990), who as a cognitive therapist encountered Ann who viewed her work situation as a secretary and her co-workers in a paranoid way. The therapist first sought to evaluate how much danger she felt and why.

Pacing and evaluating the danger—

> T: You're reacting as though this is a very dangerous situation. What are the risks you see?
>
> A: They'll keep dropping things and making noise to annoy me.
>
> T: Are you sure nothing worse is at risk?
>
> A: Yeah.
>
> T: So you don't think there's much chance of them attacking you or anything?
>
> A: Nah, they wouldn't do that.

Scaling the danger—

> T: If they do keep dropping things and making noises, how bad will that be?
>
> A: Like I told you, it's real aggravating. It really bugs me.
>
> T: So it would continue pretty much as it has been going for years now.
>
> A: Yeah. It bugs me, but I can take it.

Building up a sense of resourcefulness and a sense of self-efficacy —

> T: And you know that if it keeps happening, at the very least you can keep handling it the way you have been holding the aggravation in, then taking it out on your husband when you get home. Suppose we could come up with some ways to handle the aggravation even better or to have them get to you less. Is that something you'd be interested in?
>
> A: Yeah, that sounds good.
>
> T: Another risk you mentioned earlier was that they might talk to your supervisor and turn her against you. As you see it, how long have they been trying to do this?
>
> A: Ever since I've been there.
>
> T: How much luck have they had so far in doing that?
>
> A: Not much.
>
> T: Do you see any indications that they're going to have any more success now than they have so far?
>
> A: No, I don't guess so.
>
> T: So your gut reaction is as though the situation at work is really dangerous. But when you stop and think it through, you conclude that the worst they're going to do is to be really aggravating, and that even if we don't come up with anything new, you can handle it well enough to get by."

As we aim to facilitate the building up of a person's sense of self-efficacy, we empower the client so that he or she will begin to feel more and more resourceful, competent, and capable. This makes the *paranoia paradigm* less and less important and motivating. We begin by respecting that the person needs to view the world, others, situations fearfully, in black-and-white terms, as threatening, and so engages in less personalizing, mind-reading, and negative filtering. As this disorders the person's ability to be open, to take risks, to try new things, it reduces new learnings. By coaching new levels of self-trust and self-efficacy, it invites the client to come out and explore the world of possibilities. It facilitates the client to build up a new way to order his or her powers of thinking-emoting, speaking, behaving and relating.

Due to the inherent impairment of social communication, *re-ordering* of the paranoid personality disordering needs to include communication training, empathy development, suspension of judgment, etc.

Summary

- At the heart of all personality discovery, unpacking, understanding, and re-ordering lies the search for structure. *How* does it work? When, where, and by what thoughts and feelings do you create this? In fully understanding the structure or strategy, we can interrupt and/or refine it.

- Working with Paranoid Personality Disordering is especially challenging for a therapist inasmuch as the client will inevitably use that very program to respond to the therapeutic statements and interventions. This calls upon a consultant or therapist to establish a strong rapport.

- The magic of change lies in how we code and recode our thoughts. Recoding our memories and representations of past events or imagined future events gives us the ability to create new reference structures.

Chapter 15

Disordering "Personality" Through Anti-Social Frames

While some personality *disordering* arises from *too much conformity and sensitivity* to social mores, rules, awareness, etc. others arise from the very opposite—from too little. This especially shows up in the disordering which falls under the label of the **Antisocial Personality Disorder**.

Those who suffer from this strategy can display tremendous irresponsibility and poor judgment, along with impulsiveness, shallowness, inability to learn from experience, etc. It's enough to provoke and irritate even the best trained psychotherapists. In fact, that's often the game that goes on with such individuals. And yet, ultimately, the person's suffering from this way of thinking, feeling, acting, and speaking is more than those frames. When one's personality structure becomes warped in this way, it puts a real strain on rapport and the typical therapeutic interventions. And obviously, this particular disordering takes us right into the heart of what has been called *the criminal mind*.

Characteristics

Over the years, several different kind of formulations have developed theorizing about what primarily drives the antisocial personality disorder. These range from certain physiological characteristics of the genes, deficiencies in moral/conscience development, deficiencies in cognitive-emotive development, etc.

Ben-Aron, Hucker, and Webster's work, *Clinical Criminology* offers the following checklist for the assessment of psychopathy:

1. Glibness/superficial charm.

2. Grandiose sense of self-worth.
3. Need for stimulation/proneness to boredom.
4. Pathological lying.
5. Conning/manipulation.
6. Lack of remorse or guilt.
7. Shallow affect.
8. Callous/lack of empathy.
9. Parasitic lifestyle.
10. Poor behavioral controls.
11. Promiscuous sexual behavior.
12. Early behavior problems.
13. Lack of realistic, long-term plans.
14. Impulsivity.
15. Irresponsibility.
16. Failure to accept responsibility.
17. Many short-term marital relationships.
18. Juvenile delinquency.
19. Revocation of conditional release.
20. Criminal versatility.

Compare those characteristics with the diagnostic criteria in the DSM-IV for Antisocial Personality Disorder.

There is a pervasive pattern of disregard for and violation of the rights of others occurring since age 15 years, as indicated by three (or more) of the following:

1) failure to conform to social norms with respect to lawful behaviors as indicated by repeatedly performing acts that are grounds for arrest,

2) deceitfulness, as indicated by repeatedly lying, use of aliases, or conning others for personal profit or pleasure,

3) impulsivity or failure to plan ahead,

4) irritability and aggressiveness, as indicated by repeated physical fights or assaults,

5) reckless disregard for safety of self or others,

6) consistent irresponsibility, as indicated by repeated failure to sustain consistent work behavior or honor financial obligations,

7) lack of remorse, as indicated by being indifferent to or rationalizing having hurt, mistreated, or stolen from another.

These descriptions reveal the chief characteristics of those who think-and-feel in ways that create this disordering. There is structure in the disordering. It doesn't "just happen." To Meta-State ourselves with those kinds of thoughts-and-feelings inevitably generates a certain way of looking on the world (Meta-Programs) and you can hear it in a person's language (the Meta-Model) as well as in the larger level set of frames that govern the mind (Meta-States).

Meta-Programs Structuring of this Disordering

1) *Dissociated from empathy, not empathetically associated*
   Most theorists and therapists have noted the *lack of anxiety* in the sociopathic response pattern regarding the consequences of actions both on others and for self. Given this *obliviousness* to guilt, regret, remorse, shame, penitence, or the need to assume responsibility for one's own conduct, we experience the person as coming across without much emotion. The emotion or attitude that we sense is that of being hard and callous, uncaring, unsympathetic, selfish, etc.

   With this lack of empathy arises a *low conscientiousness* about appropriate behaviors, manners, ethics, etc. It also undermines a vigorous sense of ownership or *responsibility*. And without those guiding attitudes (Meta-States), it becomes difficult to play by the same rules as the rest of society.

2) *Self-referencing, not Other-referencing*
   At the heart of this *disordering* of personality functions, we have an extreme form of *self-referencing*. I say extreme because almost all of such a person's perceptions, thoughts, and emotions reference oneself and seldom that of others. "What's in it for me?"

"I hate injustice…to me!" As a *driving cognitive influence* this results in narcissism and supports the lack of empathy. He or she operates from self-interest in seeming disregard for others or the effects their actions have on others. In this, the individuals seem almost incapable of taking the perceptual position of another person (the second perceptual position).

3) *Present oriented*

To further complicate matters, the sociopathic personality disordering also involves an extreme form of *present time-orientation*. Such persons tend to orient only to the "now" and so show a loss of future time perspective. As a result, this leads to feeling unconcerned for the future as it simultaneously undermines the ability to plan for the future. The gestalt that emerges from this is impulsivity and inability to delay gratification. Most show a lack of inhibition as well as low frustration tolerance. Here they lack a Meta-Level frame of reference to *inhibit* their responses.

4) *Under-Responsible*

Let's add yet another characteristic to these sorting styles—*under-responsible*. In terms of accountability, they seem to hold others, the world, the system, etc. accountable for problems and difficulties, not themselves. This leads to blaming. Such persons do not operate as if "at cause" for their own lives. So when such individuals relate to others, they tend to adopt a communication style of blaming and attacking, one driven by the need to "always be right." Acknowledging error in thought and emotion comes very hard for such individuals. Most act as though the usual laws and limitations do not apply to them.

"I have a right to this."
"The world owes me."

5) *Distrusting*

These ideas as beliefs enable them to disregard the usual rules. In terms of inter-personal relations, they typically will operate from the *distrusting* sort. Supporting beliefs about the stupidity of others, that they exist to be used, etc. prevail.

6) *Black-and-White, Concrete Thinking*
More typically than not, we find that many who fall into this category operate at a very simple *concrete thinking stage*, and don't do well in abstract thinking skills—recognizing the feelings of others, personal responsibility, weighing possibilities, recognizing that words and symbols "are" not the referent, future "time" considerations, etc.

Meta-Modeling and Beliefs

In terms of the cognitive distortions which typically drive this way of ordering personality, we find emotionalizing to be common. This involves the reasoning that if one *feels like* doing something, then one has to do that thing, must do it, or cannot not do it. Such persons take *their* thoughts and feelings as true, real, indicating "reality," and do so to such an extent that they very seldom question such. Here we have the Meta-State process of believing in one's every thought and emotion.

> "Ah, so you *have to* take counsel of every anger, sense of injustice, put down, etc.? You have no other choice?"

In terms of personality skills and limitations, this results in an imperviousness to feedback, even corrective feedback. It then shows up in the seeming inability to learn from mistakes or even from painful consequences. When confronted with feedback of their errors, they dismiss such input from others as irrelevant to their purposes. If they become defensive, they will blame and accuse the speaker of trying to hurt them (personalizing).

Typically, they have developed belief systems that support their behaviors. They may regard it as "smart" to "take what you can get by with." This demonstrates "using your wits." They may even look upon cleverness in defrauding others as a mark of distinction. And, of course, with Meta-Level meaning frames like that, they have a very different way of seeing and relating to the world of people.

Denise Davis (in Beck, 1990, p. 154) introduced the following list of six beliefs that seem especially important to this way of thinking and acting:

1. *Justification:* "Wanting something or wanting to avoid something justifies my actions."

2. *Thinking is believing:* "My thoughts and feelings are completely accurate, simply because they occur to me."

3. *Personal infallibility:* "I always make good choices."

4. *Feelings make facts:* "I know I am right because I feel right about what I do."

5. *The impotence of others:* "The views of others are irrelevant to my decisions, unless they directly control my immediate consequences."

6. *Low-impact consequences:* "Undesirable consequences will not occur or will not matter to me."

Typically individuals with Antisocial Personality Disordering experience a lack of a solid sense of self. This leads to an *ego-inflation*. In other words, the almost insatiable need to "be somebody," "to have the best," "to keep up with ..." some referent person, etc. Such insecurity causes such persons to feel driven to boast of themselves and to make more of themselves than their achievements realistically permit.

Because the antisocial personality perceptions are so selectively and defensively oriented for self-protection, this leaves such individuals with a very inadequate private map of the world. And that map itself hinders new learning and growth. It prevents such persons from taking advantage of normal training and rehabilitation. This doesn't arise because the person has an inability to learn at all. Often, such individuals are very intelligent. But having learned the wrong things, the antisocial disordering prevents the reception of new or different information. Only referencing self, operating from an agenda of proving oneself adequate, and discounting others describes the kind of frames that sabotage learning.

The defective superego development of this person also prevents new learnings—learnings that would make him or her "wrong." Having no equipment or resource for coping with true guilt, this person can't allow the development of such conscience.

Sources of Origin

Adler described the sociopath tentatively as the "receptive type" variety of the "pampered life style," thus recognizing the determinants of getting something for nothing in situations of being pampered. (p. 2)

Thorne (1959) states:

> A physically attractive child of intelligence within normal limits, early learns to capitalize on behavioral attractiveness in social relations, particularly with the opposite sex. He early learns to use his wits in influencing and manipulating other people.
>
> In a typical developmental sequence, the attractive child learns to charm people, to behave so attractively that others will excuse shortcomings and withhold punishment which another child could not escape. ... Or if he is not so behaviorally attractive, he may learn that if he takes aggressively enough, he may get away with it because he knows that his relatives will not prosecute him.
>
> A typical sequence is that the developing sociopath is prematurely introduced to adult pleasures. ...[He] learns to use his wits to avoid hard work (too slow to satisfy short term gratifications) and typically fails to acquire the solid educational background which serves as a positive resource for the normal child. (pp. 319–330)

Typically, overly tolerant parents and authorities who excuse increasingly serious misconduct, hoping that the person will outgrow it, *actually reinforce it* by making it "work." As they repeatedly bail the child out of difficulties, by allowing the child to escape normal punitive consequences of misbehavior, they learn that they can get away with things. This eventually becomes the individual's *modus operandi*. They desire to take what others recognize must be earned. In doing this they disregard the reality principle.

We can even install the Anti-social personality disordering by unspoken modeling. Giffin *et al.* (1954) wrote:

> The well-integrated, mature mother does *not* immediately check on a child following an order or request; she unconsciously assumes that the order will be carried out. The neurotic mother, who immediately checks or warns that if the job is not done dire consequences will follow, merely conveys to the child that an unstated alternative exists in the mother's mind. It is frequently with this alternative image in the mother's thoughts that the child more strongly identifies.

> The child internalizes, then, not only the positive, socially consistent attitudes of the parent, but also the frequently unexpressed, ambivalent antisocial feelings. (pp. 668–684)

Therapy: Reordering the Disorder

Given this analysis of the Anti-Social Personality Disordered person, we need to assist in helping him or her shift from the rigid exclusiveness of *first perceptual position* in order to try some other perceptual position. We will also want to assist such individuals to shift out of the rigidity of the "now" thinking and balance it with the development of consequential thinking skills, planning, reality testing, weighing consequences, informed problem solving, etc. It must involve the development of empathy and social skills in order to take more personal responsibility and to develop respect for the rights, needs, and wants of others.

1) Pace the person's self-reference concerns
If pacing normally enables us to enter another's world of frames and beliefs and emotions for the purpose of understanding, trust, rapport, etc., it becomes doubly true for the disordering of the anti-

social frame. Such individuals do *not* trust. They do *not* reference much of what others say period. Begin then by pacing their concerns for getting something important to them by conducting a therapeutic interview around that subject and continually asking about the consequence of this or that choice.

"Will this get you want in the long run?"
"What possible unpleasant consequences could arise?"
"What chance would you give this scheme to work?"
"How dangerous could this be?"

This introduces another problem in working with such individuals. Such individuals typically do not and will not even consider how they could be wrong or at fault. To invite such reflection from the start will almost always backfire and evoke defensiveness. First such persons have to come to see that their choices have over the long-term caused more problems than if they had just "gone along with the system" and "played life by the rules." Therefore facilitating the person to think in terms of Advantages/ Disadvantages and rating the effectiveness of choices begins to get them to think in those ways. In this we have to first *use* their own self-referencing frames and apply them to the therapeutic process.

Inviting such individuals into the process of abstract thinking itself will oftentimes prove most challenging since it will not make sense to them, they'll feel impatient about it, and it may evoke defensiveness if they think that they have thought wrong (a Meta-State). Eventually, however, as abstract thinking skills develop …

It may also be pointed out that Anti-Social Personality Disorder is a silent menace because persons suffering from this disorder usually can't recognize the symptoms in themselves, and typically do not feel any discomfort until the disorder is quite advanced. (Beck, 1990, p. 156)

2) Gently recognize the person's Over-Identification with thoughts, feelings, being right, etc.
Another challenge involves empowering the person to break the stranglehold on the Meta-State of believing that "what one thinks or feels—one should do." This indicates that this disordering

grows from an old Aristotelian epistemology: "My map is the territory." It doesn't make the distinction between map and territory.

Given that the antisocial disordering sees and interprets disrespect and malevolence in others so easily, a therapist must exercise care to avoid evoking such. This means avoiding moralizing, judgmental comments, arguing, punishing, or putting on an impenetrable facade of toughness. Given that such individuals often love the thrill of the con—conning the therapist can become a source of pleasure. A therapist can pull the rug out from under them by admitting vulnerability to manipulation. This will make the Game of "Now I've Got You, You SOB…" less attractive.

> "I often mis-guess clients. After all, I can't read minds. So if someone lies, they lie. Nor do I even want to become a moral policeman about lying."

Use the NLP and Neuro-Semantic pattern of *Dis-Identification*, *Owning Your Power Zone*, Building a Circle of Excellence, etc.

3) Recognize the person's lack of empowerment
More often than not, the lack of true empowerment actually drives and operates as one of the meta-frames in the lives of the antisocial. After all, consider the following programs or strategies in terms of personal empowerment. Do any of them empower?

- Poor impulse control.
- An inability to plan.
- The lack of disciplining themselves for future satisfactions.
- An inability to understand or empathize with others.
- A disregard for consequences of actions.
- Reactivity.
- An inability to be wrong.

None of these characteristics describes personal empowerment. These things rather describe the lack of true personal power.

4) Recognize and address the inner hurt and defensiveness against such
Various hurts and traumas have exasperated this ordering. Most view that they have already gotten a raw deal from life and so feel

helpless and hopeless to "play the same game." They perceive that all systems (family, school, business, church, etc.) are organized against them so that they can't win. Therefore they assume that taking on and "beating the system" represents their only viable option.

Having experienced various traumatic experiences, with no good resolution, they cope with such by "not feeling" (at least dissociating from the hurt), not caring, not wanting to "think," being hyper-attentive to possible tricks and schemes of others, afraid to feel caring or tender feelings, afraid to think or feel in moral or ethical ways, etc. Their "defense" to old unresolved hurts involves moving through the world as *entitled victims* so mistreated, never wrong, always right, and ready to take revenge. Not a pretty sight nor an empowered way to live!

Accordingly, they operate from a Win/Lose or a Lose/Lose perspective. The very idea of Win/Win (collaboration, cooperation, mutual respect) seems unrealistic—a fairy tale to them.

Because of this hyper-sensitivity, using various NLP patterns for re-coding the hurt becomes valuable: the Phobia pattern, Re-imprinting, the Decision Destroyer. And because these all involve meta-stating processes, we can run these patterns conversationally as we tell stories, disclose a similar, isomorphic situation in our own lives, and speak tangentially.

5) Deal with the poorly-integrated forbidden impulses
When we set a frame that over-values our thoughts, feelings, and experiences, and assume that "if I feel something (anger, injustice, greed, lust, etc.), then I *have to* act on it," we empower every reactive and impulsive feeling to dominate our lives. This actually reduces our humanity and makes us operate more like the lower animals. The more highly developed human response involves thinking out consequences, long-term results, and taking counsel of more factors and influences than just emotions or immediate gratification.

This calls for the NLP patterns that enable us to develop state management skills:

- Gauge the quality and ecology of our states and actions.

- Develop several ways to interrupt states.

- Meta-state the experience to texture the primary emotional state with the kind of qualities and features that make them healthy and balanced (i.e. calm anger, respectful anger).

Use the basic Meta-Stating Pattern to build and install larger level and more complex states (semantic states) like proactivity, mindfulness, resilience, etc.

Summary

- It's easy to fall into the trap of assuming that something is so fundamentally wrong with the socio-pathetic that they are flawed human beings without a conscience. Here we have started from an entirely different assumption: they simply have not built the internal maps and frames that allow them to consider the impact of actions on others. This lack of empathetic mapping for a greater consciousness about the welfare of others may have arisen from poor parenting, lack of discipline, trauma, and a wide range of other things.

- Those who have disordered their personality by over-doing self-referencing, making "justice" too semantically loaded, failing to take a perceptual position from another's point of view, etc. create the larger gestalt of the anti-social personality disorder.

- To the extent that they balance these processes and develop the frames of mind that allow them to consider others, care about social rules, step aside from their own interests to view the larger picture, etc., a person can reduce the anti-social orientation.

Chapter 16

Disordering "Personality" Through Depressing

The Epidemic of Depression

The DSM-IV (1994) identifies a major depressive episode by a person having symptoms such as feeling sad or empty, lack of interest or pleasure, fatigue, feelings of worthlessness or guilt, inability to think, recurrent thoughts of death, insomnia or hypersomnia, weight loss or gain, and body agitation or slowing down.

This represents a life-threatening psycho-physiological disorder. Studies show that people who score highly on these indicators of depression have lowered lymphocyte responsiveness and immunoglobulin levels in their blood i.e., their immune systems are damaged and they are more likely to get ill (Thayer, 1996, pp. 30–31). Further, the rate of depression varies from social group to social group, and from time to time. Carefully adjusted studies (Seligman, 1991, pp. 64–65) show the incidence of depression has increased more than tenfold in the last century. This has reached the point where at any given time, 25% of people are at least mildly depressed (Seligman, 1991, p. 55). These and other statistics indicate that most "depressions" are a result of experience, not genetics (Yapko, 1992, pp. 3–4).

Alongside this apparent epidemic of depression, has come an epidemic of drug usage to attempt to treat depression. Studies show that even when drug treatment is deemed successful, "relapses" (later recurrences of depression) are more common than when psychotherapy or psychotherapy plus drug treatment is deemed successful (Yapko, 1992, p. 4). This strongly suggests that drug treatment by itself is an inappropriate solution (inappropriate in the sense that it leaves the person at a higher risk of recurrence).

Through research, we know a great deal about what kind of out-side assistance works with depression, and what kind of "assistance" does not work. We also know that 80% of individuals suffering major depression will "spontaneously" cease to be depressed in between 4–10 months (Yapko, 1992, p. 16). People normally find their own way out of depression. This also means that if any type of "assistance" continues for ten months it will seem to have solved the problem in 80% of cases. Genuinely successful strategies for assisting are those that can show benefits in the short term.

Denominalizing Depression

There are a number of things people can do that lead them to feel depressed. The NLP-based solutions will become rather obvious as we describe these depression strategies using NLP terms. Don't read this as meaning that ending depression is easy. Most of these solutions have been around for thousands of years. The challenge lies in getting people to actually stop doing the things that don't work and to begin doing the things that do. And that shall be our focus.

Depressed individuals use the very *thinking styles* that cause depression to convince themselves that they cannot, or should not, change. In fact, depression could be defined as the belief that "a person cannot or should not change." Professor of Psychology Martin Seligman calls this belief a *"permanent, pervasive explanatory style"* (1991, pp. 40–48). He describes it as part of the structure of "learned pessimism." And this is the very first thing that we will want to challenge in working with depressed persons. This also explains (in our opinion) why talking about "one person doing therapy on another" is not an appropriate metaphor in helping someone rediscover happiness.

Ericksonian therapist Dr Michael Yapko describes depression as the result of the combination of two things. One is *a style of thinking* which includes the permanent, pervasive explanatory style. The other is life. We'll have a go at defining these two things.

Let's begin with *"life."* You'd think that would be easy to define. It is not. Nominalizations don't come any more general than "life." Yapko points out that *life* itself is like a giant Rorschach inkblot. It's so undefined that you can read anything into it. By dividing up the story of your life into certain pieces, you can prove that events in life always turn out for the best. And by dividing them up in another way, a depressed person can prove that events generally turn out for the worst.

Of course, neither map *is* the territory. Neither is objectively "real." Both represent strategies for creating our subjective reality and therefore both are forms of self-hypnosis. Stephen Gilligan (1987, pp. 44–46) explains that the same strategies which can be used to produce therapeutic trance (hypnosis) can be misused to create "symptomatic trances." The depressed person can negatively hallucinate (i.e., not notice) loving individuals close by them, and can hallucinate obstacles which no-one else sees. They can numb their body so that touch no longer comforts, and regress themselves so that they relive a painful moment a million times. These are very powerful trance phenomena.

That life is cyclical is an important thing to understand about life, before we move to considering the learned pessimism style. Challenges happen every so often. Rejection, disappointment, loss, and embarrassment do occur and occur in all of our lives. When they do, a person with a "learned pessimism" style of thinking will get depressed.

In one of Seligman's studies (1997, pp. 78–79), he followed a group of 400 school students through several years of life. Those who started out with a pessimistic style were the ones who, when an event like a divorce happened, were likely to get depressed. The divorce (i.e., the life event) did not cause this depression by itself. Those with an optimistic style rebounded quickly from such events. What caused depression was the combination of painful *life events plus a style of thinking.* Because such events happen every so often, the person will appear to have a cyclical mood problem. It is not depression that is cyclical; it is life. Believing in "the cyclical nature of depression" is part of the permanent pervasive explanatory style of certain psychiatrists (Yapko, 1992, p. 124). This style itself is part of the cause of depression.

Personal Strengths

In the Personal Strengths model, when people say that their life feels hopeless they are at that moment demonstrating *the skill of chunking up* (generalizing to "their life") and associating into painful memories of the experience using the Permanent Pervasive explanatory style or frame.

Figure 16.1

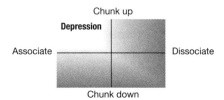

Meta-Programs and Strategies of Depression

In NLP terms (and more widely accepted terminology in brackets), the six key Meta-Programs and strategies (including Meta-Level strategies) which generate the negative trance of learned pessimism include the following. This comes from the research in Yapko (1992) and Seligman (1997):

- *Chunking up in problem situations* (permanent, pervasive explanatory style).
- *Associating into pain and dissociating from pleasure* (traumatic response).
- *Temporally orienting towards the past.*
- *Auditory-digital → Kinesthetic loop* (negative self-talk).
- *Kinesthetically shutting down* (psychomotor retardation).
- *Mapping oneself to not be "at cause"* (lack of a sense of control).

Chunking Up in Problem Situations

(The Permanent and Pervasive Explanatory Style)
Imagine the situation where a person applies for a job and fails to get it. If the person operates with a permanent, pervasive explanatory style, he or she will say, "No-one would employ me." Or, "Why do I always do something wrong?" In contrast, the person with a temporary, specific explanatory style might say, "The panel didn't understand how skilled I was in that area." Or, "I hadn't allowed myself the time to prepare well enough for the interview."

The person who depresses uses a permanent pervasive explanatory style dealing with problems. Since such people mainly think about problems, they specialize in chunking up using the linguistic form of universal quantifiers (all, always, never, etc.).

The aim of therapy is not to have such persons believe that "everything" is wonderful. Trying to "cheer up" a depressed person in this way leaves them vulnerable to the same style of thinking that caused their problem ("allness" thinking). The depressed person frequently "chunks up" in their goals for therapy as well, setting unrealistic outcomes for permanent, endless happiness (Yapko, 1992, p. 11). Successful therapy aims to teach the person to make more distinctions about what has happened and what could happen *specifically.*

Associate into Pain, Dissociate from Pleasure

(Problem Focus)
There are enormous *submodality distinctions* between the depressed cognitive style and the happy person's cognitive styles. The happy person tends to have their pleasant experiences encoded "impactfully" with large, close, and three-dimensional pictures that they can fully associate into. They code their unpleasant experiences with dissociated, small and distant submodalities. For the happy person, this means that pleasant memories are framed as very real and very significant.

Depressed people do it the other way round. They have their unpleasant experiences coded as real and the pleasant ones seem almost like false memories (because the person isn't inside their own body as they recall them). In this way, they "see" and "feel" their problems much of the time.

Solutions and positive experiences are harder to find and harder to believe in. This is the first part of the submodality structure behind the permanent, pervasive negative explanatory style. And because the depressed person mainly re-experiences unpleasant memories, the key change required involves teaching the skill of dissociating from those. Understandably, the depressed person often fears that this means "tampering with reality" (the "reality" of misery, as opposed to the "unreality" of happiness).

Temporally Orienting Towards the Past

The second part of the submodality structure behind the permanent, pervasive negative explanatory style involves the *temporal orientation*. Yapko (1992, pp. 118–121) suggests that this is the key to understanding depression: depressed persons have become stuck in looking backwards toward the past.

By way of contrast, in the disordering of anxiety, people become stuck looking towards the future, whereas for those with impulse disordering (e.g., addicted), they are stuck looking exclusively at the "now." Mental health involves a significant degree of *flexibility* in temporal orientation. The depressed person thinks of the present and future in terms of the past:

> "I know why I'm unhappy; it's because I never got over my mother's death." "My future is ruined because I'll always suffer from the confusion that I felt during sexual abuse."

Yapko emphasizes that psychotherapies which encourage a past temporal orientation are very attractive to the depressed person. And yet they also encourage them to do more of what they have already been doing that has not worked. Spending the first session of such therapy by discussing the past is a sure way to *reinforce* the hopelessness of the depressed person. The key to healing inevitably involves having the person turn around and look towards the future.

Auditory Digital → Kinesthetic Loop

(Negative self-talk, Rumination)
Seligman has pointed out that people differ in the amount that they pay attention to their internal self talk. Those who strongly attend to the language dimension are called "Ruminators" in cognitive psychology. *Rumination* in itself (using and relying on the auditory-digital sense) is not a problem. But combined with a permanent, pervasive explanatory style, this pattern cements depression in place.

Seligman (1997) says,

> The expectation of helplessness may arise only rarely, or it may arise all the time. The more you are inclined to ruminate, the more it arises. The more it arises, the more depressed you will be. Brooding, thinking about how bad things will be, starts the sequence. Ruminators get this chain going all the time. (pp. 82–83)

In NLP, we call this an *auditory digital → kinesthetic loop.* The person feels an uncomfortable feeling (K). He or she then talks about how permanent that will be and tells him or herself off (A$_d$). They next check how they feel about that (K). Not surprisingly, they feel worse. They then talk about that (A$_d$). Depressed people clearly show this strategy in their eye accessing movements. And this presents a challenge in using various NLP processes inasmuch as depressed clients will tend to talk to themselves about how the process "won't work for them," even as they engage in the process.

Kinesthetically Shutting Down

(Psychomotor Retardation)
Psychomotor retardation (Yapko, 1992, p. 94) refers to the slowing down of motor responses in depressed persons. Depressed clients often ensure this slowing of motor responses as they avoid exercise. This sets in place a cycle where lack of exercise increases insomnia, which increases exhaustion which causes a further reduction in exercise.

In NLP, we recognize that every state is affected by both internal representations and by physiology. After just ten minutes of walking briskly, most moods will lift for another 60–90 minutes thereafter (Thayer, 1996, pp. 23–24). Depressed clients usually come to the consultation in an unresourceful physiology. We can see this in the slumping down in the chair, breathing shallowly, eyes cast down to the right, and discovering that the person has barely moved over the last twenty-four hours. Attempting to work with such people in that state is like attempting to work with a drug addict while the addict is high.

Mapping Oneself as Being Not "At Cause"

(Lack of control)
Yapko points out (1992, p. 130) that the persons who are depressed often do not have a sense of themselves as able to *initiate causes* of future results. Such persons do not think:

> "If I engage in this behavior, that consequence is quite likely, whereas if I engage in this other behavior, this other consequence is quite likely."

Instead they think:

> "That behavior will happen, and I will just suffer the consequences."

This is a result of the permanent, pervasive explanatory style in relation to problems, combined with a lack of future orientation. Since sometimes, unfortunate things do happen, the depressed person becomes convinced that they "always" will. The global style of thinking means that the depressed fail to look for more precise distinctions about how they could adjust their behavior based on the feedback they are getting, in order to reach their goal. They might complain, "What's the point in falling in love; men (or women) will always leave you in the end, no matter how hard you try." Attempting to assist the person to change runs up against the same question. "What's the point of us doing NLP processes? I always end up back at the same place."

Facilitating the Demise of Depression: How Do we Do It?

1) Invite the person into the state of being "at cause"
Clearly, the structure behind depression presents a dilemma for someone wanting to assist the depressed person. Depression is both generated and perpetuated by the belief that things can't change. So the first task (and in a sense, the only task) in assisting a depressed person involves having the person experience themselves as *"at cause"* in their life.

For this reason, often our first comment with the client is to explain that we are not intending to do "psychotherapy" or "counseling" as they have known it. Instead, we plan to operate as the person's coach or consultant. We tell such persons that they are hiring us to provide advice and support to put into action a plan that will change things. This will be a collaborative relationship, in which the person will need not only to "help," but also to experimentally follow the advice we give. We have no magic way of solving problems for the depressed. But if the person follows the things we suggest, we believe that he or she will experience change.

This reflects the same deal we engage in as a consultant in the business setting. There we say, "NLP doesn't work. *You* work. NLP just explains how you work, perfectly." The other side of this is that if we are not hired as a consultant, we accept that without attempting to rescue them or to convince them. After all, others in the depressed person's life have already tried to rescue them from depression. They may have tried to cheer them up, give them gifts of time and objects, take the load off their shoulders, convince them that life is worthwhile, defend them against those who demand more of them, etc. Yet it didn't work.

No human being can *make* another human being happy. In the end, such attempts only lead to the rescuer feeling more resentful, and the depressed person feeling more hopeless. And it sets up a game. *Rescuing* is actually a dangerous game to play. It leads to increased risk of suicide as the depressed person seeks ever more frantically to indicate their need for more help, or to prove that the help has not worked. So to repeat, no one can *make* another person feel good. Even all the tricks and technology of NLP cannot do that.

The depressed person's belief that they *need* another person to save them defines, describes, and perpetuates "depression." This is not a side effect. This also explains why cooperating with it keeps the person depressed in spite of the rescuer's good intentions.

2) Pace skills and anchor resources

As noted throughout this work, the general NLP principle is that we almost always begin by pacing the skills and states which the person already uses. We then develop these. In the case of depression, the person has skills in associating into experiences, in chunking up, and in paying attention to past experience.

Anchor resourceful states from past experiences. It often takes time for the person to find any experiences that they can feel good about. Yet no person has had 100% miserable days for every day of life. At some time (even, let's say, in their childhood) this person laughed, felt proud of something they did, and enjoyed experiences. After all, they can walk, use language in talking, and dress themselves. Hypnosis is an excellent situation in which to re-access such resourceful states (Yapko, 1992, pp. 144–148).

Once a person accesses resources, change may become swift. We had one woman attend an introductory NLP training and learn the collapsing anchors process. She rang us back nine months later to say that these had been the first nine months in her life where she had not felt depressed. She said she had never sought help before, because her mother had also had a lifetime depression, and the daughter assumed that the problem was genetic. She was ringing us up to arrange a session for her mother.

3) Integrate parts and develop mindful awareness.

In the *Parts Integration* pattern, we associate into each of two opposing parts (e.g., the part that gets depressed, and the part that wants to enjoy life) and ask each part, "What is the higher intention of this part?" We do that until a shared higher intention is found. This provides a higher agreement frame for the integration.

Task the person to keep a depression diary for the first week, cataloguing all the times he or she felt depressed, and to rate those on a scale from 1–10. This provides a useful basis to explore the "exceptions" later (times when they were less depressed).

4) Coach the person in "Chunking Down" for more precision
Use Meta-Model questions to shift the person's thinking to more precise details. As a series of questions matched precisely to certain types of client comments, the Meta-Model enables us to "chunk down." The questions ask for sensory specific information. So when a client complains, "No one likes me!" by meta-modeling we inquire, "What specifically do you see or hear that leads you to believe that?" Or, "Everyone? Which people specifically do you believe don't like you?"

We not only use the Meta-Model ourselves, we also show our clients *how to challenge* their global thinking. The risk with using the Meta-Model is that many of the questions may support the depressed person's problem focus. So rather than asking, "Would no one employ you?", we instead ask a question that focuses on the counter-examples. "When has there been a time that someone did employ you?" Rather than asking, "How specifically does everything go wrong in your life?", we ask, "How specifically would something not "go wrong" in your life, if you succeeded?"

The most useful questions to ask depressed persons are solution focused questions. On this foundation Steve de Shazer, Insoo Kim Berg, and others have developed a model of change called the *Solution Focused* approach, (Chevalier, 1995). The following categories are examples of questions which guide a person to identify *what* they want and *how* to get it. When someone has an "adverse reaction" to the use of some NLP pattern, we use solution focused questions. de Shazer reports that this results in 75% success over four to six sessions.

- *Ask for a description of the outcome.* This is standard NLP outcome elicitation. Questions might include:

"What has to be different as a result of you talking to me?"
"What do you want to achieve?"
"What would need to happen for you to feel that this problem was solved?"
"How will you know that this problem is solved?"
"When this problem is solved, what will you be doing and feeling instead of what you used to do and feel?"

- *Ask about when the problem doesn't occur* (the exceptions). For example:
  "When is a time that you noticed this problem wasn't quite as bad?"
  "What was happening at that time? What were you doing differently?"

- *Ask about hypothetical exceptions with the "Miracle" question.* If there are no exceptions, use the Miracle question.
  "Suppose one night there is a miracle while you are sleeping, and this problem is solved. Since you are sleeping, you don't know that a miracle has happened or that your problem is solved. What do you suppose you will notice that's different in the morning, that will let you know the problem is solved?"

After the miracle question, you can ask other follow up questions such as:
  "What would other people around you notice was different about you?"
  "What would other people around you do differently then?"
  "What would it take to pretend that this miracle had happened?"

- *Set solution focused questions in place in the person's daily life.* We set this as a standard task for all depressed clients. Before they get out of bed in the morning they are to ask themselves,
  "What are three things that I am looking forward to today?"

When they go to bed at night they are to ask themselves,
"What are three things I valued in what happened today?"

We have had two cases of depression fully resolved where the only intervention used was to set the person the task of identifying three things they were looking forward to each day. We have found the potency of these questions extraordinary.

The person needs to know that globalized beliefs continue to be a risk even after making changes. To believe, "I've done some NLP now, so I'll never feel bad again" sets the person up for failure. Use the Meta-Model to encourage more specific expectation patterns.

5) Change submodalities to shift the focus to happiness
Given the earlier description, coach depressive persons to change the submodality features of their enjoyable experiences into more useful qualities. This may involve teaching them how to *step into* enjoyable experiences (associate into them), bring the images and sounds closer, brighten up the memory, etc. After doing two or three examples, suggest the generalization of this process. This coaches depressed persons into how to access resources by mental re-coding of thoughts.

Use the *NLP Trauma Pattern* to dissociate the person from traumatic or distressing memories. This method re-programs the brain as it invites the person to re-view a distressing memory from a dissociated position that simply watches the movie of the event from a position of comfort and interest. Do this with two or three examples and again, simply suggest the generalization of the process itself.

One elderly woman we worked with had been a Jewish child in Germany in the 1930s. When we ran the trauma resolution pattern on two incidents in her childhood, her depression lifted. The next week she reported that she was now sleeping through the night (nightmares had kept her from sleep), had more energy, and was feeling more confident. Her time-line also changed direction as a result of this intervention, so that the past shifted to being behind her (it had been in the same position as her future). This one process essentially solved her "post-traumatic depression."

Continue to ask presuppositional questions that assist clients in sorting for what is going well. With every contact after the first session, ask them what has gone well since you last met or talked. This programs in a new orientation—toward valuable and good things that count.

> "So what has changed in your life (or in your experience of the situation) that was a problem? No matter how small the changes seem at first, what is different?"

Secondly, genuinely congratulate them.

> "Wow, that's great. How did you do that?"

Then, thirdly, keep asking,

> "And what else has changed?"

6) Create a more flexible temporal orientation
Continue also using the solution focused questions that have a future orientation:

> "What are three things that you're looking forward to today?"

> "What do you want to achieve today?"

> "What will enable you to achieve that?"

Similarly, these questions will coach the person to plan ahead. All gains made in the consulting session can be carefully future paced into real life.

> "Imagine a time in the future, when in the past this would have been a problem, and tell me how it feels different now."

Time-line techniques such as the *Time Line Therapy* are a great pace and lead in regard to temporal orientation. The process for healing the past in the time-line therapy processes begins with the suggestion that the problem needs to be dealt with in there (as depressed persons suspect). But, surprisingly, the person floats into the past and then turns and looks towards the future. This is precisely the reverse of orientation that they have been missing out on before. Time-line therapy processes can be used to clear the emotions of anger, sadness and depression from the time-line.

Interestingly, we had one case where depression ended after a person cleared only anger from the time-line. No other interventions were used. The woman rang us back a week later to report that her mood had lifted immediately and remained steady. Intentionally altering the time-line direction has been an effective one session treatment for at least one client of ours also (where the past time-line had been in the same place as the future). As noted above, the treatment of depression by other means tends to alter the time-line direction anyway.

It's also important to create rich images of goals and install them on the future time-line. Sometimes depressed people will report that they have no future time-line, and the creation of one sends an important signal to the brain. In one case, our colleague worked with a woman who was told that she had only a few weeks to live. So along with other interventions, he helped her to install a future time-line. She lived a further three years, and reported that the envisioning of a future time-line inspired and gave her hope immediately.

7) Alter the client's auditory digital strategies

Usually, it also helps to alter the submodalities of the depressive's internal voice. Yapko (1992, p. 177) reports the use of submodality shifts in the person's self talk, as an effective intervention for depression. This may involve making the depressive voice like that of Donald Duck. We worked with one depressed client wherein the only overt NLP technique used was to have him do an auditory Swish pattern. We did that after the man reported that he became depressed by hearing his father's voice on the left hand side telling him that he "would never be any good."

The Swish in this case involved this voice fading away into the distance, as his own voice, powerful and affirming, came in telling him more rational beliefs. Repeating this swish several times solved the problem in the session. Richard then tested it by shouting his father's comments at his left ear. The man explained that he ran the swish himself a few times after the session, and felt that while his depression was still "possible," he had a way to solve it immediately now.

We can also create a new strategy for the auditory digital input. Our colleague, NLP Trainer Lynn Timpany, has developed a comprehensive process for doing this. She calls it *The Esteem Generator.* Many of our students report that it has enabled them to end depressive processes which have been resilient in the face of other interventions.

The Esteem Generator has three steps.

1) *Alter the auditory submodalities.*
   Begin with the unsupportive internal voice and experimentally at first, explore how you can loosen the depressive strategy.

2) *Identify the positive intention of the internal voice.*
   What is the positive intention of the voice? When that voice obtains its outcome, what does it want that's even more important than that first outcome? Continue this sequence (the Core Transformation questioning, Andreas, 1992) in order to deal with the part that has been generating the voice.

   A critical internal voice may have the positive intention such as "motivating me to be my best," or "protecting me from being embarrassed." New, more effective ways can be found to meet these intentions.

3) *Install a new strategy.*
   Begin with the old triggers for the unsupportive voice and invite the person to utter a key interrupt phrase (i.e., "Think positive!" or, "Hey wait!"). Have the person say something more resourceful inside. Congratulate them for that so that

they learn how to experience a positive feeling about having changed the old thinking. Lynn invites such persons to run through this sequence with every example they can recall, while she sets anchors and chains them on their knuckles.

8) Create the physiology of happiness

In coaching for a non-depressive strategy, it's important also to work with clients to design an exercise program that involves them in at least 15 minutes strenuous movement a day. Thayer (1996, p. 191) cites a study where depressed women were given the task of walking briskly 15 minutes a day. Those who completed the task reported elevation of mood, but only 50% completed the task. This emphasizes the importance of pacing and leading carefully as well as ensuring that clients experience themselves as "at cause."

It's also important to create a program in which any given client has a plan for laughing vigorously on a daily basis. One of our colleagues was working with a depressed and suicidal young man. He was discussing the hopelessness of his life in such somber terms, and for so long, that the situation began to feel absurd to our colleague. She began to laugh uncontrollably. Her client was first shocked. Then he felt puzzled. Finally, he joined her in laughing fully. When he stopped, his eyes lit up and he said, "Thanks! That's what I needed!" and left.

Dr Robert Holden (1993) runs the *Laughter Clinic* at West Birmingham Health Authority in Britain. He quotes William James' insight,

> We don't laugh because we are happy. We are happy because we laugh.

Holden cites evidence that laughter boosts immunoglobulin levels, restores energy, lowers blood pressure, massages the heart and reduces stress (1993, pp. 33–42). 100 laughs a day is the equivalent of 10 minutes jogging.

9) Keep the person at cause

We began with this and now we return to it. It's critical to build an expectancy of change from the first session. Indirect suggestion does this much more effectively than direct suggestion, or attempting to argue with the person (Yapko, 1992, pp. 139–142). Setting a time limit on the consulting process gives an important indirect message, "I expect this to be solved in four sessions."

You can use paradoxical suggestions also.

> "You can be just self-critical enough to really want more for yourself of the kind of things you can feel really good about."

> "Don't entertain, even for a moment, that you could be feeling better sooner than you might expect."

Experiential evidence of the possibility of change can be given using an exercise. Earlier we described the visualization exercise that we use at our trainings that involve asking a person to turn around and point to a spot, then imagining doing it and going further, and then doing it. People always go further (Bolstad and Hamblett, 1998, p. 81). When we do that, we inevitably follow up with a discussion about how our representations determine how we feel and what we achieve. This allows people to begin mapping out the idea of being "at cause."

It's important also to encourage the person to set and achieve goals. Outcomes for the sessions are set with the person, based on the specific problems they are having, and the specific Meta-Programs and strategies they are using to create these problems. It is also an important learning for the person to set small and more-than-realistic goals, and have the undeniable experience of achieving them.

For us, assisting a depressed person without the person completing tasks at home involves a contradiction of terms. Clients do not come to us to have their consulting sessions improve; they come to have their lives improve. This explains why setting tasks such as identifying three things they are looking forward to each day creates a new orientation and reminds us that we operate as consultants, not rescuers.

Reframe experiences based on the presupposition of being "at cause." From the very first comment you make to the most advanced metaphors and NLP techniques you use, everything said to the depressed person involves *reframing*. This is, in part, because the whole notion that *change can happen* represents a radical reframe for the depressed. Yet once accepted, this heralds the end of depression. And the most powerful aid to successful reframing involves your own deeply held belief that the person can change, that they will inevitably change, that life itself involves constant change.

10) Take steps to prevent suicide

Because of the potential of suicide, it's worth the risk to ask about negative responses. It is appropriate to check how far along the track of suicidal thinking a person has gone from a sense that they would be better off dead > the decision to end their life > suicidal fantasizing > concrete preparations for the act. If the person is considering suicide, consider what safety actions and precautions you will need to take. Consult your supervisor or another experienced person to discuss your decisions and their legal implications.

As a consultant, you have a right to ask that *during the period of your consulting,* the person will stay alive (otherwise your assistance is wasted). Make a *"Staying Alive Contract"* and check that they are congruently agreeing to it. Interestingly, depressed persons tend to keep such arrangements. The contract will include a method by which they can contact someone in a crisis. Decide whether that person is the consultant, a phone counseling service, or a friend or relative. In the session, rehearse this crisis contact (e.g. have them actually phone the person). Have them future pace any possible excuses they might make for not doing this ("What would make you decide not to keep this contract?") and build in reframes to ensure that even that situation leads to them contacting the person.

If the client misses a session, has not notified you before, and has been suicidal, contact them to reaffirm the Staying Alive Contract, or plan other interventions such as phoning a counseling service. Although as a consultant, you cannot ultimately *make* someone stay alive, this contract maximizes the chances that this will happen.

Summary

The RESOLVE Model and Depression

We now know the depression strategy. Depression results when a person "chunks up" in generalizations and associates into problem situations, in an orientation toward the past, while shutting down kinesthetic responses and tying oneself up in negative Auditory-Digital Kinesthetic loops. To summarize using the RESOLVE model, the recommended interventions become the following:

1) *Access and operate out from your own* **Resourceful** *state.* Establish a collaborative, consultative relationship rather than a rescuing relationship.

2) **Establish** *rapport.* Begin by acknowledging the person's pain while assessing and pacing the Meta-Programs of Towards/Away From, Time Orientation, Optimistic/ Pessimistic Attributional Style, Chunking level, Association and Dissociation patterns.

3) **Specify** *Outcomes.* Set a time limited consulting contract with outcomes. Build expectancy of change, and explain the need for tasking. Assess the need for a "Staying Alive" Contract.

4) **Open up** *the client's model of the world.* Demonstrate the power of internal representations (e.g., the pointing exercise), educate about the NLP presuppositions and reframes for resourcefulness, Meta-Model the "chunked up" descriptions to bring them back to sensory specific data, and then put them inside of a new frame. Give tasks to rehearse future orientation and positive attributional style. Identify three things to look forward to each morning, and then associate into them. Each evening identify three things you appreciate about your day. Use Solution-Focused questions.

5) **Lead** *to the Desired State.* Pace and lead to a more motivated state nonverbally. Re-access and anchor resourceful states. Use various facets of the time-line therapy model for the major emotions including "depression." Use the Trauma Resolution pattern for precipitating events (especially early in life). Rehearse new strategies; e.g. Esteem Generator to break the negative self-talk loops. Use submodality shifts to store positive memories in powerful submodalities. Place goals in one's future time-line. Plan for a daily exercise routine and sessions of laughter.

6) **Verify** *change.* Teach the person to search for and celebrate the differences in their life.

7) **Exit:** *Future pace.* Teach the person to limit generalizations (especially those that equate the past with the future) and coach the person to build more realistic expectations. Define success in achievable terms. And discuss ending of sessions clearly.

Chapter 17

Borderline Disordering of "Personality"

In the Borderline Personality Disordering we find a most difficult pattern. The very label of this disordering, *"borderline,"* makes it difficult to operationalize this style of thinking, feeling, and acting in behavioral terms. Originally, the term arose to designate a mixture of neurotic and psychotic symptoms, hence "on the border" between neurosis and psychosis. Then, over a period of time the term evolved as it was used by the psychological community, especially by psychoanalysts. Different authors used the term in very different ways, sometimes as a "garbage can" diagnosis for those whom the therapist couldn't specifically identify. Of course, that did not make for clarity! One author went so far as to describe it as "a schizotypal borderline who exhibited a psychotic structure."

At the heart of this disordering we find changeability of symptoms, variability of moods, and many intense emotional reactions as central to identifying "the borderline." Such individuals will abruptly shift from a pervasive depressed mood to anxious agitation or intense anger, or they may impulsively engage in actions that they later recognize as irrational and counter-productive. This seems to correspond to what Satir, in Family Systems, describes as "the distractor." The DSM IV offers the following diagnostic criteria for the Borderline Personality Disorder:

A pervasive pattern of instability of interpersonal relationships, self-image, and affects, and marked impulsivity beginning by early adulthood and present in a variety of contexts as indicated by *five* (or more) of the following:

1) Frantic efforts to avoid real or imagined abandonment.

2) A pattern of unstable and intense interpersonal relationships characterized by alternating between extremes of over-idealization and devaluation.

3) Identity disturbance: markedly persistent unstable self-image or sense of self.

4) Impulsivity in at least two areas that are potentially self-damaging (e.g., spending, sex, substance use, reckless driving, binge eating).

5) Recurrent suicidal threats, gestures, or threats, or self-mutilating behavior.

6) Affective instability due to a marked reactivity of mood (e.g., intense episodic dysphoria, irritability, or anxiety usually lasting a few hours and only rarely more than a few days).

7) Chronic feelings of emptiness.

8) Inappropriate, intense anger or difficulty controlling anger (e.g., frequent displays of temper, constant anger, recurrent physical fights).

9) Transient, stress-related paranoid ideation or severe dissociative symptoms.

With *variability* itself as a key hallmark of the borderline personality disorder, we need to explore the cognitive-emotive and behavioral factors that drive such variability. Obviously, the signs of such variability will show up cognitively in changing minds, flipping from one side to another (polarity jumps), cognitive extremes, either/or thinking, etc. The emotional signs will involve similar extreme flip-flops between intense ups and downs, joys and angers, total boredom, emptiness, loneliness and then excitements. Behaviorally we will see impulsive behaviors wherein the person "acts out" their affective states. Relationally, this will create instability and rocky relationships. The "borderline" strongly desires an intimate relationship and so moves toward it, then radically fears it and so moves away. This generates a "Come Closer! No, Get Away" pattern.

Conceptualization

The psychoanalytic approach took the view that the borderline personality arises from problems with object relations which involves unfinished work with early caregivers and which shows up in unrealistic expectancies. Social learning theory suggests the lack of a clear, consistent sense of self identity which then results in the lack of clear goals.

The cognitive-behavioral model focuses on the person's driving schemas (mental maps). This generally involves three central mental maps:

1) The world as dangerous and malevolent,

2) Self as relatively powerless, vulnerable, unworthy, unacceptable, and

3) Tremendous fear of rejection and abandonment.

James Pretzer (in Beck, 1990) presented the following scenario that illustrates the gestalt that results:

> "'Borderline individuals' believe that they are weak and powerless and so block [the solution of relying on their own strengths and abilities in dealing with the threats in the world.] Other individuals who believe that they are not capable of dealing effectively with the demands of daily life resolve their dilemma by becoming dependent on someone who they see as capable of taking care of them. ... However, borderlines' belief that they are inherently unacceptable block this option, since this belief leads them to conclude that dependence entails a serious risk of rejection, abandonment, or attack if this inherent unacceptability is discovered. Borderline individuals face quite a dilemma: Convinced that they are relatively helpless in a hostile world but without a source of security, they are forced to vacillate between autonomy and dependence without being able to rely on either." (p. 187)

With these dialectics on which the person vacillates comes the disordering—they feel drawn to people, but then back off in fear of being controlled, exposed, shamed, humiliated, etc. They feel afraid of the dangers of the world, but lack any internal centering of their own identity, values, and beliefs, and so dislike themselves and fear exposure.

The two most central facets driving borderlines concern their dichotomous thinking (i.e., Either/Or thinking) and lack of a solid sense of self (low self-esteeming and lack of self-efficacy). The core of a weak, powerless, unacceptable, and worthless sense of self (a Meta-State) generates very strong and intense feelings: fear, dread, shame, dependence, etc. They then filter this through the extreme thinking pattern of Either/Or thinking. The result: extreme shifts and changes, impulsiveness, love and hate, dependence and rejection, etc.

> A lack of a clear sense of self makes it difficult for borderlines to decide what to do in ambiguous situations and results in a low tolerance for ambiguity. (Beck, 1990, p. 189)

Since it takes a strong sense of self to welcome with acceptance strong negative emotions (i.e., anger, grief, fear, etc.), borderlines experience the inability to control intense emotions and so they block them off from awareness. Yet what results from this is not more control or a greater sense of self-management, but less. It results in a greater sense of one's inadequacy of skills in emotional regulation. Such individuals accordingly fear, and even hate, intense negative emotions (a Meta-State). By disparaging their emotions, they don't welcome them when small and manageable, but keep them suppressed until they hit a threshold and explode into awareness in an overwhelming way. So when the negative emotions do break through into consciousness, they feel overwhelming and life destroying. And, of course, this reinforces the belief that negative emotions are dangerous.

As borderlines recognize these experiences, they adopt a more and more disparaging and punitive attitude toward their own emotions, toward directness, toward intimacy, and toward vulnerability. They move out into the world with cautiousness—avoiding risks, guarded, always vigilant, fearful of being "controlled," etc.

Beck (1976) says that the one particular cognitive distortion of borderlines consists of dichotomous thinking.

Dichotomous thinking is the tendency to evaluate experiences in terms of mutually exclusive categories (e.g., good or bad, success or failure, trustworthy or deceitful) rather than seeing experiences as falling along continua. The effect of this 'black-and-white' thinking is to force extreme interpretations on events that would normally fall in the intermediate range of a continuum, since there are no intermediate categories. (p. 187)

This leads to the constant *polarizing* that we find in borderlines. First they view someone as totally trustworthy, then one mistake occurs, and the person becomes totally untrustworthy in their eyes. This way of perceiving governs their abrupt mood swings and dramatic behavioral shifts. It governs their coping skills in the world that they view from moment to moment as completely benign or deadly. Using this perceptual grid on themselves, they flip between being a completely flawless human being to a scumbag! Either/Or thinking also undermines their coping skills inasmuch as it makes a frustration totally "no problem" to "the end of the world" for them.

So with relationships. They totally desire others or totally can't stand them! Linehan (1987b) says that borderline individuals often vacillate between seeking dependence and actively avoiding it, "rather than being able to rely on others to a moderate degree." Relationally, all of this vacillation creates a "crazymaking" style in communicating, leaving others "never knowing where they stand" with the person.

Re-ordering the Disordering

The conceptualizations presented by Millon (1981, 1987b), Linehan (1981, 1987a,b), and Young (1983, 1987; Young and Swift, 1988) suggest, respectively, that intervention should focus on establishing a clearer sense of identity, improving skills at controlling emotions, or changing maladaptive beliefs and assumptions. (Pretzer, Beck, 1990, p. 189)

1) Gaining rapport to disprove the higher frames of danger
Given the emphasis on the role of *dichotomous, Either/Or thinking* in the disordering, the earlier we address this cognitive style, the sooner we can coach the person in more effectively managing the extreme reactions and abrupt mood swings. Yet if we simply attack such thinking without first establishing a solid and trusting therapeutic relationship, this strategy will backfire. So first comes providing an easy and solid structure for therapy that itself counter-acts the belief of the danger and malevolence of the world, which includes the therapist. Here, as therapists, our calm acceptance of the person's intense negative emotions and abrupt changes, and matter-of-factly exploring them in an easy way begins the challenge.

2) Reframing the therapeutic relationship and process
Those who suffer from the borderline disordering typically do not have a solid sense of where they stand with others. They lack a clear sense and map about inter-personal reality, including the therapeutic relationship. Therefore, as we socialize the client to the healing process of therapy it helps them to deal with their fear of ambiguity. It lets them know "where they stand" and what to expect. As we meta-comment on the person's strong anticipation of rejection and the intense emotional reactions that come out of that we invite such individuals to step aside from their old mapping in order to examine it. This begins the process of distinguishing between map-and-territory. It also communicates a very important frame, namely, "Just because I feel a certain way doesn't make it so."

3) Establishing a clear sense of direction and objective
Therapy should begin with a focus on behavior where the person would need little introspection to succeed. Borderlines will experience such as far less threatening than focusing on thoughts and emotions. This builds small successes and creates a useful momentum. It further helps with building a clear sense of where we stand with each other.

We can expect borderline clients to oscillate back and forth, wanting the intimacy of a therapeutic relationship and then fearing, "knowing for sure" that we're up to something devious, moving closer, moving away, etc. It's part of the disordering. Knowing this enables us, as therapists, to know what's occurring and to not get sucked into a defensive or care-taking posture.

4) Slowly and gently operationalizing terms and meaning

Eventually we have to gently challenge the dichotomous thinking of the client. Without doing that, we leave the person in a very limited and constricted Either/Or World with only two choices. Simultaneously, by introducing "the excluded middle," and the world of all of the in-between choices, we invite them to process that in terms of fear and dread of ambiguity. This calls for a very gentle approach as we slowly open up the world to their perspective of more choices *while we simultaneously* coach them into a more resourceful sense of self and of values.

As we Meta-Model the specifics of the borderline's words, language, and conceptual mapping, we invite them to begin to operationalize what trust and distrust (treachery), security and insecurity means. We invite them to map out *how they will know*. This also provides opportunities for them to reality test their new mapping by offering counter-examples from their own experiences. Slowly, this will begin to de-nominalize their over-generalized map that has failed to see things in degrees, steps, and stages.

5) Modeling the acceptance of negative emotions

Given that borderlines dread and fear negative emotions so much and have little concept of how to do that, one of the most powerful therapeutic interventions involves *modeling* how to do that for them. As a therapist, if we demonstrate that we can and do *accept* our own negative emotions, and intense ones, and that we can just talk about them, and about how we are in our core self much more than our emotions, this invites the client to begin to build similar maps.

So in modeling our own acceptance, even appreciation, of negative emotions, of our fallibility, and of texturing our states with various resources, we model the art of state management and impulse control. This separates self and emotions, self and thoughts, self and the functions or powers of one's self. As it does, it makes room so that the person can simply notice thoughts-and-emotions, acknowledge such, and welcome them. Building up this Meta-State begins to deframe the old Meta-States that comprise the borderline disordering.

Structurally, to experience the borderline disordering one brings the Either/Or Dichotomous Thinking state to bear upon one's self, others, the world, etc. This creates the two polar opposites in each of these conceptual categories. It explains where the person goes in their abrupt polarizing from one side to the other.

Figure 17.1

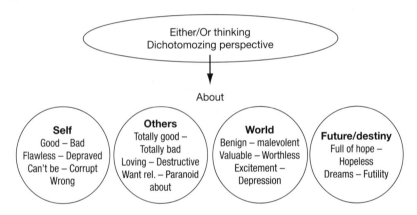

6) Distinguishing Map/Territory
To deframe this complex Meta-State format, we outframe the Either/Or thinking itself, quality control it as we "run an ecology check" on it, reality testing it, etc. Any NLP and Neuro-Semantic pattern that underscores the map/territory difference assists this learning.

7) Setting Meta-Frames for Resourcefulness
Since borderline clients also have meta-stated themselves with rejection and hate about their emotions, we will want to coach them into a number of Meta-Level moves. This is "dangerous" to their old disordering frames. It invites lots of self-reflection and

the danger is that they will do so from the old frames of self-contempt, fear, dread, etc.

So we need to preframe the Meta-Level move with comfort, pleasure, "just an exercise" in merely observing and noticing, doing so in a kinder and gentler way, etc. Once we establish this, we can then invite our clients to reject their rejection of emotions, to accept their rejection and to accept their negative emotions by reframing them as "just emotions," "just somatic body responses to thoughts," and as "just energies that come and go." All of this begins to break down the old frames that have held the borderline disordering together.

Outframing in terms of bringing thoughts and feelings of value, acceptance, dignity, etc. to bear upon their "sense of self" provides a powerful intervention. Here again, meta-modeling self-definitions, operationalizing how they know to define something as they do, exploring where they got that map, how well it serves them, etc. counters the current self-disordering. It facilitates the client's developing a clearer sense of identity, recognizing themselves as a part from their functions. This then makes feedback more safe and therefore acceptable.

Now over to Richard and Margot.

When Borderlines say, "Your Therapy won't work with me!"

When people feel depressed or anxious, they often seek therapeutic help. And when people psychotically break with "reality," others often seek help for them. But when someone is angry or hyper-critical (with themselves and others) they don't necessarily believe they need help. And, others will not necessarily want to help them. If they do seek help, their therapists frequently wish they had not because of their "critical," "hostile," "resistant" approach. Over and over, they communicate in effect, "Your therapy is bullshit, and your tricks won't work with me!"

Early on in our work with NLP, we naively believed that NLP change processes would work with all our clients as they did with ourselves. The clients would do the process, and then they would change. Then they would thank us, and leave. Instead, what we found was that a small group of people told us that none of the processes worked, that NLP was "just a set of tricks," that they felt really angry with us for promising things we didn't deliver, and that they wanted to come back and do some more. This surprised us. We would apologize. We would promise to try to do better. Yet even saying such things only made the problem worse. Since then we've learned to detect such responses earlier and respond in ways that quickly enable these people to turn around 180°.

Searching for a not-too-blatantly insulting name, psychiatrists landed on *"Borderline Personality Disorder"* to describe this kind of responding. Michael noted in quoting from the DSM-IV, that the Borderline Disorder is defined in terms of emotional impulsivity, instability, emptiness, and anger at both self and others. Much of what we have here will also be useful in work with persons diagnosed with Dependent, Antisocial, Histrionic, Narcissistic or Obsessive-Compulsive personality disorders.

The term "Borderline" refers to an old, pre-DSM belief that someone with this disorder was on *the borderline between sanity and insanity.* While we doubt that the Borderline Personality Disorder "exists" as a separate physical condition, we do propose that there are processes that can help a person suffering from emotional impulsivity and confusing feelings of emptiness and anger.

"What's so fucking wrong with being borderline?"

In NLP, we see the core characteristic of people diagnosed with "Borderline Personality Disorder" as *a severe sequential incongruity.* In external relationships this is expressed in swings from idolizing another person and desperately wanting to be with them, to despising them and wanting to escape the relationship. Such a person's relationship with themselves shows up in swings from apparent arrogant self-promotion to self-hatred and disgust. Cognitively, this means constant polarity responses; the person mismatches their own and others' experience continuously.

Emotionally this creates confusion about who they are and what they want, resulting in feelings of frustration, anxiety, depression, emptiness and hopelessness. The person's final behavior may be deliberately self destructive (e.g., suicide attempts, self mutilation), destructive of others (e.g., physical fighting, smashing objects, explosive shouting) or dangerously impulsive (e.g., drug abuse, binge eating, reckless driving). It is as if they are at war with themselves, and with anyone else who gets in the way of this primary target.

People with higher "hostility" scores on the widely used Minnesota Multiphasic Personality Inventory (MMPI) are more likely to smoke, drink alcohol excessively, be obese, have high cholesterol levels, and consume more caffeine (Williams and Williams, 1993, p. 80). They are also five times more likely to die before the age of fifty (Williams and Williams, 1993, p. 54).

This fits with the results we see in people diagnosed as "borderline." 56% have anxiety disorders, 41% have a major depression (Crits-Christoph, 1998, p. 545) and 69% have an addictive disorder (Santoro and Cohen, 1997, p. 90). These other problems, which may first bring the person to a therapist, are also harder to change using cognitive (NLP style) therapy when in a person diagnosed as borderline (Crits-Christoph, 1998, p. 549) because they will mismatch the therapy process itself as noted earlier.

"Why does this shit always happen to me?"

Research to date rules out even a genetic *component* in the development of BPD (Crits-Christoph, 1998, p. 546). Neurological studies show that the borderline person has more right brain activity (perhaps more emotional processing than logical processing) and an over-responsive noradrenaline system. Yet, this is just another way of saying that such individuals are angry! The most significant thing known about the origin of the problem is that 70–79% of these people have suffered severe physical or sexual abuse or endured serious trauma in very early childhood (Crits-Christoph, 1998, p. 545; Santoro and Cohen, 1997, p. 4).

Traditional psychotherapists have proposed (Kernberg, 1986, p. 142) that during these traumatic early events, healthy repression (or healthy dissociation) was not possible because the child had not developed the skills to manage just stepping aside from an emotion and merely observing it. Instead, the state dependent memory of each traumatic event has been fully split off from the rest of the "personality." This results in a vast array of "parts" conflicts. This psychoanalytic proposal actually precisely fits with the NLP frame.

The problem before us at this point concerns what to do about it. Results of treatment with antidepressant, anti-anxiety, and anti-psychotic drugs have at best been inconsistent, and at worst useless (Woo-Ming and Siever, 1998, pp. 562–564). Behavioral therapy has been shown to reduce impulsive behavior, but not the emotional instability of people with BPD (Crits-Christoph, 1998, pp. 547–548).

Interestingly, one study revealed that 12 months after a year of psycho-dynamic therapy (based on the "Self Psychology" model), 30% of clients no longer met the borderline criteria (Crits-Christoph, 1998, p. 548). This is an impressive result, and emphasizes several points that Cognitive Therapists (therapists using techniques similar to NLP) have made about the disorder.

They describe it as an Identity level disorder (Layden *et al.*, 1993, p. 7) based on core beliefs about the self, such as, "I am unloveable," and "I am broken." Because the person believes, "This is who I am," they resent therapeutic attempts to change less central beliefs as "I can't manage this particular task." They are inclined to say, "If you think *a person like me* can change that, you don't know how serious this is!" In this description, we have many Meta-Level states and frames which set and protect the disordering.

The Self Psychology model (Kohut, 1971) sees problems such as "borderline personality disorder" as resulting from damage in the healthy development of a "love of self." The model holds that when a three-year-old child says, "Look at me! Aren't I great!", functional parents will respond by mirroring this excitement (e.g., "Wow—that's amazing!"). But when the mirroring available is seriously inadequate, the child becomes fixated at this "level of development." By creating an empathic environment, the Self Psychology practitioner aims to create a relationship in which clients can explore their swinging between idealization of others and grandiose, self obsessed rage, and grow beyond child-like responses.

Cognitive therapists point out that "borderline" persons have whole areas of life where they function in a successful and adult way. On the other hand, the state dependent memories which have been split off (the "parts" of the mind that generate the borderline symptoms) function with a thinking style similar to that of a pre-school child.

Even the sensory system (the VAK representations) used to store the traumatic responses is determined by the early age of the events which created it (Layden *et al.*, 1993, pp. 28–33). Events before age 12 months are usually stored kinesthetically and auditory tonally, and events before age 2 years are stored kinesthetically, auditory tonally, and visually. Only after this time does effective auditory digital information get layered into the memories. Mary Anne Layden and colleagues recommend using kinesthetic experiences (such as relaxation and kinesthetic anchors), guided visual imagery (such as the NLP Trauma Pattern), and techniques based on voice tone (e.g., trance) to access and heal the earlier memories.

Imagine a client, one minute telling you that he or she wants you to save him or her from a catalogue of shitty situations, and the next minute that *you* are the one causing one of those situations. What *skills* is this person demonstrating? Diagnosing this from the *Personal Strengths model,* we see demonstrated skills in chunking down (to "the shitty details") and dissociating from the experience.

"Don't you tell me I mismatch!"

Several key Meta-Programs and strategy variables drive persons diagnosed as Borderline. These include the following:

Figure 17.2

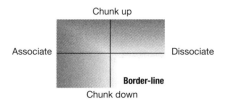

1) Sorting by self
The person is convinced that almost everything happening is hap-pening *for* them. This leads at times to paranoia: "Why did you say that? What are you trying to tell me?" At other times it leads to interpersonal conflict: "You knew I didn't want you to do that. Why did you do it?" The person is not fully separating out first position (seeing through their own eyes) from second position (seeing through the other person's eyes). In communication theory terms, they have confused problem ownership (Bolstad and Hamblett, 1998, pp. 73–77). In traditional psychotherapy terms, they have "diffuse boundaries."

2) Sorting for differences (mismatching)
The person sorts for what they disagree with, and what doesn't fit. This means they are continuously aware of how life *does not* live up to the ideal. In therapeutic relationships, this results in them identifying even very small differences between what a therapist said and did, "You said you'd tell me the truth; how come you never mentioned before that you… "

Even much of the person's language (auditory digital) processing is taken up with mismatching themselves (telling themselves off). In their early life, mismatching originally served as an important skill that protected them from being totally overwhelmed by pow-erful others. But now, it has become an uncontrollable reflex response to almost every event. As a Meta-Program, *sorting for dif-ferences* is a useful and essential one for creativity, and psycholog-ical independence. Yet as with any Meta-Program, its compulsive use creates problems.

3) Chunking across and Either/Or thinking

Part of the process of mismatching involves what is called in cognitive psychology "transductive reasoning" (Layden *et al.*, 1993, p. 38). As the person leaps from one state to another, and one opinion to another, they fail to chunk up and identify general principles behind these separate events. There is a lack of meta-analysis, and, in Meta-State terminology, an absence of Meta-States such as a strong sense of self. (Hall, 1996)

Another result of mismatching and polarity-based thinking involves perceiving things as *either perfect or ruined.* "My haircut was a disaster today. I'm going to kill myself." This is connected to chunking across, because the person has no higher category to experience the specific event as "a part of." In the example, the haircut is *all there is.* There's no "self" above and beyond the events of the moment, so that the bad haircut is the only evidence of self to measure success by.

When the person asks, "Am I loveable?" or "Am I competent?" in mapping these strategies, only the immediate evidence is assessed. What's the danger here? It lies in that, in relation to other people, one "mistake" can provide enough evidence to the borderline person to feel that their very life is threatened.

4) Present temporal focus

The previous example demonstrates how the person assesses most decisions by reference only to the present moment. "Do I want to use this heroin? Why not? It'll stop the pain right now!" They respond based on the principle, "Out of sight; out of mind." In developmental terms, this is described as "lack of object permanence."

The same process often creates anxiety about relationships, because as soon as the other person in the relationship leaves the room, the borderline persons feel abandoned. It also results in the person having a "consistent convincer strategy," (i.e., a lack of trust) which means that he or she never feels fully convinced by previous experiences.

5) *Away from motivation*

Many decisions, such as decisions to commit suicide or use drugs, are a result of moving away from pain without any evaluation of what the person actually wants instead.

6) *Sequential incongruity*

The combination of the above Meta-Programs makes it more difficult for the person to hold in mind two differing responses (e.g., being annoyed at what someone did, at the same time as loving them). They experience such polarities sequentially, each one mismatching and moving away from the previous response. They frequently feel split off from ("positive" or "negative") parts of their own experience.

"Help me change (but don't make me do anything different!)"

The borderline disordering system, described above, is actually a very resilient one. It has to be in order to enable the person, with the limited resources of a young child, to survive severe trauma. Further, the person does not identify this *personality system* as the problem. He or she will rather identify feelings of anxiety, frustration, emptiness, depression, or even the endless succession of absolute bastards who seem to intrude as "the problem."

1) *Get permission to identify mismatching*

For us, the first step in helping such persons to make lasting change involves *identifying this extreme mismatching style*. This also involves setting up a consulting relationship in which we have permission to help them identify and change this style that actually generates the unpleasant states which they want to change.

Bob (for so we will name him) came to one of our weekend trainings. We used a visualization exercise that involved individuals turning around and pointing behind them with their arm. They would then return to the front and imagine themselves going further, and noticing what they would see, feel, and say to themselves if their body was more flexible and they could turn around further. Then they turn around again and notice how much further they go (Bolstad and Hamblett, 1998, p. 81). Yet unlike the great majority who do this with great results, Bob wasn't impressed.

Bob: Well, I think I went further the first time. It didn't work for me at all.

Margot: That's right, it didn't because you didn't do the process the way I described it. I said to imagine what it looked, felt, and sounded like to go further, and you talked to yourself inside about how this probably wouldn't work for you....Right?

Bob: Hmmm. Probably. Yeah, I guess so.

Margot: And that's probably the way you've been doing a lot of other things too. You're already good at talking skeptically to yourself. If you want to get a *different* result in your life, then it's worth using these exercises the way we actually describe them, and *only* do what we describe. You just did more work than you needed to. Now lets do that one more time, the new way.

Before using central change processes, we use "the pointing process" as an opportunity for people to mismatch. This acts as a "mismatching detector." In order to mismatch the instructions given, a person needs to override the internal visual, auditory, kinesthetic representations suggested. Since the most likely way to do that is by talking to themselves, Margot drew Bob's attention to that and then asked Bob to mismatch his mismatching (Meta-State his mismatching with mismatching). She commented that if he kept mismatching, he is just doing the same old thing every time. The only way to mismatch is follow our (new) method.

This is a simple application of the technique Milton Erickson identified for use in this situation. Erickson (1980) wrote:

> When sufficient material has been obtained from the aggressive, hostile, antagonistic, defensive, uncooperative patients to appraise their unfortunate behavior and attitudes and to judge their type of personalities, they are interrupted by an introductory paragraph of mixed positive and negative, seemingly appropriate and relevant

remarks addressed to them in that form of language they can best understand at that moment. However, concealed and disguised in these remarks are various direct, indirect, and permissive suggestions intended to channel their reactions into receptive and responsive behavior. (p. 301)

2) Shift to a consulting mode

We prefer to inform clients explicitly that they need to change their Meta-Programs in order to get their desired results. In doing so we are setting up a very specific type of "therapeutic alliance" or "consulting."

In this arrangement, we make suggestions as to processes which they could use to change. If they follow these processes, they will get the results they want. If they want to keep us hired as a consultant, they need to actually follow the recommendations. We emphasize that processes must be followed precisely in order to get the desired results. We like to clearly describe this consulting arrangement before starting "formal" NLP interventions.

Consistently, we have found "borderline" persons able to be more resourceful when helping someone else to change, rather than when trying to change themselves. Accordingly, we teach them to utilize this *resourceful helping state* by becoming their own therapist. We simply provide supervision of their therapy.

For example, in helping a person learn to sort for what is going well in their life we may ask them, as a task, to take time each evening and identify three things that went well in their day. We then say that we've had people return to tell us that they tried this, and it just made them feel bad. Obviously, they didn't do the task as instructed. Instead they thought of the first thing that went well, and then thought about *how hard* it had been to think of that one thing (one Meta-Level), and then they *worried* that they might not be able to think of two more (another Meta-Level), and then wondered what that *meant about them as a person* (a third Meta-Level). Understandably, they felt bad about all of this. Yet they had not performed the task given.

To be this "confrontational," we have to use rapport skills very subtly because such persons will be on the alert for "tricks" and will mismatch body posture if they detect the therapist's attempt to match. We also have to genuinely tell the person what *behaviors* they have done which indicate to us the functional areas of their life. This differs from saying, "You're wonderful," a claim which would directly contradict the person's Identity level beliefs (Layden *et al.*, 1993, p. 60). Instead, we say, "I was impressed with the time you spent helping other course participants. It made our job easier." This positive feedback provides a model of sorting for positives that we want the person to learn. Even when the person disparages it, it still has usefulness as a genuine feedback, and as an example of how we come to believe that the person can change.

3) Acknowledge and use the mismatch limitations

As consultants, there are limits to our help. When a person compulsively has to mismatch, this often prevents us from taking him or her through some standard NLP pattern. On such occasions we have found it useful to ask the person to run their own NLP processes while we serve as a coach.

Instead of saying, "See yourself in a movie theater, and move back to the projection booth," we say,

"Here's how the NLP Trauma pattern works. Now, just run that through by yourself until you've solved the problem, and come back and check in with us then."

Certainly, we need to set limits on how much time we are willing to spend with this person, who, remember, is capable of demanding and dismissing "endless" convincing and reassurance. We aim primarily to model new strategies, such as self-reassurance, and then have the person run these strategies themselves.

The following change processes are only applied within the context of the consulting relationship as described here. With them, we have found that many "personality disorders" can be reversed in weeks, rather than years. Without preframing this relationship from the start, we often lose the ability to help effectively since our presence itself becomes a powerful trigger for mismatching.

4) Check for suicidal thinking

Therapists are often contacted by people in a crisis who may be experiencing extreme anxiety, depression or frustration (see Bolstad and Hamblett, 1999a, b, & c). At such times, it is appropriate to check how far along the track of suicidal thinking the person may have gone, as well as what violence the person has previously been involved in or contemplated.

At that point, assess for yourself whether you feel safe working with this person. Being a consultant does not mean being a martyr. Ask that during the time of your consulting the person commits him or herself to staying alive and to take time out from being with others if they feel anger escalating dangerously. To make these contracts work requires rehearsing the person (and possibly others who live with them) through the process of getting help in a crisis. We often ask people that while they are in the session with us, they practice contacting a support person by phone.

While we ultimately cannot "make" a person stay alive, or guarantee that they won't injure others, as a person in the therapeutic role we are legally responsible for taking all reasonable steps to keep clients and others safe. As you familiarize yourself with this aspect of this work, develop as many safety processes as possible.

5) Accessing resources

One of our major aims in working with borderline clients involves generalizing skills from functional areas of life to areas where their unresourceful states are triggered (Layden *et al.*, 1993, p. 38). The challenge here involves how to even begin talking positively with someone who mismatches. Yvonne Dolan (1985, pp. 29–43)) discusses a number of ways to do this without triggering mismatching behavior. These include the use of interspersed embedded suggestions and presuppositional language. Perhaps the most famous example comes from Erickson who commented to an angry youth diagnosed with personality disorder.

> *"How surprised* will you be when you find next week that you've completely changed?"

The young man replied, "I'll be bloody surprised!"

In so replying, he thereby accepted all the positive presuppositions in Erickson's comment. Dolan explains her method of using such language within metaphor to enable the person to make internal representations of enjoyable experiences, without feeling that they are "required to" as part of some "technique." Such enjoyable experiences can be anchored and re-accessed later in the session.

Even direct utilization of the person's most obvious resources can make a significant difference. Dolan tells the story of Alice, a 25 year old with a history of violence and suicide attempts (Dolan, 1985, pp. 146–149). While she refused to discuss "therapeutic" topics with Dolan, Alice eagerly discussed her interest in craft and needlework.

Dolan told her "You can really find a way to use all your abilities in a way that lets you win."

To which Alice's response was characteristically "You're nuts!"

However, she began to smile and interact socially more frequently after this, and then excitedly came in one day to announce that she had found a job as a bouncer in a rough local bar. Her previous skill at fighting served her well! Within a year she was working in the same bar as a bartender, and had begun a college degree in psychology.

6) Coach in the ability to match and move towards
Teaching the person to sort for agreement and positive results is an important base from which change processes can actually work, rather than being incorporated into a long line of failures. Dolan explains (1985, pp. 50–57) how to convert a person's habitual, *"No"* responses into *"Yes"* responses by carefully restating the client's disagreement and concluding with a negative tag question.

Suppose the person says, "I'd rather just give up on this."

We might reply, "You'd rather **not** be here?" or "There are lots of better places to be, are there **not**?"

In our experience, mismatching can be directly confronted and reframed as a choice which, while important in childhood, has now become overused. We set the person the conscious task of deliberately sorting for agreement, by asking, "What is going well for me?" and, "What do I agree with here?" We will frequently ask the person to refrain from discussing any negative responses or experiences for certain time periods, making a commitment to discuss only what is going well and what they agree with. Solution focused therapy questions also focus our conversation in this direction. Two types of Solution focused questions can be used to elicit such times and are discussed more fully in the chapter on depression (Chevalier, 1995).

1) Ask for a description of the person's outcome.

2) Ask about when the problem doesn't occur (i.e., exceptions to the complaint). If there are no exceptions, then ask about hypothetical exceptions by using the "Miracle" question. "Suppose one night there is a miracle while you are sleeping, and this problem is solved. Since you are sleeping, you don't know that a miracle has happened or that your problem is solved. What do you suppose you will notice that's different in the morning, that will let you know the problem is solved?"

We can interrupt language or verbal mismatching as they run in a number of ways. One involves asking the person to restate the therapist's instructions to them in their own internal voice. Another is to overload the internal auditory channel of language by having the person count down from 1000 in increments of seven, while running the process. We have found that clients become extremely excited to find that techniques actually work for them once they employ their auditory digital process in a useful way, rather than in self criticism.

7) Healing early trauma
Use the standard NLP techniques for healing trauma, such as the *Dissociation Trauma Pattern* (Bolstad and Hamblett, 1998, pp. 109–112, 118–120), *Time-Line Therapy* techniques (James and

Woodsmall, 1988; Hall and Bodenhamer, 1997) and *Re-Imprinting Pattern* (Dilts, Hallbom, and Smith, 1990).

These techniques address what both cognitive psychology and self psychology agree is the original problem in most cases of borderline disordering. These techniques will only be successful once the consulting relationship has been established, and mismatching has been effectively dealt with.

Visualization and anchoring meet the requirement of accessing non-verbal methods for change in BPD, as referred to by cognitive psychologists Layden *et al.*, 1993, pp. 86–94). These techniques also give the person temporal flexibility (the ability to look into the past, present and future), which is a key to healing depression and anxiety as well as impulsive behavior (see Bolstad and Hamblett, 1999d, p. 6).

8) Coaching people to chunk up (go Meta) to integrate
The *"Parts" Integration process* and the *Core Outcome process* (Bolstad and Hamblett, 1998, pp. 44–49) enable people to integrate split off areas of the neurology which have been operating separately from the resources of the adult person. This involves asking the person to identify the higher positive intention of any split off "part." To answer the following questions, they have to generalize. They have to rehearse themselves through an important skill often underdeveloped in borderline disordering.

"What do you get through that behavior?"
"What higher intention does it serve?"
"And when you get that, what does that give you that's even more important?"

Because these split off "parts" have previously expressed themselves sequentially, one challenge in integrating them involves ensuring that they are available and accessed ready for integration. Sometimes people who learn NLP and other models that create a positive orientation often become so skilled at accessing resourceful states, they don't have full contact with "parts" which generate damage in their life. As a guide, it's useful to check that you have in fact re-accessed fully the part that was separated out (e.g., by having the person step back into a time when that part "that caused the problems" was running things).

9) Facilitating clear "first and second positions"
Clearly understanding this pattern is usually a priority in managing the consulting contract with someone diagnosed as a "borderline." This relationship provides a great opportunity for both to develop more effective ways of experiencing relationships in general.

We prefer to first teach the problem ownership model for cooperative relationships (Bolstad and Hamblett, 1998, pp. 73–77). This model is useful both for the client to use in their own relationships, and for their helper to use in the interaction with the client. Change agents who lose track of problem ownership put themselves at risk of various sorts of destructive relationships with clients (e.g. confusing sexual relationships, explosive conflicts and ever-more-frantic attempts to "rescue: the client from their own personality).

The model says that a client who feels upset, worried, resentful, frustrated, angry, fearful, or otherwise unhappy with the consulting situation or some personal issue *"owns a problem."* What's the appropriate approach at this point? To shift into second position so that we begin to think from the client's perspective. This includes using skills which maintain rapport (i.e., matching the client's behavior, acknowledging his or her concerns, and listening). It includes using verbal skills which help the client clarify outcomes and safely create his or her own solutions.

Advice giving, criticism, lecturing, interrogating and other directive skills, which may be quite safe in the no-problem situation, are not appropriate responses when a client gives signals that they "own a problem" (i.e. are upset). In this context, they will often resist direction. The two most effective verbal skills in this situation are:

> *Reflective Listening*
> "So the problem you're experiencing is… " "You want to…"

Open, Solution-Focused Questions
"What would it take for you to have solved this?" "Can I just check, what needs to be different here?"

On the other hand, when we are upset, worried, resentful, frustrated, angry, fearful, or otherwise unhappy with the consulting situation or some personal issue, we *"own* a problem." This doesn't equate to "fault." It only means that *we* are the ones who *want to change something.* When my problem is with some issue unrelated to the consulting situation, I use my own solution generating skills to solve it. But when my problem is related to some behavior of a client's, I will choose to communicate to that person in some way. In this case, I am responding from first position (thinking from my own perspective).

Advice giving, blameful criticism, lecturing, interrogating and similar skills are, again, *not* very effective. The most useful verbal skill for the situation where I "own a problem" is to describe my problem clearly. Doing this gives the client information about the sensory specific behavior that generates the problem, rather than my theory about their internal intentions, or my judgment of that behavior. Instead of saying:

"You were careless about our agreements,"

I communicate more specifically:

"You arrived half an hour after the arranged start time for this session."

I can also tell the client about any concrete effects the behavior has on me, and about the nature of my undesired state. I communicate with an "I" message format:

"I have a problem I'd like some help with…X, when… The effect on me is… and I feel… "

"I have a problem I'd like some help with. When you arrive late to the session, I find I need to re-plan what we're doing. I get quite frustrated."

367

In real life, problem ownership constantly changes. In the middle of assisting a client to solve her relationship problems, I may discover that she has values and attitudes which I deeply resent. I need to monitor the situation, to identify when it becomes appropriate to shift from reflective listening to an I message. Certainly, if I send an I message, my client may well feel uncomfortable about that; they may even feel "angry," "humiliated," or "insulted." Therefore, before re-sending or re-explaining my I message, I now need to respond to this new client problem with reflective listening. I do this until the client indicates that they feel understood (usually by nodding). We are then back in rapport enough for me to send a revised I message. The result is a kind of "dance" which we term "the two step," and which leads towards win-win conflict resolution. This dance moves clearly between second and first positions.

Here is an example:

> *Consultant:* "There's something I wanted to mention before we start. The last two sessions we've started half an hour later than arranged and I've needed to re-plan what we're doing. It's starting to frustrate me."
>
> [A description of problem in an I message, from First Position]
>
> *Client:* "Shit! So now I have to clock in or get my pay docked? What is this crap!"
>
> [Client indicates he now owns a problem, having heard the I message]
>
> *Consultant:* "You think I'm being over the top."
>
> [Reflective listening, from Second position]
>
> *Client:* Nods
>
> [Feels understood and so is back in rapport]
>
> *Consultant:* "Well I guess it may seem silly. I want to find a way to get the feeling that we're achieving what we plan to."

[Re-sending a modified I message]

Client: "Well I just can't handle this. It's like school. Sometimes I have a bad day, and I don't find it easy to get up for these early morning sessions."

[Client indicates he still owns a problem]

Consultant: "It's the morning sessions that make it most difficult?"

[Reflective listening]

Client: Nods

[Feels understood and so is back in rapport]

Consultant: "Okay; I'd really like to solve this so that it works for both of us. So one way would be to change the time of the sessions. What other solutions would work for you?"

[Beginning win-win conflict resolution]

Summary

- This last interchange demonstrates how helping people diagnosed as "borderline" disordering (and other severe mismatching responses) can be very challenging. But remember, *challenging,* not impossible. Creating a safe and conscious therapeutic relationship with such individuals enables them to become aware of "mismatching" as a style, to quality control it, and to choose it when it enhances things.

- Since "borderline" disordering involves a person *not knowing* his or her world, we want to provide clear and definite boundaries, guidelines, and communications. This means inviting clients "on board" and enabling them to benefit, to have "control" of the healing processes.

- Borderline disordering may seem very difficult, yet NLP and Neuro-Semantics have many patterns that can effectively empower such persons to transform their inner mappings and outer response patterns.

- Richard and Margot have noted that many of their clients have expressed profound gratitude for the personal transformation they have initiated and experienced. They have shifted from feeling despair about their life to feeling confident that they can have all the benefits they see others around them getting.

Resourceful State

Identify strongly mismatching clients.
Be clear about your own problem ownership issues.
Check your own safety working with this person.
Accept and model the acceptance of negative emotions.

Establish Rapport

Use rapport skills subtly.
Use tag questions when restating the person's concerns.

SPECIFY Outcomes

Contract as a consultant more so than a therapist.
Set limits on your input, establish strong boundaries.
Ensure the resolution of any immediate crises.
Include safety arrangements in your contract.
Use solution focused questions.

Open up the person's model of the world

Access positive resources indirectly using metaphor, congruent compliments, presuppositional language and embedded suggestions.
Coach clients to identify the mismatching strategy.
Reframe mismatching and other Meta-Programs as the best choice at earlier times.

Leading (change techniques)

Heal trauma with the Trauma Pattern, Time-Line processes, Re-imprinting.

Heal "parts" conflicts using Parts Integration, Core Outcome processes, Meta-Stating Integration Patterns.

Facilitate the flexibility of consciousness in second and first positions, problem ownership, communication skills, etc.

Set the person tasks to install more useful Meta-Programs.

Verify Change

Invite clients to verify their own change using solution focused questions.

Exit /Future Pace

Invite clients to future pace their own changes as a task.

Chapter 18

Disordering "Personality" Through Histrionic Disordering

Characteristics

The diagnostic criteria in the DSM-IV for Histrionic Personality Disorder involve the following:

A pervasive pattern of excessive emotionality and attention-seeking, beginning by early adulthood and present in a variety of contexts, as indicated by five (or more) of the following:

1) is uncomfortable in situations in which he or she is not the center of attention,

2) interaction with others is often characterized by inappropriate sexually seductive or provocative behavior,

3) displays rapidly shifting and shallow expression of emotions,

4) constantly uses physical appearance to draw attention to self,

5) has a style of speech that is excessively impressionistic and lacking in detail,

6) shows self-dramatization, theatricality, and exaggerated expression of emotion,

7) is suggestible, i.e., easily influenced by others or circumstances,

8) considers relationships to be more intimate than they actually are.

As a result of this kind of personal drama and emotionality in their basic style in living, they tend to live on "an emotional roller coaster" with lots of ups-and-downs. In relationships, others perceive them as charming, but shallow, exciting but demanding, warm but overly dependent. Thus they experience interpersonal relationships as stormy and ungratifying. At the heart of this ordering of self lies "an overly dramatic, or histrionic, presentation of self."

Slavney (1978) found that self-dramatization, attention seeking, emotional instability, and seductiveness were ranked as most diagnostically important and most confidently recognized. In these frames lie this particular kind of disordering.

The Driving Meta-Programs for Histrionic Disordering

The histrionic person tends to sort *globally,* and to therefore speak in all-inclusive terms. "These things just always seem to happen to me." In so generalizing, they leave lots of counter-facts out of consideration, and all too quickly jump to conclusions. Given this way of over-generalizing, what happens to the attention and thinking of such individuals? It becomes diffuse and impressionistic.

Additionally, in this disorder people typically speak in strong dramatic ways, with a great deal of hyperbole. Often they will use a theatrical intonation with dramatic non-verbal gestures and facial expressions. This reflects perhaps a *reactive style, very associated* into immediate emotions, and *impatient.*

As a consequence of the lack of focus on details, such individuals tend to settle for impressionist knowledge of things. So instead of thinking about things in a reflective way, they tend to jump to rash conclusions and react emotionally before thinking. Their thoughts jump to exaggerated global ideas thereby making their emotions very intense and labile.

This results in experiencing a general distractability, suggestibility, and deficiency of general knowledge. And these things make for a weak problem-solving style. Fleming (in Beck, 1990) writes:

> The histrionic patient's characteristic thought style leads to several of the cognitive distortions outlined by Beck (1976). Since these patients tend to be struck by impressions rather than thinking things through, they are especially susceptible to dichotomous thinking. They react strongly and suddenly, jumping to extreme conclusions, whether positive or negative. Thus, one person is seen immediately as wonderful, while someone else is seen as a totally awful person. Because they feel their emotions so strongly, and lack sharp attention to detail and logic, histrionic patients are also prone to the distortion of over-generalization. (p. 218)

Histrionic clients adopt romantic views in relationships which then set them up for high expectations. When they feel disappointed in these, they act out in dramatic outbursts, temper tantrums, and manipulative uses of anger.

Driven primarily by the emotional want of *approval*, while simultaneously feeling basically inadequate, the historic disordering deepens the desperate feeling for approval. This leads to overusing cuteness, physical attractiveness, charm, seductiveness, playfulness, etc. as their "performance" is designed to get approval. And, seductively, this usually works—*at first*. Eventually, however, this wears thin. Those disordered by the histrionic pattern become overly demanding of attention and of constant reassurance. *Indirectness* governs their style, rather than assertive directness, in asking for what they want. What drives their internal desperate feelings for approval? Their lack of a clear sense of identity which sets them apart from others. Their over-use of Other-Referencing as a Meta-Program distinction. They see themselves primarily in relation to others and tend to avoid deepening their own self-knowledge via self-reflection.

Therapy: Reordering the Disorder

Inasmuch as global, impressionistic, and emotional thinking and reasoning ("emotionalizing") drives this ordering of personality powers, therapeutic intervention must focus on these cognitive facets and assist such persons to shift to a different way of mapping things. This will include developing the flexibility of consciousness to balance their current strengths and strategies with a more detailed, systematic, solution-focused thinking, a self-referencing for values and visions, a self-esteeming, and a more reflective approach.

1) Invite and evoke thoughtfulness

Allen (1977) commented that we need to "teach the hysteric to think and the obsessive to feel." (p. 317)

Barbara Fleming (Beck, 1990) adds:

> However, the very nature of the histrionic's dysfunctional thought style means that he or she comes to the session with an approach to life diametrically opposed to the systematic, structured nature of cognitive therapy. (p. 218)

This calls for coaching the person to step into the *first perceptual position* and learning how to view the world, others, time, etc. through one's own eyes, ears, and skin. Given the nature of this disordering, rapport and trust typically come easily. With most, they are given. After all, histrionic clients *need* our approval. Use this. "I want you to do something for me. It may feel very strange and weird at first, but trust me, this will empower you in ways that I can't fully explain right now."

The rapport building to do with this population is that of matching or pacing their belief, thinking, and feeling that they "have to" have approval. As we so pace, then we can begin to lead them to the new and undeveloped skill of self-referencing, indepth thinking about their own values, visions, and outcomes. At that point, one of the first tasks becomes altering how we reward the person, and for what. At first this means shifting away from giving attention, interest, or approval from their entertaining drama (including their dramatic stories), cuteness, emotionally absorbing tales of woe, adventure, etc., and rewarding detailed and reflective thinking, focused attention, competence, assertiveness, attention to specifics.

Here we utilize the principles of NLP Anchoring to *shape* the behavior and responsiveness of the client. By attending, showing interest, and "rewarding" with "ah has" and "mmmms" we gently nudge them into a new orientation. The focus of our therapeutic work with such persons will involve nudging them from the drama (and seduction) of rescuing them from their problems as we enable and empower them to tap into their own resources.

At this point several dangers exist. As a therapist, we can easily become seduced into the role of a savior and rescuer. Danger also exists for the histrionic. After all, the very idea of *not* playing the old games (the ones that have protected and secured them to date) and moving out to the unknown territory of personal empowerment can feel very frightening.

Because the problems of the histrionic become exacerbated by their global, impressionist thinking style, another therapeutic intervention, involving helping them monitor their thoughts and identify specific cognitive distortions, becomes an important tool. Fleming writes,

> The process of identifying thoughts and feelings is the first step toward making gradual changes in the problematic thought style of histrionics, while also serving the function of focusing attention on their emotions, wants, and preferences. (p. 223)

Meta-modeling the global orientation with specific questions begins to build the specific sorting. "How can you tell if you achieve your goal?" "What will you see, hear, or feel?" "What criteria will you apply to it?"

2) Use Precision thinking to set desired outcomes
We can both invite a more reflective way of thinking while providing a sense of safety by using the NLP pattern for Well-Formed Outcomes. Securing an agreement about what a full and balanced life would look like that can balance integrity with oneself and healthy relationships with others gives a sense of safety and the beginning of a new way of thinking, i.e., precisely defining an outcome and "chunking it down" to a step by step process.

Since the histrionic does not screen out distractions, but mentally bounces all over the place, building up the skill of concentrated focus becomes important. We accomplish this by coaching the client regarding how to focus on one issue at a time, how to align all of the distracting *attentions* with his or her highest *intentions* (a meta-stating pattern), and how to align all of the higher levels with the primary level behavior.

With regard to their passion, desire, and skill for flare—pace it by encouraging them to write dramatic rational responses to their cognitive distortions. They can replace them with more vivid and compelling responses.

Because histrionics very frequently over-use the *visual* system (e.g., vivid imagery, impressionistic pictures, and movies in their head), another therapeutic process involves helping them to balance their internal processing with words. This helps one to stop overloading the imagery as a See—Hear circuit. We can also coach the client to *externalize* any internal *voices* to which the person may be responding to in a dramatic way. Externalizing the voice provides a powerful method for creating a more rational response to one's own thoughts.

3) Meta-State the histrionic structure
In this disordering, a person experiences a sense of inadequacy about the "self," and a belief in the importance of "performing" using dramatics, cuteness, entertaining drama, etc. This belief, in turn, means that such individuals set "the need to perform to get approval" as a Meta-Level state *about* their self. This presupposes yet another higher frame, "my self-worth and value is conditional. It's conditioned upon the approval of people. Without their approval, I am nothing." It is this structure of beliefs and ideas about the "self" that drives the program that results in this disordering.

Recognizing this, it makes sense that the very processes that may cure the disordering may seem very scary and unacceptable to them. Fleming has noted this Meta-State structure in the following as "frightened by the idea … of 'reasonable.'"

> Even patients who come to see the advantages of thinking more
> clearly and using assertiveness may become frightened by the idea
> that if they learn to become more 'reasonable,' they will lose all the
> excitement in their lives and become drab, dull people. Histrionics
> can be lively, energetic, and fun to be with, and they stand to lose
> a lot if they give up their emotionality completely. (Beck, 1990,
> p. 230)

This presupposes yet another Meta-Level state (beliefs) that hold
the system in place. What would it mean to give up all of the emotionality and drama? It would mean my life would become more
dull. It means I will never have the energy or excitement I now
have. It will mean I don't know who I will be. No wonder such
change seems so fearful.

Structurally, having regular traumas, dramas, and big emotional
scenes offers histrionics a way to experience emotionality in life.
This is usually *not* a conscious awareness even if they may feel and
even insist that they need to "let it all out" at times. Such individuals also frequently insist that they have no choice but to get terribly depressed and upset about all of the terrible things that have
happened to them. "I have to. That's just the way I am."

We can use this. We can have them "schedule a trauma." Fleming
notes,

> Patients can pick a specific time each day (or week) during which
> they will give in to their strong feelings (of depression, anger, tem-
> per tantrum, etc.). Rather than being overwhelmed whenever such
> feelings occur, they learn to postpone the feelings to a convenient
> time and keep them within an agreed-upon time frame. This often
> has a paradoxical effect. (p. 230)

4) Gently coach them through the processes
Histrionics frequently can lose interest and become bored very
easily. Therefore taking things in small steps allows them to learn
how to "make contact" with the world and use their consciousness
to take interest. This develops their own proactivity and reduces
the reactivity.

Assertiveness training provides another very important skill for the histrionic. It builds up more of a sense of self as they learn to know their own mind and emotions, what they want, and to directly ask for it. This increases their sense of self-efficacy and reduces their feelings of inadequacy and neediness.

There are numerous NLP and Neuro-Semantic patterns that we can use: from Re-Imprinting, using the Swish Pattern to create "a me for whom disapproval is no problem," to the Decision Destroyer, to meta-stating oneself with self-referencing in a way that maintains good relationships, to the Pleasure and De-Pleasure Pattern for obsessive-compulsions.

Summary

- Whatever map we build throughout the years of growing up will take us somewhere. They all work. But a great many take us to pits of despair and others to dead-end streets that limit our choices. Mapping my sense of self as inadequate and needing constant approval inevitably drives me to despair or to drama.

- Yet if it's just a map, then it can be changed. We can refuse and reject old toxic maps that hinder our personal empowerment and choose new maps. Remapping the extreme Other-Referencing of the histrionic personality disordering involves some simple but very basic transformations.

- Anticipating and coping with the fearfulness of inviting the approval dependent person is central and highlights the importance of establishing a solid therapeutic relationship. Then we can coach the person to become aware of the kind of thinking that has created the distress, along with all of the "secondary gains" or positive intentions behind such. We do this for the express purpose of safeguarding those while adding new benefits.

Chapter 19

Disordering "Personality" Through Narcissism

Narcissistic Personality Disorder

Characteristics

The DSM-IV describes the Narcissistic Personality Disorder using the following diagnostic criteria.

A pervasive pattern of grandiosity (in fantasy or behavior), need for admiration, and lack of empathy, beginning by early adulthood and present in a variety of contexts, as indicated by five (or more) of the following:

1) has a grandiose sense of self-importance (e.g., exaggerates achievements and talents, expects to be recognized as superior without commensurate achievements),

2) is preoccupied with fantasies of unlimited success, power, brilliance, beauty, or ideal love,

3) believes that he or she is "special" and unique and can only be understood by, or should associate with, other special or high-status people (or institutions),

4) requires excessive admiration,

5) has a sense of entitlement, i.e., unreasonable expectations of especially favorable treatment or automatic compliance with his or her expectations,

6) is interpersonally exploitative, i.e., takes advantage of others to achieve his or her own ends,

7) lack of empathy: unwilling to recognize or identify with the feelings and needs of others,

8) is often envious of others or believes that others are envious of him or her,

9) shows arrogant, haughty behaviors or attitudes.

Given these general characteristics, the narcissistic person disorders his or her powers around three central features: grandiosity, hypersensitivity to evaluation, and lack of empathy. By thinking, believing, and feeling themselves to be special and unique, they distance themselves from others, and exaggerate their own importance, skills, and destiny. This way of thinking also moves them into a superior position as it makes others inferior, thereby undercutting their ability to put themselves in the place of others. Yet, because their self-esteeming *depends* conditionally upon others recognizing and acknowledging their superiority and central importance—any kind of negative feedback becomes very threatening to them. Herein lies one of the paradoxes about this particular disordering of personality.

Meta-Programs that Drive Narcissism

To almost the same extreme, only in the opposite direction to the histrionic, the narcissistic person over-does and exaggerates *self-referencing* in an exclusive way. This exaggerated self-referencing style prevents them from shifting consciousness to do some other-referencing. This parallels the opposite struggle to the histrionic disordering.

Various theories, most of them from the psychoanalytic field, have arisen in an attempt to explain why and how a person gets stuck in such self-referencing. Millon (1969), using the social learning theory, posits that it arises, not from maternal deprivation, but from parental over-evaluation. It begins with parents who respond to their child in a way that *over-inflates* the child's sense of self (self-worth, self-value, self-specialness). The child then internalizes this, and so uses external validation (e.g. praise, approval, recognition, etc.) as signaling their specialness.

Narcissistic disordering also involves *personalizing* events. Such persons interpret time, space, causality, relationships, etc. in a highly personal way. This faulty way of processing information leads them to attend too much to the praise and criticism of others. Believing in their specialness, they feel so exceptional that they *expect* admiration, deference, and compliance from others. And that expectation can easily slide into *demanding* it. Further, they typically take any lack of cooperation with their grandiose fantasies as a personal insult.

As they disorder themselves more and more through over-valuating themselves over others, they come to live more and more for flattery, indulgence, favoritism, and entitlement. These become their central frames-of-mind. They perceive themselves as different from others in important ways. If they happen to have an actual or culturally valued talent or physical attribute, this tends to reinforce their superior/special schema or frame (which, of course, operates as Meta-States).

The narcissistic disordering also depends upon *black-and-white thinking* that polarizes and dichotomizes. This enables them to separate people into those that they consider special and then the regular and average people, whom they disdain. This all-or-nothing thinking style feeds their extreme mood fluctuations and prevents them from accepting things "in between" the highest of highs or lowest of lows.

Because they adopt a negative relationship to feedback, they will *discount* any negative feedback, or distort it, or rage against it as unfair and unknowing. Instead, they always take counsel of the highest frame, their specialness and need for recognition. Frequently they may assault someone whom they perceive as threatening their superiority. This can give many of the narcissistic volatile and destructive impulses. Davis (in Beck, 1990) says that "the personality disorders most likely to overlap with narcissism are histrionic, antisocial, and borderline."

Though they perceive in a self-referent or internally referent way, they value not the internal world, but the external world most. They value the best clothes, homes, cars, jobs, etc. This makes them externally oriented in terms of their values, and therefore often unaware of their internal world of thoughts, ideas, emotions, or those of others.

They typically think of themselves as "sensitive" persons, but only sensitive to themselves, not to others. Their sense of entitlement also causes them to not tolerate discomfort very well. This illustrates another Meta-Program: *under-responsible*. They assume little responsibility **for** themselves or **to** others since they operate from the assumption of entitlement. This leads them to conclude that others stand responsible **to** and **for** them. Others "should" attend to them, recognize their specialness, make special allowances for them, etc.

External signs of the narcissistic disorder involve lots of constant attention to grooming, fitness, and wardrobe. They have a hyper-concern for personal appearance and comfort. And because they view themselves as special, they will ask for (or demand) special concerns. Further, temper tantrums, verbal harangues, and various kinds of abuse may evidence the person's belief that others should primarily concern themselves with making them happy and comfortable.

The entitlement syndrome leads to assuming that they exist above the regular rules that govern society. Their specialness exempts them. This can cause them to behave in anti-social ways. It moves them to think that they have the right to criticize everybody, but are above receiving such back.

Treatment for the Re-ordering of this Disorder

1) Establish a collaborative relationship
More often than not, it's problems with relationships and depression which drive individuals suffering from narcissism to therapy. Consequently, working with the narcissistic disordering means we have to work to develop a collaboration with someone who has emotional investment in "being superior."

We can begin pacing by validating and exploring the need of such persons to succeed and to achieve as we get them to think about doing so in terms of long term hedonism, rather than short-term pleasure.

"In the long-term will this get you what you want?" "In the long-term, will people work cooperatively to support your goals?"

By using this to tap into the motivation of such persons, we can then begin identifying cognitive distortions, lack of empathy, etc. and how such traits do not serve them in the long term. Doing this allows us to begin the therapeutic process.

2) *Reduce the cognitive distortions*
Treatment must involve decreasing the cognitive and perceptual distortions. We do this by bringing up the limiting beliefs which disorder the person's powers, and in building up new skills. These include taking second perceptual position in order to develop empathy for others, referencing the values and emotions of others, recognizing their specialness, and cooperating as a team player.

As a therapist, we will need to challenge and outframe the person's All-or-Nothing thinking. Using that kind of thinking and applying it to one's sense of self, thinking about others, life, destiny, the importance of approval, etc., creates some severe limitations in the sense of options. Continually inviting the client to "run an ecology check" on this thinking is important. So is coaching a person to engage in continuum thinking skills. "To what degree may this feedback have some accuracy?"

3) *Strengthen ego strength*
Since these individuals operate from a phobia of criticism (hypersensitivity to evaluation), the paradox is that by empowering them, they have less of a need to stay focused on self, and more ability to extend beyond their fragile ego boundaries. We can use the Swish Pattern for this, Owning our Power Zone, Developing a Circle of Excellence, etc.

Once we have accomplished that, we can then work with the person with regard to de-sensitizing that automatic semantic reaction to criticism, changing their beliefs about feedback so that they can learn to use it and profit from it. Davis (Beck, 1990) has proposed,

> The patient could purposely plan to request feedback from others. In structuring this exposure, it would be beneficial to start with feedback that is likely to be positive. Positive feedback is a more tolerable point from which to begin taking emotional risks and examining the role of personal thoughts and interpretations. (p. 250)

Exercises that help one to break the all-or-nothing thinking thereby enable them to become more discriminating in the attention they give to evaluation. This can enable them to stop the mind-reading, and directly inquire about feedback.

4) Empathy skill development

To assist with a person's development of empathy involves helping them to do some "role reversals" and role playing exercises so that they can get practice shifting their consciousness from self-referencing, to other referencing. Using a number of NLP patterns for stepping in and out of various perceptual positions supports this, as trance identification, and the As If Frame.

New belief statements can help in reframing and altering perspectives: "Other people's feelings matter too." "Give someone else a compliment." "Let someone go ahead of you in line." "Everyone is unique in some way."

Davis (Beck, 1990) offers the following list of "alternative beliefs" that will counter-act the narcissism. To set and solidify these kinds of ideas provides the kind of mental and emotional frames that reorders everything.

> Be ordinary. Ordinary things can be very pleasurable.
> One can be human, like everyone else, and still be unique.
> There can be rewards in being a team player.
> I can enjoy being like others, rather than always having to be better.
> I can choose to be a member of a group and not always the exception.

I can go for long-term respect from others instead of short-term admiration.

Other people have needs and opinions that matter too.

Colleagues can be resources, not just competitors.

Feedback can be valid and helpful. It's only devastating if I take it that way.

No one owes me anything in life.

Thinking about real situations can be healthier than being preoccupied with exaggerated dreams.

I don't really need constant attention and admiration from everyone to exist and be happy.

Superiority and inferiority among people are value judgments and thus always subject to change.

Everyone has flaws.

Everyone is special in some way.

I can choose to be accountable for my own moods. To let the evaluation of others control my moods makes me dependent on them and out of control.

Summary

- Narcissism as a personality disordering is not about being "selfish," it's about lacking the kind of ego strength and sense of self that empowers us to own and affirm ourselves without needing to put others down. Lurking below all the bluster and drama of the narcissist is a very frightened and insecure person who posits his or her value and worth on conditions of recognition of specialness and superiority.

- Undoing the disordering within this pattern means establishing a solid sense of self, putting it upon an unconditional basis, and then empowering the self so that one can extend oneself for the sake of others.

- The danger in dealing with many of the personality disorderings lies in forgetting that there's a structure and strategy to these experiences. When we do, we can also fall into the trap of mere labeling and moralizing.

- All of the personality disorderings arise from the mismapping of things. Yet every mapping had some original positive intention. Aligning ourselves with that enables us to become a colleague and companion to the person so disordered so that we can facilitate a much better structuring of thoughts and feelings, speech and behaviors.

Chapter 20

Disordering "Personality" Through Avoidance

Characteristics

That which primarily drives the disordering of personality that we label the *Avoidant Personality Disorder* involves a pervasive avoidance at the level of behavior, emotions, and cognitions. Thus, the DSM-IV gives the following diagnostic criteria:

A pervasive pattern of social inhibition, feelings of inadequacy, and hypersensitivity to negative evaluation, beginning by early adulthood and present in a variety of contexts, as indicated by four (or more) of the following:

1) avoids occupational activities that involve significant interpersonal contact, because of fears of criticism, disapproval, or rejection,

2) is unwilling to get involved with people unless certain of being liked,

3) shows restraint within intimate relationships because of the fear of being shamed or ridiculed,

4) is preoccupied with being criticized or rejected in social situations,

5) is inhibited in new interpersonal situations because of feelings of inadequacy,

6) views self as socially inept, personally unappealing, or inferior to others,

7) is unusually reluctant to take personal risks or to engage in any new activities because they may prove embarrassing.

Karen Horney (1945) described this type of personality disordering as an "interpersonally avoidant" person.

> There is an intolerable strain in associating with people, and solitude becomes primarily a means of avoiding it. ... There is a general tendency to suppress all feeling, even to deny its existence. (pp. 73–82)

> On little or no provocation he feels that others look down on him, do not take him seriously, do not care for his company, and, in fact, slight him. His self-contempt ... make[s] him ... profoundly uncertain about the attitudes of others toward him. Being unable to accept himself as he is, he cannot possibly believe that others, knowing him with all his shortcomings, can accept him in a friendly or appreciative spirit. (1950, p. 134)

Given this way of functioning in the world, the disordering of this avoidant style motivates a person to over-use avoidance as *a coping mechanism* for dealing with his or her fears of rejection, abandonment, criticism, and unpleasant negative emotions. As one thinks and believes that avoiding things is the best strategy, values it, only knows it as a coping mechanism, and begins to define oneself by that, the person orders and structures self and responses in the image of the avoidant style.

Driving Meta-Programs and Meta-Model Distinctions

At the heart of the Avoidant Personality Disorder lies a Meta-State of *conditional self-esteem*. The person views his or her **self** as conditionally valuable or worthwhile, and dependent upon the confirmation, approval, and acceptance of others. This gives lots of power and meaning to mistakes, criticisms, negative feelings, etc. to totally devastate a person's sense of self. Unlike the histrionic who similarly feels inadequate and needy of approval and performs for it, the avoidant disordering decides it's too dangerous to take that chance.

Along with this comes a *personalizing and emotionalizing* of problems, conflicts, and negative feedback. Operating from the adaptation sort of *judging*, such persons take whatever happens in their life field as reflective of them, of their value, lovability, worth, etc. These individuals then *judge* every negative emotion (from embarrassment to shame, to feeling rejected, etc.) as indicative of their general unacceptableness. From fear of this, they move away from the events and experiences that evoke this dread. This also leads them into judging and contempting their **self** as inadequate, unworthy, and unacceptable.

Given this schema of self-inadequacy, they then typically engage in *mind-reading* others as they assume that others also are contempting, despising, and rejecting them. To any kind of disclosure or exposure of their humanity (i.e. fallibility), they feel vulnerable to rejection and disapproval. Therefore they adopt a *placating* communication style, trying to please people in order to get approval. This makes them unassertive in relationships, living behind facades, and always *moving away from* things. This *away from* motivation leads them to not only physically and behaviorally avoid fearful situations, but they also avoid their internal states of thoughts and emotions. This makes them not very psychologically astute about their states or their cognitive distortions.

This low tolerance for dysphoria (negative emotional states) moves them to immediately avoid emotional awareness, which thereby causes them to *not* learn from them or use them for growth. They develop a Meta-Level structure inside of *disgust and rejection of negative emotions,* especially anger, stress, frustration, but also discomfort, fear, embarrassment, etc. They believe that they should always feel good, the other people rarely feel scared, embarrassed, bad, upset, etc. They believe that if they allowed themselves to feel dysphoric, such negative emotions would totally engulf them and they would never recover.

Like other disorderings, this also reflects the use and operation of the *black-or-white, Either/Or* perceptual filter. They either exist as good loving and adequate persons or as totally inadequate, bad, and unacceptable persons.

Therapy: Re-ordering the Disordering

This way of "doing personality," or experiencing our powers of our person, operates primarily from a Meta-Level belief of inadequacy and unworthiness of **self** and then uses the coping mechanism of **avoidance** to always and only *move away from* anything and everything that highlights that. It operates in an *Either/Or* way by *judging* self and other's internal thoughts-and-emotions (mind-reading) as inadequate.

1) Build up a solid sense of self
First and foremost in reordering people in this situation, we must re-structure the person's cognitive format. At the heart of the self-schema of the avoidance disordering, we have such limiting belief maps as the following:

> "I'm defective," "I'm unlikeable," "I'm different," "People don't care about me," "If people really knew me they would reject me," etc.

Typically, early experiences with a highly critical and rejecting parent can install this kind of cognitive distortion. When that happens, then yet another belief arises, namely, that criticism, disapproval, or rejection "is" terrible, awful, unacceptable, etc. So from "the 'is' of identity" wherein the person over-identifies his or her "self" and self-definitions with the responses of others, and the demand for total acceptance as the only basis for self-acceptance, then comes the "is" of predication, predicating (asserting) that any information about inadequacy and fallibility "is" terrible.

Re-structuring self-definition will obviously play a most crucial role.

> "Upon what basis do you value or dis-value a human being?" "What makes a person loveable, likeable, and acceptable?" "From what source did you come up with this criteria?" "How well does it serve you?" "Does it enhance your life?"

Then providing instructions for how to *unconditionally* value and esteem one's self, or to cut out the rating of self entirely as unproductive enables a person to deconstruct the old conditional esteeming.

For designing and re-designing a person's self-definition, we can use an educational approach to how we distinguish between a person's "self" as a human *being* and a person's "abilities" as a human *doing*. This separates the Meta-Level structures of "self-esteem" (worth, value, dignity) as beingness, and "self-confidence" as the faith we have in our abilities to actually *do* something.

Because those who have disordered in this way through judging their self as inadequate, readily believe in their inadequacy.

"If anyone judges me negatively, the criticism must be true."

"If others really knew me as I am, they would not like me."

"It's dangerous for people to get too close; they may see the real me."

"If I make a mistake, others will dislike me."

We can therefore use various NLP processes of the Swish Pattern, Circle of Excellence, Belief Change patterns, meta-stating "self" with acceptance, appreciation, and esteem, etc.

2) Coach for reflectiveness on mistakes
This structuring of personality makes relationships, friendships, and therapy tentative inasmuch as such persons will constantly stay vigilant to anything that they might possibly read as disapproval, criticism, or rejection. Therefore the first step in helping involves assisting avoidant persons in becoming **reflective** of this, rather than **reactive**.

We can do this by bringing up and treating the person's fears of rejection as the source of the cognitive distortion. We can do the same kind of *outframing* on the person's over-used coping mechanism of avoidance. As we "run an ecology check" on these ways of responding, we quality control how useful, productive, enhancing, etc. they are.

> "How well does it serve you to over-load with meaning the acceptance or rejection of others?" "How well does avoiding things serve you?"

By flushing out and identifying the extent such persons judge themselves, we can shift to yet a higher level. We can outframe the judging by judging the judging.

> "What a stupid and judgmental way to treat a human being!" "I will refuse to judge and evaluate my total self based upon a few facets of myself." "What others think or say about me does not establish 'the last word' about me. I am so much more than my thoughts and emotions."

And because the expectation of rejection can become so habitual, one may need to constantly bring *acceptance* and *acknowledgment* to bear upon this.

> "I can expect that my mind-and-emotions will jump to judge myself harshly, and I accept this as the results of some old dysfunctional programming."

3) Re-Orienting the person from away-from to toward
Part of the reordering also involves shifting the driver Meta-Program of *away from* so that the person can also have the choice of moving *toward*. Judith Beck and Christine Padesky (in Beck, 1990) wrote this:

> Patients are aware, to some extent at least, of their behavioral avoidance. They invariably criticize themselves in global, stable terms: 'I'm lazy,' 'I'm resistant,' 'I'm passive-aggressive.' Such pronouncements reinforce beliefs about being inadequate or defective and lead to hopelessness. Patients don't see that their avoidance is their way of coping with uncomfortable emotions. They generally are not aware of their cognitive and behavioral avoidance until such a pattern is made clear to them. (p. 264)

They have developed the Meta-Level structure of *hating* their negative emotions. This shows up in such beliefs as: "It's bad to feel bad." "I shouldn't feel anxious." "One should always feel good." So not allowing themselves to experience the negative emotion and learn from it—they always move away from such experiences. Now they need to give themselves to, step by step, begin to experience the negative emotion, knowing that it exists *only as an emotion*, and that they do not need to read it as signifying anything more.

This changes the ordering of things. Now they can begin to *approach* their negative thoughts and emotions, backtrack them to the higher level ideas and beliefs from which they come, reflectively reality-test them for accuracy, and consciously choose when to move away from and when to approach. They can then use the scientific attitude of testing their automatic thoughts to check out their reality. They can check out their thinking for cognitive distortions. "There I go again, trying to avoid thinking about the negative awarenesses that create these negative emotions."

4) Raising frustration levels by acceptance
Now they can practice the paradox of "avoiding the old avoidances!" Doing this leads them to raise their tolerance of negative emotions about criticism, disapproval, and rejection. Now they can practice "staying with the emotion" in order to learn from it, and to backtrack it to the thoughts that gave birth to it. Beck and Padesky write:

> Repeated experiences like this may be necessary to build tolerance for dysphoria and to erode patients' dysfunctional beliefs about experiencing uncomfortable emotions. To desensitize patients, a hierarchy may be constructed that outlines increasingly painful topics to be discussed in therapy. The therapist can elicit patients' predictions of what they fear will happen before they discuss each succeeding topic, test out the predictions, and accumulate evidence to contradict their fault beliefs (e.g. 'It'll be too painful to discuss,' 'If I start feeling bad, I'll never get out of the feeling,' etc.) Patients can also construct hierarchies for assignments outside of therapy to increase tolerance for negative emotions. Such

assignments can be labeled 'dysphoria practice' or 'anti-avoidance activities.' (p. 271)

As a result of learning to "answer automatic thoughts" (a Meta-State), they person learns to *not* avoid the thoughts-and-emotions that pop through consciousness, but address them and reality-test them. In this way, the person can practice using a strong confident anti-avoidance internal voice to speak to and stand up to habituated cognitive non-sense.

"Just because I feel something does not make it so."

"Just because I have a negative thought of inadequacy or feeling of being criticized by someone doesn't mean I need to run and avoid things."

"If I give in to this fear, I only reinforce it. Every time I stand up to it and avoid this avoidance, I strengthen my resolve."

"I refuse to give all of my power away to the thoughts and opinions of others about me—I esteem myself as having value and loveability."

In this way, a complete restructuring about self and the role of fallibility occurs so that the person develops a good relationship with their realization (in thoughts-and-feelings) about mistakes, acceptance, criticism, etc. As this de-constructs their phobia to disapproval, it enables the person to build a new kind of center for him or herself.

Summary

- Once again we have seen how a basic perception and coping style can be exalted to the place where it becomes a disordering influence. There's nothing wrong with avoiding things. Many things should be avoided. But when *avoidance* becomes our *modus operandi*, our basic and only coping skill, and the way we define ourselves—we disorder all of the rest of our thinking, emoting, speaking and behaving powers making us less and less effective.

- Reordering in this case, as in the case of so many other nom-inalized "Personality Disorders" involves identifying fully the over-used and over-valued frame, aligning with its positive intentions, and then balancing it with other resources and responses. This makes for more of a sense of options, choices, and control.

- Working with those disordered by avoidance can be difficult in that too much directness can activate the program to avoid *you*. As a therapist, let this caution you to gain rapport, build a supportive therapeutic relationship, provide an understanding of the desired resources, and then go slow and gentle at first.

Chapter 21

Disordering "Personality" Through Dependence

Characteristics of the Dependent Personality Disorder

The most obvious feature that drives this disordering of personality springs from the thoughts-and-feelings of *dependency* on others. Persons with this internal organization look upon others as more adequate, intelligent, capable, important, and valuable than themselves. Thus, an inner sense of *inadequacy* also drives this way of thinking and feeling. And because of this schema of inadequacy, the dependent person over-copes by depending and attaching to others.

The DSM-IV describes the Dependent Personality Disorder using the following diagnostic criteria:

> A pervasive and excessive need to be taken care of that leads to submissive and clinging behavior and fears of separation, beginning by early adulthood and present in a variety of contexts, as indicated by five (or more) of the following:

1) has difficulty making everyday decisions without an excessive amount of advice or reassurance from others,

2) needs others to assume responsibility for most major areas of his or her life,

3) has difficulty expressing disagreement with others because of fears of loss of support or approval,

4) has difficulty initiating projects or doing things on his or her own (because of a lack of self-confidence in judgment or abilities rather than a lack of motivation or energy),

5) goes to excessive lengths to obtain nurturance and support from others, to the point of volunteering to do things that are unpleasant,

6) feels uncomfortable or helpless when alone because of exaggerated fears of being unable to care for himself or herself,

7) urgently seeks another relationship as a source of care and support when a close relationship ends,

8) is unrealistically preoccupied with fear of being left to take care of himself or herself.

Driving Meta-Programs and Meta-Model Distinctions

Given this description of the dependent disordering of personality, it immediately becomes obvious that such persons operate primarily via the *Other-Referent* Meta-Program distinction. They reference off of others and external sources and have a rather weak ability to reference their own thoughts, emotions, values, beliefs, etc. Something holds them back from that. Some taboo prevents and/or prohibits them from that kind of self-trust.

Further, in terms of response to stress, they choose the *passive response pattern* rather than the aggressive one, they typically will *move away from values* more than approach values. They move away from being rejected and disapproved. They move away from assuming knowledge, skill, information, resources, etc. And they do this to move toward being protected, kept safe and secure, and toward things being made all right by others.

Such persons also typically operate in *an associated way* with the experiencing of their emotions, and that, in turn, leads them to "emotionalize" and "personalize" most readily and effectively. Thus in terms of "adaptation" to the world, they operate from the

Judger Meta-Program, and so they apply harsh judgments to themselves, but not to others. This moves them from blaming to *placating* as their communicational and relational style.

Unlike others who operate from fear, these individuals more typically naively *trust* and believe in people and therefore want to attach and depend upon them. Given that frame and coping style, they will act in under-assertive ways, not leveling about their thoughts-emotions, or wants, and not taking responsibility to do such, hence *under-responsible.*

The inadequacy schema also encourages the over-use of the *modal operators of impossibility.*

> "I can't stand criticism." "I can't speak up for myself." "I can't stand being alone."

Further, thinking in *Either/Or and black-and-white* dualities (dichotomous thinking) typically characterizes this disordering. "A person is either completely competent and independent or completely helpless." "A person is either completely right or completely wrong."

At a Meta-Level, one of the worst fears of those disordered by the ideas and feelings of dependency involves fear of autonomy, fear of independence, and even the fear of not needing others. The Either/Or thinking helps to exaggerate these fears since the person doesn't process oneself as partially dependent in some ways on others and partially independent in other ways. For them, the choices seem dichotomous. "Either you depend on others, please them, not get them angry or you stand on your own, alone and without good relationships."

Treatment: Reordering the disordering

Numerous problems and Axis I diagnoses can bring a person with the Dependent Personality Disordering into therapy. Foremost among these are depression, then anxiety disorders, self-doubt, insecurity feelings, psychosomatic problems, alcoholism, relationship problems, adjustment problems, etc.

1) Coach to activate the person's own responsiveness
To treat this disordering, we must first address the self-inadequacy schema which drives the coping pattern of over-attaching, cling-ing, and depending which then, in turn, results in non-assertive hinting, passivity, passive-aggressiveness, victim-thinking, etc. Simultaneously, if we can address the black-and-white thinking, then such persons can begin to think in terms of steps, stages, and continua for becoming more resourceful. They can then begin to learn to become gradually more separate from significant others and to increase their own sense of self-esteem and self-efficacy.

Here *meta-modeling with Socratic-like questioning* that evokes the person's own thinking, deciding, concluding, reasoning, emoting, etc. will facilitate more and more empowerment and self-trust. In this, shifting into more and more of the role of a *coach* or *facilitator* becomes useful. The danger for the therapist in working with this population occurs from the very submissive, cooperative, pleasant and placating style of the dependent disordering. Such clients can easily hook a therapist's authority needs and get him or her to play the "Great Expert" if the therapist isn't careful. So the bait becomes: "All I want is just for you to tell me what I need to do." How could you give them *that? That's* what they came for, or so *they* think.

Knowing the structure of this disorder, we know that they actually have come for something more, something bigger, something more grand. They came to grow up out of the dependency pat-terns and to set new and higher frames for their own personal empowerment, something that currently scares them so that they can't go there. Therefore, it becomes a therapeutic intervention to *not* play the great Expert, but even to frustrate such clients in this very thing and *not* give them answers. This takes a good bit of skill and even more *art*. As therapists we will want to invite and facili-tate *their* thoughts and feelings, hold them responsible for their recovery, and even provoke them to discover their powers through exercises and tasks.

2) Facilitate the meta-move to a higher level of awareness
To enable the individuals who suffer from this disordering to dis-cover their powers and to step up into higher frames of autonomy,

individuality, empowerment, etc. we need to invite them to "go meta" to their cognitive style, cognitive distortions, to the old frames that have become less and less effective, and to take an intentional stance so that they build up a new map about independence and inter-dependence.

Making this meta-move will empower such clients to also see, recognize, and interrupt the old schemas that have driven their experiences of dependency. Such persons typically do not have a lot of introspective awareness about their thoughts and feelings since they generally give that up as they acquiesce to others. So self-management training for them will involve self-monitoring, self-evaluation, and self-reinforcement at Meta-Levels.

3) Invite a meta-NO response to some of the old frames
Facilitating the meta-move will also enable these clients to catch their self-contempting, their self-defining of inadequacy, their perfectionistic standards, their Either/Or thinking, etc. Then, from that level, they can learn to run an ecology check on their *style of thinking-feeling and coping.*

In the cognitive therapies and in NLP, we frequently use the task of writing out an Advantage/Disadvantage list on these patterns. Doing this typically flushes out secondary gains that accrue to persons via depending and attaching. These often involve having someone take care of them. And more often than not, it involves a subtle form of "power." Barbara Fleming writes:

> There often are some compelling reasons for the dependent person to be ambivalent about changing. Although the person struggling with helplessness may feel that he or she has no power, taking the helpless role can actually be very powerful and reinforcing ... and this role can be difficult to give up. If the patient can be helped to identify what would be lost if he or she were less helpless, it may be possible to find a more constructive substitute. (Beck, 1990, p. 303)

Fleming further recommends drawing a continuum from dependence to independence as most useful in assisting a client in recognizing the many steps in between the extremes of total dependence and total independence. Doing so breaks the Either/Or thinking and makes it less frightening to make progress in small steps.

Systemic issues arise with this disordering since the family and friends may not want the person to become more autonomous, independent, and assertive. They may like the system of interactions with the person always complying, submitting, and placating. Therefore preparing them for such disruptions becomes another therapy issue.

Summary

- We all experience "dependency" and we experience it throughout our lives in one form or another. The kind of *dependency* described in this chapter, however, that disorders personality involves a dependency upon others for approval, decision-making, thinking, etc. In other words, the dependency of one who has not yet recognized, claimed, and taken full ownership of his or her powers of personality—thinking-and-feeling (the private powers) and speaking and acting (the public powers). Having not differentiated themselves enough, such persons then disorder themselves by failing to develop sufficient independence so that they can then enter into relationships from a position of strength and experience inter-dependency.

- This disordering isn't genetic, inherited, or destined. It arises as a function of the developmental mapping that one makes which calls into question and doubts one's right, privilege, and responsibility to give approval to one's own values and visions.

- For the therapist to facilitate a client in this reordering of this pattern, he or she must be careful *not* to perpetuate the dependency. To enter into a conspiracy and simply transfer the client's feelings of dependency to the therapist only complicates matters, and shows a lack of professional understanding and behavior.

Chapter 22

Obsessive-Compulsive Disordering

Obsessive-Compulsive Personality Disorder Characteristics

In the recent movie staring Jack Nicholson, *As Good As It Gets*, we have a classic picture of a person suffering from an obsessive-compulsive way of moving through the world. He wanted to "control" his world and make it "perfect" and so had developed many particularities that made him odd and "difficult" to get along with. He knew it was a problem, was seeking relief, yet it wasn't until a larger frame of reference (e.g., a woman) came into his life that he began adjusting his obsessive-compulsive map. Ultimately, it is "just a map," although those caught up in that particular "frame world" experience it as "real," "the way it is," and self-perpetuating. And that, by the way, actually describes every one of these "personality disorders."

The DSM-IV describes the central features of this disordering using the following diagnostic criteria:

> A pervasive pattern of preoccupation with orderliness, perfectionism, and mental and interpersonal control, at the expense of inflexibility, openness, and efficiency, beginning by early adulthood and present in a variety of contexts, as indicated by four (or more) of the following:
>
> 1) is preoccupied with details, rules, lists, order, organization, or schedules to the extent that a major point of the activity is lost,
>
> 2) shows perfectionism that interferes with task completion (e.g., is unable to complete a project because his or her own overly strict standards are not met),

3) is excessively devoted to work and productivity to the exclusion of leisure activities and friendships (not accounted for by obvious economic necessity),

4) is overconscientious, scrupulous, and inflexible about matters of morality, ethics, or values (not accounted for by cultural or religious identification),

5) is unable to discard worn-out or worthless objects even when they have no sentimental value,

6) is reluctant to delegate tasks or to work with others unless they submit to exactly his or her way of doing things,

7) adopts a miserly spending style toward both self and others; money is viewed as something to be hoarded for future catastrophes,

8) shows rigidity and stubbornness.

The Source of its Origin

Proposed ideas for the origin of this disordering are many. Beginning with the psychoanalytic idea that it arises from inappropriate and inadequate toilet training, this has generated the now common recognition of the "anal character" and characterized by such skills as obstinance, orderliness, and parsimony. Other psychoanalysts have focused on overly rigid and punitive toilet training along with over-control and conflict. Harry Stack Sullivan theorized that these problems develop out of interpersonal relationships and low self-esteem. Therefore to cope, such individuals become superstitious and believe in verbal magic and ritualistic magic.

The theme of interpersonal and intra-personal insecurity dominates in other theorists. This refers to the person's desperate feelings of insecurity, their need for security and the various mechanisms used to gain control over self and the environment. Too much rigidity, demand for conformity, painfulness of mistakes, etc. feed this insecurity. Early experiences of sexual abuse are also often used as a reason for the need to constantly wash the hands.

The cognitive-behavioral models see these influences as resulting from and in schemas of perfectionism, rigidity, and intolerance for mistakes. As a result, such persons pay extreme attention to details, over-control their own thinking-and-emoting, develop a rigid and inflexible stance about how things should/must be done, become moralistic and demanding, dogmatic, perfectionistic, indecisive, and emotionally block. Such describes this way to disorder human thinking-feeling, speaking, and behaving, which in turn, creates numerous limitations and difficulties.

Driving Meta-Programs and Meta-Model Distinctions

Given this description, what drives this Obsessive-Compulsive disordering? It operates primarily from a mental-emotional state of *conditional self-esteem*, a perspective that then sorts for threats and dangers to the self. As it then takes on, primarily, an *away from* posture, such persons then defensively view the world using an *Aristotelian thinking-emoting style*. They want to know "the right way" to do things. They perceive things in Either/Or terms, in Black-and-White categories. Of course, this then creates a *methodical procedure* style in terms of how such individuals adapt themselves to life. Rather than moving through the world as an observer and just perceiving, they adapt by making the world fit their mental maps about how things "should" be. And they focus on *details and specifics* using their *black-and-white* perceptual filtering.

Given these Meta-Programs, such people also use (and over-use) the *modal operators of necessity*. You can hear it in their self-languaging. Their talk will be full of "shoulds," "musts," and "have tos."

"I must not make mistakes." "I should always be in control of myself." "I have to get this assignment done perfectly." "I should keep this old lamp; I might need it one day." "I should

be doing something more productive than wasting time reading this novel."

Given all of this internal pressuring, demanding, and ordering,
such persons then develop with an over-consciousness (and conscientiousness) about morals, rules, and procedures. They consistently sort most things in terms of "right and wrong," "good and
bad," and "moral and immoral" concepts. Given this, they move
toward goals and goal-fulfillment in a *perfectionistic* way, i.e., they
demand flawless performances or performances that meet unrealistically high standards. And, of course, that can generate disappointment, depression, discouragement, and a negative attitude.

Karen Simon and James Meyer (in Beck, 1990) describe the obsessive-compulsive personality as operating from the following
assumptions:

"There are right and wrong behaviors, decisions, and emotions."

"I must avoid mistakes to be worthwhile."

"To make a mistake is to have failed," and "Failure is intolerable."

"To make a mistake is to be deserving of criticism."

"I must be perfectly in control of my environment as well as of
myself," "Loss of control is intolerable," and "Loss of control is
dangerous."

"If something is or may be dangerous, one must be terribly upset
by it."

"One is powerful enough to initiate or prevent the occurrence of
catastrophes by magical rituals or obsessional ruminations."

"If the perfect course of action is not clear, it is better to do
nothing."

"Without my rules and rituals, I'll collapse in an inert pile."
(pp. 314–316).

These driving cognitive schemas further illustrate the *Judger* Meta-Program which such individuals use in adapting themselves to life. In terms of the Meta-States that drive their lives: their over-valuing of control, safety, perfection, and morality form their primary frames of reference. Their black-and-white thinking posits all-or-nothing choices in their map of the world and this underlies their rigidity, procrastination, and perfectionism.

Treatment: Reordering the Disordering

What brings such individuals to therapy? Some of the "problems" that bring obsessive-compulsive persons into therapy include anxiety problems, indecisiveness, procrastination, psychosomatic problems (headaches, backaches, constipation, ulcers, etc.), sexual disorders, and depression. Sometimes others force them to go due to their rigidity, demandingness, and lack of flexibility. They almost never consider their attitude of their focused attention, need for control, or fear of mistakes the problem. And *that*, of course, only confirms the structure of their disordering and prevents the structure itself from being questioned.

1) Quality control the results and outcomes
People who learn and highly develop the skills of mentally obsessing and emotionally compulsing hardly ever think that *that* is the problem. They view *those behaviors* as just the necessary requirements for "making sure of things," "protecting myself against dangers," "insuring that things go well," etc. They may not like the results and consequences, but they "just know that their way of thinking" is right and necessary.

Begin then by assisting them to *quality control* their lives. Run the ecology check by continually checking:

> "Do you like this feeling of having to check the doors twelve times every time you leave for work?" "How much does this checking behavior enhance your life and enable you to achieve the things you want to achieve?"

Once we have a commitment about this, then we can set the frame that if something is not working, and we know that it doesn't work, we will not keep proving its non-functioning and dysfunctional nature. We will try something else. We will try something new and different—anything but the thing we know that does not work.

2) Welcoming the fallible nature of human existence

The Meta-Level structuring that generates the obsessing and compulsing in the first place, in terms of "the strategy" that makes it work, involves non-acceptance of insecurity, fallibility, and humanity. Refuse to know and accept yourself as a fallible human being, and you begin to disorder yourself for insecurity and protective moves. Those suffering from the obsessive-compulsive style feel uncomfortable about their emotions of anxiety and worry, and so they reject such. We can see this Meta-Level structuring in the following statements:

> "I don't want to work on this assignment because I won't be able to do it perfectly."

> "I feel that I must avoid mistakes if I'm to feel secure and worthwhile."

> "I can't stand to think about leaving things unchecked."

These feelings, ideas, and beliefs set the frame at the Meta-Level and so define the world they live in. At the heart of this disordering then lies this cognitive distortion. People think of their "self" as a human *doing*, rather than a fallible human being. They refuse and reject the fact of human insecurity. Herein lies paradox. The more I accept my fallibility, that I have a fallible brain and so misperceive, mis-think, mis-believe, misunderstand, etc., the more I accept my fallible emotions and that I mis-emote, and my fallible speaking and behaving, the more comfortable I feel with my fallibility. Conversely, the more I refuse to accept my fallible insecurities, the more insecure I feel.

The most basic insecurity which drives all of the coping of those who obsess and compulse involves the meta-frame that demands that they "do" and "be" right. Permission has been taken away from them to be "wrong." And as "being wrong" is tabooed, rejected, hated, despised, etc., insecurity increases. Paradoxically, experiencing permission to be "wrong" and still maintain personal dignity, wholeness, value, confidence, etc. decreases the need to be absolutely right and safe.

When people "can't" be wrong, when they can't acknowledge their insecurities, fears, worries, errors, etc., and then base their "self-esteem" upon being right, they set frames that prevent them from being human, from being authentic, and from accepting their humanity.

Conversely, when they access thoughts and feelings of conditionality and apply such to their self-concept, they become *conditionally valued* human beings. If they *identify* their self as totally a product of their actions, thoughts, emotions, etc., they thereby are never allowed to feel safe as a human being in all their wondrous fallibilities. Here also we can Meta-State the obsession with a sense of "grace," unconditional love and value.

This explains why so many will therefore begin to focus on external things—rituals, words, procedures, rules, money, status, things, degrees, etc. Such individuals refuse to allow themselves to relax. They attribute relaxing as meaning that they "are wasting time" and not being productive. And above all things, they must produce. Most also highly value their worrying and ruminating, thinking that such actually helps them.

Reordering this structure involves bringing *acceptance* to one's "self," and re-inventing oneself upon an entirely new basis. It involves accepting and esteeming one's self *unconditionally*. Since *permission* to accept and welcome the imperfect, the human, and the fallible seems to centrally drive this disordering, reversing this means restoring permission and giving new meanings to error, mistakes, fallibility, etc.

"I give myself permission to accept my insecurity, fallibilities, and mistakes."

"This means that I don't have to strive for perfection." "This means I can accept my anxiety about such realizing that such comes from the old beliefs of measuring myself by my external actions."

Patterns that enable us to therapeutically coach a person to this new re-ordering include using the Meta-State pattern for Self-Acceptance and Self-Esteeming, using the Swish Pattern to "the me for whom being fallible is no problem," and reframing the meaning of ambiguity, insecurity, etc.

3) Meta-Model the generalizations and necessities

Since obsessing and compulsing frames involve both high level and usually fuzzy concepts and the modal operators of necessity, we can coach and educate clients about such by meta-modeling. This involves challenging and disputing the old Either/Or thinking pattern so that such individuals can use their brains to think in terms of degrees, steps, stages, and continua.

Further, given the All-or-Nothing thinking pattern that applies "allness" to things—giving oneself permission to learn to chunk things down into smaller and more manageable pieces and thinking in terms of doing it in steps and stages allows the person to slowly retrain their way of coping with the world.

Taking a meta-position to the dichotomous thinking of Either/Or helps one to reduce the judgments against self and others for imperfections. As a result this leads to new levels of tolerance, acceptance, and flexibility. It frees one up from the rigidity and dogmatism.

4) Tasking for imperfection

A paradoxical and yet powerful therapeutic intervention involves tasking clients with purposefully making "three mistakes every day" and noticing the thoughts and emotions that emerge, listen to the internal voices that might be activated, while giving themselves permission to be human, rather than trying to play the God Game. This exercise will typically flush out various internal voices that the person has lost awareness of, the internal critical mother and father voices that keep taking permission away and that demand perfection. Then we can change the coding of those voices (turning down the volume, putting the voice in the little finger, hearing them as Elmer Fudd, etc.), answering the voices with new meaning frames, and/or integrating the voices as legitimate parts with positive intentions.

Summary

- There's a positive intention behind the skills that make up the strategy of the Obsessive-Compulsive disordering. It's a real art. Not everybody can do it. It takes a particular structure in terms of how to think, feel, believe, value, etc. in order to pull it off.

- Yet this strategy can also be messed with, which in a way is what clients pay therapists to do. "Mess with this strategy so that it becomes just one of many choices that I have. Help me to expand my options."

- Obsessive-compulsive disordering, like so many other "personal disorders" involves over-doing some good things and lacking a balance with some other skills. By finding the structure to the experience, we can interrupt it and re-design new and better ways to move through life in a productive and happy way.

Chapter 23

Disordering "Personality" Through Becoming Addictive

Defining Addiction

According to O'Brian and McKay (1998) at any given time, 6% to 7% of Americans show diagnostic signs of substance dependence (p. 127). In this research, substance is used in the strict sense of substances such as alcohol, cocaine, cannabis, or opiates. The research excluded nicotine and caffeine dependence, as well as behavioral dependence such as compulsive gambling.

While we will here focus on *substance use,* the same interventions will work with any addictive problem. Today we no longer question that the level of addiction in our societies is a serious problem. Alcohol alone is implicated in half of all driving fatalities, a quarter of all suicides, a third of all assaults, and in the medical cause of death for 100,000 Americans a year. (Dorsman, 1997, p. 2)

In trying to define dependence, psychiatrists and others refer to more than just excessive use, and to more than a psychological sense of needing the substance (American Psychiatric Association, 1994, pp. 108–9). They refer to what counselors call ambivalence (Miller and Rollnick, 1991, pp. 36–47) and what in NLP we call *sequential incongruity* (Bandler and Grinder, 1982, pp. 179–188). This means that in an ongoing sequence, a person accesses the part of their neurology that wants to use the substance and then the part that doesn't want to use it.

For example they may take more of the substance than they originally planned to. They may make attempts to stop, or say they want to stop using the substance, and then carry on using it. They may abandon other activities important to them, as a result of using the substance. They may continue using the substance despite actually suffering persistent, painful problems as a result of this use. They may even have tried to stop using the substance, and experienced extreme discomfort (called "withdrawal"). In short, an addiction occurs where one part of a person wants one to stop, but (and that word "but" is used intentionally) another, apparently more powerful part does not want one to stop.

Personal Strengths

What "strength" does the person with an addiction have? Such a person may have any of a number of general personality profiles. The key lies in the tendency to associate into and out of the addictive process sequentially. In using the Personal Strengths model it is more appropriate to work with the more intact skills of "chunking up and chunking down."

Figure 23.1

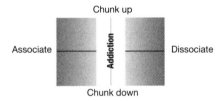

People Naturally End Most Addictions

There are a large number of programs that assist people in stopping using addictive substances including the famous "12 Step" programs such as AA (Alcoholics Anonymous). However, contrary to popular belief, *most people break free of addictions on their own.*

Several surveys by the institution for Health and Aging (University of California) show that drinking problems up to the level where blackouts occur almost always disappear before middle age, without medical assistance, as do most teenage drug addictions (Peele, 1989, p. 66). Over two-thirds of those addicted people who stop drinking alcohol, do so on their own with no help. 95% of the 30 million Americans who have quit smoking in the last decade or so, did so without medical or AA style help. (Prochaska *et al.*, 1994, p. 36). These people have better long term success than those who choose treatment programs: 81% of those who stop drinking on their own will abstain for the next ten years, as compared with only 32% of those who are going to AA. (Trimpey, 1996, p. 78; Ragge, 1998, p. 24)

The same seems to hold true for *lifestyle-based "addictions."* In 1982, Stanley Schachter announced the results of a long-term study into obesity. He set out in the early 1970s with the idea that while most overweight people can lose weight, few ever keep it off. In two separate community based studies, what he actually found was that 62% of obese people succeeded in taking off an average of 34.7 pounds and keeping this weight off for an average of 11.2 years. Those who never entered weight loss programs showed better long term weight loss. Incidentally, he stumbled on the finding that many smokers give up smoking on their own. He followed up this variable too, and again found that those who attended treatment programs did not do as well as those who gave up on their own! (Schachter, 1982, pp. 436–444)

What about so-called "hard" drugs?

In a 1982 study of morphine use, 50 surgery patients were given uncontrolled use of morphine for 6 days. Though they used far more than street addicts, they all decreased the use of the drug and stopped with no problems after their discharge from hospital. Of USA soldiers who used heroin in the Vietnam war (and most did), 73% became addicted and displayed withdrawal on return. Authorities were terrified, expecting a huge surge in addiction numbers.

In fact, 90% simply stopped once they got back to America. Researchers noted,

> It is commonly believed that after recovery from addiction, one must avoid any further contact with heroin. It is thought that trying heroin, even once, will rapidly lead to re-addiction … Half the men who have been addicted in Vietnam used heroin on their

return, but only one in eight became re-addicted to heroin. (Peele, 1989, pp. 167–168; Trimpey, 1996, p. 78)

How Medicalization Reinforces Addiction

Addiction has been described by AA as an uncontrollable physical disease, and alcoholics are told that "just one drink sets off the uncontrollable disease process again." Research, however, consistently invalidates this claim.

In 1973, Psychologist Alan Marlatt gave alcoholics heavily flavored alcoholic drinks and found that as long as they *believed* the drinks were alcohol-free, they drank only normal amounts. On the other hand, alcoholics who *were told* their drink contained alcohol began to drink compulsively, even though their beverage contained none. Such studies have been repeated numerous times under varying conditions. Those who *believe* that they are powerless once they have had a drink of alcohol, do far worse in long term studies.

One four year study followed up 548 diagnosed alcoholics initially treated at 8 different AA centers, and found that while only 7% had managed abstinence, 18% were now social drinkers with no instances of drunkenness. In this study, those who most strongly agreed with the AA "disease model" of alcoholism were the most likely to still be heavy problem drinkers four years later (Ragge, 1998, pp. 32–34).

Consider the 90% of Vietnam veterans who gave up heroin use after their return. What caused them to become addicted in the first place? Did they have a disease that other Americans their age missed the gene for? No.

They were placed in a situation that produced extreme incongruity. One part of them kept them in a war zone, where another part of them suffered extreme pain. They suppressed the awareness of that pain with heroin, just as the surgical patients in the hospital study cited above suppressed their pain with morphine. After their return to the United States, 90% of the veterans found that they no longer had the pain. Just over 10% still had severe unmet needs on their return. The others simply stopped because the need had stopped. They were never "powerless" over the drug, they were overwhelmed by their own inner yearnings; remarkably sane, understandable yearnings. We do not need the idea of "disease" to explain this process.

Stanton Peele (1989) emphasizes this:

> When narcotics relieve pain, or when cocaine produces a feeling of exhilaration, or when alcohol or gambling creates a sense of power, or when shopping or eating indicates to people that they are being cared for, it is the feeling to which the person becomes addicted. No other explanation about supposed chemical bondings or inbred biological deficiencies is required. And none of these other theories come close to making sense of the most obvious aspects of addiction. (p.151)

The medicalization of addiction has even more unfortunate side effects when the person actually stops using and terminates treatment. They are then told that their very feeling of being completely okay is proof that they have a disease! This is a classic double bind which is contradicted by the vast majority of addicts who recover permanently on their own.

How "Confrontation" Reinforces Addiction

Imagine a psychotherapist working with a client who has a sequential incongruity. The client gets drunk and then wishes he or she did not do that. The therapist decides that the part of them that wants to stop is "right," and begins to argue and "confront" the client from that point of view. What will happen?

The result is predictable. The client will argue from the other side. This then leads to the belief that "denial" and "rationalization" are "personality characteristics" of addicted people. Yet five decades of research has shown no correlation between denial and addiction (Miller and Rollnick, 1991, pp. 9-10). Actually, the only character trait associated with addiction is the feeling of ambivalence about the addictive substance. Consider that!

However, denial has been shown to increase as a result of confrontative treatment programs. In fact, the longer a person remains in a "12 Step" addictions program, the higher they score on measures of guilt, defeat, fear, and other personality characteristics usually associated with addiction (Ragge, 1998, p. 25).

In NLP we operate from the presupposition that *resistance indicates the lack of rapport*. Several meta-reviews of research studies show that in predicting outcomes with addiction, *therapist style* plays a more important role than the content of the therapy. And, the style most effective is less confrontational, more empathic, and uses more communication skills (Finney and Moos, 1998, p. 160; Miller and Rollnick, 1991, pp. 4–7).

Even within one session, the use of "confrontation" and labeling ("Face up to it! You're an alcoholic!") have been shown to increase client arguing and denial (Miller and Rollnick, 1991, p. 9–10). This is extremely important to understand. At least one book claiming to present an "Ericksonian Approach" to addictions counseling urges the use of extreme confrontation (Lovern, 1991). Yet addiction itself is not evidence of a personality based on denial and argumentative rationalization. So aggressive approaches such as John Lovern's actually create the problem they claim to solve.

What Works?

Glowing reports of success at addiction treatment centers often disguise the fact that over 80% of clients do not complete the programs (Trimpey, 1996, p. 78). Because their own publicity is so pervasive, 12 Step Programs tend to appear successful, yet this success has been hard to demonstrate in research.

Dr Keith Ditman, head of the Alcoholism Research Clinic at the University of California, studied three groups of alcoholic offenders randomly assigned by a court to AA, to a medical clinic or as controls (no treatment). In the follow-up period 69% of AA clients re-offended and 68% of clinic clients. Only 56% of the controls did (Ragge, 1998, pp. 21–22). While two studies emerged in 1997 suggesting that AA groups fared as well as cognitive behavioral approaches, there is no justification for the claim that 12 Step groups are the only effective solution to addiction. They represent one of several choices now available for social support in the process of change.

We do need to remember that most people recover from their addictions on their own. This raises several questions. What has happened in these people's lives? Research on 2700 British smokers showed that, at the time they stopped, they often changed their job, altered their relationship, or otherwise solved some lifestyle problem. Also, they stop when they "lose faith in what they used to think smoking did for them" while creating "a powerful new set of beliefs that non-smoking is, of itself, a desirable and rewarding state." (Marsh, 1984).

The program which shows the highest effectiveness in meta-analysis of research on addiction is *social skills training*—the kind of training we offer in our *Transforming Communication course* (Bolstad and Hamblett, 1998). Using roleplay and coaching, this training teaches people how to state their own concerns clearly and non-blamefully, how to listen effectively to others' concerns, and how to work towards solutions that suit both them and others. The most effective approach to addiction is not in fact to deal with "the addiction," but to solve the interpersonal problems in the person's life (Finney and Moos, 1998, p. 157). To use an analogy, most addiction treatment is like setting up AA clinics for the soldiers in Vietnam. What really works is *bringing them home.*

The second most successful treatment program for addictions, in meta-analysis of the research, is *Brief Motivational Interviewing* (Finney and Moos, 1998, p. 157). This is based on a model developed by James Prochaska, John Norcross, and Carlo Diclemente. These researchers interviewed 200 people who quit smoking to find out what happened (Prochaska *et al.*, 1994). They then followed up with studies of people who had given up a number of other addictions, and in doing so they found very similar patterns. Amazingly, Motivational Interviewing is delivered in a four-session format, which makes it the briefest treatment available in the field. The methodology of Motivational Interviewing does not focus on the content of the addiction (e.g., by educating people about the dangers of drinking), but on the process of becoming motivated to quit.

The Six Stages of Change

Prochaska and DiClemente (Prochaska *et al.*, 1994; Miller and Rollnick, 1991, pp. 14–18) found that *successful self-changers* cycle through a series of six stages. Helping a person at one stage requires an entirely different approach to helping someone at another. The authors describe resistance as a result of applying a change strategy designed for the wrong stage of change (e.g., treating a person in the contemplation stage as if they should be ready for action). We have diagramed the stages below:

Summary of the Model

We will shortly consider in more depth how to utilize NLP interventions in this sequence that has been shown to work with addictions. We will also discuss how to identify the stage the person is at. Summarizing the effective responses to each stage we have:

1) *Pre-contemplation.* The person doesn't consider the addiction an issue at this stage and so refuses to collude with the problem, and simply seeks permission to give information.

2) *Contemplation.* The person seesaws between wanting to change and wanting to use. Explore values with the person and use NLP decision-making processes.

3) *Commitment.* The person says he or she really wants to change. Help set goals and provide tasks for the person to check out the intention to act.

4) *Action.* Once the person becomes ready to act, elicit and alter the old strategy for using, and then integrate the conflicting parts to resolve the problem.

5) *Maintenance.* Build a new lifestyle by integrating change at the level of mission, values, and time-lines. Then teach interpersonal skills, state changing skills, and health skills.

Figure 23.2

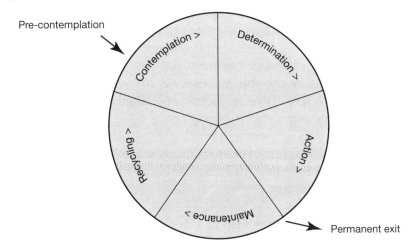

6) *Recycling.* Future pace the person through possible future lapses to a life beyond "recovery" to ensure that they can quickly respond to any new challenges.

1) Pre-contemplation

At this stage the person is not consciously aware of the sequential incongruity that others might consider "an addiction." At this stage, people do not "own the problem." Useful help at this stage aims at creating a situation where the person accepts help. What can we do?

- Obtain permission to provide information and act as a consultant. An effective consultant knows their facts, shares information respectfully, listens to the person's response, and leaves the decision-making to him or her.

- Refuse to cover up the incongruity for the person, while not trying to "convince them" to act on it. Aim simply to assist clients in becoming more aware of what is happening. The use of effective communication skills becomes crucial at this time. This includes the ability to send a clear *I message:*

> "When you arrived home two hours later than you arranged, it meant I ended up missing out on the movie we were going to. I felt really disappointed because I'd been looking forward to going with you."

It includes being able to respond to the person's reaction with reflective listening before restating your concern in a new I message:

> "You think I'm over-reacting. You just forgot, and you're sorry about that." (*Transforming Communication*, Bolstad and Hamblett, 1998)

- Present advantages for changing rather than simply using *away-from* motivation. Research shows that "towards" motivation is extremely important in shifting from pre-contemplation to contemplation, while reducing internal conflict is more significant in moving from contemplation to actual commitment. (Prochaska, *et al.*, 1994, pp. 162–171)

2) Contemplation

At this stage the sequential incongruity is most obvious. The person now becomes engaged in the change process, and oscillates between wanting to change, and wanting to ignore the problem. They may say, "Sure, it's a hassle; but I think I can manage it." At this stage we assist with contemplation. It is tempting to try to rush the person through the whole change process, yet that is typically unsuccessful.

Where incongruity is severe, the person can often present a plausible demonstration of readiness for action over the 30–60 minutes of a consulting session, but still demonstrate complete disinterest in change outside of the session. Particularly where the person has had experience of confrontative "Recovery" programs, they have often learned to present only the part that wants to change within the session. To be helpful, the session needs to contact both sides of their ambivalence:

- Elicit values and set goals to help the person identify what they want to do about the problem.

- Without attempting to force a decision, explore the risks of continuing with the problem behavior to elicit the away-from motivation and to reduce the perceived risks of changing.

- Invite the person to state why change would be useful. Do this by pointing out all the advantages of continued using and asking why they'd want to change.

- Use the NLP Parts Integration process to enable the person to access and integrate both sides of the ambivalence about changing.

3) Commitment

Every so often, a window of opportunity opens within the contemplation stage, when the person shows evidence of commitment. Such evidence might include:

Stopping presenting reasons why the problem behavior is "okay."
Making motivational statements (e.g., "I need to change this!").
Discussing what it would be like to have changed.
Experimenting with change processes, or with stopping the problem behavior.

We can strengthen *commitment* in a number of ways:

- Identify and utilize the person's usual motivation strategies and Meta-Programs. Carol Harris (1999) offers an excellent assessment and utilization guide in the context of weight loss dealing with more than ten core Meta-Programs. She suggests pacing each of these while designing goal setting and visualization.

- Coach the person to set goals for change. Solution focused questions are extremely useful here: "How will you know that this problem is solved?" "When is a time that you noticed this problem wasn't quite as bad? What was happening at that time? What were you doing differently?"

- Reframe the problem as changeable.

- Negotiate a strategy for changing.

- Set achievable tasks which presuppose commitment. Such tasks could include monitoring the behavior to identify how often it occurs and when it doesn't occur. The person's response to these tasks allows you to assess whether they are ready for the action stage yet (Overdurf and Silverthorn, 1995 A, pp. 29–32).

4) Action

Once we have evidence that the person has begun to take action, the action stage involves replacing the person's old "problem" strategy with a new one (called "countering" by Prochaska). This can be done on a number of different levels, including:

- Elicit the person's strategy or strategies for using the addictive substance (Overdurf and Silverthorn, 1995 A, pp. 32–34). What is the sequence of thoughts which the person regularly uses from the beginning (when not thinking about using) to actually using? Strategies are triggered by some external event which they see or hear, or by a physical sensation. Often it will involve some sequential incongruity (e.g., telling themselves they shouldn't use the substance, and then adding to the stress until they feel they have "justified" giving in to their desire to use). Using strategy notation, an example of someone who smokes cigarettes after each meal, the strategy might look something like this:

$$V^e \to V^r \setminus K^i \to A_d \setminus K^i \to K^i / K^i \to A_d \to K^e$$

Figure 23.3

Trigger	Operation	Polarity operation	Test (comparison)	Exit (A)	Exit (B)
V^e	$\to V^r \searrow K^i$	$p \to A_d \searrow K^i$	$\to K^i / K^i$	$\to A_d$	$\to K^e$
See meal finished	Remember cigarette and feel enjoyable feeling	Say to self "It's wrong to smoke! This is terrible!" and feel guilty	Compare feeling of guilt to feeling of smoking	Say to self "Damn it! Why should I have to feel bad!"	Smoke cigarette

Possible addiction strategy

We can interrupt this strategy at a number of different places:

- Design a visual swish from the trigger image to an image of oneself as a resourceful person who no longer smokes. The power and the risk of this method are demonstrated by a case of a man who came to see us because he smoked while playing the piano. After a visual swish from the image of the piano, he reported that he no longer felt like smoking when he thought of the old trigger. A year later we met him and found that he had never smoked while playing the piano again (he found other places!). It is important to clear all possible triggers.

- Directly alter the strategy in a key way, such as having the person smoke a cigarette before the meal, or having them always smoke two cigarettes where they would have smoked one. Anything that disrupts the strategy will tend to work if the person has actually decided to stop.

Milton Erickson, acknowledging that an alcoholic needed to be "sincere" before his work would succeed, gives several examples. In one case (Lankton and Lankton, 1986, pp. 26–27) he worked with a man who came in for treatment for alcoholism. Erickson elicited his strategy for drinking, and found that he would sit at a bar and drink a beer, followed by a whiskey chaser, and repeat this process until drunk, one drink at a time. Erickson told him that next time he went to the bar, he was to order three whiskeys and three beers and to line them up in a row. As he drank each drink, he was to curse Erickson, in prescribed ways. The tamest was: "Here's to that damned Doctor Erickson; may he drown in his own spit!" That was the end of the therapy. The man came back three months later to thank Erickson for curing his addiction. He was unable to drink with these alterations to his strategy.

- Enable the person for more powerful reframing and meta-modeling skills so that the person can challenge his or her own auditory responses at either the polarity operation or at the exit. For example, instead of talking to oneself about how wrong it is to smoke, the person might learn to talk about how good it would be to have healthy lungs. Or instead of saying, "Why should I have to feel bad?" the person might ask, "How could I feel even better than I feel when smoking?"

Using these skills would lead the strategy in an entirely different direction. Cognitive behavioral therapy focuses most fully on these sort of language challenges (Lewis, 1994, pp. 117–146). The Rational Recovery system for changing addictions has the person identify the internal submodalities of the voice with which the addicted "part" speaks (e.g., when it says, "Damn it, why should I have to feel bad!"). This voice is called the "beast." The person then learns to identify that when it says this, it means itself or the part that wants the addiction, rather than the person. This technique further dissociates the person from the addictive part. In NLP terms, the only reason for doing this would be to prepare for the next intervention. Namely:

- Turn the comparison into an integration of the two conflicting parts. Use the Parts Integration pattern to integrate the part that feels guilty smoking on the one hand, with the part that enjoys the feeling of smoking on the other. You can do this linguistically using Tad James' Quantum Linguistic patterns. (James 1996, p. 58)

An NLP Practitioner once asked me how she could stop smoking, which she had attempted for some time. I asked her what was the intention of the part that smoked. She said to have her relax. I then said,

"Please listen carefully. Does that part realize that anything less than completely stopping smoking isn't totally getting you the relaxation you want?"

She actually couldn't hear what I had said. Why? Because to understand the question requires simultaneous accessing of both the conflicting parts. After I repeated the question several times, she went away none the wiser consciously, and reported some months later that she hadn't smoked since that moment.

Notice the structure of what I said: "Anything less than completely stopping [the problem behavior] isn't totally getting you [the higher positive intention of that behavior] regarding what you want."

A third NLP method of resolving the parts conflict is the older Six Step Reframe, described in a 12 Step context by Chelly Sterman (1991).

- Use Time-Line Therapy or Re-Imprinting to clear the cause of the addiction from the person's time-line. John Overdurf and Julie Silverthorn clear three things using this method: the representation of the first use of the substance, the root cause of the addiction, and the unconscious decision to become an addict (1995 B, pp. 31–32). These may have all occurred at the same moment, or they may be widely spread apart in time. We have had the experience of simply clearing the root cause of addiction and having a person unable to access the craving for cigarettes any further.

5) Maintenance

Maintaining change requires different skills from making the initial shift. A person could congruently stop drinking alcohol in the office, and then find him or herself without any resources to cope with interpersonal conflicts at home. This explains why actually teaching communication and conflict resolution skills offers such an effective technique for ending addictions. Maintenance involves building a new life without the addictive process. Accordingly, we can:

- Teach Conflict Resolution Skills (Bolstad and Hamblett, 1998) including: problem ownership, reflective listening, I messages, Win-Win solution finding, and skills for resolving values collisions. This intervention alone is often the most successful change program known for ending addiction.

- Release any other harmful emotions, decisions, or beliefs from the time-line using some *Time-Line* process or *Re-Imprinting*. Albert Ellis points out that the addicted person may have self imposed limitations at several levels of Dilts' neurological Levels model (Lewis, 1994, p. 153). These could include environmental limitations (only having friends who use the problem substance), behavioral and capability limitations (e.g., not knowing how to respond to the feeling of craving), belief limitations (e.g., "It's not fair that I can't drink alcohol when I want."), and identity limitations (e.g., "I am a broken person."). We can elicit these limiting beliefs, clear them from the time-line, and/or replace them using any NLP belief change process.

- Coach the person to create a new sense of mission for his or her life, and align values and goals to support this mission. The belief of AA is that this sense of mission needs to involve connecting to a "higher power." In her work that challenges AA and its twelve step program, Charlotte Davis Kasl (1992) has invited clients to rewrite the twelve steps. However, even her re-writings of the last step seem remarkably similar to the original (which was "Step 12: Having had a spiritual awakening as a result of these steps, we tried to carry this message to others and to practice these principles in all our affairs").

- Coach the client in *State Changing skills* such as using a relaxation anchor. It is important to check that solving the addiction will actually solve the person's problems. It is quite possible for a person to have anxiety difficulties or depression at the same time as an addiction. In such a case, using the NLP Trauma Cure to heal the origin of anxiety may solve the addiction. Remember the 90% of Vietnam veterans who were cured of heroin addiction simply by returning home.

- Help the person explore how to keep their body healthy. Because feeling healthy itself is a positive motivator psychologically, many writers suggest that physical health problems may encourage cravings for unhealthy substances. (Kasl, 1992, pp. 186–211)

- Run the person's old strategy for addiction with the new content of health. For instance, using the previous example, the smoker's strategy after a meal was to think of how good a cigarette would feel, and then tell himself off. Then, feeling guilty, he would compare this discomfort with the imagined pleasure of smoking, say, "Why not!" and so light up.

To re-run this strategy healthily, we might say during a trance induction, "Sometimes you may find yourself digesting the successes in your life, and imagining achieving an even healthier lifestyle. You can react against that, telling yourself you shouldn't ask too much of life, but when you compare how suffocating those limits feel, you'd probably just say, 'Damn it; why should I have to feel bad about asking more of life!' and find yourself reaching for the planning diary!"

6) Recycling

It is generally unusual in NLP to recommend planning to recycle a change process at a future time. Yet Richard Bandler precisely suggested that for addiction treatment (Bandler, 1989, Tape 3; Overdurf and Silverthorn, 1995 B, p. 33). In future pacing beyond the possibility of a future "lapse" we reframe any time the person "uses" again as part of long term success. The very concept of a "lapse," Bandler points out, suggests that the person will have not been using for some time. James Prochaska (1994) simply says,

> A lapse is not a relapse. If one swallow does not make a summer, one slip does not make a fall. (p. 227)

Re-read that last sentence. To future pace success, you may:

- Arrange a follow-up session some months into the future.

- Plan strategies to deal with stressful events, including re-contacting you for help.

- Design reframes to remind the person that they can easily restart their new life with the strength that comes from their new learnings.

Future pacing is one thing, but the context of successful change is that when you look back on it, it seems almost silly to have been worried about how to maintain it. The 95% of smokers who give up smoking without any help do not spend the rest of their life in "recovery." They have better things to do! Charlotte Davis Kasl says she prefers the term *"Discovery"* for this final state rather than recovery. "Discovering suggests opening, expanding and growing."

Summary

- Addiction involves a profound ambivalence about a behavior, resulting in sequential incongruity. Yet most people faced with such a situation will recover on their own.

- Research shows that successful assistance of someone wanting to end an addiction is very different from the endless, confrontative, labeling approach of the recovery industry. The stages of the Motivational Interviewing model parallel the RESOLVE model for work using NLP (Bolstad and Hamblett, 1998, pp. 107–108). These are:

  1) *Resourceful States for the consultant* (Pre-contemplation).
     The person is not aware of the incongruity.
     Get permission to consult before starting.
     Use clear communication to clarify concerns.
     Present positive advantages of changing.

  2) *Establish Rapport* (Contemplation).
     The person alternates ambivalently between wanting to change and not wanting to change. Reflect on the experience and ambivalence about changing (e.g. using parts integration and eliciting values.

  3) *SPECIFY Outcome* (Commitment).
     As the person talks about really wanting to change, help him or her set goals.
     Utilize appropriate Meta-Programs.
     Reframe problem as changeable and discuss strategy for change.
     Provide tasks for the person to check out their intention.

  4) *Open Up the person's Model of the World* (Action; A).
     As the person becomes ready to act, elicit and alter the old strategy for using.
     Meta-Model and reframe old languaged responses

5) *Leading* (Action; B).
   Integrate parts.
   Use Time-Line Processes or Re-Imprinting.

6) *Verify Change* (Maintenance).
   Confirm that the person has built a new lifestyle.
   Teach conflict resolution skills.
   Integrate change at the level of mission, values, and time-line.
   Teach skills for both state changing and for healthy living.
   Run new content through the old strategies.

7) *Exit* (Recycling).
   Future pace the person through possible lapses to discovery and delight.

Chapter 24

Disordering "Personality" Through Anxiety-ing

The Craze for Anxiety

As an emotional state, *anxiety* brings more people into psychiatric treatment than any other (Beletsis, 1989, p. 264). 33% of all people visiting their doctor have anxiety as a key complaint. A similar percentage of the general population will develop a "clinically significant anxiety disorder" at some time in their life (Barlow, Esler and Vitali, 1998, p. 312).

The DSM-IV (1994) psychiatric manual describes anxiety in three ways.

1) Prolonged anxiety includes symptoms such as feeling restless, fatigued, keyed-up, irritable, suffering from muscular tension, and being unable to sleep or concentrate.

2) Acute anxiety attacks (panic) are even more intense responses and include heart pounding, sweating, shaking, difficulty breathing, chest and abdominal pain, nausea, dizziness, and extreme fear (of death, insanity or loss of control).

3) Many people suffer from one of the above types of anxiety, but cope with it in ways which become other symptoms: alcohol and drug use, extreme and involuntary dissociation responses, eating disorders, compulsive rituals, violence and other behaviors designed to avoid the anxiety. Twice as many women as men report anxiety as such, and this seems related to men's preference for certain of these other behaviors. (Barlow, Esler and Vitali, 1998, p. 290)

Understandably, a plethora of medications such as Valium (diazepam) have been used to treat anxiety. Yet there is little evidence that drugs, used alone, reduce the frequency and severity of anxiety, and users have been shown to exhibit the same level of fear and avoidance behavior after the drug treatment as before (Franklin, 1996, p. 7). Again and again though, cognitive NLP-style change processes have been compared to diazepam and related drugs and shown to be far more successful. (Barlow, Ester and Vitali, 1998, p. 310)

Unfortunately, the craving for a quick-fix (such as pills seem to offer) is implicit in the very nature of anxiety. Conversely, longer-term psychotherapy feeds into the very nature of the problem by creating dependency (Beck and Emery, 1985, p. 171). What works is what NLP offers: short term change processes which give the person back control over their own state.

Denominalizing Anxiety

We begin by defining anxiety as a state. Notice that the DSM-IV criteria for anxiety are described almost entirely by *internal kinesthetic* indicators. Yet when the DSM-IV wants a synonym for anxiety, it uses a purely cognitive one: "apprehensive expectation." This is important. We experience anxiety as a physical response, and yet it cannot be generated without certain constructed internal representations (visual, auditory or kinesthetic) of "possible" future events.

A person seeing a spider may make a huge internal picture of a spider crawling towards them, and then feel the resulting fear ($V^c\backslash K^i$). Another person may create the sound of an entire hall of people laughing and shouting at their humiliation and feel the fear of that ($A^c\backslash K^i$). Another may create the feeling of slipping off a high place and falling so well that they feel as if they are falling, and feel the fear of that ($V^c\backslash K^i$).

These are *synesthesias*. This term describes a representation in one sensory system which is simultaneously linked to one in another system. The pictures, sounds, or physical sensations simultaneously generate an internal set of sensations described by the person as "anxiety." Longer-term anxiety can be sustained by strategies which place A_d (the language of self-talk) in the sequence. A person may imagine failing an exam, talk to themselves about how terrible that would be, and pick up an increasing sense of panic about what they are saying ($V^c \leftrightarrow A_d \setminus K^i$).

We can also feed back into the system the initial results of the original synesthesias. A pounding of the heart resulting from thinking about the spider can lead to speculation about a heart attack, and to increased pounding ($V^c \setminus K^i \leftrightarrow A_d \setminus K^i$). Such physical escalation is the source of panic attacks, as opposed to longer term anxiety.

Bandler and Grinder (1976, p. 101) identified such *synesthesias* as the source of most fears and anxieties. They noted that the person with anxiety is not necessarily sure what triggers their kinesthetic responses. The response seems "automatic" to them. At times their conscious theory about the cause is quite different to the unconscious strategy which we would elicit. A person may tell you she has a fear of "success," but actually generate panic by internal images of social rejection and public failure. (Beck and Emery, 1985, p. 213)

Like all such anchored responses, the original trigger for anxiety may generalize to related situations. The DSM-IV has a category called *Generalized Anxiety Disorder.* We consider the anxiety here to be "free floating" and not related to any specific trigger. Research by cognitive psychologists (Beck and Emery, 1985, p. 94) suggests that this whole category is mythological. Triggers always exist, but are not always consciously recalled by the person. Why? The anxiety may be triggered by a set of situations which are apparently unrelated (though all often lead to the same ultimate feared consequences for the person e.g., humiliation, death).

Another reason is that often the internal representations used to generate the anxiety are of events which do not, or did not, exist in the real world. A person may have a phobia of snakes even though they have never seen a real snake. They do this by imagining what it would be like to be fatally attacked by a snake, stepping into that image and feeling the fear as if it had happened. A movie like *"Jaws"* is often followed by a wave of new phobia sufferers for this reason. The movie is quite safe, but the internal images are not.

Personal Strengths

In terms of *the Personal Strengths model,* when a person tells us about a phobia of elevators we recognize the demonstration of the skill with "chunking down" (to the details of the elevator) and "associating into" the experience. The synesthesias operate from coding the experiences as associated (i.e., mentally stepping into a plane crash). Very specific (chunked down) cue situations produce this result (as contrasted with depression, where "everything" feels bad).

Figure 24.1

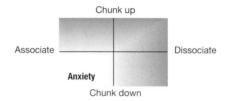

The "As If" World

Why do anxiety "sufferers" run these annoying synesthesias?

Ericksonian therapist David Higgins (in Yapko, ed., 1989, pp. 245–263) points out that all of us live in an *"As if"* world. In order to act, we make certain guesses about what will happen. Technically, while these guesses are all "hallucinations," they have the potential to generate hope or fear, happiness or pain. This is an active ongoing self-hypnotic process, and is potentially healthy.

In anticipating future challenges, we estimate the significance of the challenge, and the strength of our resources to respond to that challenge (Beck and Emery, pp. 3–53). Some fear realistically appraises a serious challenge level, and usefully mobilizes the body to deal with such challenge by increasing the pulse and breathing rate, and mobilizing the muscles etc. Severe anxiety, however, is a disorder of *the "As if" process.* The anxious person (as opposed to the person who realistically fears a current threat) demonstrates certain "cognitive distortions." They make certain key submodality and strategy shifts to do this. Which ones? The following are typical:

1) *Sorting for the future.* By attending to potential future events to the exclusion of present and past, the person becomes unable to access resourceful memories, or effectively use resources at hand. A person who spoke to a crowd of 1000 people and loved it last week may panic as they think about repeating that tomorrow.

2) *Sorting for danger.* The person pays more attention to potential risks and less to potential safeties. They do this by using focused "tunnel vision" and its auditory and kinesthetic analogues. For example, a person afraid of public speaking may see only one angry looking person staring at them, and not notice those smiling. A person with chest tightness may pay attention to that and speculate about its cause, rather than feeling the comfort in their hands.

3) *Associating into internal representations of danger.* This describes the very opposite of the submodality shift which we work with when we use the NLP Phobia/Trauma Resolution pattern.

4) *Increasing the significance of the danger.* Anxious persons increase submodalities such as size and closeness on the feared object or situation. This makes the threat seem greater than one's resources. At the same time, these persons also diminish the submodalities of their own resources and memories of success. A person afraid of public speaking may see a room of huge eyes staring at them, and so shrinks into the floor. They may do this by "talking up" the power of the audience to reject and humiliate them.

5) *Unrealistic evaluations as a result of increasing the sense of danger.* Rather than grading risk (e.g. "On a scale of 1–10, how risky is this?"), anxious people act as if any danger equals total danger. Persons with a phobia of flying, for example, may estimate at normal times that the risk of harm from a flight is one in a million (1:1,000,000). At the time when the airplane takes off they may estimate it as 50:50,

and with slight turbulence at 100:1 in favor of a crash (Beck and Emery, 1985, p. 128). They may then bring into play a series of beliefs about what "has to happen" in such situations (e.g. "I have to get out of here." "I have to take my pills.").

Another such set of beliefs may involve the estimate of the importance of what others think of them and their responses. Doing something embarrassing in public may be estimated as likely to result in physical consequences every day for the next sixty years. In the state of anxiety, the person generates a whole separate set of beliefs to which they respond. We call this a sequential incongruity.

6) *Not being "at cause."* While we all can create synesthesia patterns, anxious people run them more frequently and with less conscious awareness. This leads to the belief that their feelings just happen, or are caused by the environment, rather than being a result of their attention to representations of "danger."

7) *Physiological activation.* Anxious people act in several ways to activate their body. They attend to their in-breath rather than their out-breath. They walk and move more, and often allow less time for sleep than other individuals. They breathe through their dominant nostril (Rossi, 1996, pp. 171–2). Ernest Rossi points out that this partly keeps them in the alertness phase of the normal rest-activation cycle for prolonged times. Where anxiety peaks at a certain time in the day, this indicates a damaged rest cycle reaching critical level at that time.

Anxiety and Depression

Earlier we examined the structure and treatments for depression. A person can run strategies which generate anxiety and those which generate depression. Both conditions involve sorting for what is wrong and associating into unpleasant experiences. However, the two sets differ, and it may help to distinguish them before we consider how to resolve anxiety.

In the case of depression, the focus is on past experiences—failures, losses, and defeats which have already happened, and which are fixed facts. The depressed person may not even have a future time-line about which to feel anxious, let alone in which to formulate goals. That person's comments about life and self will therefore be based on a "permanent pervasive style" of explanation:

"This is the way I and other things are; everything is like this, and it always will be."

The depressed person has understandably little interest in doing anything, because he or she expects failure:

"What's the point, it only gets you to the same place I've always been…nowhere."

Such a person may become hopeful about specific tasks (and then use the patterns that we call "anxiety"), but generally the depressed person has given up in trying to avoid the kind of pain which the anxious person runs from.

The anxious person focuses on potential future defeats, failures, and losses. The anxious person considers these disasters as being possibly avoidable, if only he or she can escape in some way from certain feared events. This leads to the style of explanation of being more tentative, conditional, and more focused on particular events:

"If I can only avoid elevators (or crowds, thinking about death, etc.), then I might be able to escape this terror."

This means that the anxious person has objectives, but is unable to reach them. Such people fear failure. They do not give up on doing everything (unless they finally got depressed about their anxiety), but give up on doing the things they fear—the triggers for the anxiety.

How Do We End Anxiety?

There's more to this question than meets the eye. Anxiety itself is driven by *an attempt to avoid* some feared consequence. The "simple" solution to anxiety for the person with a spider phobia seems to be to never think about, or come into contact with, anything to do with spiders. For the person with anxiety about loss of self-control, the "simple" solution is to never be in a situation where loss of self-control is even remotely possible.

Of course these are impossible goals. Yet many people with anxiety clutch at the illusion of such solutions in the form of drugs, distractions, lifestyles totally organized around the fears, and around dependent relationships where they cannot let another person out of their sight or reach. What we usually call "secondary gain" (the accidental advantages which the problem brings to life in terms of sympathy, avoidance of challenges, etc.) is really primary gain in anxiety conditions. These are often the immediate aims of the person with the anxiety.

As a therapist, we first need absolute clarity about the person's concerns regarding our role. We do not want to create such illusory solutions as presenting NLP as a series of tools which will *automatically* solve the problem regardless of what the person does. Another example would be offering to become the person's total life support system: "Call me any time!" This is not wise.

Being a "magician" can be very satisfying. Yet it pales in comparison to the joy of empowering those driven by anxiety so that they learn to perform their own magic. Our role must focus on becoming a coach or consultant to the person.

Frame it as the anxious person has simply hired you to provide advice and support in putting a plan into action that will change things. Make it a collaborative relationship in which the person will need to "help" and to experimentally follow the insights and patterns we provide. We have no magic way of solving the problems for people. Yet if our anxious clients will practice and do the things we suggest, they will experience positive changes. As a time-limited arrangement, it is important to arrange at the start to meet for a specific number of sessions with an eye on the end point (typically two or four).

There's another side of this. If a client does not hire us as a consultant, we fully accept that and do not enter into a therapeutic relationship. In practice, this becomes important. If we suggest some task (such as having the person identify three things they achieved that day) and the person does *not* actually *do* the task, we don't suggest any other tasks in the hope of "finding one that works." In such situations, we will explore *what he or she did* instead of the task, and seek to discover how that created undesired results.

The following five sets of NLP tools are intended to be used inside this context in order to reverse the "cognitive distortions" of anxiety.

- Reframe Anxiety and its Symptoms.
- Access Resources and Solutions.
- Teach Trance and Set Relaxation Anchors.
- Alter the Submodality Codings.
- Create more Integrated Beliefs.

1) Reframe anxiety and its symptoms
We begin with an educational approach. We first point out *the value* of normal fear responses as we explain the structure of problematic anxiety as generated by perceptual distortions and synesthesias. This allows anxiety to simply become a signal which clients need to identify in order to adjust perceptions of situations, and then to behave differently.

We then elicit the triggers which the person has been using to generate anxiety and search for the submodality distortions which increase the significance of the threat. We have resolved anxiety about public speaking on a number of occasions by simply having the person notice the image they hold in mind when they think about such. They typically have narrowly focused their perceptions on certain people in a way that distorted the size of their eyes so that they are very much enlarged. Frequently, once people access their triggers, they can change them without further explanation. The unrealistic evaluations being made by the person can be checked at this time. Resilient beliefs will require some of the later techniques, but people anxious about all the things they "need to get done immediately" may be intrigued to find that they have incorrectly evaluated the need.

One fun way to produce submodality shifts even at this initial exploration involves using the playful type of intervention Richard Bandler demonstrates in *Magic in Action* (1984). Working with Susan, a woman who experiences panic when her family are late home, Bandler says: "Let's say I had to fill in for you for a day. So one of the parts of my job would be if somebody was late I'd have to have the panic for you. What do I do inside my head in order to have the panic?" (p. 9)

Susan replies "You start telling yourself sentences like…"

Richard interrupts "I've got to talk to myself".

She continues, "…so and so is late, look they're not here. That means that they may never come."

Bandler asks, "Do I say this in a casual tone of voice?"

Tad James has modeled this pattern and put together a pattern that he calls The Logical Levels of Therapy, which has more recently been updated by Hall (*The Sourcebook of Magic*, 1997).

We can also reframe kinesthetic triggers which feed a panic cycle (e.g. $V^c\backslash K^i \rightarrow A_d \backslash K^i$). Point out that the feeling of faintness is just the same as the feeling of being "giddy" with excitement; that the feeling of labored breathing and dizziness is the same feeling as when dancing fast; that the feeling of hot and cold flushes is like the feeling of being in a sauna and cold pool; that anxiety-based numbness in hands or jaw is like having a hand fall asleep while leaning on it absorbed in TV, etc. (see Russell Bourne's article "From Panic to Peace: Recognizing the Continua," in Yapko, ed., 1989, p. 214).

2) Access resources and solutions

We next assist clients by identifying and building inner resource experiences to cope with the situations found difficult. Anxious people sort for danger, and so, when asked to find a resource experience, they will often access their most challenging and scary times. That's where their brain goes. We inform them that this simply represents a Meta-Program choice and that they can change it by simple rehearsal. We described two types of Solution Focused Questions to elicit such times which we described more fully in the chapter on Depression. (Chevalier, 1995)

1) *Outcome questions:* Ask for a description of the person's outcome.

2) *Exception questions:* Ask about when the problem doesn't occur (the exceptions).

If the person cannot find any exceptions, then ask about hypothetical exceptions using the "Miracle" question.

"Suppose one night there is a miracle while you are sleeping, and this problem is solved. Since you are sleeping, you don't know that a miracle has happened or that your problem is solved. What do you suppose you will notice that's different in the morning, that will let you know the problem is solved?"

Invite clients to begin using Solution Focused Questions in daily life. Before getting out of bed in the morning, they are to ask themselves, "What are three things that I am looking forward to today?" Prior to going to bed at night, they are to ask themselves, "What are three things I achieved today?" You will find that the potency of these questions is extraordinary.

3) Teach trance and set relaxation anchors

One simple way to build resources is to teach clients to relax physiologically. This includes showing them how to actually stop tightening muscle groups, to pay attention to the out-breath rather than the in-breath, to breathe through the non-dominant nostril (Rossi, 1996, pp. 171–2), and to orient towards enjoyable internal imagery. Here we aim to coach clients to go into a trance on their own, using anchors under their control. Such anchors can be set by the person in the therapy.

Working with students who have exam anxiety, for example, we have often completely solved the problem by inducing a trance, having the person make a gestural anchor with their non-dominant hand (which will be free when they are writing) and testing the anchor afterwards. The person then uses the anchor in the exam. Typically we have people reporting, "That was the most relaxed exam I've ever had in my life." Anchoring paces the anxious person's personal strength of associating into experiences.

Many of our more generally anxious clients comment after an initial 15 minute trance induction, "This is the most relaxed I have ever been," Yet for them, this is only the beginning. The person also needs to commit to using this process on a regular basis. And "regular," Ernest Rossi points out (Rossi 1996, pp. 279–313) means several times a day. This re-establishes a natural ultradian rest cycle. With Rossi, we have found that many anxious clients will have no further problems if they arrange every 90 minutes to rest for ten minutes lying on the dominant side (thus opening the non-dominant nostril).

Yoga teacher, Debra Lederer with Michael Hall (1999) have presented a whole series of yoga exercises for relaxation (*Instant Relaxation*). These provide a way to build and reinforce the relaxation answer to the point where it can be used as a resource in a great many other contexts.

4) Alter the submodality codings

Submodality change techniques give us a phenomenal flexibility in removing the triggers of anxiety. We have already discussed altering the submodalities of an experience so that it is coded in a more normal way (e.g., so that we see the eyes of people in a feared audience as normal size rather than large and glaring).

We can use other submodality changes to do this with flair. In *Magic in Action,* Bandler demonstrates the use of a Visual Swish to end a woman's panic about her family dying in an accident. That is, he had her rehearse through seeing the image of the accident *replaced instantly* by the image of her as much more resourceful and confident. He then used the Dissociation Trauma pattern to resolve another woman's agoraphobia. Versions of these processes have also been used outside the field of NLP by cognitive psychologists (see Beck and Emery, 1985, pp. 215–231) and Ericksonian therapists (see Russell Bourne in Yapko ed., 1989, p. 217).

We can solve most one-situation anxiety problems (e.g. examination anxiety) by simply changing the submodality of time perspective. A technique from *Time Line Therapy* (James and Woodsmall, 1988) that James uses is to use the fact that the anxious person is looking towards the future.

> If you would, I'd like you to think of an event about which you're fearful,…fearful or have anxiety about. When you have one, I'd like you to float up above your Time Line again. Go out into the future—one minute after the successful completion of the event about which you were anxious. (Of course make sure the event turns out the way you want.) And I'd like you to turn and look towards now. Now where's the anxiety? Notice how you chuckle. Fear and anxiety have no existence outside of time. (p. 45)

The Dissociation Trauma pattern is the most well researched of all NLP interventions for panic (see Einspruch, Allen, Dennholz and Mann, Kosiey and McCleod, and Muss for examples). We have taught this process to psychiatrists in Sarajevo for use with survivors of one of history's most horrific wars.

Margot took one woman through a trauma resolution pattern on the entire war experience. She began quite tearful, announcing in English, "I hate the war; and I hate talking about it!" She said she had experienced nightmares every night since the war. For her, sounds were powerful anchors, and the sound of explosions produced uncontrollable panic.

The previous week someone had organized a fireworks display in Sarajevo. Rationally, she knew she was safe, yet her panic put her right back in the war situation. She ran into a nearby house and hid in their basement until the display was over. After attempting unsuccessfully to explain the trauma process to her (her knowledge of English was limited), Margot simply asked her to imagine

447

being in a movie theater and ran the process. Her movie went from the time before the war to the time after it, a period of over three years.

Margot then asked her to think of the fireworks and find out how it felt now.

She laughed.

Next, Margot asked her to remember some of the worst times from the war, and check how they were. She gazed ahead with a dazed expression.

"So how is it?" we checked.

"Well, she said, with a smile, "I'm seeing the pictures, and it's as if they're just over there, and I'm here."

The entire process had taken twenty minutes.

5) Create more integrated beliefs

Anxiety and panic responses make people incongruent with the rest their life. In NLP we describe this incongruency as the result of "parts." It is as if the part of a person which is in control at the time of the panic or anxiety has its own intentions, its own beliefs, and its own behavioral choices. And all of these are quite different to the intentions, beliefs, and choices when the person feels calm.

On the surface, there is no reason for a grown man or woman to be afraid of elevators. Yet when the anxious person moves near the elevator, a whole different set of beliefs about what might happen activates the particular anxiety response. The person then chooses from a range of behaviors not normally used, all the while *not* accessing skills he or she usually values.

Several techniques allow information to flow from the rest of the person's neurology into the areas where one generates the anxiety. One of the simplest is the *Eye Movement Integrator* (Andreas, 1992, pp. 9–11) in which the person accesses their memory of a situation of anxiety (visually, auditorially, and kinesthetically) and follows the practitioner's finger movements as they move from one side of the client's face to the other, horizontally, vertically and obliquely.

A similar technique, marketed outside of NLP, is *EMDR* (Shapiro, 1995). Francine Shapiro explains,

> One of the simplest ways of describing EMDR effects is to say that the target event has remained unprocessed because the immediate biochemical responses to the trauma have left it isolated in neuro-biological stasis. When the client tracks a moving finger or attends to a hand tap, tone, or even a fixed point on the wall, active information processing is initiated to attend to the present stimulus.

In other words, your brain knows how to fix stuff as soon as you access both sides of it at once. In our experience, even highly anxious individuals can be taught to process their own material at home by using a variation of the technique, such as accessing anxiety triggers while juggling.

Several other techniques in NLP generate integration by starting with the behaviors of the "part" active during anxiety, and chunking up until the general resources of the whole neurology are accessed. One is *the Mind Backtracking Technique* (Hall and Bodenhamer, 1997, p. 35) in which you begin with the irrational auditory digital thought and ask repeatedly,

> "And behind that thought whirling in your mind lies another thought. So as you allow yourself to notice, what thought do you find back there?"

Our own version of this process is *Ascending States* (Bolstad, 1998, p. 17) in which the person attends to the kinesthetic experience of anxiety and asks repeatedly, "As you are aware of that, what arises from underneath that?" We've also used this as a one-session treatment for anxiety.

Another set of integration techniques includes *Core Transformation* (Andreas, 1992, pp. 3–5), *Meta Transformation* (the same process restructured in terms of Meta-Levels), and *Parts Integration.* In these, the person identifies the intention of the problem behaviors and then asks repeatedly,

"And if you have that intention fully and completely, what even more important thing do you get through having that?"

Our colleague Lynn Timpany's *Esteem Generator* technique combines this with the installation of a new auditory-digital strategy for those who have run a self-critical internal voice. Lynn's new strategy begins with the old triggers for the unsupportive voice, has the person say a key interrupt phrase (like "Think positive!" or "Hey wait!"), has them say something more resourceful to themselves, and then has them congratulate themselves and give themselves a positive feeling about how they changed their thinking. Lynn has the person run through this sequence with every example they can recall. Using this technique before we get people to do group presentations in our Master Practitioner course has solved most of the anxiety problems we used to cope with.

Finally, a wealth of NLP techniques for changing beliefs can be used to alter the irrational beliefs once they have been accessed (notice that while they are kept separate in the panic part of the person, the person does not experience them as real and does not "need" to change them). Some level of integration needs to occur for belief changes to access the part of the neurology generating the problem belief.

Summary

- As the most common undesired state in psychotherapy, anxiety is generated by a number of synesthesias from representations of potential future dangers to kinesthetic activation.

- The structure of anxiety-ing involves sorting for potential future dangers, associating into them, and exaggerating their importance through the submodalities of "real," "close," "now," "compelling," etc. All of this results in unrealistic evaluations of the danger, and in a sense of the person's emotional state being out of their control.

- Using the *RESOLVE model of therapy* (Bolstad and Hamblett, 1998, pp. 107–108) we summarize the responses we have found effective thus:

1) Resourceful State

Establish a collaborative, consultative relationship rather than a magical or dependent one.

2) Establish Rapport

Acknowledge the person's difficulty.

Assess and pace Meta-Programs (especially Towards and Away From, Time Orientation, Association vs. Dissociation) and physiological arousal.

3) Specify Outcomes

Set a time-limited consulting contract with outcomes.

Build expectancy of change and explain the need for completing tasks at home.

4) Open Up the Client's Model of the World

Coach about the structure of anxiety and elicit the triggers used.

Reframe anxiety and its physical symptoms as manageable.

Use solution-focused questions to build resources.

5) Leading to Desired State

Practice and teach physiological relaxation, including muscle and breathing control.

Set relaxation anchors.

Alter the submodalities of the triggers using swishes.

Apply the Trauma Resolution pattern to all triggers.

Teach the person to alter time perspective to looking back from the future.

Teach the person the Eye Movement Integrator or a variant of such.

Use techniques which chunk up to core states (Mind Backtracking, Ascending States, Core Transformation, Parts Integration).

Consider using belief change or strategy installation to complete a new response setup.

6) *Verify Change*

Teach the person to celebrate their new ability to relax.

7) *Exit: Future Pace*

Use the new time perspective to have the person in the future looking back towards now and seeing the changes.

Chapter 25

You and Your "Personality"

"I never leave home without my personality."

Every day when we wake up and move through the world we manifest an expression of ourselves in the way we walk, talk, interact, and gesture. We manifest it by the things we do, the places we go, the people we choose to be around. We manifest it in our clothing, our lifestyle, our grooming, etc. We manifest what we call "a personality" style.

We have noted throughout these chapters that we do not so much "have" a *personality* as we *manifest* a personality. The way we *order* and disorder our thinking, feeling or emoting, our use and management of our body, our languaging, and behaving shapes and forms the kind and quality of "personality" that we experience. By the time we enter into adult life we have pretty much solidified most of our central and highest beliefs, ideas, values, visions, and identifications. As these higher frames become solidified and we treat them as "real," they seem stable and sometimes even permanent or unchangeable. It's out of that gestalt that arises the sense that "our personality is pretty much set by five or eighteen" or some other early age.

Yet as we have seen, it only *seems* so. That most of us *feel* it so only testifies to the power and stability of the higher frames of mind and how we can carry them around with us for years without them changing very much. In fact, the even higher frame of reference that we *think and believe* that "personality" is a solid "thing-like" entity only further ensconces it from our remaking and transforming and protects it in a frame that allows little alteration. This illustrates further the self-organizing influence of a higher frame that works as an attractor in a system.

As we have applied the Cognitive Behavioral model of NLP and Neuro-Semantics to "personality" in this work, we have underscored repeatedly that "personality" is something we *learn,* something we *do*, and something that we *perpetuate* by the way we set frames in terms of beliefs, values, and expectations. Given that, we can *unlearn, redo, and reframe* "personality" and reinvent ourselves. We have showed and illustrated numerous NLP patterns as the technology of transformation for engaging in that personality altering process.

Where are you with your "personality?" To what extent do you like the "personality" that you've learned to map out for yourself? How well has it served you? How well does it continue to enhance your life? How would you like to alter, transform, and refine your "personality?"

Having traced many of the NLP and Neuro-Semantics models for looking at the very structure of experience, we have only initiated the beginnings of how to treat this non-thing of "personality" as truly a process. There is a strategy to "personality." It does have order, elements, component pieces and parts of the sub-processes of thinking-emoting, referencing, speaking, and acting. It also has a Meta-Level structure that operates as a system of interactive parts. Meta-States provide a way to track the non-linear nature of the feedback and feed forward processes involved in how we map from experience to the higher frames of mind.

This book has been far from exhaustive. It's more like just the beginning of mapping the wild and wonderful domain of how we recognize ourselves as *persons*, and then solidify our sense of self over time to create our "personality." Knowing that *you* are so much more than any of these experiences, anything you've been through, anything you've thought or could think, anything that you have felt or could feel, may you allow yourself to map out new structures that will tap into your full resources and empower you to be at your best. Life is a journey, may yours be lived with passion and compassion, with insight and practicality, with fun and productivity.

Chapter 26

Personality and the Matrix

One of the most recent developments in Neuro-Semantics is the creation of *the Matrix Model* (2002). This model combines and unifies all of the individual pieces, patterns, models, and processes of NLP and Neuro-Semantics into one structure. It does so by distinguishing two *process matrices* by which we create our sense of reality (the Meaning matrix and the Intention matrix), the one *foundational or grounding matrix* wherein we experience things (the State matrix), and five *content matrices* built around five categories or concepts (Self, Power, Time, Other, and World). Together these operate as a complete neuro-semantic system with primary and meta-feedback and feed forward loops.

What does this have to do with "personality"? Everything. The meanings and intentions that we build and map about our Self affects our sense of "personality." So do our mappings about our Power or Resourcefulness to handle things. This leads to our meta-sense of self-confidence in our abilities and self-efficacy in facing reality on its own terms. Our conceptual mappings about Time affect the time-zone we live in, past, present, or future and our flexibility or rigidity in moving between these temporal concepts. There are Time emotions. Regret, bitterness, old unfinished business and nostalgia, that are emotions of a past orientation. Hope, anticipation, worry, impatience and anticipatory fear are emotions of a future orientation. Patience, presence, lost in the moment and impulsive are some emotions of the present time orientation.

The Other or Relationship matrix affects our sense of self in the eyes of others, our social self, and the emotions of wanting approval, being loved, connected, valued, unvalued, judged, etc. The World matrix refers to all of the worlds that we have maps for navigating, from the physical world, to the world of work, career, sports, finance, politics, and so on. These too reflect and reveal the mappings we create or have inherited about ourselves.

Since we create meaning by labeling things, events, and ideas; associate emotions with meanings, set them as a frame of reference, and evaluate them; it is through such meaning-making that we participate in inventing our personalities. This power allows us to begin the process of re-inventing ourselves. Via our meaning-making powers and powers of intention, we can re-construct a new map for how to *be* in the world, relate to others, relate to ourselves, think and feel about ourselves, and so on.

In this way the Matrix Model provides an over-arching framework for how we use events, experiences, ideas, words, feelings, and circumstances and begin to construct or map our conceptual understandings. For more on the Matrix Model, see the book by that title.

NLP and Neuro-Semantic Resources and Patterns

Throughout these pages we have mentioned numerous *Transformation Patterns* that come from the field of Neuro-Linguistic Programming (NLP) and from Neuro-Semantics. In Chapter 12 we detailed many of the more central patterns. Yet there are a great many more, probably 100 to 200 NLP Patterns, and another 100 Neuro-Semantic Patterns. The following works provide the majority of these.

Neuro-Linguistic Patterns

The Sourcebook of Magic (1997, Hall and Belnap)
The User's Manual for the Brain (1999, Bodenhamer and Hall)
Using Your Brain for a Change (1985, Bandler, ed. by Andreas)
Transforming Communication (1998, Bolstad and Hamblett)
Pro-fusion (1998, Bolstad and Hamblett)
NLP: the New Technology (1997, Andreas and Faulkner)
The Heart of the Mind (1991, Andreas and Andreas)
Change Your Mind and Keep the Change (1987, Andreas and Andreas)
Time Line Therapy and the Basis of Personality (1998, James and Woodsmall)
Adventures with Time-Lines (Time-Lining, 1997, Bodenhamer and Hall)
Reframing (1985, Bandler)
Changing Belief Systems (1991, Dilts)
Core Transformation (1991, Andreas)
Figuring Out People: Design Engineering Using Meta-Programs (1997, Hall and Bodenhamer)

Neuro-Semantic Patterns

Meta-States: Mastering the Higher Levels of Your Consciousness (2000, 2nd ed., Hall)
The Structure of Excellence (1999, Hall and Bodenhamer)
Dragon Slaying (1996, Hall; 2000, 2nd ed.)
Meta-States Patterns (2001, Hall)
Meta-States Certification Training Manual (2000, Hall)
Advanced NLP Flexibility Using General Semantics (2000, Hall)
Frame Games: Persuasion Elegance (2000, Hall)
Secrets of Personal Mastery (2000, Hall)
Games for Mastering Fear (2001, Hall and Bodenhamer)

Bibliography

Adams, P. (1998). *Gesundheit*, Rochester, VA.: Healing Arts Press.

Adler, R. (1999). "Crowded Minds" in *New Scientist, Vol. 164,* No. 2217, pp. 26–31, December 18, 1999.

Allen, K. (1982). *An Investigation of the Effectiveness of Neuro-Linguistic Programming Procedures in Treating Snake Phobias.* Dissertation Abstracts International, 43, 861B.

American Psychiatric Association Diagnostic Criteria, from DSM-IV (1994). Washington DC, American Psychiatric Association.

Andreas, C. (1992). *The Aligned Self: An Advanced Audiocassette Program: Booklet,* Boulder, CO: NLP Comprehensive, Boulder.

Andreas, Steve; Andreas, Connirae (1987). *Change Your Mind and Keep the Change,* Moab, UT: Real People Press.

Andreas, Steve; Andreas, Connirae (1989). *Heart of the Mind,* Moab, UT: Real People Press.

Andreas, Steve; Faulkner, Charles (1994). *NLP: The New Technology of Achievement,* NY: William Marrow and Company.

Andreas, S. (1999). "What Makes A Good NLPer?", *Anchor Point, Vol 13,* No. 10, pp. 3–6, October 1999.

Arieti, S. (1948). "Special logic of schizophrenic and other types of autistic thought" in *Psychiatry,* 11, pp. 325–338.

Assagioli, Roberto. (1965). *Psychosynthesis: A Manual of Principles and Techniques.* New York: Penguin.

Bandler, Richard; Grinder, John (1975). *The Structure of Magic, Volume I: A Book about Language and Therapy,* Palo Alto, CA: Science & Behavior Books.

Bandler, Richard; Grinder, John (1979). *Frogs into Princes.* (ed. Steve Andreas), Moab, UT: Real People Press.

Bandler, Richard; Grinder, John (1981). *Trance-formations: Neuro-linguistic Programming and the Structure of Hypnosis* (ed. Connirae Andreas), Moab, UT: Real People Press.

Bandler, Richard; McDonald, Will (1988). *An Insider's Guide to Submodalities,* Capitola, CA: Meta Publications.

Bandler, Richard (1993). *Time for a Change* (ed. Daniels), Capitola, CA: Meta Publications.

Bandler, Richard; LaValle, John (1996). *Persuasion Engineering,* Capitola, CA: Meta Publications.

Bandler, Richard (1989). *Creating Therapeutic Change* (Training sessions recorded on set of 7 videotapes), Boulder, CO: NLP Comprehensive.

Bandler, Richard; Grinder, John (1982). *Reframing: Neuro-linguistic Programming and the Transformation of Meaning,* Moab, UT: Real People Press.

Bandler, Richard (1984). *Magic in Action,* Cupertino, CA.: Meta Publications.

Bandler, Richard (1988). Videotaped Client Sessions #2 and #4: Paranoid Schizophrenia, Boulder, CO: NLP Comprehensive.

Barlow, D.H., Esler, J.L. and Vitali, A.E. (1998). "Psychosocial Treatments for Panic Disorders, Phobias and Generalised Anxiety Disorder" in Nathan, P.E. & Gorman, J.M. (1998). *A Guide to Treatments that Work,* NY: Oxford University Press.

Barnaby, W. (1995). "Saner Views of Schizophrenia" Briefing, The Royal Society, London.

Bateson, Gregory (1972). *Steps to an Ecology of Mind,* New York: Ballatine.

Baxter L. R. (1994). "Positron emission tomography studies of cerebral glucose metabolism in obsessive compulsive disorder." *Journal of Clinical Psychiatry, 55,* Supplement, pp. 54–9.

Beck, A.T., Emery, G. with Greenberg, R.L. (1985). *Anxiety Disorders and Phobias: A Cognitive Perspective,* NY: Basic Books.

Ben-Aron, M.H.; Hucker, S.J.; and Webster, C. (1985) (Eds.). *Clinical Criminology,* Toronto: M. & M. Graphics.

Bergin, A.; Garfield, S. (1994). *Handbook of Psychotherapy and Behavior Change,* NY: Wiley & Sons.

Berry, P. (1961). "Effect of Colored Illumination Upon Perceived Temperature" in *Journal of Applied Psychology,* 45(4) pp. 248–250.

Bolstad, R.; Hamblett, M. (1999D). "Time Line Therapy And Identity Change" in *The Time Line Therapy Association Journal, Vol 13,* pp. 5–7.

Bolstad, R. (1995A). "An NLP Model of Personal Strengths" in *Anchor Point, Vol 9:3,* March, pp. 34–38.

Bolstad, R. (1998). "Beyond Self" in *Anchor Point, Vol 12,* Nov 12, December, pp. 9–17.

Bolstad, R. (1995C). "NLP and the Five Elements" in *Anchor Point, Vol 2,* No. 2, July.

Bolstad, R. (1995B) "R.E.S.O.L.V.E.: An NLP Model of Therapy" in *Anchor Point, Vol 9:8,* August, pp. 12–14.

Bolstad, R.; Hamblett, M. (1997). "Questing: Aligning Change With Life's One Great Search" in *Anchor Point, Vol 11,* No. 4, pp. 3–12 and *Vol 11,* No. 5, pp. 3–16; April and May.

Bolstad, R.; Hamblett, M. (1999). "Visual Digital: Modality of the Future?" in *NLP World. Vol 6,* No. 1, March.

Bolstad, R.; Hamblett, M., (1998). *Transforming Communication,* Auckland: Addison-Wesley-Longman.

Bolstad, Richard (1996). "NLP: The Quantum Leap" in *NLP World, Vol. 3,* No. 2, July, pp. 5–34.

Breggin, P. (1992). *Toxic Psychiatry,* London: Fontana.

Briggs Myers, I. Manual: *The Myers-Briggs Type Indicator,* Palo Alto, CA: Consulting Psychologists Press.

Brockman, W.P. (1980). "Empathy revisited: the effects of representational system matching on certain counselling process and outcome variables", *Dissertation Abstracts International* 41(8), 3421A, College of William and Mary, p. 167.

Cairns-Smith, A.G. (1996). *Evolving The Mind: On The Nature Of Matter And The Origin Of Consciousness,* Cambridge: Cambridge University, Cambridge.

Cameron, Norman (1959). "The Paranoid Pseudo-Community Revisited", *American Journal of Sociology, Vol. 654,* pp. 52–58.

Caplan, P.J. (1995). *They Say You're Crazy,* Reading, MA: Addison-Wesley.

Carkhuff, R.R.; Berenson, B.G. (1977). *Beyond Counselling and Therapy,* New York: Holt, Rinehart and Winston.

Chevalier, A.J. (1998). *On The Client's Path,* Oakland, CA: New Harbinger.

Condon, William S. (1982). "Cultural Microrhythms" pp. 53–76, in M.Davis (ed.) *Interactional Rhythms: Periodicity in Communicative Behavior,* New York: Human Sciences Press.

Crits-Christoph, P. (1998). "Psychosocial Treatments for Personality Disorders" pp. 544–553, in Nathan, P.E. and Gorman, J.M. *A Guide to Treatments that Work,* NY: Oxford University Press.

DeMares, R. (1998). "Interspecies Communication"at www.dolphininstitute.org, Dolphin Institute.

Denholtz, M.S.; Mann, E.T. (1975). "An Automated Audiovisual Treatment of Phobias Administered by Non-professionals". *Journal of Behaviour Therapy and Experimental Psychiatry,* 6: 111–115.

Diamond, M. (1988). *Enriching Heredity: The Impact of the Environment on the Brain,* NY: Free Press.

Dilts, R.; Hallbom, T.; Smith, S. (1990). *Beliefs: Pathways to Health and Well-being,* Portland, OR: Metamorphous Press.

Dilts, Robert (1990). *Changing Belief Systems with NLP,* Cupertino, CA: Meta Publications.

Dilts, Robert; Grinder, John; Bandler, Richard; DeLozier, Judith; Leslie Cameron-Bandler (1980). *Neuro-linguistic Programming, Volume I: The Study of the Structure of Subjective Experience,* Cupertino, CA: Meta Publications.

Dilts, R. (1983). *Roots of Neuro Linguistic Programming.* Cupertino, CA: Meta Publications.

Dilts, R.B. (1994–5). *Strategies of Genius, Volume I, II, and III,* Capitola, CA: Meta Publications.

Dilts, Robert; Epstein, Todd (1995). *Dynamic Learning,* Capitola, CA: Meta Publications.

Dolan, Y.M. (1985). *A Path with a Heart,* NY: Brunner/Mazel.

Dorsman, J. (1997). *How to Quit Drinking Without AA,* NY: Prima.

Einspruch, E. (1988). "Neuro-linguistic Programming in the Treatment of Phobias" in *Psychotherapy in Private Practice,* 6(1), pp. 91–100.

Ellis, Albert; Harper, Robert A. (1976). *A New Guide to Rational Living,* Englewood Cliffs, NJ: Prentice-Hall, Inc.

Erickson, M.H. (1953). "The therapy of a psychosomatic headache" in *Journal of Clinical and Experimental Hypnosis,* 4, pp. 2–6.

Erickson, M.H.; Rossi, E.L. (1979). *Hypnotherapy: An Exploratory Casebook,* NY: Irvington.

Erickson, M.H. ed. by Rossi, E.L. (1989). *The Collected Papers of Milton H. Erickson on Hypnosis: Volume 1*, NY: Irvington.

Eysenck, H.J.; Eysenck, S.B.G. (1991). *The Eysenck Personality Questionnaire, Revised*, Sevenoaks, Kent: Hodder and Stoughton.

Eysenck, S.B.G.; Barrett, P.T.; Barnes, G.E. (1993). "A cross-cultural study of personality: Canada and England" in *Personality and Individual Differences*, 14, p. 1–10.

Finney, J.W.; Moos, R.H. (1998). "Psychosocial Treatments for Alcohol Use Disorders" pp. 156–166, in Nathan, P.E. and Gorman, J.M. *A Guide To Treatments That Work*, New York: Oxford University Press.

Franklin, J.A. (1996). *Overcoming Panic*, Australian Psychological Society, Carlton, Victoria.

Freud, Sigmund (1924). *The Loss of Reality in Neurosis and Psychosis, Volume XIX, The Complete Psychological Works of Sigmund Freud*. NY: Basic Books, Inc.

Freud, Sigmund (1936). *The Problem of Anxiety*, NY: Norton.

Gazzaniga, M.S. (1976). "The Split Brain In Man" in Thompson, R.F. (ed.) *Progress in Psychobiology*, San Francisco: W.H. Freeman and Company.

Gendlin, Eugene T. (1964*). Personality Change,* New York: John Wiley & Sons.

Genser-Medlitsch, M.; Schütz, P. (1997). "Does Neuro-Linguistic Psychotherapy Have Effect? New Results Shown in the Extramural Section." Martina Genser-Medlitsch and Peter Schütz, ÖTZ-NLP, Vienna.

Giffin, Mary; Johnson, Adelaide; Litin, Edward (1954). "Antisocial Acting Out," *American Journal of Orthopsychiatry, Vol. 24*, pp. 668–684.

Gilligan, S.G. (1987). *Therapeutic Trances,* NY: Brunner/Mazel.

Goodwin, P.A. (1988). *Foundation Theory,* Honolulu, HI: Advanced Neuro Dynamics.

Greenough, W.T.; Withers, G.; Anderson, B. (1992). "Experience-Dependent Synaptogenesis as a Plau-sible Memory Mechanism" pp. 209–229 in Gormezano, I. and Wasserman, E. (ed.), *Learning and Memory: The Behavioral and Biological Substrates,* Hillsdale, NJ: Erlbaum & Associates.

Hagstrom, G.C. (1981). "A microanalysis of direct confrontation psycho-therapy with schizophrenics: using Neuro-linguistic Programming and delsarte's system of expression" from California School of Professional

Psychology, available in Dissertation Abstracts International 42(10) 4192-B.

Haley, J.; Hoffman, L. (1967). *Techniques of Family Therapy,* NY: Basic Books.

Hall, Michael (1998). *The Secrets of Magic: Communication Excellence for the 21st Century.* Wales, UK: Anglo-American Books.

Hall, Michael (1988). "Personality as Neurologically Energized Holographic 3-D States & Meta-States." Unpublished monograph. ET Publications.

Hall, Michael (1995, 2000). *Meta-states: Managing the Higher Levels of Your Consciousness,* Grand Jct., CO: Neuro-Semantics Publications.

Hall, Michael (1996c). *Languaging: The Linguistics of Psychotherapy,* Grand Jct., CO: ET Publications.

Hall, Michael (1996). *The Spirit of NLP: Mastering the Art,* Wales, UK: Crown House Publishing.

Hall, Michael; Bodenhamer, Bob (1997). *Mind-lines: Lines for Changing Minds,* Grand Jct., CO: ET Publications.

Hall, Michael; Bodenhamer, Bob (1997). *Figuring Out People: Design Engineering Using Meta-programs,* Wales, UK: Anglo-American Books.

Hall, Michael (1997, 1998). Series on Belief Change Pattern, *Anchor Point* (Nov, Dec. 1997, Jan, Feb. 1998), Salt Lake City, UT: Anchor Point Associates.

Hall, Michael; Bodenhamer, Bobby G. (1997). "The Mind Backtracking Technique" in *Anchor Point, Vol 11,* No. 6, June.

Hall, Michael (1997, 1998). *NLP: Going Meta: Advanced Modeling Using Meta-levels,* Grand Jct., CO: ET Publications.

Hall, L.M. (1995). "The New Domain of Meta-States in the History of NLP" pp. 53–60 in *NLP World, Vol 2,* No. 3, November.

Hall, L. Michael (2000). *Frame Games: Persuasion Elegance.* Grand Jct., CO: Neuro-Semantics Publications.

Hall, L. Michael (2000). *Secrets of Personal Mastery: Advanced Techniques for Accessing Your Higher Levels of Consciousness.* Wales, UK: Crown House Publishing.

Happold, F.C. (1970). *Mysticism.* Harmondsworth, Middlesex: Penguin.

Harris, C. (1999). *Think Yourself Slim.* Shaftesbury, Dorset: Element Books.

Hatfield, Elaine; Cacioppo, John; Rapson, Richard (1994). *Emotional Contagion,* Cambridge: Cambridge University Press.

Hischke, D.L. "A definitional and structural investigation of matching perceptual predicates, mismatching perceptual predicates, and Milton-model matching" in Dissertation Abstracts International 49(9), p. 4005, undated.

Holden, R. (1993). *Laughter: The Best Medicine,* London: Thorsons.

Ivey, A.E.; Bradford Ivey, M.; Simek-Morgan, L. (1996). *Counseling and Psychotherapy: A Multicultural Perspective,* Boston: Allyn and Bacon.

Jablensky, A.; Sartorius, N.; Ernberg, G.; Anker, M.; Korten, A.; Cooper, J.E.; Day, R.; Bertelsen, A. (1992). "Schizophrenia: manifestations, incidence and course in different cultures. A World Health Organization ten country study." In *Psychological Medicine,* Supplement 20, pp. 1–97.

Jacobs, B.; Schall, M.; Scheibel, A.B. (1993). "A Qualitative Dendritic Analysis of Wernicke's Area in Humans: Gender, Hemispheric and Environmental Factors" in *Journal of Comparative Neurology,* 327.1, pp. 97–111.

Jacobs, L. (1980). "A cognitive approach to persistent delusions" in *American Journal of Psychotherapy,* 34, pp. 556–563.

James, T. (1995). "General Model For Behavioral Intervention" in *Time Line Therapy Practitioner Training Manual* (Version 3.1), Association, Honolulu, HI: Time Line Therapy.

James, Tad; Woodsmall, Wyatt. (1988). *Time Line Therapy and the Basis of Personality,* Cupertino, CA: Meta Publications.

James, Tad (1996). *Prime Concerns: Using Quantum Linguistics to Increase the Effectiveness of the Language we Use,* Honolulu, HI: Advanced Neuro Dynamics.

Jayakar, Pupul, J. Krishnamurti (1986). *A Biography,* London: Arkana.

Jaynes, Jaynes. (1976). *The Origin of Consciousness in the Breakdown of the Bicameral Mind,* Boston, MA: Houghton Mifflin Company.

Jensen, E. (1995). *The Learning Brain,* San Diego, CA: The Brain Store.

Johnson, Stephen M (1985). *Characterological Transformation: The Hard Work Miracle,* NY: W.W. Norton and Company.

Johnson, Wendell (1946/1989). *People in Quandaries: The Semantics of Personal Adjustment,* San Francisco: International Society for General Semantics.

Jones, P.B.; Rodgers, B.; Murray, T.M.; Marmot, M. (1994). "Child developmental risk factors for adult schizophrenia in the British 1946 birth cohort" in *Lancet*, 344, pp. 1398–1402.

Jung, Carl (1964). *Man and his Symbols,* NY: Dell Publishing Co.

Kasl, C.D. (1992). *Many Roads, One Journey: Moving Beyond the 12 Steps,* NY: Harper Perennial.

Kernberg, O. (1986). *Object Relations Theory and Clinical Psychoanalysis,* Northvale, NJ: Jason Aronson Inc.

Kipper, D.A. (1986). *Psychotherapy Through Clinical Role Playing,* NY: Brunner/Mazel Co.

Kleinman, A. (1991). "The Psychiatry of Culture and the Culture of Psychiatry" in *The Harvard Mental Health Letter,* President and Fellows of Harvard College, July.

Kohut, H. (1971). *The Analysis of the Self,* Madison, CN: International Universities Press.

Kopelowicz, A.; Liberman, R.P. (1998). "Psychosocial Treatments for Schizophrenia", pp. 190–211 in Nathan, P.E. and Gorman, J.M. *A Guide to Treatments That Work,* NY: Oxford University Press.

Korzybski, Alfred. (1941/1994). *Science and Sanity: An Introduction to Non-Aristotelian Systems and General Semantics,* (5th. ed.), Lakeville, CN: International Non-Aristotelian Library Publishing Co.

Kosiey, P. and McLeod, G. (1987). *Visual Kinesthetic Dissociation in Treatment of Victims of Rape. Professional Psychology: Research and Practice, 18* (3): 276–282.

Kubie, Lawrence S. (1957). *Explorations in Social Psychiatry*, (ed. Alexander H. Leighton, John A. Clausen, Robert N. Wilson). "Social Forces and the Neurotic Process" (pp. 79–99, 409–410), NY: Basic Books Inc. Publishers.

Lakoff, George; Johnson, Mark (1980). *Metaphors We Live By,* Chicago: University of Chicago.

Lankton, S.R.; Lankton, C.H. (1986). *Enchantment and Intervention in Family Therapy,* NY: Brunner/Mazel.

Lavoie, G.; Sabourin, M. (1980). "Hypnosis and Schizophrenia: A review of experimental and clinical studies" in Burrows, G.D. and Dennerstein, L. (eds) *Handbook of Hypnosis and Psycho-somatic Medicine,* pp. 377–419, New York: Elsevier/North-Holland Biomedical.

Layden, M.A.; Newman, C.F.; Freeman, A.; Byers Morse, S. (1993). *Cognitive Therapy of Borderline Personality Disorder,* Boston, MA: Allyn and Bacon.

Lewis, B.A. (1996). *Sobriety Demystified,* Santa Cruz, CA: Kelsey & Co.

Lewis, Bryon A.; Pucelik, R. Frank (1982). *Magic Demystified,* Lake Oswego, OR: Metamorphous Press.

Long, W.L. (1997). "Schizophrenia: Youth's Greatest Disabler" in *Internet Mental Health,* British Columbia: Schizophrenia Society, www.mentalhealth.com.

Lovern, J.D. (1991). *Pathways to Reality,* NY: Brunner/Mazel Co.

Macroy, T.D. (1985). "Linguistic surface structures in family interaction" in *Dissertation Abstracts International* 40(2), 926 B, UT: Utah State University, 133.

Madjar, I. (1985). "Metapersonal perspectives on health and illness" in Boddy, J. (ed.) *Health: Perspectives and Practices,* Palmerston North, New Zealand: Dunmore Press.

Mann, L.; Beswick, G.; Allouache, P.; Ivey, M. (1989). "Decision workshops for the improvement of decisionmaking: skills and confidence" in *Journal of Counseling and Development, 67,* pp. 478–481.

Marlatt, G.; Gordon, J. (1985). *Relapse Prevention: Maintenance Strategies in the Treatment of Addictive Behaviors,* NY: Guilford Press.

Marsh, A. (1984). "Smoking; habit or choice?" in *Population Trends,* 37: 20.

Marshall, I. (1989). "Consciousness and Bose-Einstein Condensates" in *New Ideas in Psychology, 7,* pp. 73–83.

Masson, J. (1993). *Against Therapy,* London: Harper Collins.

Mathews, G.; Deary, I. (1998). *Personality Traits,* Cambridge, England: Cambridge University Press.

Miller, George A.; Galanter, Eugene; Pribram, Karl H. (1960). *Plans and the Structure of Behavior,* Toronto: Holt, Rinehart and Winston Co.

Miller, S.D.; Hubble, M.A.; Duncan, B.L. (1996). *Handbook of Solution Focused Brief Therapy,* San Francisco: Jossey-Bass.

Miller, W. (1985). "Motivation for treatment: a review with special emphasis on alcoholism," in *Psychological Bulletin,* Vol 98 (1), pp. 84–107.

Miller, W.R.; Rollnick, S. (1991). *Motivational Interviewing,* NY: Guilford Press.

Millon, Wm. Theodore (1981). *Disorders of Personality, DSM-IV and Beyond*, London: John Wiley & Sons.

Mortensen, P.B.; Pedersen, C.B., Westergaard, T.; Wohlfahrt, J.; Ewald, H.; Mors, O.; Andersen, P.K.; Melbye, M. (1999). "Effects of Family History and Place and Season of Birth on the Risk of Schizophrenia" in *The New England Journal of Medicine*, February 25, Vol 340, No. 8.

Munshaw, Joseph; Zink, Nelson (1997). "SD-A Self-Organizing Toolbox," *Anchor Point, Vol. 12*, July, 1997, pp. 23–29.

Muss, Dr D. (1991). *The Trauma Trap*, London: Doubleday Co.

O'Boyle, M. (1995). "DSM-III-R and Eysenck personality measures among patients in a substance abuse programme," in *Personality and Individual Differences*, 13, pp. 1157–1159.

O'Brien, C.P.; McKay, J. (1998). "Psychopharmacological Treatments of Substance Use Disorders" pp. 127–155 in Nathan, P.E.; Gorman, J.M. *A Guide To Treatments That Work*, NY: Oxford University Press.

O'Connor, J.; Seymour, J. (1990). *Introducing Neuro-Linguistic Programming*, London: Harper Collins.

O'Connor, J.; Van der Horst, B. (1994). "Neural Networks and NLP Strategies: Part 2," in *Anchor Point, Vol 8*, No. 6, June, pp. 30–38.

Overdurf, J.; Silverthorn, J. (1995). "Recovering Options: The Transformation of Addictive Processes" in *Anchor Point:* Part A: Vol. 9, No. 6, June, pp. 29–35; Part B: Vol. 9, No. 7, July, pp. 31–36.

Peele, S. (1989). *Diseasing of America*, Boston, MA: Houghton Mifflin.

Perris, C. (1989). *Cognitive Therapy With Schizophrenic Patients*, London: Cassell.

Pomare, E.W.; de Boer; G.M. Hauora: (1988). *Maori Standards of Health*, New Zealand Department of Health and Medical Research Council, Wellington.

Prochaska, J.O.; Norcross, J.C.; Diclememnte, C.C. (1994). *Changing For Good*, NY: William Morrow & Co.

Ragge, K. (1998). *The Real AA: Behind the Myth of 12 Step Recovery*, Tucson, AR: Sharp Press.

Rahula, Walpola (1955). *What The Buddha Taught*, Oxford: Oneworld.

Rhue, J.W.; Lynn, S.J.; Kirsch, I. (eds) (1997). *Handbook of Clinical Hypnosis*, Washington DC: American Psychological Association.

Rose, S. (1992). *The Making of Memory,* NY: Bantam.

Rosenhan, D.L. (1973). "On Being Sane In Insane Places" in *Science,* January 19, pp. 250–278.

Rossi, E.L.; Cheek, D.B. (1988). *Mind-Body Therapy: Ideodynamic Healing in Hypnosis,* NY: W.W. Norton & Company.

Rossi, E.L. (ed.) (1980). *The Collected Papers of Milton H. Erickson on Hypnosis: Volume IV,* NY: Irvington. (Innovative Hypnotherapy.)

Rossi, E.L. (1996). *The Symptom Path To Enlightenment,* Pacific Palisades, CA: Palisades Gateway Publishing.

Rusten, J. (ed.) (1993). *Theophrastus: Characters,* Cambrige MA: Harvard University Press.

Santoro, J.; Cohen, R. (1997). *The Angry Heart: Overcoming Borderline and Addictive Disorders,* Oakland, CA: New Harbinger.

Satir, V.; Baldwin, M. Satir (1983). *Step By Step,* Palo Alto, CA: Science and Behavior.

Scagnelli-Jobsis, J. (1982). "Hypnosis with psychotic patients: A review of the literature and presentation of a theoretical framework" in *American Journal of Clinical Hypnosis,* 25, pp. 33–45.

Schachter, S. (1982). "Recidivism and self-cure of smoking and obesity" in *American Psychologist 37:* pp. 436–444.

Schachter, S.; Singer, J.E. (1962). "Cognitive, social and physiological determinants of emotional state" in *Psychological Review, 69* (12) pp. 379–399.

Schneider, K. (1923). *Psychopathic Personalities,* London: Cassell.

Seligman, Martin, E.P. (1975). *Helplessness: On Depression, Development and Death,* San Francisco: Freeman.

Seligman, Martin E.P. (1991). *Learned Optimism,* NY: Alfred A. Knopf.

Shapiro, F. (1995). *Eye Movement Desensitisation and Reprocessing,* NY: The Guilford Press.

Sheitman, B.B.; Kinon, B.J.; Ridgway, B.A.; Lieberman, J.A. (1998). "Pharmacological Treatments of Schizophrenia", pp. 167–189 in Nathan, P.E. and Gorman, J.M. *A Guide to Treatments That Work,* New York: Oxford University Press.

Sterman, C.M. (ed.) (1990). *Neuro-Linguistic Programming in Alcoholism Treatment,* NY: Haworth Press.

Thayer, R.E. (1996). *The Origin of Everyday Moods,* NY: Oxford University Press.

Thorne, Frederick (1999). "The Etiology of Sociopathic Reactions," *American Journal of Psychotherapy, Vol. 13,* pp. 319–330.

Toivonen, VM. (1993). "SIPP: The Subsystems Inventory of Psychological Phenomena" in *Anchor Point,* Vol 7:6, June.

Trimpey, J. (1996). *Rational Recovery,* NY: Simon & Schuster.

Whitmont, E.C. (1991). *The Symbolic Quest: Basic Concepts of Analytical Psychology,* Princeton, NJ: Princeton University.

Wilber, Ken (1985). *No Boundary,* Boston, MA: Shambala.

Wilber, Ken (1996). *A Brief History of Everything,* Boston MA: Shambhal.

Williams, R.; Williams, V. (1993). *Anger Kills,* NY: Harper Collins.

Woodsmall, Wyatt (1996). "What is Wrong With Logical Levels," IANLP Conference, April 26, Austin, Texas.

Woo-Ming, A.; Siever, L.J. (1998). "Psychopharmacological Treatment of Personality Disorders" pp. 554–567 in Nathan, P.E.; Gorman, J.M. *A Guide To Treatments That Work,* NY: Oxford University Press.

World Health Organization (1992). The ICD-10 classification of mental and behavioral disorders: diagnostic criteria for research, World Health Organization, Geneva, World Health Organization, "Mental Health", WHO Fact Sheet N130, Geneva, August 1996.

Yapko, M.D. (ed.) (1989). *Brief Therapy Approaches to Treating Anxiety and Depression,* NY: Brunner/Mazel.

Yapko, M.D. (1992). *Hypnosis and the Treatment of Depressions,* NY: Brunner/Mazel.

Yapko. M., (1981). "The Effects of Matching Primary Representational System Predicates on Hypnotic Relaxation" in *American Journal of Clinical Hypnosis,* 23, pp. 169–175.

Zeig, J.K. (1980). *A Teaching Seminar with Milton H. Erickson,* NY: Brunner/Mazel.

Zink, Nelson; Munshaw, Joseph (1997). *SDA—A Self-Organizing Toolbox,* Salt Lake City, UT: *Anchor Point Associates, Vol 11,* July, pp. 23–29.

Index

Authors: